INTRODUCTION TO
CONTEMPORARY CULTURAL STUDIES

This is the first in an occasional series of introductions to modern studies under the general editorship of Professor Malcolm Bradbury. Longman has also published *Introduction to American Studies*, edited by Malcolm Bradbury and Howard Temperley (1981).

INTRODUCTION TO CONTEMPORARY CULTURAL STUDIES

Edited by David Punter

LONGMAN
London and New York

LONGMAN GROUP LIMITED
Longman House, Burnt Mill, Harlow
Essex CM20 2JE, England
Associated companies throughout the world

*Published in the United States of America
by Longman Inc., New York*

First published 1986

BRITISH LIBRARY CATALOGUING IN PUBLICATION DATA

Introduction to contemporary cultural studies.
  1. Great Britain—Civilization—1945-
  I. Punter, David
  941.085   DA566.4
ISBN 0-582-49366-8

LIBRARY OF CONGRESS CATALOGUING IN PUBLICATION DATA

Main entry under title:

Introduction to contemporary cultural studies.

  Bibliography; p.
  Includes Index.
  1. Great Britain—Popular culture—History—20th century—Addresses, essays,
lectures. 2. Great Britain—Civilization—1945-   —Addresses, essays, lectures. 3.
Great Britain—Popular culture—Study and teaching (Higher)—Addresses, essays,
lectures. 4. Great Britain—Civilization—Study and teaching (Higher)—Addresses,
essays, lectures. 5. Culture—Study and teaching (Higher)—Great Britain—Addresses,
essays, lectures.
  I. Punter, David.
  DA589.4.158   1986   941.082   85-11288
  ISBN 0-582-49366-8

Set in 10/11pt Linoterm Times
Produced by Longman Group (FE) Limited
Printed in Hong Kong

CONTENTS

Contents

ACKNOWLEDGEMENTS

I am grateful to The Women's Press Ltd & George Brazilier Inc for permission to reproduce extracts from *Faces In The Water* by Janet Frame (1980). My thanks are also due to the contributors for making my life as editor an easy one; and to Lorna Smith for her considerable help with the Index.

PREFACE

I began collecting together the various essays which comprise this book in 1982. As a survey of British culture since the war, and of the study of that culture, it is obviously patchy; in particular, there is almost no attention to film, partly because it is hoped this will be the subject of a further volume in the same series.

Since 1982, many features of British cultural life – in the widest sense of culture – have changed; many more have not, and it may well be the sense of persistent, grinding atrophy which rings truer than claims for mobility, development, or even determinate regression. As I see it, it is the task of the cultural critic to attempt to assess, in relation to the records of culture but also in relation to the representative experience of the individual, the sociopsychological meanings which lie behind the observable data of change and stasis; and there are many attempts in these pages to do just that.

My own principal observation of the last three years has been of moving into a society where the quotidian experience of freedom is ephemeral; and where, instead, the reified forms of hierarchy, which themselves represent a power proposed as unchallengeable, loom ever larger on the horizon. It needs hardly to be pointed out that this tendency is in direct contradiction of governmental rhetoric; but there is nothing too surprising in that. In absense, it is as though we are no longer invited to deal for ourselves with the cardinal differences involved in being human – differences of race, culture, gender, age, class – but instead we are invited to view these differences as massive dead forms, around which we must tread with care for fear of awakening ghosts. I would interpret this psychoanalytically as a phenomenon of bad dependence, a robbing of the potency of action, and a consequent reliance on quasi-parental authority writ large; but others, from their different subject positions, may of course see things differently.

Norwich 1985

Introduction

CULTURE AND CHANGE

DAVID PUNTER

This book is designed as an introduction to the study of contemporary culture. I hope that it will be of value not only to students beginning courses at universities, polytechnics and other colleges, but also to many other readers, and in two slightly different ways. On the one hand, it provides an introduction to some of the ways in which contemporary culture actually is approached, and thus to some of the methods which are used, some of the theories which are relevant, and some of the ways of working which have been found productive through educational experience. On the other, in the course of this the book naturally provides an introduction to some of the basic forms in which that culture actually occurs: forms in the sense of media – there are accounts here which are based in literature, in television, in advertising, in music, and so forth – and in the sense of significant topics and themes, the concerns which structure contemporary culture – divisions of race, class, gender; ways in which we imagine the past, the present, the future; contemporary hopes and anxieties; the real social structures within which we live and within which our subjectivity is formed.

In collecting these essays, I have tried to keep in mind two basic co-ordinates: that 'contemporary' be interpreted as covering the period after the Second World War, and that the focus of each essay be British. In both cases, it is the exceptions which prove the rule: phenomena which affect us today cannot be explained without reference back to the recent past; and there are areas of British culture which make no sense without considerable reference to the international forces which have operated and continue to operate here, on it. In soliciting the essays, I chose not to suggest a definition of 'culture' to which all the writers might want to adhere, because I suspected that this would be constraining, and that, for readers in search of a definition, I could offer more by allowing the writers to work within their own parameters. I recognize that this means that more definitional work must reside with the reader; but this seems to me precisely the point.

I should also say that I have found the process of collecting and editing the volume immensely stimulating. In some cases I found myself with topics on my hands which, in my view, required attention; in other cases I knew of writers and thinkers from whom I very much wanted a contribution; in still others, I was aware of schools of thought, working tendencies, which, I believed, should be represented if the book were going to offer a realistic account of the work in contemporary cultural studies which is proceeding and developing in the various appropriate sites. The essays emerged from these various beginnings. I made one more comment to the contributors: which was that I very much wanted them to consider their own choice of form. There are forms which have become conventionally associated with the 'academic', and others which have become associated with specific ideologies: I wanted some of these to be represented, but I also wanted to offer a space within which individual writers could select the appropriate shape for their comments, something particularly important in a field where there is, of necessity, constant change and a constant search for the appropriate form amid the diversity of forms offered us by the wider proliferation of media. Only the reader, of course, will be able to decide for him- or herself on whether this tactic has produced useful results.

In writing this introduction – an introduction to an introduction – there are various things which I have decided not to do, because they have turned out to be unnecessary. It is not necessary, for instance, for me to attempt an account of contemporary social history, because this is provided in Arthur Marwick's essay; nor of the genesis and development of contemporary cultural studies, because this is offered by Tony Dunn. Likewise the future directions of contemporary cultural studies are spoken of eloquently in the fourth section of the book. So what I have instead chosen to do is, first, to describe in brief the essays which follow, and the sections into which they fall; and second, to take up some of the themes which seem to me to offer links and bridges between the essays, and to make some suggestions about how they might relate to our general cultural preoccupations, and how they might provide keys for unlocking some of the secrets of contemporary cultural life.

The book is divided into four sections; that was not my original plan, but has emerged as appropriate in the light of the material which the contributors have provided. I am therefore assuming that it reflects, in some sense, the reality of the study and research processes which the book represents. Section A, called 'Cultural frameworks', contains three essays which give us some essential backgrounds: to British social history since the Second World War, to the development of the media during that period, to the parallel and dialectically related evolution of cultural studies. Even in this section, there is no claim that the 'coverage' offered is comprehensive: and certainly there is no such claim in the three sections which follow.

Section B, called 'Cultural studies and methodology', offers three accounts of developments in the pedagogy of cultural and communication studies. The third section, the largest in the book, is called 'Topics in contemporary culture', and offers a range of such topics, treated in diverse ways: television comedy, science fiction, comics, school textbooks, rock music, youth styles are all themes which appear here in various guises, as do many of the key political issues of these years: racism, the clash of different cultures, gender, education, fears of terminal war. The fourth section contains four essays which appear to me to suggest future directions in which the study of contemporary culture might go. I should like now to say a few more words about each of these essays, concentrating where possible on connections between them, in order to help with the construction of meaningful shapes and patterns which is, I take it, the task of interpretation.

Arthur Marwick's 'A social history of Britain 1945–1983' (Ch. 1) offers us precisely that; but also much more. The essay serves, for instance, as a warning against over-simplification. It is all too easy to try to read the post-war period as a unified whole; by calling attention to the breaks and changes of direction which have characterized social evolution and social policy during that period Marwick helps us with the task of seeing history in terms of 'significant wholes'. Perhaps most significant of all, and certainly controversial, is his assertion that the Falklands War marks a break in history, and thus in our culture; this underlines a sense, which can also be found in later essays in the volume, that we might be witnessing a critical moment in British culture, a moment when acceptances which have come to seem 'traditional' may no longer be holding, and when the task of contemporary interpretation thus becomes all the more vital.

It is, however, true that that sense of the 'critical moment' is one which has tended to recur in the increasingly fast-moving world of contemporary culture; and Roger Sales, in his essay 'An introduction to broadcasting history' (Ch. 2), reminds us of several such moments in the recent past, and above all of the critical impact which broadcasting has had on political life and on social attitudes. In particular Sales helps us to notice again that forms of culture which we have all too easily come to see as 'natural' are, of course, nothing of the sort: his accounts of the genesis of television, of the battles between state monopoly and so-called 'independent broadcasting' call to mind the fact that things could have been otherwise, that at those critical cultural moments decisions are taken – or evaded – and that the outcome of those decisions is related to a complex interplay of individuals and social forces. There are languages in the criticism of contemporary culture which talk in terms of 'strategies of power', and other languages which might prefer the terminology of 'corridors of power': we too, as readers and critics, have our choices to take about the appropriateness of those languages and of the ideologies which underlie them.

The name of Richard Hoggart occurs in Marwick's essay and in Sales's; it recurs, with other key names, in Tony Dunn's account of 'The evolution of cultural studies' (Ch. 3), which moves us from the culture itself towards the actual forms and modes in which it has been and is being interpreted. Contemporary cultural studies has been, from its outset, a primary site for intellectual contestation, and Dunn gives us a sense of what that contestation has been about. In particular, he picks out the way in which the study of British culture has been informed and influenced from the outset – and particularly through the influence of *New Left Review* – by theory transmitted from continental Europe, and this despite the overwhelming fertilization of British culture, not by Europe but by the United States. Behind this curious collision, there are obviously important forces at work, and they have partly structured 'indigenous' British criticism (Hoggart, Raymond Williams, Stuart Hall, the Birmingham Centre for Contemporary Cultural Studies).

The essays in Section B can be seen as more practical accounts of some of the conflicts which Dunn outlines. Anne Beezer, Jean Grimshaw and Martin Barker demonstrate for us (Ch. 4) the fact, so easy to forget, that theory is not the same as method: we do not simply grasp a theory in its totality, rather we come to see its meaningfulness – or lack of it – by testing its efficacy on actual objects of study: here advertisements, women's magazines, teenage reading matter. There is also a significant polemic behind this essay, one which has enduring importance for the criticism of contemporary culture: do those theories which set out to demonstrate for us the ways in which subjectivity is 'constructed' by societal forces really act to generate discriminating descriptions of the 'reading act'? In both Dunn's essay and this one, the name of Althusser occurs, and we are invited to consider whether the model of relations between society and the subject which Althusserian Marxism offers is adequate; and, indeed, adequate for what specific purposes? Beezer, Grimshaw and Barker also write within a context where a major determining factor is the evolution of feminism; and some of their arguments reappear, in different guises, later in the book.

In 'Critiques of culture: a course' (Ch. 5), Jon Cook further narrows and intensifies the focus by describing not merely a specific course in cultural studies, but also some of the difficult emotional content of pedagogic activity. The intellectual context in which this course emerged is clearly spelled out, and relates back to dominant figures already mentioned in the book: Marx, Freud, Marcuse, Althusser, the feminist theorists and writers might provide us, if we attend to their work with discrimination, with tools for analysis, though these tools will be useless unless we also attend to the actual process whereby they may be transferred into the hands of students, rather than being used as blunt instruments. There is a genuinely democratic use of theory, and a use which borders on the terroristic: by trying to articulate the authority structures and institutional contexts within which teaching actually occurs we become more able to discern the difference, and at the same time we engage with the reflexivity which we need in order to elaborate our own feelings about the materials with which our culture confronts us.

By this point in the book, I hope it will have become clear that 'cultural studies' embraces a heterogeneous group of activities; Derek Longhurst's 'Communication studies: definitions and problems' (Ch. 6) isolates one of these emphases, and sets out to provide a statement about its specific value to students. There is here again an engagement with theory and with how we may be able to demonstrate its value – or rather, the value of rendering it articulate, for there is no such thing as a theory-free view of the world. There is also a further version of the complex combination of academic subjects and disciplines, already alluded to by Dunn, which attended the birth, some with blessings and some with imprecations, of communication studies and its cognate disciplines. And there is some attention to 'contemporaneity' in a different sense; we live in a period where the very processes of information are undergoing serious alteration and development, and it is Longhurst's contention that we need to pay attention to these developments – computerization, information technology, electronics – if we are to resist that nostalgic tendency within contemporary cultural studies which serves as our inevitable attempt to 'naturalize' the unfamiliar and the frightening.

The third section of the book could have been much larger; but here, at least, are seven topics within the contemporary culture which should be engaging our attention. Terry Lovell offers us an account of 'Television situation comedy' (Ch. 7) which has ramifications far beyond the specific genre. One of the enduring difficulties of cultural studies has been the problem of dealing with 'popular' forms. All too often, work in contemporary cultural studies has looked like an army of sledgehammers attacking an increasingly shy nut, and a nut, furthermore, with an unexpected resistance to being cracked. By judicious use of theory derived from Freud and Tzvetan Todorov, Lovell raises the question of our own role as 'readers' of cultural texts, and thus turns the analysis of production and consumption into an account of the actual process of reception. She also raises an all-important issue for cultural studies, and indeed for any intellectual discipline: by what means do we pick and sort the actual object of study? By 'author', by genre, by form, by internal structure?

Louis James, in ' 'Science fiction' and the 'literary' mind' (Ch. 8), works with another popular form and explicitly calls attention to the tangential relation between such forms and the traditional criteria of criticism. High culture, mass culture, popular culture, these are terms among many which have been used to effect discriminations, but they are also terms, as we need to recognize, which are themselves in a constant process of flux as the relations between classes and sub-groups in society alter and re-form. Like Longhurst, James reminds us that massive change is with us even now, change in the technology of information and perception, and that this will inevitably be producing change, perhaps as yet inarticulate, in the imagination. It might be that, in respect of these changes, science fiction, with its insistence on imagining the future in its different possible guises, occupies a privileged position which has little to do with the 'excellence' of the work under discussion; it might also be that we have ourselves to find new forms of 'writing' with which to cope with these changes.

Alec Gordon's essay, 'Thoughts out of season on counter culture' (Ch. 9), is in one sense a detailed account of a specific historical moment, and at the same time an investigation into the process of historical and cultural categorization. It is about 1968, about a certain kind of romantic utopianism, about the New Left (all topics already alluded to); but it is also about how culture is mediated through time, about the stories we make up to account for difficult or intractable material, and in this sense it looks forward to the essays by Richard Johnson and Bernard Sharratt later in the book. Raymond Williams is discussed again, and in a new context, one which offers us some comments about how specific categories of his – the selective tradition, residual, dominant and emergent ideologies – might be usable in a genealogy of cultural viewpoints. And again, there is a polemic here: there is, obviously, a view which would say that effective study pre-supposes system; but what, Gordon asks, if 'system' itself is an 'effect of history', another one of our ways of subduing that which tends to exceed the bounds of a particular historical world-view?

The structure of Eileen Aird's essay, 'Gender, education and change' (Ch. 10), returns us to the problem of the uses of theory by providing, on the one hand, an empirical account of the problems of education in a gender-divided society and of some of the attempted solutions – or rectifications – of the relations of dominance which obtain at every level of study; and on the other, a way of relating these phenomena to some of Freud's concepts of male and female sexuality, taken in the historical context within which that theory was constructed. And, of course, this is not an 'external' matter: the site which Aird is describing is one where we have all been, and one which has inscribed us all on behalf of the society in whose service education perforce operates. As with many of the other essays, I would hope that this one could be read as a reflexive account of what actually happens to the educators and the educated in a society based on hierarchies of gender, race and class, and in a society, furthermore, which has at the moment sacrificed the political will to modify or ameliorate the effects of those hierarchies.

Within that triplicity of powers, I believe it is fair to say that race is, so far, the least effectively worked in the context of contemporary cultural studies. David Wright's 'Racism in school textbooks' (Ch. 11) embarks on this overwhelmingly difficult subject, at a crucial level. As so often, it is primarily a question of attempting to 'defamiliarize' that which appears familiar and thus unquestionable, in this case geography textbooks which are in wide use and yet are increasingly at best irrelevant to the society in which we live and, at worst, insulting to a vast number of members of that society (and thus to all of us). There is an extent to which what Wright is dealing with is unconscious; and, looking back to previous essays, we may begin to sense that the discernment of conscious and unconscious levels in cultural forms is of primary importance. There is also an implicit argument about power, the power of the written word, especially when sanctioned by specific institutions: nowhere in contemporary culture are we dealing with a pleasing quasi-scientific neutrality, or if we are we are missing the essential connections between culture and the social forces which generate it and hold it in being.

It is power and the written word which, in different ways, are also at stake in 'Textuality/sexuality' (Ch. 12), by Susan Bassnett and Keith Hoskin. The main issue is a general one: how can we see the ways in which every cultural 'text' is structured by issues of sexuality? More specifically, are there particular forms (and Bassnett and Hoskin are concerned with rock music and video) which question established relations? New technology, new languages, new power relations: are we witnessing real change, or further and more adept reticulations of a social formation with unprecedented powers of survival and incorporation? Or, to put it another way, what is the relative autonomy of culture within society? Bassnett and Hoskin return us also to the Falklands War, and now in a more symbolic mode, appropriate in an age where symbolic readings of the text, informed by theorists such as Jacques Derrida and Hélène Cixous, are proliferating.

My essay 'The unconscious and contemporary culture' (Ch. 13), is also informed by such symbolic readings, and addresses itself to ways in which we might get 'under the skin' of various familiar experiences: youth styles, constructions of the future, class attitudes, ways in which the 'literary' is mediated and received. One of the aspects of intellectualism which we are warned against by writers as diverse as Derrida and Michel Foucault is the habit of closure, the supposition that interpretations of phenomena can be arranged into neat and teleological patterns: I have tried to guard against this, and at the same time to take on some of the arguments about narrative which also emerge in the essays by Dunn and Johnson. We live by making narrative: fictions are not superstructural, but function as ways in which we survive the experiences of incomprehensibility. The short pieces which comprise my essay attempt to be self-reflexive about that construction of narrative.

The first essay in the final section of the book is by Richard Johnson, and is called 'The story so far: and further transformations?' (Ch. 14). It has as its basis a particular practice, that of the Birmingham Centre for Contemporary Cultural Studies, and it has a relation to arguments we have already glimpsed: about the primacy of the political in the structuring of culture, about 'interdisciplinarity', about the role of the New Left, about consciousness and subjectivity. Johnson also addresses the role of Marxism in cultural studies directly, in terms of significant metaphors of circulation and capital. Over the course of the whole volume, I would hope that the debate between 'culturalism' and structuralism has come to have some meaning; Johnson takes this as the site of his argument, and suggests some ways in which precisely this contradiction of approach and methodology might be seen as laying down lines into the future.

John Broadbent, in his 'Site visit: local cultural interpretation' (Ch. 15), can be seen as taking up the argument from the previous two essays, mine and Johnson's, in the sense that he is also resisting the impulse towards the global and the teleological while specifically addressing the question of what immediate analysis of our present predicament, and our real feelings about it, might yield in terms of a set of perceptions of the underlying purposes behind contemporary cultural life. His essay is simultaneously an account of a set of actual pedagogic and experiential practices, a series of workshops run by the Development of University English Teaching Project, at the moment the major attempt in Britain to generate a reading of culture by those within the institutions which are primarily responsible for interpreting it. The prospects of crisis and terminality are perceived in the terms in which we actually experience them in our everyday work: as redundancy, closure of options, professional sterility, collapse of authority. Broadbent's attempt is to validate a version of education as itself a 'form of life' worth living, as against the élitist and power-loaded structures which are privileged increasingly by our political masters. There is also an implicit argument about the nature of psychoanalytic interpretation, and about the consequent importance of myth as a key to understanding the present predicament.

But where, after all, are the crucial myths? Lorna Smith's essay, 'Women beyond culture', (Ch. 16), takes it as axiomatic – as, now, have many other writers – that the major myths can be apprehended only through an attempt to deal in the suppressed but returning forms of the feminine. For us, it may be that such forms can be dealt with only as madness: but again, madness is a culturally constructed category, and it may be only through the extraordinary and uncategorizable experience that we can experience the deficiencies of present culture.

Again, there is a specific modulation here of psychoanalysis, and a specific version of the relations between language and the self, narrated through the reading process itself as it affects the (female) individual: silence, a new relation between bodies and spaces, a new version of the inner significance of alienation, perhaps these are some of the ways through to a new projection of the future; and thus, necessarily, to a new and broader conception of the implications of the present.

The nature of 'spaces' as objects of interpretation is integral to the essays by Johnson and Broadbent; Bernard Sharratt, in his 'Towards the cultural study of time' (Ch. 17), takes up the other essential co-ordinate of our perceptions, in order to demonstrate how this most unquestionable of all elements in our experience is itself socially and culturally constructed. That element of 'construction' is reflected in the 'mosaic' form of the essay; the emphasis on the importance of our imaginings of the future, already present in several of the essays, here becomes focal particularly in relation to Marxist views of what might be available to replace the restrictive and damaging forms of capitalism. Capitalism, we might say, is uniquely the economic form without a future, because it exists only in a fantasy world, a universe which, despite the obvious economic facts, is taken to be continually expanding; this cannot be separated from the restriction of imagination which capitalism must therefore necessarily impose on consciousness, but, as Sharratt points out, this is precisely the difficulty: how to perceive restriction when it has become woven into the very fabric of our culture and our lives.

I am aware of having been writing so far as an editor, as an educator, and as a pluralist. There is a sense – touched on in many of these essays – in which those three orientations are of necessity linked. In the remaining part of this introduction to an introduction, I shall be writing from a different place, from my own convictions about the importance of contemporary cultural studies as a potent force in the constellation of practices and behaviours and conceptualisations which we refer to as culture; and I shall thus also be speaking more subjectively, and from my own experience of what some of the vital conscious and unconscious themes appear to be in the world immediately around us.

All culture is 'political'; that is to say, it has to do with the ways in which people live and with the structures of power which impose themselves on those forms of life. Writing, however, in 1984, the connections between culture and politics are in many respects difficult to see. The British situation is, as always, a peculiar one, and there are many historical factors at work.[1] There is, for instance, the nature of the party political system. Perry Anderson reminded us, years ago, of the absence of a native Marxist sociology in Britain[2]; he could have added to that the absence of a mass Communist party, an absence which we take as a fact of life but which, in an advanced industrial

European nation, is eccentric. There is no space here to go into the historical reasons for this; but it could be argued that Communism, because of its unique hold on a conception of world-change and thus on the future, should precisely be the political philosophy which carries the imagination and which continually reminds us of long-term goals.

In Britain, only the Labour Party would seem at all likely to perform this function, but there are many blocking mechanisms: the rhetoric of the trade union movement, so vital in past decades, has become fossilized; the Labour party itself has not proved adept at generating links with an intelligentsia, and has, indeed, perhaps not considered it worthwhile. Long-term thinking is replaced by a politics of short-term goals, underlining the worrying side of democracy, the endless ability of particular parties to shelve large-scale problems in the hope that they will recur in embarrassing form under the next government. It is only in a climate such as this that the intellectual pretensions of the New Right could be taken seriously; the void gets filled with the cliquey pseudo-philosophy of monetarism and élitism, Milton Friedman and Roger Scruton, the theorists of acceptance and control.

In connecting these forces with culture, I am implicitly supposing that culture does not rest at opera and high theatre, or even at television and sport. Culture in its widest sense can be taken as akin to the older phrase, 'quality of life'.[3] Few people in positions of political power are thinking about what 'quality of life' might be like in the Britain of the future, and when they do they become branded as mavericks – Tony Benn in the Labour party, Edward Heath among the Conservatives. There are also local efforts of importance; I think particularly of the metropolitan councils of London and Liverpool. But, of course, it is precisely these bodies which are now under threat of dissolution. There are, as I have said, conscious and unconscious forces at work in society; one does not need to adopt a conspiracy theory in order to suggest that the abolition of these councils will not be accidental, but will fit neatly into the foreshortening of institutional and national perspective which is essential if we are to continue to operate and believe in a form of economic organization which clearly has now only a short life ahead of it.

In saying that, I am not referring to any imminent possibility of internal change, still less revolution; the one-dimensional society which Herbert Marcuse described has effectively damped down and bought off most of the agencies for such change.[4] But, seen from a wider perspective, this is of decreasing importance: in the context of the Third World, and particularly of the fictional status of the present world banking system, the kinds of culture which the West is generating look increasingly precarious, yet we are still treated by our political leaders to a diet of charades: a meaningless conflict between the West and the Soviet Union, an incomprehensible supposition that individual Western nations can somehow 'balance their books' while the rest of the world, and those portions of our own inner cities which have already gone into internal exile, are in flames.

That might seem a melodramatic way of putting it (unless you live in Toxteth, or in that area which used to be Toxteth until it was conveniently renamed, along with the Windscale nuclear power station); but it remains necessary to emphasize as strongly as possible the unique character of social and cultural change in the late twentieth century. We can take an apparently much lesser example: the book as a form. As I write, plans are going ahead (if the funding can be found) for the institution of a new 'library' which will link together hundreds of existing libraries in a single European data-base. The implications are enormous. The book itself, with all its connotations of authority, possession, development, will become what Derrida terms a 'trace'[5]: a collection of data available in various forms, the geographical location and physical existence of which will become increasingly irrelevant as the process of 'circulation' becomes more immediate and more complex.

The great mistake would be to think that this is merely a change of form, a superstructural change below which all will go on much as before. To believe that would be to suppose that our own subjectivity will remain the same while the webs of information change. One consequence, of course, is already becoming apparent: the instantaneous interchange of information entails a change in our whole conception of privacy, and thus a change in the concept of the individual. When, as individuals, we think of the state of our bank balance, we no longer imagine stacks of pound notes; similarly, as the concept of the book recedes we shall find ourselves with new imaginings, and we will thus be located differently in space and time.

We come, therefore, upon a different definition of the text, a definition which is still evolving but which may have little to do with the printed and bound volume. Just so, in the evolution of television, we come upon different and changing definitions of time and flow: making the leap from commercial to drama-documentary, from news to serial, requires particular mental processes, ones of which we had no previous need and which therefore require internal adaptation. In every age, there is the 'new': what is different is the pace with which the new is evolving, and also the complexity of mental activity necessary to keep up with that pace.

The major change, for the West, is marked by feminism; by the gradual re-emergence of half of the human race into a position where it can be recognized and reckoned with. That change is, of course, a change for women; but it is also a change for men, of a massive kind. It is also, again, a change in conceptualisation and imagining. If we are to recognize the underlying structures of the world as phallomorphic, how far must the revision go? The world itself? The very concept of system and order? Is it these assumptions which have to be discarded in the course of a reorganization of power and 'quality of life'?

And here again we confront a question about the reality of cultural change. It could be said that feminism has so far made major gains: gains in terms of equality of opportunity, in terms of employment, in terms of representation, in all the senses of that manifold word. The 'happy' scenario would be that we are seeing the beginnings of a revolution which will proceed apace, gaining more adherents, smoothly altering the social formation. History demonstrates, however, that major change rarely occurs like that. At the moment, it could be suggested, feminism is able to take advantage of a certain elasticity within apparently liberal societies; but that elasticity has its own functions, and it may well stop short of any real handover of power.

The worst scenario is terrifying indeed. We live under the threat of nuclear war. The symbolic force of Greenham Common is that, if only we can tap the peaceful energies which have to do with the female, somehow that threat can be rolled back. But what if the reverse were the case? When threatened, people in power become frightened and angry; macho masculinity, at the end of its tether and facing the rise of the feminine with terror and anxiety, might indeed take the final step. Rather, so such a force might argue, that the world should cease to exist than that we should hand over our power. The end of the phallic is said to be destruction; let us, then, prove it.

I mention this scenario, not because I believe that there could be any such conscious argument; it would be an obvious lunacy. But the world does not work in rational terms. Order is kept by the imposition of boundaries; at least, that is the male account. What do you do when those boundaries come under threat? There is the boundary of gender to be 'protected' against invasion; there is also the ethnic boundary, increasingly eroding in the 'multicultural' urban societies of the West. And there is, on top of, or below, all this the futurelessness of capitalism, already mortgaged to the oil suppliers and increasingly invested in a level of technology which may prove useless.

What, then, does this mean for students of contemporary culture? What it certainly does not mean, I would say, is that the work of criticism and interpretation should be abandoned in the face of apparently disastrous societal pressures.[6] That would be precisely to collude with the overt and covert purposes of those in power, to abandon hope in the face of the governments of blind anger which are now operating in Britain and other Western countries – and in doing so, of course, those governments are enacting our own fear of change, because they have massive mandates. What we need to investigate is not some conspiracy whereby clever politicians hoodwink us, but rather a massive phenomenon of anxiety which makes it seem, to a vast number of people, as though it is only through punishment, exclusion, victimization, that we can move forward into the future. What is at stake is not political manipulation but the social and individual imagination; and this is why the study of culture, however we define the term, is of crucial importance to an understanding of our present predicament, because it is in cultural representation that we can get at the materials the imagination is working on and the forms in which it is dealing with time and space, hope and fear.

What, then, do the cultural theorists have to say to us? We need to be clear that there is no cultural theory of the Right. The body of ideas we work with, the hypotheses about human behaviour and society which inform our thinking, are largely derived, whether we like it or not, from the two great 'nineteenth-century radicals', Marx and Freud. Endlessly though we may bend and criticize their theories – and rightly so – they will not go away. And they converge on one point: that we are not our own masters or mistresses, that behind what we take for responsibility there lie other forces, deep in the psyche and out in the social formation, which influence our actions. There is plenty of argument in these essays about the contemporary significance of Marx and Freud[7]; and there is also discussion of the great debate which has occupied the last decade of cultural studies, between 'culturalism' and 'structuralism', between theory and the 'poverty of theory', a debate which itself goes back to roots in Marx and Freud. But another 'great debate', I would say, is now opening up, and its terms are somewhat different: a debate about subjectivity, about the ways in which the self is formed, and about the true meaning of individual and social agency.

I do not wish here to adumbrate that argument, although many of the essays touch upon it. What I do want to suggest is that the nature of subjectivity is becoming the site for research and thought, and for very precise reasons. Despite their implicit and explicit revolutionary content, Marxism and Freudianism cannot escape coloration by history; and under the present circumstances, they tend to appear as determinisms. In this sense, they cease to offer alternatives to the dreadful hold of 'that which is'; on the contrary, they become contributions to despair, and in that sense they collude with the new conservatism. They collude by robbing us of agency; they collude by translating a specific powerlessness into an eternal fact of life.

What power might we exert as students of contemporary culture? The power, I would say, of forming concepts of the familiar and the unfamiliar, the natural and the contingent. As we go to work in the morning, or to the dole queue, we are subjected to a barrage of information and image; the power of those who construct and transmit that information and those images lies in their ability to make us believe that these signs are natural, inevitable, that there is nothing puzzling or peculiar about advertisements for lung cancer. It is the power of hegemony; of gaining acquiescence by cutting out the processes of questioning.[8] Yet every man-made object which we stare at or absorb can be subjected to interpretation, however tiny – as, of course, Marx and Freud demonstrated.[9] And it is through that work of continual interpretation that we can try to keep pace with change, and, indeed, to move alongside and beyond it, sensing the processes by which control is exerted, describing the familiar in terms of the unfamiliar, performing those small everyday acts of estrangement which will encourage questioning and resistance.

We can see it, for instance, at the level of nationality; and one of the questions which lies implicitly behind many of the essays here is about what it means to be British. 'British-ness' – and the many regional, class-based, group-based terms which lie uncomfortably within it – is not a 'given', but a constructed entity; unless we help to deconstruct it, it will be constructed around us, and will fit us like a shrinking suit of armour. What, we might ask, does it promote? What does it exclude? What does it prioritize? In what images is it summarized? In whose service does it operate?

As I write this, there has recently been on television a programme about rituals in the Masai tribe. It was a fascinating programme, but, as more than one reviewer pointed out, it contained a very odd moment. This was when, at a supposedly crucial point in the ritual, a honeycomb was produced. The television camera, avid for information and for the effective image, closed in on this honeycomb, whereupon a brief exchange between two Masai was heard. 'They are', observed one, 'looking at the honeycomb'. 'They must', whispered another, 'be mad'. One of the reviewers came up with an apt analogy: what if a group of people from a widely different culture came to England and went to a cricket match, but spent their whole time watching the heavy roller?

The point of the metaphor is that contemporary cultural studies is a unique subject in that its objects of attention are not predefined. It is up to us as students to determine what the significant objects are; and even in the act of doing that, we are already performing an activity of criticism and interpretation. Those cultural objects which are 'privileged' may indeed have stories to tell, if only they can be properly unpacked; but so may the most insignificant of advertisements, the least noticed pieces of social behaviour, the most apparently innocent tricks of speech.

It is for this reason, to return to an earlier point, that we need to be reluctant to offer a definition of culture; to define it is already to collude in a hierarchy of meaning, and one which, even if temporarily valid, is now likely to be out of date before it has come into focus. Who would have predicted, five years ago, that computers would mean more to the average twelve-year-old than to their parents? Or that the Tolkienesque fantasy of the game 'Dungeons and Dragons' would have become a major cultural force for the young? Or that the whole business of career structures would have undergone such radical revision? As the picture shimmers into view – and this is to use an image from Roland Barthes – we need indeed to photograph it, and to assess it[10]: but we must not make the mistake of supposing that, when we look up from our interpretative labours, it will still be there.

But neither – although this may seem like a contradiction – must we suppose that it has gone away. Freud uses an extraordinary image of the unconscious which is of continuing value. He supposes that we are looking out over Rome, or over some other ancient city, and seeing it as we would today. a conglomeration of ancient ruins, modern tenements, civic buildings. But then he asks us to imagine that what we see is not this accumulated Rome, but rather *all* the cities of Rome there have ever been, a different one each century, each decade, each minute, all still existing and superimposed one upon another. This, he says, is a representation of the unconscious, from which nothing ever goes away.[11] But it is also a representation of history: change and retention are the twin facts of our subject, and the paradoxical base from which we must begin.

The fundamental question can be put another way. What is work? For Hegel, as for many other thinkers, work is the human essence[12]; it is through the transformation of nature and of ourselves that we validate our humanity. But patterns of work change, and they are changing faster now than at any previous stage of history. What, as students, we are engaged with is also work; our problem is to find a process of work, interpretative work which can stand in the most useful relation to the changes going on around us. This may entail fast movement, fast discarding, a great deal of provisionality, even a residence in the transient which goes against all the canons of masculine achievement; nevertheless, the alternative is to become fossilized while we speak. These essays are examples of work, and some of those examples will seem more valid to you as a reader than others; but whatever the case, they can only attain to their true validity if they are seen as stages in a process, a process in which the student of contemporary culture participates, and the purpose of which becomes increasingly urgent as the succession of contexts and frameworks becomes increasingly rapid.

Norwich 1984

NOTES AND REFERENCES

1. See E. P. Thompson, 'The Peculiarities of the English' (1965), in *The Poverty of Theory and Other Essays,* Merlin 1978, pp. 245–301.
2. See Perry Anderson, 'Components of the National Culture', *New Left Review,* No. 50 (1968), pp. 3–57.

3. See Raymond Williams, *Keywords: A Vocabulary of Culture and Society,* Fontana 1976, pp. 76–82; and *Culture,* Fontana 1981.

4. See Herbert Marcuse, *One-Dimensional Man: Studies in the Ideology of Advanced Industrial Society,* Routledge and Kegan Paul 1964.

5. See Jacques Derrida, 'Edmond Jabès and the Question of the Book' (1964), in *Writing and Difference,* trans. A. Bass, Routledge and Kegan Paul 1978, pp. 64–78.

6. Theodor Adorno, 'Cultural Criticism and Society' and 'The Sociology of Knowledge and its Consciousness', in *Prisms,* trans. S. and S. Weber, Neville Spearman 1967, pp. 17–49.

7. See also particularly Juliet Mitchell, *Psychoanalysis and Feminism,* Allen Lane 1974; Rosalind Coward and John Ellis, *Language and Materialism: Developments in Semiology and the Theory of the Subject,* Routledge and Kegan Paul 1977; Jane Gallop, *Feminism and Psychoanalysis: The Daughter's Seduction,* Macmillan 1982; Coward, *Patriarchal Precedents: Sexuality and Social Relations,* Routledge and Kegan Paul 1983.

8. See Antonio Gramsci, 'The Study of Philosophy and of Historical Materialism' and 'The Modern Prince', in *The Modern Prince and Other Writings,* trans. L. Marks, International Publishers, New York 1957, pp. 58–75, 135–88.

9. See, e.g., Marx, 'Economic and Philosophical Manuscripts' (1844), in *Early Writings,* introd. L. Colletti, Penguin 1975, pp. 279–400, and, of course, *Capital* (1867–94) itself; also Freud, *The Psychopathology of Everyday Life* (1901), in *Standard Edition of the Complete Psychological Works of Sigmund Freud* (23 vols.), ed. J. Strachey, Hogarth Press 1953–73, VI.

10. See Roland Barthes, e.g., *Camera Lucida: Reflections on Photography,* trans. Richard Howard, Cape 1982.

11. See Freud, *Civilisation and its Discontents* (1930), in *Standard Edition,* XXI, 69–70.

12. See Hegel, e.g., the arguments on desire in *The Philosophy of Subjective Spirit* (3 vols.), ed. M. J. Petry, Reidel, Dordrecht 1978, III, 43–59.

Section A
CULTURAL FRAMEWORKS

Chapter 1

A SOCIAL HISTORY OF BRITAIN 1945–1983

ARTHUR MARWICK

While Britain may well seem a conspicuously static and conservative society, with the only significant theme since 1945 that of decline in almost everything, there have been in detail many changes in living standards, lifestyles, and attitudes. In particular, the relatively free-wheeling society of the late 1960s and early 1970s differed markedly from the tight and excessively traditionalist society of the late 1940s and early 1950s. A primary task of any historical survey must be to get the periodization right: first, to pin down, as far as this is possible, the main points of change; secondly, to avoid the travesty of presenting the period since 1945 as one undifferentiated whole to be treated simply topic by topic, as if 'family' or 'leisure' or, indeed, 'socialism' signified exactly the same thing in 1945 as in 1980. Thus this survey is divided into three chronological sections (with a final coda to bring the story as up to date as possible): the period of post-war reconstruction and establishment of social consensus, lasting till the late 1950s (let us say 1957); the period of 'cultural revolution',[1] of upheaval in cultural forms and social attitudes, closely linked to sharply rising living standards, under way in the later 1950s, assuming critical mass in 1959, and ending with the economic crisis of 1973; and, thirdly, the subsequent period of very obvious economic difficulties and marked social dissidence. Only with the Falklands War of the summer of 1982 did it become clear that yet another turning point in social history had been reached.

Running through the entire account are five major themes. First, the legacy of the Second World War: was the war a crucial factor in Britain's industrial decline, or was that decline (as Martin Wiener has argued[2]) already deeply rooted in British society by the end of the nineteenth century?; did the war experience encourage social welfare, classless democracy, and a healthy pride in British culture, or did it merely (as Angus Calder has maintained[3]) shunt Britain more firmly on to the iron rails of conservatism? The second theme involves the question, 'what went wrong?'. How did the victorious power of 1945, soon to be lauded abroad for its welfare state and 'quiet revolution' in social relationships, become by the 1970s 'the sick man of Europe'? Thirdly, the all-pervasive topic of class; and fourthly that of what, elsewhere, I have termed 'secular Anglicanism'[4]: is it true that the spirit of tolerance which historians of earlier periods have attributed to the Anglican compromise persisted in secular Britain?; if so, has it fostered stability or stagnation? Fifthly, I take the issue with which I began as a major theme in itself: the torrential release (as I see it) from Victoria social controls which characterized British society at the very heart of the period under review.

RECONSTRUCTION AND SOCIAL CONSENSUS, 1945–1957

In his study *The Wasting of the British Economy* Professor Sydney Pollard has stressed the important war-led expansion 'in some of the most promising sectors like vehicles, aircraft and electronics' and in emphasizing Britain's economic *advantages* in 1945 he lists the following:

> . . . strong social cohesion and no waste of effort in searching out war criminals and collaborators, no loss or change of territory, the psychological boost of victory, immense technological superiority over all others except the Americans, an industrial machine in much better shape, high prestige as a provider of quality exports to world markets, a sound financial system, and traditional links by language and culture with many of the best and most rapidly growing export markets overseas.

'Looking back', Pollard concludes, 'it is not at all evident that the British, given their starting handicap, were bound to fail; on the contrary, in 1945 they looked hot favourites.'[5] War-time needs brought new active industrial capacity to areas becoming industrial wastelands in the inter-war period, and new economic resources, such as roads, bridges and harbours, to remote areas which had been equally, if less conspicuously desolated. For a decade or so ahead, there were positive economic gains, yet the re-emphasis on heavy industry was not necessarily a long-term blessing; productivity in the coal industry, battered, betrayed, and bitter for so long, remained low. To wage war, Britain sold off overseas assets, obliterated her export trade, and ran up massive debts. A not unjustified sense of victory gained by unlimited fortitude and sacrifice, and a feeling that following a 'people's war' the people should indeed enter the promised land of peace and plenty meant that there could be no acceptance, as perforce there had to be in devastated continental countries, of the desirability of draconian restraints on consumption in favour of productive investment.

During the war there had been wholesale government control of major sectors of the economy. The Labour government returned to power in 1945 was by conviction committed to overall planning, social engineering, and the centralized direction of the economy. It sought to achieve these aims through nationalization of the major industries, the Distribution of Industry Act (1945), the channelling of new investments to 'development areas', and the building of new towns. There were important successes; although the great freeze-up of 1946–47 combined with the rundown of the coal industry produced the temporary unemployment figure of 800,000, by 1950 Britain could quite properly be described as a full-employment economy; and the vital export target of 75 per cent up on the best pre-war figures was also achieved. Slow, if undramatic, economic expansion and steady diffusion of modest prosperity continued under the Conservatives, though the recessions of 1952–53 and 1956–57 revealed the continuing vulnerability, beneath the surface prosperity, of the older industrial areas. While Labour brought about increased concentration of industry in the hands of the state, the processes of private industrial concentration accelerated in the 1950s. The weakness of Labour's nationalization programme was that it did not greatly change the personnel of those in control of industry: many of the new managers were the same old private managers with, often, simply a token trade unionist being added to the board. In the 1950s we have a picture of major state enterprises, and major private enterprises, largely run by the same class of people, collaborating and carving up the economy, but deeply hostile to any genuine individualistic small-business enterprise. The iron and steel industry, never effectively nationalized by Labour, was denationalized by the Conservatives: it is difficult to believe that the formal rubric made, or would have made, any significant difference.[6]

Labour's centralized planning also had the weakness of mistaking forms for reality. In Britain too much influence rested in the hands of traditionalist civil servants and overly theoretical professional economists: there was lacking the direct, common-sense drive towards productive investment in industry, in railways, in roads, in canals, and in renewing the environment which characterized the continental countries, where the level of serious practical education of higher civil servants was far above that of their public-school and Oxbridge counterparts in this country. Whatever success the Labour government and its propaganda campaigns achieved in the way of enthusing the people for such slogans as 'Export or Perish' was thoroughly dissipated in the 1950s when politicians spoke more of consumption and living standards at home than of production and winning export markets abroad.[7]

Already by the 1930s government social policy, in what was then spoken of as the 'social service state', affected four main areas: the maintenance of income (of a sort) whenever ordinary earnings were interrupted or brought to an end, whether because of unemployment, injury, bad health, or old age; health; housing; and education. The setting up of the welfare state (1945–48) involved the attempt to co-ordinate these four aspects into one unified social plan, the addition of the positive policy of maintaining employment, and the crucial switch from *selectivity* (providing services only for those who could prove need) to *universality* (providing the services for the entire community). The experience of war, the liberal traditions of the social service state, as well as labourist and socialist ideology, played a part. The setting up of the famous Beveridge Committee in 1941 owed most to the new pressures and new concerns with social policy generated by the war.[8] The main body of the Beveridge Report of December 1942 offered detailed proposals for a universalist national insurance scheme: but the report also assumed the implementation of the other aspects of a comprehensive welfare state, in particular economic policies directed towards the avoidance of mass unemployment, and a National Health Service. To meet the needs of war, a nationalized Emergency Hospital Scheme had already been created.

It was in education that the one major social reform of the war-time government was enacted (1944). In that it made 'secondary education for all' a reality the Butler Education Act had immense positive social implications; in that it established the distinction between grammar and modern schools, it also had considerable negative ones. The responsible minister, R. A. Butler, came from the Conservative élite and was a strong upholder of the public schools; these were left untouched. A further important measure was enacted by the caretaker Conservative government which held office between the resignation of the war-time coalition and the election of the Labour government: Family Allowances represented the fullest expression of the universalist ideal, in that they were paid to all families, rich or poor, were financed from general taxation, and were themselves subject to tax. The National Insurance Act (1946), which amalgamated all the main forms of interruption of earnings, also applied to all classes, though it retained the principle of the insurance contribution; benefits were, as Beveridge had insisted, on a flat rate, though at a higher level than envisaged by Beveridge (but still not high enough to keep up with the cost of living). Since the insurance principle was maintained there had to be another system to provide for those who did not have a satisfactory contribution record. While, therefore, the 1948 National Assistance Act formally abolished the old Poor Law, it did retain, in the National Assistance Board, a revised form of the hated Unemployment Assistance Board of the 1930s.

In the main the new National Health Service (enacted 1946, effective in 1948) embodied the universalist principle: it was entirely open to everyone, and, apart from certain specified extra services, it was entirely free. Against the opposition of the Conservatives, but building upon the Emergency Hospital Scheme of the war years, Aneurin Bevan, the responsible minister, was able to institute a nationalized hospital service. Between 1946 and 1948 there were many battles between the doctors and the government before the overwhelming majority within the profession decided to come into the scheme, on the understanding, however, that they would be paid on a capitation fee basis, not as members of a salaried service. Much criticism was soon to be levelled at the 'tripartite' administrative division of the NHS: new regional hospital boards for the hospitals; new local executive councils for the general practitioners; old-established local authorities for many other services. Be that as it may, the variety of community health services offered by the local authorities amounted to an impressive advance on the patchiness of pre-war years. Economic shortages meant that there were great deficiencies in the early years in physical facilities. The demand for medicines of all kinds, as also for dentures and spectacles, proved to be enormous, and while this was in large part a measure of the wilful neglect of the 1930s, it also drew attention to the fact that the human capacity to consume free medicine is practically inexhaustible. The Korean War provided the occasion for the introduction of health service charges in 1951–52.

There were great difficulties in the way of changing the explicitly selective basis of existing housing legislation: council housing, as housing acts made clear, was specifically 'for the working classes'. Both the English and Scottish Housing Acts of 1946 retained this phrase though Bevan, and Joseph Westwood, in respectively introducing the two Acts, explained that the phrase would be taken as meaning 'all sections of the working population'. The phrase 'for the working classes' was, at last, dropped in the Housing Act of 1949 which now made subsidies available for conversions and renovations. Throughout, the rights of tenants were firmly upheld as against those of private landlords in Rent Control Acts of 1946 and 1949. As late as 1951 local authorities were allowed to authorize only one privately-built house for every four they built themselves. Under the new Conservative government, an equal division was made between private housing and local authority housing. After January 1953 local authorities were empowered to license smaller private houses without question, and larger ones on their merits; thus 28.5 per cent of all houses completed in 1954 were constructed by private builders.

In education not much was achieved beyond the bare implementation of the provisions of the 1944 Act, though modest advances became possible in the 1950s. By January 1955 the number of pupils remaining at school till the age of seventeen and beyond was twice what it had been in the 1930s, though in England and Wales it was still only 7.9 per cent of the total age group. The actual quality of educational provision in any particular area depended very much on the local authority. It was after the Conservatives' return to power in the 1950s that the Labour-controlled London County Council opened the first comprehensive school; other areas shortly followed in seeking to overcome the segregation at 'eleven-plus' between grammar and secondary modern education. There were important developments in university education, with the proportion of students drawn from the lower-middle class and working class being higher than ever before, though the odds were still against a university education for a working-class child.

In the 1950s the radical Right of the Conservative party argued that as the country grew wealthier the Welfare State should 'wither away'. Yet by the later 1950s the Welfare State was not as much a matter of serious political controversy as political speeches and newspaper articles might suggest. Arguably, the main forces behind subsequent developments in social policy depended more on medical advances, innovations in social theory, and greater professionalization and professionalism than on party politics. At any rate, by the end of my first period, that is to say around 1957–58, the Welfare State was firmly established, functioning effectively, and while subject to criticism from the knowledgeable for still being too limited and piecemeal in approach (dealing with sickness rather than with health), the entire concept was subject only to attack from an isolated minority on the right.[9]

The people of the United Kingdom can be grouped in various ways: by nationality (Irish, Welsh, Scottish, etc.); by race ('white', 'black', 'brown', etc.); by religion (Anglican, Catholic, Non-conformist, etc.); by region ('Northerner', 'West Countryman', 'Londoner', 'Highlander', etc.); by class ('middle-class', 'working-class', etc.); by sex; and by age (children, youth, old-age pensioners). The latter two are brought together in the fundamental unit in which, at the same time, relationships and tensions are often most clearly exemplified, the family. The most important, though the most controversial to evaluate and the most difficult to define, is class.

If we study the popular vocabulary of the late 1940s and early 1950s we find widespread and quite precise use of the phrase 'working class' or 'working classes', and a rather more varied and less precise use of 'middle class' and 'middle classes' as well as 'lower-middle class' and 'upper-middle class'. There was less agreement over the use of the term 'upper class': many of those who might be thought, by objective criteria, to have belonged to such a class preferred to refer to themselves, and would often be described by others, as 'upper-middle class'. For myself, I prefer the simple phrase 'upper class' to describe what Sir Ian Fraser (in a private letter written in the 1930s) shrewdly defined as that 'reservoir of persons economically free and accustomed to responsibility from an early age' who, in a later refinement of Richard Crossman's, enjoy 'an ease and amplitude of life' denied to the overwhelming majority, and who, as a matter of objective fact, exercised, if they chose to, a dominance in the spheres of power, authority, wealth, and income totally disproportionate to their numbers, and who have a distinctive culture and lifestyle of their own, basically centred on the most celebrated public schools and on the more prestigious Oxford and Cambridge colleges.[10] I estimate this class as making up about 3 per cent of the population in the years after 1945[11]; the phrase 'upper-middle class' is then better applied to the upper segment of the class below, a segment enjoying considerable prestige and affluence, but without the disproportionate dominance of wealth and power. Once upon a time it was argued that the growth of large-scale industrial organizations and the so-called 'managerial revolution' had replaced old-style capitalists with salaried managers: in fact, owners of capital in the 1940s and 1950s were often also managers; successful managers usually acquired capital. Thus there was in fact quite a clear class distinction between major businessmen on the one side, who, combining managerial power with capital ownership, formed part of the upper class, and mere managers on the other, who were part of the middle class.

There was little ambiguity about the composition of the working class. Of the total employed population, well over 60 per cent did manual work of one sort or another, ranging from unskilled road work to the craftsmanship of the engine driver or mechanic. Manual workers and their families formed the working class, in which should also be included small shopkeepers and publicans in working-class areas. Foremen and floor managers occupied an ambiguous position on the fringes, as did the technicians in many of the newer industries. If we mark off the upper class and the working class, we are left with the middle classes, amounting to over 30 per cent of the population. Setting aside all the subtle shades of distinction which exist within all social classes there remains quite an important, though far from rigid, line between the lower-middle class of, essentially, clerical and other types of white-collar worker, and the 'true' middle class of small businessmen, managers, and professionals.

The disruptions of war had affected class and relationships between classes. The most important single development was the change in status and bargaining power of the working class. Resorting as necessary to strikes, the workers were able to exploit the very high demand for labour engendered by the necessities of war to push their real earnings up by well over 50 per cent. The much-commented-on 'mixing' of social classes during the war was more in spirit than substance, but undoubtedly there was new upper-class and middle-class concern that, having played so crucial a role in the war effort, the workers should not be plunged back into the economic depression of the

Introduction to contemporary cultural studies

inter-war years. The egalitarian policies mooted during the war and carried out by the Labour government after the war did not, as many hoped, alter the basic social structure, but in a general way they favoured the working class. High taxation during and after the war hit the upper-middle class hardest, lowering the barriers between it and the rest of the middle class. Overall, the war strengthened the solidarity and self-awareness of the working class. Thus there was both disintegration of class boundaries and consolidation within classes.

The advent of the Labour government in 1945 did not mean that the upper class necessarily relinquished power. Of Labour leaders, Hugh Dalton, Sir Stafford Cripps, and John Strachey could scarcely be described as anything other than upper-class; Clement Attlee, the new Prime Minister, undoubtedly thought of himself as middle-class and was usually perceived as such by political opponents; but as the son of a prosperous well-connected Victorian solicitor who had been able to indulge the young Attlee with a private income, he belonged to that upper professional group which was already in the nineteenth century moving into the upper class. The Haileybury school magazine in November 1945, able to congratulate itself on the election only of one Conservative old boy, directed its encomiums towards its four Labour old boys and its first ever Prime Minister, to whom it extended congratulations, 'proud that he is a son of Haileybury, and confident that he would not fail his high trust'.[12] In any case, the Conservatives were back in power after 1951, by which time, however, there had been a slight shift in the balance of forces within the party: there were more representatives of such new growth areas as investment trusts, insurance, property development, advertising and public relations, entertainment, and communications. Whatever party was in office, the higher civil service continued to be dominated by the upper class; of the successful candidates for open entry to the administrative class in 1949–52, 74 per cent came from Oxbridge.[13] High politics was a traditional occupation for the denizens of Sir Ian Fraser's 'reservoir'; otherwise, the city, the diplomatic corps, or the higher civil service. But in a new age, upper-class figures were moving into other jobs as well. After Eton and Balliol, the Hon. John Godley (later Lord Kilbracken) joined the *Daily Mirror*, in preference to becoming a diplomat.[14] By the mid-1950s journalism, publishing, films, radio, television and advertising had become classic refuges for the upper class.

In her meticulous social survey of the Oxfordshire town of Banbury, conducted between 1948 and 1951, Margaret Stacey concluded that 'it was impossible to ignore the existence of upper-class people', which in so far as it (the upper class) 'sets the standards and aspirations of traditional social class attitudes . . . is important out of all proportion to its size'. While 'members of the traditional upper class in the Banbury district were all educated at one of the major public schools', a common educational background was not a specific middle-class

26

characteristic. This makes sense: the middle class recruited from all sections of society. On the other hand, Professor Stacey found, a 'majority of the working class received only an elementary education while a much higher proportion of the middle class received a secondary education'.[15] A strong middle-class self-image comes through from this comment from a woman civil servant who clearly envisaged a three-class society, with herself in the middle, or lower-middle:

> I definitely think of myself as middle-class. It is difficult to say why. I had a typical middle-class education (small private school and secondary school). I have a middle-class job and I live in a middle-class district. But none of these things would make me middle-class in themselves. If I had been clever enough to get a higher post or professeion, or rebellious enough to chose a more attractive manual job, I should not thereby have changed my class. Nor should I change it by living in a different district. Besides, my education and job and residence (to a certain extent) were determined by the fact that my parents were middle-class so it is like the old riddle of the hen and the egg. Income has something to do with it though not in itself a deciding factor nowadays as many working-class people get higher pay than the lower middle-class, and many upper-class 'new poor' get less.[16]

Historians have argued that, for the late nineteenth and twentieth centuries, the distinction between 'respectable' working class and 'rough' working class was at least as significant as that between working class and the lower-middle class. After 1945 this does not appear to be the case; on the whole the working class presents an homogenous appearance, and a self-confident one, with little aspiration after middle-class values.[17] For all that, the basic fact remains: to be working-class meant performing manual work, most usually under arduous, uncongenial, or just plain boring circumstances. When it came to 'life chances' members of the working class were still at a serious disadvantage compared with all other sections of society. Individual members might move upwards, but conditions within the working class, not excluding working-class attitudes themselves, discouraged educational aspiration. Class is a crucially important phenomenon in post-war British society, still of much greater significance than the other distinctions referred to a few paragraphs back. Yet, though strikes continued to be frequent throughout the 1940s and 1950s, it is difficult to maintain that anything which might be described as class conflict seriously menaced the cohesion of British society, appallingly evident though class divisions were throughout the hierarchies of politics, industry and education.

If we come to the question of actual living standards, the period of 'reconstruction and social consensus' does divide rather more sharply into two than is the case with other areas. No understanding of post-war society would be complete without an emphasis on austerity. Rationing, imposed in war time, continued. In 1948 weekly allowances per person were 13 oz of meat, 1½ oz of cheese, 6 oz of butter and margarine, 1 oz of cooking fat, 8 oz of sugar, 2 pints of milk and one egg. Bread, which had never been rationed in the darkest days of war, was rationed between July 1946 and July 1948. A common shabbiness prevailed, for clothes rationing did not end till March 1949; many other restrictions and controls were lifted in 1950. Housing shortages in the immediate post-war years were highlighted by the rash of prefabs around the cities and on urban wasteland, by the frequent need for young couples to live with in-laws, and by the phenomenon of the squatter. From 1954 rationing was ended, the housing shortage eased, and largely because international terms of trade moved in Britain's favour, a greater variety of foodstuffs became available in the shops. Yet the unifying and continuing factors are more important. The critical point about the post-war years was the high level of demand for labour, mainly caused by the needs of reconstruction and the great surge of demand which had been dammed up during the war. By the end of the war earnings had already gone up by 80 per cent, whereas the cost of living had gone up by only 31 per cent. By various agreements ratified in the immediate post-war years the average working week was reduced from 47 or 48 to 44 or 45 hours. In the late 1940s, wage rates moved slowly upwards; so also did prices. With fair success, the Attlee government endeavoured to secure agreement to a policy of 'wage restraint'. Wages and prices continued their upward drift in the 1950s. For all the harassment of rationing, shortages, and prosperity, already by 1951 the nation as a whole was healthier and fitter than it had ever been before. Children in all sections of the community were taller and heavier than in 1936. In 1950, for the first time, infant mortality fell below 30 per thousand.[18]

The upheavals of the Second World War had some effect on the social roles of men and women, but broadly it would be true to say that right through the 1950s, the roles and rewards of men and women continued to be governed by the old traditions, the husband's tasks clustering round his function as principal breadwinner, while a wife's clustered round her function as homemaker and child-rearer. In sexual matters, within an ambience of reticence and even ignorance hard to credit today, the old 'double standard' undoubtedly still prevailed, even after the excitements and opportunities of war had added a further twist to the story of women's sexual emancipation. Geoffrey Gorer's survey conducted in January 1951 brought out that just over half the men and nearly two thirds of the women interviewed expressed disapproval of sex before marriage, while 43 per cent of this total sample admitted to having had a sexual relationship before or outside marriage, with 47 per cent giving an emphatic denial.[19]

The war had, in many instances, disrupted marriages and family life. Divorces reached a peak of 60,000 in 1947, ten times the pre-war figure. The passing of the Legal Aid Act two years later opened the possibility of divorce for many who had previously been deterred by the expense. By the middle 1950s there were about 25,000 divorces a year. Yet, of those divorced, three quarters re-married. The really important historical trend can be seen in the figures relating to women in the 20–29 age group: in 1911 only 552 out of every thousand women in this age group were married; in 1951 731 were married. There was a brief baby boom' in the immediate post-war years, with the birth-rate reaching a peak of 20.5 per thousand in 1947. Thereafter, the birth-rate levelled off again, and it became apparent that in almost all sections of society deliberate family limitation was being practised. Of all children born in 1955, 5 per cent were illegitimate.[20] It is a commonplace that the technological innovation and social engineering of the period adversely affected the close network of the traditional extended family. Yet still in the later 1950s, though re-housing and slum clearance programmes were well under way, many of the old working-class communities still existed virtually intact. Leisure activities, which boomed as the war ended, remained characteristic of the pre-war years. Blackpool, Scarborough, the Isle of Man prospered. Cinema attendances reached a peak in 1946, and remained high, till slow decline began to set in in the early 1950s; the wireless retained much of its war-time prestige, only seriously losing out to television after the middle of the 1950s; football enjoyed a golden age.[21]

In the 1940s the grown-up generation provided the semi-outcast figure who shocked the respectable and outwitted the sluggish government: the spiv. With the early 1950s there came the first nationally recognized figure representative of the detachment of youth from the rest of society and representative also of the fact that for the first time working-class youth could take an initiative in determining styles: the teddy boy. One particular national institution served as a fundamental influence on the lives of almost all young males, National Service. For most men National Service meant boredom and waste, though few denied receiving any personal benefit at all. It is a moot point whether National Service really served as a force for social control, or whether, by breaking family links, disrupting apprenticeships, opening new horizons, imposing new and sometimes brutal stresses it was a potential agent of social disruption.[22] Probably its greatest significance was in helping to preserve that slightly archaic quality which is such a striking facet of British life in the post-war era.

Old-fashioned text books used to write of the 'popular mood' of 1945, of the electorate voting for social reform, for socialism even. Without doubt, during the war there was a definite move to the left throughout all classes of society. But we should never forget that in 1945, although Labour had a crashing majority in the House of Commons, 39.8 per cent of the electorate voted Conservative, and 20 per cent did not bother to vote at all. However, when discussing prevailing social ideologies it is not the popular vote itself that is important, but the beliefs of influential people and their understanding of the popular will. Looked at that way, there was a left-of-centre consensus in Britain which actually gathered in strength during the 1940s, and which was qualified in a rightward direction, rather than obliterated, by the Conservative victories in the 1950s. Though the Conservatives took the House of Commons in 1951, Labour's popular vote had actually both continued to increase, and was greater than that of the Conservatives. In 1955, however, the Conservatives capitalized on their years in office, on the divisions within the Labour party, and on the taste, sedulously fostered by the Press, for 'freedom' and consumerism. The disastrous and immoral Suez venture (1956) of the Eden Conservative government seemed a bitter divider of opinion at the time, yet was remarkably quickly pushed into the background.[23] Suez was significant as a demonstration that the end had definitely come to Britain's power to pursue imperial ambition. Contrary to what is often said, there is actually very little evidence that the loss of empire had any very serious impact on the psychology of the British people. Secular Anglicanism prevailed, loyalty towards the monarchy demonstrably increased.[24] Britain, on the surface at least, was a country without domestic strife, with high civic loyalty and low political participation, save at general elections. Behind the facade, or scarcely even behind it, was an overweening complacency, characteristic of the Conservative party and shared by many in the Labour party: a conviction that the British way of doing things was not just correct, but eternal. Critical voices, 'the Movement', 'the Angry Young Men', were raised from the early 1950s onwards; but though they contributed to later critiques, their impact at the time was no more than what one would expect of middle-class coteries.

THE CULTURAL REVOLUTION, 1958–1973

Vital components of the cultural revolution were the mutually interreacting forces of new technologies and sharply rising living standards. The waging of war had had important repercussions for British science, and, aside from the more obvious consequences, some invaluable indirect ones for medicine. However, here I am concerned with those technologies which directly interacted with consumer society. It was not that the British economy had suddenly moved into a new era of soundly-based expansion: but annual growth rates of 2 to 3 per cent were sufficient to generate growing affluence. Earnings from banking, insurance, and shipping services, together with growing investments in Britain by multinational corporations, were sufficient to keep international payments in the appearance of balance, even though British exports were losing out against foreign competition. Britain profited from the general expansion of trade throughout the industrial world, and shared in the continuing exploitation of the under-developed world. Though Conservative governments (till 1964 and 1970–74) and Labour governments (1964–70) did much harm to British industry by violent changes of course in their opening years of office,[25] there was underlying continuity of the notions of the mixed economy, demand management, and the comfortable divine right of the big battalions (now increasingly international ones) as against genuinely individualist enterprise. The fruits seemed good. Back in 1951 the average weekly earnings of men over twenty-one had stood at £8.20 per week. A decade later the figure had almost doubled to £15.35; in 1966 it was £20.30, in 1968 £23.00, in 1969 £24.80, in 1970 £28.05, and in 1971 £30.93. Of course, there was a whiff of inflation around as well. Between 1955 and 1960 retail prices rose by 15 per cent; by 1969 they were 63 per cent higher than in 1955. But against that, weekly wage *rates* rose 25 per cent between 1955 and 1960, and had risen by 88 per cent in 1969. When overtime is taken into account, we find that average weekly *earnings* rose 34 per cent between 1955 and 1960, and 130 per cent between 1955 and 1969. This last figure was almost exactly matched by the average earnings of middle-class salaried employees, which rose 127 per cent between 1955 and 1969. While prices of food and other necessities were steadily rising, the prices of small cars, in relation to earning power, were falling, and many products of new technology, such as television sets and washing machines, were, despite inflation, actually costing less.[26]

Of the new leisure and labour-saving products of technology, by far the most popular was the television set. Still a rarity in the early 1950s, sets were to be found in 75 per cent of homes by 1961, and in 91 per cent of homes by 1971. Next in popularity were refrigerators and washing machines. In 1956 only about 8 per cent of families had refrigerators, but by 1962 32 per cent had them, and by 1971 69 per cent; at this time 64 per cent of families had a washing machine. Telephones and motor cars were not quite so democratically distributed. By the end of the 1970s only about 50 per cent of households had a telephone, whereas 52 per cent had the use of at least one car, with 11 per cent having the use of at least two cars. The expansion of car ownership moved slowly in the 1950s, but accelerated rapidly in the early 1960s: 2,307,000 cars and vans in 1950; 3,609,000 in 1955; 5,650,000 in 1960; 9,131,000 in 1965; 11,802,000 in 1970.[27]

For the sake of brevity I shall discuss the cultural revolution itself under five rather clumsily wide-ranging and also overlapping headings. First, the general *attack upon*, and *release from*, the *social controls and conventions* established in Victorian times. This was not a political movement, and included the 1960 Betting and Gaming Act, which turned Britain into a racketeers' paradise, the entirely new phenomenon of the 1960s of drug abuse among young people, and the relaxation of censorship following the failure of the prosecution for

Introduction to contemporary cultural studies

obscenity in 1960 of the publishers of *Lady Chatterley's Lover,* as well
as the great 'civilized society' reforms of the middle and later 1960s.
Corporal punishment, still inflicted in the first post-war years, had
been abolished in 1948, but hangings continued, till in 1965 capital
punishment was abolished as a five-year experiment; in 1969 abolition
was made permanent. The 1967 Abortion Act made possible abortions
on medical or psychological grounds, and even made it possible to get
an abortion on the National Health Service. The National Health
Service (Family Planning) Act of the same year permitted local
authorities, for the first time, to provide contraceptives and contraceptive advice. Then, the Sexual Offences Act, also of 1967, ended the
barbarous tradition whereby a homosexual act between two consent-
ing adults in private was a criminal offence; social discrimination
against homosexuals, of course, could not so readily be swept away.
The Divorce Reform Act of 1969, described by Dr Shirley Summer-
skill as a 'Casanova's charter', seemed to most people to offer freedom
from an irksome and unjust social control. The Matrimonial Property
Act of 1970 established that a wife's work, whether as a housewife
within the home or as a money-earner outside it, should be considered
as an equal contribution towards creating the family home, if, as a
result of a divorce, that had to be divided. The Equal Pay Act, also
1970, was not intended to become fully effective for another five years,
and even then there were many loopholes; but at least these two Acts
took further the attack upon Victorian assumptions about the inequality of women. Acts of Parliament must never be mistaken for the
reality of social change: but in fact the reality of change was everywhere to be perceived in fashion, in a new frankness in conversation
and in print, and in all the things summed up under the label 'permissiveness'. (The advent of the contraceptive pill undoubtedly contributed to more liberated sexual attitudes and behaviour, but the
evidence suggests that it was not actually in wide use before the late
1960s).[28]

My second heading is *cosmopolitanism,* which I take to include the
manner in which intellectuals and artists began consciously to break
with the cosy insularity of the post-war era, and the way in which, at a
more general level, there was an openness to American and continental developments. Though it is not within my brief to go into detail
here, I'm thinking of the advent of the New Left, of the impact of
cultural theories transmitted from the USA, of the interest in structuralism, as also, at a more mundane level, of the effects of foreign
travel and the growing taste for foreign foods and foreign restaurants.

Third, and most complex, *new attitudes to class.* The literary, and
quintessentially minority, movements of the early and middle 1950s,
'the Movement', 'the Angry Young Men' and 'kitchen sink', laid stress
on the importance of provincial, as against metropolitan life: but the
Movement writers at least were more closely associated with the

provincial universities than with the provincial working class. It would be absurd to claim that class distinction, and the condition of the working class in particular, had not been seriously and honestly presented before the late 1950s.[29] But it was a fundamental and characteristic feature of the cultural revolution that class differences were made unambiguous and explicit. In no way was 1960s society 'classless', but the working class, largely because of its increased spending power, was now *visible* in a way that it had never been before; some of its most talented escapees held the limelight, and while doing so made no attempt to eschew their origins. The key work in revealing the working classes as neither inert victims, nor idealized heroes of the future revolution, was Richard Hoggart's *Uses of Literacy*, first published in 1957.

My fourth heading is the power of, and preoccupation with, *youth*. At root this was an economic phenomenon related to the spending power created by the new technological high-wage society. Youth, of course, could mean different things depending upon the standpoint. The 'Angry Young Men' were certainly not youths. But their writings, and the publicity which surrounded them, helped nonetheless to create the notion of a culture led by individuals of a rather younger age than had hitherto been usual; there was a kind of 'shunting' effect – intellectuals were now fifteen or twenty years younger than they used to be, so the age of popular entertainers and fashion-setters, too, was shunted back by fifteen or twenty years. To hand were spending power, encouragement of, and means towards, self-expression – mass-produced but stylish clothes and, above all, the new rock-based popular music. Finally, the various influences come together to help create *distinctive cultural artifacts* which were both products of the cultural revolution and served to define and extend it.

A crucial aspect of the liberalization of the 1960s was the major development in the realm of higher education. Many colleges, particularly in the spheres of art and design, were upgraded, as were teacher training colleges; quasi-university status was given to leading colleges of technology – rechristened polytechnics, their degrees were awarded by one *national* body (a sharp break with tradition, this), the Council for National Academic Awards (CNAA), founded in 1964; certain colleges of higher technology became full universities, and totally new universities were created: Sussex, York, Kent, Warwick, Lancaster, East Anglia, Essex and Stirling. The student movement of 1968 was relatively mild, and in many ways imitative, compared with the French example – secular Anglicanism at work again perhaps. It took its sharpest forms in the austere environment of Essex, or the cramped urban quarters of the London School of Economics. In four big demonstrations against American policies in Vietnam the pendulum of violence swung forth and back: March, violent, non-violent, violent (the 'Battle of Grosvenor Square'); October, so non-violent that there was much self-congratulation over British tolerance and stability. Youth was certainly not made an enemy of by established society; and a section of it, at least, was incorporated in the political nation, by the lowering of the voting age in 1971 to eighteen.

There were profound changes in other sectors of education as well. By 1964 the arguments against the eleven-plus by sociologists, psychologists, and committed social egalitarians were becoming almost deafening. The new Labour government in July 1965 issued Circular 10/65 calling upon all local authorities to submit proposals for establishing comprehensive schools. Great impetus was certainly given to the replacement of education divided between secondary modern and grammar schools by comprehensive schooling but within a context of great confusion and inconsistency. Government intentions in regard to direct grant schools were far from clear; local authorities anyway had plenty of licence to go their own ways. Confusion was confounded, inconsistency confirmed when the new Conservative government, in June 1970, issued Circular 10/70 which stressed that the reorganization of secondary education was entirely a matter for the local authorities. Thus there was no unified comprehensive system; but at least deep inroads had been made into a system which, with more than a whiff of Victorianism about it, had essentially selected those from deprived backgrounds to go to secondary modern schools, and those from relatively privileged backgrounds to go to grammar schools.

Where innovation most in accord with the other changes that have been discussed took place was in the primary schools. For long enough children had been reared under the shadow of the Victorian faith in the three Rs. One of the first major initiatives towards bringing imaginative new approaches to curriculum design came from a private source, the Nuffield Foundation. In 1964 the Schools Council for the Curriculum and Examinations was set up, with finance coming from the local education authorities. From the Schools Council came many initiatives towards making the primary school curriculum more flexible, more imaginative, and more enjoyable. Of course, just as many respectable and far from wrong-headed citizens deplored what was happening in the universities, old and new, and argued that the spread of comprehensive education was destroying the high academic standards once the pride of the grammar schools, so there were many who thought that primary school children were being given far too much latitude while failing to learn the necessary basic skills.

To a degree these changes benefited the working class, mostly they benefited the middle classes. Though there was a new emphasis on, real gains for, and a reappraisal of attitudes towards, the working class, the essential contours of the British class structure did not alter much. There was some rather wild theorizing about the *embourgeoisement* of the working class, but when a man had to work long hours of overtime in conditions which continued to be distinctively unpleasant in order to achieve a middle-class standard of living, clearly he was still working-class.[30] At the other end of the scale, while the range of achievements which might permit socialization into the upper class continued to widen, the dominance of the class itself was little shaken. Meantime, other social divides had come to the fore. Of the thousands of black men and women who came to Britain during the Second World War to work as civilians or members of the armed forces, the majority returned home on the establishment of peace. But they returned to disillusionment and unemployment. Until 1952, America was the pre-ferred new home for migrant West Indians – it was nearer and richer than Britain. But in that year the United States introduced a virtual ban on West Indian immigration, with the result that they turned to Britain, then still suffering from labour shortages. A peak was reached in 1962, when 34,000 West Indians arrived. This coincided with a greater inflow of immigrants from the Indian sub-continent, pre-viously strictly controlled at source by Indian government refusals to grant passports to its nationals – a control ruled unconstitutional by the Indian Supreme Court in 1960. Rumours of impending legislation to control immigration into Britain only increased the numbers trying to enter the United Kingdom. The new immigrants settled in the poorer parts of London (almost a third of all immigrants), in the West Mid-lands, in Bradford, and in other run-down urban areas. In August 1958 violent race rioting broke out between local whites and the heavy concentration of West Indian immigrants in Notting Hill, West London (177 people were arrested). Attempts to control immigration began with the Immigration Act of February 1962; attempts to deal by law with race discrimination began with the Race Relations Acts of 1966 and 1968. The unconstructive confusion of the British response to race relations forms perhaps the most clearcut condemnation of the spirit and consequences of secular Anglicanism. The 1960s was a decade of striking success for organized Scottish nationalism, and, to a lesser degree, for Welsh nationalism, which, however, did at least achieve the triumph of the Act of 1967 which placed the Welsh lan-guage on a par with English in Wales. But secular Anglicanism was strong enough even in the Celtic hinterlands to ensure that there was no real threat to the unity of the United Kingdom. Feminism was only just beginning to stir into action at the beginning of the 1970s, and here, too, there was none of the obsessive violence of the con-temporary American SCUM (Society for Cutting Up Men). Published in 1970, Germaine Greer's seminal feminist tract, *The Female Eunuch*, was to prove as influential in the 1970s as Hoggart's *Uses of Literacy* had been in the 1960s.

There remains to be mentioned one oppressive and all too visible phenomenon of the 1960s: the destruction, in the name of redevelop-ment, low-cost housing, planning, architectural innovation, freedom for the motor car, and quick profits for the influential, of the urban environment. Urban motorways and uninhabitable high-rise flats were to be the unacceptable face of the cultural revolution. For all that, British society had broken out of the straitjacket of dullness and conformity which had pinioned it since Victorian times. It would be wrong to exaggerate changes in everyday life; yet it would be fair to say that there was a new hedonism abroad in the land, that life was lived with greater gusto than ever it had been since the evangelicals set their stamp upon the mores of the middle class. Many of the changes, such as the new feminist movement and the citizens' rights movement, just apparent at the end of the decade, only really moved on to their full strength in the 1970s.

DISSONANCE AND MANIFEST DECLINE, 1973–1982

The search for historical watersheds is a notoriously unrewarding one: the Autumn of 1973 when the oil-producing nations doubled their prices and when world trade slid into recession is one of the most clearly defined watersheds in recent history. Paradoxically, it was at the same time that Britain began to develop her own oil resources in the North Sea; but rather than a chariot of fire against recession these were to serve as little more than a rapidly shrinking defensive moat. In the years of optimism too much investment had been channelled down the easy slope into the service industries; now, in fiercely adverse world conditions, Britain's industrial base went into alarming decline. More than any other European country Britain found its economy dominated by such multinationals as Exxon, Ford, and Texaco (American-owned), Rothmans (South African-owned), Bowater (Canadian-owned), Shell (jointly Dutch and British-owned), British Petroleum and Unilever (both British-owned). Multinationals compounded a basic weakness of Britain's over-large, inadequately integrated industrial units: remoteness from the real problems and concerns of the shop floor. In 1973, the failing Conservative government of Edward Heath at last took Britain into the European Common Market. From the middle of the decade a marked economic and social orientation towards Europe was very apparent: as older ocean-going ports closed down, new European container terminals opened up. Although Labour was returned to office in 1974, there was a definite trend towards 'orthodox' market-oriented and monetarist economics and towards commercialization at the expense of state initiatives. In its own large public expenditure cuts (1978) the Labour government was responding to the demands of the International Monetary Fund whose assistance was required in the wake of the 1976 crisis. Commercialization is seen strikingly in the way in which private companies began to take over the sponsorship of artistic and sporting events.

The economics of the later 1970s had their most disastrous outcome in the mounting levels of unemployment. The percentage of un-employed out of the total number of employees stood at 2.6 per cent in 1970, rising to 3.5 per cent and 3.8 per cent in 1971 and 1972 respectively, with a drop back of 2.7 per cent in 1973 and 2.6 per cent in 1974; in 1975 it rose to 4.1 per cent, in 1976 to 5.7 per cent, in 1977 to 6.2 per cent, with a slight remission in 1978 to 6.1 per cent, then up again in 1979 and on into 1980. By the end of 1981 unemployment in Britain was at the two million mark and a year later it was three million and still steadily rising. The other economic ill much commented upon, of course, was inflation. Seemingly under control toward the end of the 1970s, it rose sharply to unprecedented heights in the early 1980s, coming down somewhat in 1983, but at the expense of an intolerable level of unemployment.

There had been some changes of direction in the Welfare State during the 1960s. In the realm of income security the major changes were the abandonment of the idea of flat-rate benefits (in 1959 – the principle was extended by the Labour government in 1966), the retreat from the principle of universality which Conservative and Labour experts both now felt was wasteful of resources in that it spread inadequate benefits too thinly across the entire nation, the introduc-tion (in 1965) of the idea of redundancy payments, and the deliberate seeking out of sources of deprivation ignored during the first stage of the setting up of the Welfare State. The most important Act of the 1960s was the 1966 Ministry of Social Security Act which sought, among other things, to remove the stigma which still deterred many deserving individuals from applying for National Assistance by replacing it with Supplementary Benefits. Supplementary Benefits, in many respects, were administered in a flexible way sensitive to indivi-dual needs. But there were two obnoxious features: the 'wage-stop' designed to ensure that Supplementary Benefit did not act as an encouragement to the workshy by offering more than they would normally obtain in employment (but, in effect, placing certain people in a 'poverty trap'); and the 'cohabitation rule' which meant that single, separated, or divorced women claiming benefits could have them stopped if it was discovered that they were cohabiting with a man who could then be held to be providing them with financial support. On the more constructive side the National Insurance (Old Persons and Widows Pensions and Attendance Allowance) Act of 1970 directed new benefits towards the disabled and the very old.

From what was said in the opening paragraphs of this section one might expect a general curtailment of the Welfare State in the 1970s. Actually, until the reassertion of Victorian dismal science after 1979, the major innovation was the Employment Protection Act of 1975 whose provisions covered the right not to be unfairly dismissed, entitlement to a written statement of terms and conditions of employment, guaranteed pay, time off work for trade union duties, and also redundancy pay, minimum periods of notice, and maternity rights. The Act could not of itself serve as a protection against industrial recession; nor could various job-creation schemes, including the Employment Subsidies Act of 1978. The Labour governments sought to achieve the aim of income maintenance in old age through linking Social Security pensions with the cost-of-living index, and through pressing for the adoption of private schemes whose basic feature was the provision of a pension related to the level of earnings upon retirement. Themselves a reaction to inflation, these policies, as became clear by the end of the decade, were in turn menaced by inflation and economic crisis. Still, in 1978–79 the Government spent a total of £16,490,000,000 on Social Security benefits, compared with £3,410,000,000 in 1968–69.

In health the significant developments going back to the late 1950s were: completely new attempts to deal seriously and sensitively with the problems of mental health (the epoch-making Mental Health Act was passed in 1959); the steady increase in a larger range of health service charges; the attempt to remedy the worst shortages of both hospital accommodation and medical personnel, successful on the whole, at least until the economic crises of the mid–1970s; the re-organization – much criticized – of the whole structure of the medical services in the early 1970s; and the growth of private medical schemes. It is difficult to disentangle the many continuing successes of the health service from the tales of despondency and gloom; however by the 1980s there were legitimate doubts as to the seriousness of the Conservative government's commitment to the basic principles of the National Health Service. In education, universalist principles were resumed by the Labour government after 1974, when it moved forward with a policy of directly absorbing public-sector grammar schools into comprehensive schools and indirectly asserting pressure on independent schools to join in by withdrawing their direct grants. There was much debate over whether or not the absorption of grammar schools into comprehensive schools meant a lowering of standards.

A more traditional social history would have given more attention than I have so far to the institutions of the British Labour movement. Britain has the oldest, the most coherent, and the most consciously organized working class in the world. While there can be no escaping the fact that much of Britain's weakness is due to deficiencies in Britain's élites, there is much also in the view that serious problems have been caused by the way in which the British working class over more than a century has become deeply entrenched in a defensive, hostile, and essentially conservative set of attitudes towards the rest of society, the rest of the world, and above all towards the problems of economic innovation and growth.

Engrained in this deep conservatism of British society is the immutable belief that workers must at all costs defend their existing position, that it is the duty of management to manage, and that workers should not concern themselves with larger issues of productivity or economic success. The Labour government after 1945 proved, in practice, to be deeply hostile to the idea of industrial democracy. The matter was not revived in any serious way until the 1970s. The whole saga of industrial democracy in the later 1970s tells us much about the contemporary trade-union movement and its attitudes, and very much suggests, not that radical, disruptive ideas were taking over, but that the traditional stance had shifted little. However, with a Labour government back in office after 1974, and a General Council of the TUC, together with the most influential trade-union leader of the time, Jack Jones of the Transport and General Workers Union, strongly committed to their own version of industrial democracy, the matter was very much back on the agenda. Furthermore, the Labour government began to surmise that the extent of worker participation in management in European countries, particularly West Germany, might have something to do with their greater economic success. In his first address as Prime Minister to the Labour Party Conference in 1976, James Callaghan spoke of successive governments having 'failed to ignite the fires of industrial growth in the ways that Germany, France, and Japan, with their different political and economic philosophies, have done'. Worker participation schemes, on government directions, were introduced into the British Steel Corporation, British Leyland, and Chrysler.

Yet there was still great resistance to the whole concept from within the trade-union movement itself: opposition was particularly strong from the Electricians, the Engineers, and the General and Municipal Workers. Among the public at large, it appeared that something over half of all adult employees did favour worker participation in management, but that most people were against industrial democracy being imposed by law. There was public opposition, too, among trade unionists as well as non-trade unionists, to the TUC scheme, whereby worker directors would be nominated through trade unions; there was also opposition to any idea of worker directors being in a majority on boards. As governments so often did in such circumstances, the Callaghan government in December 1975 appointed a Committee of Enquiry, under the chairmanship of Lord Bullock. The Bullock Committee had an enormously difficult task in front of it and in the end produced a majority report, a minority report, and a note of dissent. Basically the Bullock Report proposed that its scheme for industrial democracy would only come into practice in a company where at least one-third of the employees expressed the wish for such an arrangement. But where the scheme did come into effect workers' representation on the board would be controlled entirely by the trade unions. It was on this point that the minority – desiring that representation should be directly from the work force as a whole, not through the unions – split from the majority. An elaborate scheme for the composition of boards would ensure that though in appearance there would be 'parity' between employers and employees, the addition of a co-opted 'third group' meant that workers (or in effect, union) representatives could never be in a majority, and thus could always escape responsibility for serious or unpopular decisions. At the same time the Report went out of its way to stress that unions would still retain their traditional independence.

As was to be expected, the proposals were not well received. Employers drew back now from the prospect that industrial democracy might become a reality; liberals (in all parties) joined with the minority in opposing the vesting of control of workers' representation exclusively in the hands of the unions; and such union leaders as John Lyons, General Secretary of the Electrical Power Engineers Association, expressed the old reservations: 'Employee representatives on boards à la Bullock will tie the unions into the management process'. Thus when the Labour government came to frame its own proposals on the subject they departed quite perceptibly from Bullock. The government proposed a two-tier scheme, with worker representation only on a 'Policy Board', not involved in the day-to-day running of the company, which would be reserved to a more traditional 'Management Board' exclusively composed of the usual 'professional' managers; even on the Policy Board, workers' representatives would have no more than one third of the seats. Elections for these seats would be carried out by the work force as a whole, not through trade unions. Once more, little had been done to implement the proposals by the time the Labour government fell from office.[31] The present Thatcher government has shown no inclination whatsoever to take the matter up.

British trade unions came increasingly under fire for their alleged propensity to go on strike. Actually, till the end of the 1960s, the record of British trade unions for days lost due to strike action was not noticeably worse than that of most other industrialized countries. The problem in the 1960s had been that of the 'unofficial' or 'wild-cat' strike: short, unexpected strikes, called without official union support, not globally particularly significant, but damaging because of their very unpredictability. In the 1970s the pattern changed, with more massive strikes officially sponsored by the very large unions; these strikes certainly suggested a very grave difference, in a time of gathering economic recession, between powerful unions on one side, and government and organized society on the other. By the middle of the 1970s, British strike figures were considerably worse than those of any of our European competitors. The only country with figures manifestly worse than those of the United Kingdom was the United States.[32] The fact that the only country with a worse record than Britain's was that bastion of untrammelled private enterprise, the United States, might suggest that a basic weakness was a failure to establish, as in the main European countries, an orderly round of industrial relations bargaining.

The phenomena of flying pickets and secondary picketing had been introduced in the early 1970s. Then in 1974 the miners' leaders deliberately acted to restrain violence. But the issues remained live ones even during the period of relative peace in industrial relations in the middle 1970s; then violence flared in July 1977 during the strike at the Grunwick film-processing factory in West London, and in the steel strike of 1980. The new type of picketing was little more than an up-dating and intensification of the activism of the hunger marchers of the 1930s; it became open to legitimate criticism when it interfered with the livelihood of employers and employees not in any way directly involved with the particular strike in question.

The sense of dramatic change between the bustling optimism of the cultural revolution and the depression-bound 1970s was heightened by the arrival of IRA terrorism on the British mainland, militancy and violence in industrial relations, National Front provocation and police over-reaction, all involving the first deaths in civic strife on the British mainland since the police strike at the end of the First World War (the IRA campaign of 1939 being excepted). Yet many of the liberating trends of the later 1960s continued and expanded. Despite talk of 'the new piety', there was no going back to the sexual taboos of the 1940s and early 1950s, though no doubt the feminist movement, which developed rapidly, had some success in demonstrating that what might be sexual liberation in a male-dominated society was not necessarily quite that in a society which respected women's attitudes and aspirations. It appeared, indeed, that many women were learning to treat total sexual involvement, the romantic ideal of a mere dozen years earlier, as a deadly drug to be sedulously avoided. Though more in evidence in middle-class than working-class areas, the growth of citizens' rights movements in what had formerly been a rather apathetic political culture was noteworthy. Homosexuals began to organize to make the letter of the law also the reality and the spirit.

Other trends, longer term and less inspiriting, also continued. Economic recession re-intensified distinctions between social classes and, even more disastrously, racial tensions and hostilities.[33] At the beginning of the new decade there were frightening incidents of violence and destruction of property at St Annes in Bristol, Brixton in South London, and Toxteth in Liverpool, fuelled by economic deprivation, racial indignity, and police insensitivity. For awareness and comprehension of such incidents the British people were dependent upon Press and television. While there had been much to commend in British television (first under the BBC monopoly till 1954, thereafter with the creation of commercial television under two competing mono- polies), the history of the British Press had provided small ground for comfort. Continuing concern in governing circles was evident from the fact that the Royal Commission which reported in 1948 was followed by a further one, reporting in 1977. The later Commission noted the accelerating trend towards mergers and closures, and the chronic condition of financial crisis in which the national Press found itself. Nine great combines controlled the overwhelming bulk of the British Press, four of them, in the last analysis, controlled from outside Britain. Apart from the menace of mergers and multinationalism, the Commission also identified four other serious problems: the invasion of privacy by 'investigative' reporters; the weakness of the Press Council in preserving high journalistic standards; the growing control of the only alternative source of information, television, by the news- paper companies; and poor industrial relations:

> One debilitating legacy to national newspapers from the post-war days of
> easy profits and weak management has been the exceptionally high earnings
> of print workers and a disposition among publishers to yield easily to threats
> of unofficial action. Industrial relations in Fleet Street have been
> notoriously bad for a generation and their improvement has been the
> regularly falsified hope of everyone who has attempted to set the industry
> on the path of modernization.[34]

Throughout 1979, indeed, *Times* newspapers were paralysed as man- agers and men failed to agree over the introduction of computerized techniques. When their representatives appeared on television to ex- press their differences and, ultimately, to explain their agreements, it was the British class system itself which was being paraded: on the one side, the public school accents of the managing director, Marmaduke Hussey, on the other the London accents and ungrammatical construc- tions of the SOGAT leaders.

Were political and social values changing?; was secular Anglicanism a busted flush? It could be argued that it was the continuing vigour of the Anglican tradition which permitted a relatively peaceful accom- modation to consumerism, participation, youth culture, and feminism. Arguments that Britain was becoming a corporatist state also seemed exaggerated.[35] That ordinary Members of Parliament have been losing influence since the late nineteenth century is a historical truism. That MPs carry less respect than they once did among their peer groups in the upper and middle classes is also true; how much they actually meant to the masses in the nineteenth century is a moot question. But direct influence upon Parliament and government by vested interests and pressure groups is nothing new whatsoever. As modern society has become more complex, so the balance of forces behind political decision-making must become more complex. Political commentators have focussed attention on such pressure groups as: the Child Poverty Action Group whose campaigning and lobbying did much to bring about the introduction of Child Benefits; the Abortion Law Reform Association and the Society for the Protection of the Unborn Child which between them provided much of the ammunition for the parliamentary debates on abortion; and the National Association for Mental Health which did much to reorientate the National Health Service towards this traditionally neglected and suspect area.

The Conservative government collapsed at the beginning of 1974 because of Heath's unwise confrontation with the miners. In the February election Labour polled half a million less votes than they had in the election they lost in 1970, but the Conservatives lost still more seriously at the hands of Nationalists and Liberals. With 37.9 per cent of votes cast the Conservatives returned 297 MPs; Labour with 37.1 per cent of votes cast actually returned 301 MPs; the Liberals with 19.3 per cent had 14 MPs, the Scottish Nationalists with 2 per cent and the Welsh Nationalists with 0.6 per cent had 7 MPs and 2 MPs respectively. Harold Wilson ran a minority government till October when he chose his moment for a further general election. This time Labour polled 39.2 per cent of all votes cast to 35.9 per cent for the Conservatives. Despite a tiny majority, and despite the desperate sterling crisis of the late summer of 1976, Labour under Wilson, then Callaghan, seemed to govern with some confidence: the 'Social Contract', essentially Attlee's wage restraint policy with a grandiose name and legal sanctions, proved effective in controlling inflation. However, as Callaghan prolonged his government into the dismal winter of 1979 (the 'Winter of Discontent'), deep stresses and divisions became very apparent in the Labour party. Nevertheless, the general election of 1979 no more showed that Great Britain had become a country of reactionary conservatism than the result of 1945 showed it had become socialist: 43.9 per cent of those voting voted Conservative, but 36.9 per cent still voted Labour, with nearly 30 per cent not voting at all. So it would be a mistake to see the Conservative election victory as marking anything like a revolution in British social and political values. Self-evidently, most of those who believed in consensus politics or some form of collective socialism continued to do so. On the other hand, since the early 1970s there had been a steady re-emphasis on the part of most leading politicians in both parties on the values of thrift and enterprise. As inflation rose sharply, greater weight was given to arguments that above all it was the duty of governments to provide the preconditions for a stable economic environment in which each individual could plan his future on a rational basis. The Labour party with its genuine roots in the working class was a unique phenomenon on the world political scene. Many of its members saw it also as the custodian of the broad consensus which had achieved important reforms in the 1940s and the

1960s: some of these, early in 1981, established the Social Democratic Party.

CODA AND RECAPITULATION

It was far from clear at that point in time in 1982 that there would not be a great resurgence of the Labour party, and indeed a successful reaction among consensus Conservative politicians against the right-wing tenets of the Conservative leader, Margaret Thatcher. But in the summer, in an affair which future historians will find incomprehensible, as indeed most Europeans of all political persuasions found it at the time, the British government, having failed to take effective precautions to warn off the Argentine, found itself involved in a war with that country to restore British sovereignty to the Falkland Islands. After the recapture of the islands, an heroic adventure with respect to the servicemen involved, the tides of opinion began to run strongly for Mrs Thatcher and all she stood for. Now the privatization of the British economy and the dismantling of the universalist Welfare State became substance, no longer just threatening shadow. That there was to be no effective resistance in the near future was clarified by the convincing Conservative victory in the general election of June 1983.

The country which, in 1940, had faced its greatest crisis ever with remarkable unity, which had come through the 1940s with fortitude and determination, and which in the 1960s had surprised the world with its innovative energies, was run-down and perhaps more obviously divided than it had been since the nineteenth century. A country which, in its more cloistered corners, could rear great talent (as achievements in science and medicine revealed) had failed to tap the genius of its people but instead nurtured its conservatism, defensiveness, and xenophobia. The Second World War had brought pride, much change, but still more complacency. Not so much a rigid but an infinitely resilient class structure, with its strong educational and cultural frame, had endured, so that too many of the same sort of people continued to take too many wrong decisions. Deep and obvious inequalities brought a seepage of morale, damaging divisions and confrontations, a reluctance to become involved in the nation's problems, and above all lost to society that which the spurned and discriminated-against, given encouragement, could have contributed to the common weal.

NOTES AND REFERENCES

1. This view, of course, is contentious: the notion of a 'cultural revolution', for example, is in effect dismissed by John Hill in 'Working Class Realism and Sexual Reaction', in *British Cinema History*, eds James Curran and Vincent Porter, Weidenfeld 1983, pp. 303–11. My own arguments are more fully developed in *British Society since 1945*, Allen Lane 1982, Part Two, and in *'Room at the Top* and *Saturday Night and Sunday Morning* and the "Cultural Revolution" in Britain', *Journal of Contemporary History* XIX, 1 (1984), pp. 125–51.
2. Martin J. Wiener, *English Culture and the Decline of the Industrial Spirit, 1850–1980, Cambridge University Press* 1981.
3. Angus Calder, *The People's War*, Cape 1969.
4. *Social Change in Britain, 1920–1970,* Birkbeck College 1970, and *British Society since 1945*. The concept has been welcomed in reviews by, among others, John Vincent, *Sunday Times* (2 May 1982), and Paul Addison, *History* (October 1982).
5. Sydney Pollard, *The Wasting of the British Economy,* Croom Helm 1982, pp. 124, 186.
6. For nationalization and economic policy generally, see Pollard, *Wasting* and *The Development of the British Economy*, Edward Arnold 1962; and Reuben Kelf-Cohen, *British Nationalisation 1945–1973*, Macmillan 1973.
7. The motor industry is the classic case of private industry preferring soft options at home to winning markets abroad: Pollard, *Development,* p. 381.
8. José Harris, *Beveridge*, Oxford University Press 1977; Addison, *The Road to 1945,* Cape 1975, Ch. 8; Marwick, *Britain in the Century of Total War*, Bodley Head 1968, pp. 304–13; *The Home Front*, Thames and Hudson 1976, p. 130.
9. The best accounts are *Penelope Hall's Social Services of England and Wales* (9th edn) eds J. Mays, A. Forder, and O. Keidan, Routledge and Kegan Paul 1975; and Eric Butterworth and Robert Holman, *Social Welfare in Modern Britain*, Collins 1975.
10. Fraser to Miss Stanley, 11 May 1930, BBC Written Archives, Acc. no. 1420; R. H. S. Crossman, *The Diaries of a Cabinet Minister* (3 vols.) Hamilton 1975–77, Vol. 2, p. 190. See Marwick, *Class: Image and Reality in Britain, France and the USA since 1930*, Collins 1980, Chs 9, 15.
11. Arriving at a satisfactory figure is incredibly difficult: see in particular W. D. Rubinstein, *Wealth and the Wealthy in the Modern World,* Croom Helm 1980, and *Men of Property*, Croom Helm 1981. Recent Marxist writers would see the 'capitalist class' as much smaller than this, but then I am far from sure that the upper class is a capitalist class: see J. M. Scott, *The Upper Class in Britain*, Macmillan 1982.
12. *Haileybury and Imperial Service Chronicle* (9 Nov. 1945).
13. R. K. Kelsall, *The Higher Civil Service in Great Britain,* Routledge and Kegan Paul 1955, p. 142.
14. J. R. Godley, *Living Like a Lord*, Gollancz 1955, p. 56.
15. Margaret Stacey, *Tradition and Change: A Study of Banbury,* Oxford University Press 1960, Ch. 8.
16. Mass Observation Archives, file 3073.

17. Marwick, 'Images of the Working Class since 1930', in *The Working Class in Modern History*, ed. Jay Winter, Cambridge University Press 1983, pp. 215–31.
18. B. S. Rowntree and G. R. Lavers, *Poverty and the Welfare State*, Longmans 1951.
19. Geoffrey Gorer, *Exploring English Character*, Cresset Press 1955, pp. 12–51.
20. Throughout this essay vital statistics are culled from the relevant volumes of *Annual Abstract of Statistics*, HMSO.
21. James Walvin, *Beside the Seaside*, Allen Lane 1978, pp. 126–55; and *Leisure and Society 1830–1950*, Longman 1978, pp. 149–57; Roger Manvell, *The Film and the Public*, Penguin 1955, p. 217.
22. *Called Up*, eds P. Chambers and A. Landreth, Wingate 1955, and King George's Jubilee Trust, *Citizens of Tomorrow*, King George's Jubilee Trust 1955.
23. Leon Epstein, *British Politics in the Suez Crisis*, Pall Mall 1964, pp. 147ff., citing British Institute of Public Opinion Polls.
24. Philip Ziegler, *Crown and People*, Collins 1978.
25. See Michael Stewart, *The Jekyll and Hyde Years*, Dent 1977.
26. Marwick, *British Society since 1945*, pp. 117–18.
27. Central Statistical Office, *Social Trends*, No. 10, HMSO 1980, pp. 30–3.
28. Christie Davies, *Permissive Britain*, Pitman 1975; Michael Schofield, *Sexual Behaviour of Young People*, Longmans 1965.
29. See for example the films *Love on the Dole* (1941), *The Ship Builders* (1943), *It Always Rains on Sunday* (1948) and *The Brave Don't Cry* (1953).
30. See especially Ferdynand Zweig, *The Worker in an Affluent Society*, Heinemann 1961, and David Lockwood, 'The "New Working Class" ', *Archives Européennes de Sociologie*, I, 2 (1960), 248–59.
31. Robert Currie, *Industrial Politics*, Oxford University Press 1979, pp. 274–83; *Report of the Committee of Enquiry on Industrial Democracy* (Bullock Committee), HMSO 1977.
32. International Labor Office, *Year Book of Labour Statistics 1983*, ILO, Geneva 1983, Table 29.
33. See especially Thomas Cottle, *Black Testimony*, Wildwood House 1978.
34. *Royal Commission on the Press: Final Report*, HMSO 1977, p. 5.
35. The chief academic protagonist of this view is Keith Middlemass. See his *Politics in Industrial Society*, André Deutsch 1979; also Michael Moran, *The Politics of Industrial Relations*, Macmillan 1977.

Chapter 2

AN INTRODUCTION TO BROADCASTING HISTORY

ROGER SALES

> The stage but echoes back the publick voice.
> The drama's laws the drama's patrons give,
> For we that live to please, must please to live.
> (Dr Johnson)

The learned Doctor suggests that every society gets the theatre it deserves. The opening nights associated with British broadcasting, particularly the first commercial television transmission in 1955, question such optimistic equations between the 'publick voice' and the 'drama's laws'. Radio and television, hailed as the biggest theatres in the land, have a nasty habit of echoing the voices of their political rather than public patrons. All those glowing tributes to the cultural significance of broadcasting sit uneasily alongside the fact that structural decisions and developments have never been major general election issues. Those who bleat away about the sacred power of the off-switch are recommending a primitive weapon in what has always been a sophisticated political battle. Politicians may claim the divine right to make the 'drama's laws', although broadcasting mandarins and producers always want to develop and interpret them as they see fit. The echoing stage is sometimes filled with a single voice, but it is more likely to ring with the competing cries of its political and professional patrons. The argument is invariably about what the great British public either wants or needs, yet their voice is no more than a stage whisper. This essay will consider the first forty years of British broadcasting in order to provide some of the background to contemporary debates. Two issues will receive special attention in the post-war period. First of all, the advent of ITV in the 1950s will be considered as an example of the power of political patronage to determine the overall shape of broadcasting. Secondly, the 'Fourteen Day Rule' will be discussed to illustrate the vulnerability of day-to-day current affairs programming to more indirect forms of political pressure.

RADIO REITH

It is still well nigh impossible to write about British broadcasting without a balanced comment on its founding father, Lord Reith. Although he left the BBC in 1938 to run Imperial Airways, it took more than a while for the news to sink in. Those who did register his departure wondered why even a high flyer should want to desert those mighty imperial airwaves. The Director General of the BBC was a very real power in the land. Tenure of this unelected vocation transformed Reith himself from an obscure engineer into the great social engineer. His message for the infant medium of sound broadcasting was that it had to be as morally sound as a church bell. He wanted it to take the high cultural road and educate popular taste rather than merely pander to the lowest common denominator. There was thus a heavy stress on the best that had been thought, written, known and heard. Reith's book of prophecies, *Broadcast Over Britain* (1924), was a mixture of the theocratic ramblings of a Carlyle with the cultural poise of an Arnold. He quoted with approval a statutory old lady's statutory remark that the wireless was such a 'friendly thing'. The early broadcasters were also friendly things, even though they could be rather patronizing ones. They tried to prove their friendship by offering to share their cultural wares.

The unresolved question was whether the wireless could be a friendly and a controversial thing at the same time. Reith came to describe his own politics as being 'vaguely Liberal'. He sometimes conjured up the shade of another grand old man, Gladstone, when seeking a more precise definition. He believed fervently that broadcasting ought to be free from government control in its day-to-day affairs. Such freedom from the state would allow it not only to raise cultural standards, but also to level up democratic awareness and responsibility. Radio Reith may have preferred to talk at rather than with its audience, but it still wanted to put controversial items on the agenda. It was the politicians rather than broadcasters who were afraid of this particular combination of the friendly and the controversial. Reith thus found himself impaled on the horns of a familiar old liberal dilemma: he wanted freedom from the state but his original licence to breathe came through the state. The tensions inherent in this position surfaced during the General Strike of 1926, before the British Broadcasting Company had been transformed into a public corporation. The Company had had a broadcasting monopoly since the beginning of 1923, so when the newspapers were closed down it assumed a significance out of all proportion to its size or track record. Churchill was all for committing infanticide, but Reith insisted that all of the show and some of the substance of independence had to be preserved. Stanley Baldwin and others supported this stand in the belief that, left more or less to his own devices, Reith would hold a balance that was heavily weighted in favour of the government. He did not disappoint his political patrons. He penned a sentence which nearly says it all when he reflected upon these events in his autobiography, *Into the Wind* (1949): 'if there had been broadcasting at the time of the French Revolution, there might have been no French Revolution'. He was dealing specifically with the way in which accurate news bulletins supposedly scotched rumours, although this reflection on the French Revolution needs a wider context. Reith felt that it was his duty as the managing director of a national company to act in the national interest, which he interpreted along the lines of not broadcasting anything which might help to spread the strike and thus damage the nation.

The details of Reith's actions during the strike, for instance the fact that he tarted up Baldwin's scripts but went along with the decisions, sometimes reluctantly, to keep Labour leaders and other potential mediators away from the microphone for as long as possible, have often been used to suggest that he was nothing more than the gaffer's man. He was, however, as angry as anybody when the Royal Charter which created the British Broadcasting Corporation continued an earlier ban on controversial broadcasting. The politicians had chosen to ignore a recommendation of the Crawford Committee that a 'moderate amount of controversial matter' ought to be permitted. Reith was successful in getting this ban lifted in 1928. The politicians could still muzzle programmes that were too controversial and nobody could stop them. A series entitled *The Citizen and His Government*, which was to have contained both a fascist and a communist, was regarded as being out of bounds. The politicians were of the opinion that the wireless proved its friendship, to them as well as to the audience, by steering clear of controversy. The proper place for such matter was deemed to be the House of Commons. The BBC's political patrons have always jealously guarded their own sphere of influence. They did not want the studio to replace the Commons as the main forum for debate. They even regarded the reporting of their great deliberations as the thin end of the wedge, so it was not until 1941 that the BBC secured adequate gallery facilities at Westminster for home broadcasting. It is to Reith's credit that direct censorship of programmes by politicians was the exception rather than the rule. Such editorial independence was nevertheless purchased at the expense of crusading zeal. Reith tended to play it safe by narrowing down the angle from which the politicians could shoot at him. The Director of the troublesome Northern Region was told that his judgement was at fault when he included an interview with hunger marchers in a programme. Members of the crusading Talks Department, which had produced some abrasive programmes on unemployment, were not even speaking to each other by the middle of the 1930s. Reith continued his General Strike policy of tipping the balance in favour of the government of the day. Opponents of the National Government could not get within shouting distance of a microphone until the 1931 general election gave them a right to broadcast over Britain. Opposition spokesmen were not allowed to respond to budget broadcasts until 1934. The major parties provided Reith with definitions of what constituted a major party. They even cobbled together lists of acceptable political hacks. The politicians were sometimes given complete freedom to make their own current affairs programmes, as happened with a series ironically named *The Debate Continues*.

Reith's safety-first policy, which was implemented by a burning bush known as the Administrative Department, both preserved and proscribed editorial independence. Reith took the Imperial Airways job because it seemed to be a stepping stone to the distinguished and stretching political career which he had always hankered after. He was also using the BBC as a passport to Whitehall during his final years as Director General by insisting that controversy was not too controversial. The progressive edge to his distinctive brand of liberal paternalism was certainly blunted when his ideals became institutionalized. The BBC became the experts on the pronunciation rather than the practice of controversy. Penelope Fitzgerald captures the spirit of Radio Reith perfectly in *Human Voices* (1980), a period piece about broadcasting at the beginning of the Second World War. She describes it as 'a cross between a civil service, a powerful moral force, and an amateur theatrical company that wasn't sure where next week's money was coming from'. Reith, a truly eminent Victorian, was a firm believer in administrative efficiency and moral elevation. The waste-paper-basket and the Bible between them could bring about a national revival. He was also just enough of a showman to take part in some in-house dramatic productions. He apparently did an amusing turn as one of the broker's men.

THE BBC AT WAR

Reith's departure did not alter overnight the moral and vocal tone of British broadcasting, although it became harder during the war to subscribe to some of his more Victorian standards. J. B. Priestley was one of the broadcasters who ventured to question the soundness of sound broadcasting. He was given a seven-minute slot after the *Nine O'Clock News* on Sunday nights to deliver a series of *Postscripts*, which were aimed at maintaining morale on the Home Front in the aftermath of Dunkirk. *Picture Post* described the talks as putting the 'ordinary person's point of view in simple, straightforward, heartening language'. Priestley's fireside chats certainly seem to have kept those home fires wide awake. His praise for the heroisms of daily life nevertheless developed into a more controversial argument. He moved on from extolling the virtues of cockney pride, rustic wisdom and northern wit to suggest that there were still two nations, the rulers and the ruled. He reminded his large audiences that they might have to win the peace as well as the war. Such fighting talk worried the BBC politicians as well as the men from the Ministry of Information since peace aims were out of season. It was therefore decided to make Priestley an offer he had to refuse: he could continue to give the *Postscripts* but only on an occasional basis. His response was a satire on Reithland called *Goodnight Children*, which began its short London run on 5 February 1942. The stage is set in the English Broadcasting Corporation's regional studio somewhere in Barset, which is run by Commander Copley, an old sea dog who hates broadcasting and the 'temperamental Johnnies' involved in it. Reith's top administrative brass were often the genuine article. The producers under Copley's command have all been banished from Radio House by Rudolph Persimmon, the Head of Drama who has not recovered from the fall of Old Vienna. He is thus totally oblivious to the English regions, although rumour has it that he once 'borrowed a fur coat and an interpreter and spent half a day in Manchester'. Members of the crew of the good ship Barset include Fairfax Haycraft, a vain announcer who is unable to get that hint of Westminster Abbey out of the voice, and Moya Gronova, a European pianist with a past but no future. The new Deputy Assistant Director General, who has been seconded from the Civil Service, drops into the studio unannounced to get his first impressions of broadcasting. Tristan Sprott and the other producers dutifully oblige: 'the whole thing comes out of the spout watered down for safety . . . economy . . . and for stupidity'. Every hour is children's hour on the friendly, avuncular EBC, says Priestley playfully. More seriously, he was arguing that the wireless could and should be used as a platform for discussion and an agent of change rather than as a 'friendly thing' whose programmes were watered down to keep politicians and old ladies happy.

The politicians have always had, in theory, the absolute power to check that the broadcasting balance is in their favour. The BBC's Charter was renewable on a payment by results basis. Committees of inquiry were appointed by politicians to adjudicate on this weighty matter, although their recommendations could be ignored if they did not suit the party in power. Politicians were also in charge of jigging the gigocycles, fixing the licence fee and determining how many hours were to bring about the broadcasting day. They bobbed up on boards and advisory panels with monotonous regularity. The Ullswater Committee, which reported on broadcasting policy in 1936, confirmed the policy that in 'serious or national emergencies' these potential powers for absolute control ought to be realized. It might be expected, then, that the BBC became totally dependent on its master's voice during the war. Yet, despite stricter financial controls and the political appointment of programme advisers, the Corporation actually managed to shake itself free of some of the restrictions of the past. Its increased size, together with a fragmentation from the centre, helped. The BBC doubled up during the war and, although the Regional Network was mothballed, whole departments donned the fur coat and exiled themselves to the provinces. The lack of a clear policy about the aims and objectives of broadcasting in war also gave the BBC unexpected room for manoeuvre. Detailed plans had been drawn up before 1939 to define the Corporation's institutional position, or lack of it, in the event of hostilities, but they did not take on board the possibility of a 'phoney' war. It was in this lull before the furious storm that the BBC, true to its tradition of improvised theatricals, effectively established its war-time credentials. Evelyn Waugh was not amused by such fly-by-wire programming. Angela Lyne hits the bottle and the radio switch as simultaneously as she can in *Put Out More Flags* (1942). This novel does nevertheless suggest perhaps the main reason why the BBC, against the odds, actually increased its independence: those monumentally stupid asses at the Ministry of Information were a danger to themselves not others at the beginning of the war. The Forces Service, with its mixture of light music and entertainment, was launched in February 1940 during this 'phoney' war period. The BBC, more by accident than design, not only enhanced its independence, but also managed to place a heel and a toe more obviously on the low cultural road.

The dispute over Priestley's *Postscripts* shows that the top brass within the BBC, often in consultation with other interested parties, were quite prepared to gag a particular speaker or programme. The members of *The Brains' Trust* were allowed to turn their great minds to the question of how, or perhaps it was why, a fly lands upside down on a ceiling, but they could not discuss pay ceilings for women in the armed and auxiliary services. Politicians successfully protested against an undignified political quiz in a show called *Everybody's Mike*. The BBC politicians agreed that a brick had been dropped in suggesting that politics had anything to do with vaudeville and so hurriedly dropped this part of the pilot programme. Such interventions usually came after a particular proposal had gone through at least the initial planning stages within the BBC. In other words, there was not a concerted attempt to take programme conception and execution out of the hands of the various production departments. The majority of programmes operated within the prevailing consensus on war aims and thus escaped the blue pencil or the studio switch. The BBC was even left to and with its own devices in the sensitive area of overseas propaganda. The 'V For Victory' campaign originated within the BBC and not some government department. It proved that rookie producers were capable of transforming a 'friendly thing' into a weapon of war. The campaign did come under closer political scrutiny, through the Political Warfare Executive, as broadcasts to occupied countries had to be consistent with the latest tactical thinking. Even so the BBC found itself involved, actively rather than passively, in this and other areas where a consensus had to be negotiated.

Both Reith's patrician liberalism and Priestley's populist radicalism belonged to the world of the nineteenth-century crusade rather than the twentieth-century communications network. The fact that they both came out against commercial television suggests that the divisions between them may not have been as great as *Goodnight Children* implies. The real change that took place during the war concerned the way in which the BBC was prepared to discard the mantles of these Victorian sages and prophets in favour of snappier garments. As suggested, the increasing emphasis on variety and light entertainment tended to undermine orthodoxies about sound broadcasting. The Forces Service weakened the moral force. Similarly, the gradual professionalization of news coverage, together with the belief that broadcasting was essentially a journalist's medium, marked a shift of gear. Reith had certainly not ignored news. He fought one of his hardest battles against the press barons for greater freedom and independence. In its early days the BBC was forced to be totally dependent on Reuters reports and had to schedule its bulletins so that they did not compete directly with the evening newspapers. Things improved considerably in the years immediately before the war, although BBC News did not cover itself with glory when covering some of the early campaigns. A. P. Ryan did much to improve journalistic standards and his work was built on by William Haley when he assumed special responsibility for News in 1943. The creation of the *War Report* unit in 1943 and the appointment of Haley as Director General in 1944 indicate changes in priorities. The BBC was on its way to becoming the hunting ground for newshounds as well as culture vultures. Harold Nicolson, who was on the Board of Governors at the time of Haley's appointment, felt that a mere journalist could not undertake 'the cultural job' of running the BBC. It was during the war that the BBC's cultural role came to be defined in less Arnoldian terms. The war reporters went on bombing raids over Germany, but their main function was to cover the opening of the Second Front. Their job was to take the mike on a hike to where the action was and to let it record history in the making. *War Report* symbolically took over Priestley's old slot after the *Nine O'Clock News*. Although the *Nine O'Clock News* became almost a cliché in the propaganda films of the period, this particular slot did not become the flagship in the schedule until as late as October 1938. Reith was opposed to the whole practice of scheduling and suspicious of the audience research work on which such slick calculations were based. An Audience Research Unit had been set up in 1936, but even in the post-war period Reith maintained that such activities could be cut without too much damage. Radio Reith operated within a system in which the audience cannot choose but hear. *War Report,* with its carefully scheduled slot and location reports, looked forward to the twentieth-century communications network. Gucci cowboys with stopwatches were going to inherit the air.

COMMERCIAL TELEVISION

The BBC came of age during the war, but the celebrations were over almost before they had begun. Although Churchill's war-time broadcasts had struck the keynote in the 'war of words', he now seemed anxious to strike at the BBC itself. He had long harboured a grudge against Reith for not letting him broadcast about India in 1933, which may provide a subsidiary reason behind Reith's failure to establish himself as an effective war-time minister. The BBC's belief that a platform should only be provided for politicians from within a narrowly defined consensus was always vulnerable to the maverick who came in from the cold. Churchill and his supporters also believed that the BBC had not played fair by them in the 1945 general election. According to this interpretation, the road to 1945 was paved with lyrical broadcasts about the virtues of a planned economy. The BBC was placed in its customary role as everybody's Auntie Sally, even though the real villain of the piece as far as the Conservatives were concerned was probably the Ministry of Information. Tensions increased as Labour proceeded apace with its nationalization programme, for the BBC's monopoly inevitably became part of the wider political dogfight. The Beveridge Committee, which was belatedly convened in 1949 to conduct the necessary inquest on broadcasting, isolated monopoly practice as the key issue. This Committee did not give the BBC an easy run for the licence money. It was concerned about the way in which the Corporation minimized controversy, prevented minorities from ever turning themselves into majorities and indulged in 'innocent nepotism' in the choice of presenters and participants. Beveridge had always fancied himself as a broadcaster more than the BBC did. One of his solutions to the creative and administrative dangers of monopoly was to suggest that the BBC ought to be more responsive to 'ceaseless vigilance' and 'careful criticism' by outside bodies. He was realistic enough to recognize that watchdogs could be a problem as well as a solution and so proposed that they in turn ought to be watched. The Committee formulated proposals for a Public Representative Service which, as it was to be given a seat on the Board of Management, stood some chance of success. It also recommended that devolution to the regions might safeguard against a complacent bureaucracy. Despite some muddled thinking over what constituted a vested interest, the Report contained impressive and constructive solutions to the real and potential dangers of a broadcasting monopoly.

The Committee was still in session when Lord Simon, the Chairman of the Governors, provided disturbing evidence to support the view that watchdogs needed watching. He took it upon himself in October 1950 to ban a repeat of a television play by Val Gielgud called *Party Manners*. This play follows the political fortunes of Kit Williams, an Eton and Oxbridge socialist, who moves smartly over to the Atomic Board when he learns that his days in the Cabinet are numbered. An election looms on the horizon so his old comrade, Jim Ballard, urges him to publish a recent report on nuclear power as its optimistic conclusions are felt to be enough to buy the public voice and secure another period of office. Publication would, however, also reveal nuclear secrets to potential enemies. Kit eventually rejects Ballard's overtures, despite the tempting rewards that are dangled in front of him. He is more influenced by the Earl of Eltham, the former owner of the stately home now used by the Atomic Board, than by any ethical headaches about the freedom of information. The good earl is reduced to being a butler and argues with impeccable logic that a 'decanter of port will go round a table, but it won't go round the world'. New master and new retainer end up drinking twice too often to this. Kit's eyes are now opened to the fact that his party merely makes 'the underdog the overdog' and the more outrageous Eltham has the nerve to suggest that 'the only consistent political belief held by the English is that all politicians are funny'. Simon was bound to have been offended by other cracks against career politicians since they were too close to the bone. He claimed in *The BBC From Within* (1953) that it was strongly represented to him by 'individuals of weight and judgement' that the play held 'leading British statesmen up for contempt in a way which was improper and undesirable'. This was going too far, as *Party Manners* was only a skit of dubious quality, without the bite of *Bill Brandt*. The fact that Simon would not name the weighty individuals only fuelled the speculation that they were not, as they say, unadjacent of the higher reaches of the Labour party. By a strange coincidence, Labour was holding its Annual Conference at Margate, firing up the faithful for the next general election, when simple Simon struck. The wave of protest that greeted his rash decision showed that it was unwise for even the Chairman of the Governors to try to impose his will on both the Director General and programme policy. The incident set a number of people besides Beveridge wondering what might be achieved if the watchdogs did not bark quite so loudly. Those who hold yesterday's leading British statesmen up to contempt still run the risk of a single ticket to Radio Barset.

The initial political wrangle over the Beveridge Report concerned the majority recommendations for regionalization as part of the over-all scheme to make the BBC more flexible and accountable. The debate concerned the possible role to be played by local politicians on regional boards. The Earl of Eltham would no doubt have hooted with laughter at the sight of national politicians discussing the burning issue of whether elected representatives could say their piece on broadcasting policy. Such arguments came to represent a turning point about which broadcasting did not turn since the narrow Conservative victory in the October 1951 general election switched the spotlight onto Selwyn Lloyd's minority report. He rejected the majority recommendations for improvements and safeguards as he believed that monopoly was as out-of-date as divine right. Reith had unwisely intervened in this post-war debate to intone the praises of the 'brute force of monopoly', which he saw as representing the only way of maintaining spiritual and cultural standards. The BBC was a beast, but a just beast. Selwyn Lloyd came to rest his case on the unfortunate implications of this particular phrase, which was also kicked around both the Commons and Lords during the subsequent debates on commercial television. It is therefore an understatement to describe it as an own goal.

The 1951 general election was the first one in which politicians availed themselves of television facilities to broadcast over Britain. Their programmes did not, however, bother to deal with the politics of broadcasting. It was only after the result was safely in the bag that television, rather than the more firmly established radio, became the battleground for those Conservatives who were determined to break the 'brute force' of the BBC's monopoly. Television had been closed down at the very beginning of the war after just under three years of active service. As it was only being received by about 20,000 homes in the London area on 10-by-8-inch screens, it was little more than a twinkle to the eye. Coverage was resumed at the beginning of June 1946 in time for the Victory Parade. Television quickly re-established its supremacy in the field of outside broadcasts, but it was still the most vulnerable outpost of the BBC's empire. The facilities at Alexandra Palace were primitive, although the wise monkeys at Broadcasting House tended to give them the blind eye. The Cinderella service was a late and not very welcome arrival at the broadcasters' ball. The major item on the agenda was the creation of the Home, Light and Third networks rather than the development of television. A reminder that television was still regarded as a flashy junior partner in the old family firm came when the service found itself without a Director, and thus a seat on the all-important Management Board, in the post-war reconstruction. The snub was withdrawn in 1950 although Norman Collins, the man tipped by himself and others for the job, was passed over. It went instead to George Barnes, the Director of the Spoken Word, no less.

Collins decided that London commercial television would belong to him and, as one of the few experts available, became an important figurehead for the monopoly-busters when he resigned from the BBC in a blaze of publicity. He teamed up with Sir Robert Renwick, C. O. Stanley and other captains of industry who did not want to play monopoly according to the BBC rules. Although their company, Associated Broadcasting Development, came to present commercial television as the people's birthright, the target audience for their public relations campaign was in fact exclusive rather than inclusive. They were primarily concerned with educating the educated and influencing the influential. This was also true of the Popular Television Association, which became the umbrella pressure group for commercial television later on in the campaign. Collins and Christopher Mayhew, one of the leading lights of the rival National Television Council, staged a great debate about the future of broadcasting at the Oxford Union, yet they were reluctant to court the common people. Both sides opinion-polled the proles, but that was as close as they wanted to get to the people whose television service they were squabbling about. The larger advertising agencies, such as J. Walter Thompson, and the big electronics firms, such as Pye, came out strongly in favour of commercial television. Market researchers, merchant bankers and public relations buffs also rallied to the cause. In the early days cinema, theatre and press interests tended to be wary of commercial television. The campaign would never have succeeded if it had just been confined to these dynamic, resolute sections of the business community. A small group of MPs was prepared, however, to move the argument into the political arena. The associations between these honourable members and the businessmen were far from being tenuous ones. Fingers were in the Pye or anywhere else that paid well enough. These interests were always scrupulously declared. Mr Speaker returned to the democratic days of the early nineteenth century to find a ruling which declared that a personal interest was not in fact a personal interest 'if it is shared with the rest of Her Majesty's subjects'. This did not mean that everybody was entitled to a slice of the financial action. It was merely taken to indicate that the poorest he or she that is in England could watch the programmes along with the greatest he or she. The declaration of individual interests at least prevented unjust questions from being asked about Conservative party funds.

The parliamentary debates on the future of television, which sprawled out over a couple of years, were claimed by both sides to be among the most significant of the age. Broadcasting was invariably presented as the most important means of influencing society, which explains why society was not allowed to influence broadcasting. The BBC supporters' club was strong on rhetoric. They conjured up visions of Ariel locked in combat with Caliban, the Ark of the Covenant threatened by the Golden Calf and money lenders at work in the temple of the arts and music. The spectre of Americanization haunted their arguments: canned food should not be allowed to produce canned programmes and cereals had to be prevented from packaging serials. These supporters were not so strong on parliamentary tactics as they never really believed that the commercial lobby had the necessary clout. There was also a feeling that the whole question was above the sordid realities of party politics rather like previous debates on the prayer book. Lord Hailsham, a pillar of the National Television Council whose maiden speech in the Lords had nevertheless been an amusing attack on Simon's handling of *Party Manners*, put a more damaging case against his own party. He argued in the debate on June 1954 that the crucial point was the underhand way in which the issue had actually entered the political arena:

> If the Government had harboured the intention of introducing a revolutionary principle into our broadcasting system, it was merely playing with popular opinion not to put it in an Election programme. This is a disreputable piece of chicanery, and it can be described in no other language. It is not simply the absence of a mandate; it is a deliberate concealment, so far as one can judge, of a vital element in a political programme, which either was or ought to have been, well within the contemplation of the leaders of the Party at the time of the General Election.

Two of the oldest tricks of the politician's trade are to raise the question of a mandate and to wonder why the whips are on. Hailsham was no fool when it came to debating-club rules, although his argument that commercial television ought to have been offered to the electorate was difficult to deny. Those who tried to do so got themselves in an awful mess by claiming that the public voice could only be solicited when there were concrete alternatives. Commercial television was therefore ruled out because it was merely a concept. Such an argument would change politics at a stroke if it ever became a universal truth.

Even with the mixed blessings of hindsight, it is difficult to be precise about the reasons behind the success of the pressure group for commercial television. Many Conservatives out in the sticks craved a token piece of privatization, so the BBC's monopoly became a sitting duck as far as the constituency parties were concerned. Although Churchill himself had no love for commercial television, he was the last person to rally support for the BBC. The Labour party probably made a tactical error in threatening to reverse legislation, particularly on sponsored programmes, thus polarizing the debate in a way which suited Conservative Central Office. Cynical observers of the parliamentary scene noticed that the threat to make commercial television an election issue helped to get it through the last phases of the democratic process. The MPs attached to the Conservative Broadcasting Study Group tended to be new and relatively inexperienced, but they did manage to bend he seasoned ear of Lord Woolton, who was one of the Cabinet Ministers with responsibility for broadcasting. The evidence about how he in turn persuaded the Cabinet is still not available, although as a successful party chairman he always had the option of reminding everybody that he was in touch with the grass roots. The Conservatives minimized the risk of opposition within their own ranks, as well as drawing Labour's sting, by eventually opting for spot advertising in natural breaks rather than the more controversial system of sponsorship. They were very fortunate to have quotable opponents like Reith. Simon seemed to be playing for their side as well not just over *Party Manners*, but also with some disparaging remarks he made about commercial broadcasting in the West Indies. He was taken to court and had to grovel out effusive apologies. Walter Elliot fastened onto the noble lord's plight in the debate of 15 December 1953 with his customary elegance. Finally, the mighty host of speakers which thundered away against the evils of trivialization and vulgarity had little commitment to television. They often shared the same prejudices against it as the BBC's own top brass. Thus perhaps the most important tactical decision of the campaign, officially taken almost immediately after the 1951 general election, was to go for television rather than radio. The BBC did not surrender its sound monopoly, to another Conservative government, until 1972.

The Television Act which created commercial television was given the final nod on 30 July 1954. It established an Independent Television Authority to erect transmitters, dish out contracts, collect the rent and keep a beady eye on programme standards. The Authority was given a ten-year lease on life and was to operate under more or less the same payment-by-results scheme as the BBC. Those who wrestled with the academic dilemma of exactly what this Authority was independent of were treated to a comparison with the free Press rather than the free Ritz. Although the contractors were ever so strictly forbidden from editorializing and thus broadcasting their own political opinions, advertising came under the different heading of natural facts of life. The commercial barons who had skulked in their tents during the great debate now experienced dramatic conversions on the road to prosperity. Twenty-five private armies went forth to battle. Granada won the weekday contract for the northern marches. The money came from a theatre and cinema chain and the inspiration from Sidney Bernstein, the fabled El Sid of Granada. ABC belatedly picked up the contract for weekend programming in both the Midlands and the North after another outfit had been forced to retire hurt. Some of the money came from the Associated British Picture Corporation. Associated-Rediffusion (A–R) snatched the opportunity to provide weekday programmes in London, which was thought at the time to be the glittering prize. Financial support came mainly from British Electric Traction, although Associated Newspapers also had a stake until the going got too tough for them. Norman Collins and friends snapped up the contract for weekend programming in London and weekday in the Midlands. Their precarious finances forced them into the arms of the Incorporated Television Programme Company, which had originally been their main rival for the London weekend contract. ITPC had been turned away empty-handed because it was felt, not without justification, that its directors were already too powerful. Prince Littler, Val Parnell and Lew Grade between them controlled the important theatrical agencies as well as the big variety theatres. ATV which included Collins as well as these showbiz giants, was thus something of an unholy alliance. The company was also patched up by the *Daily Mirror* group when it hit the financial rocks a little later on. The BBC supporters' club had argued that, for all the stirring speeches about free trade and enterprise, the Television Act would merely strengthen existing monopolies. This came to pass. Monopoly interests which had opted out of the first scramble for contracts, such a Beaverbrook Newspapers, eventually had to get in on the act. The spoils did not go entirely to traditional Conservative supporters, as E Sid's bank manager could prove. The 'free switch' did nevertheless favour those who were committed in a big way, not so much to free enterprise, as to monopoly capitalism.

A–R displayed its wares to the public with an opening night at the Guildhall on 22 September 1955. More people tuned into the death of Grace Archer on dear old steam radio. ATV opened up shop a couple of days later. Both companies were in grave danger of going up in smoke like Grace Archer as the admen decided to play their own waiting game. The television barons had to deliver the audience before they would deliver the goods. Even the audience, in whose name the great crusade had been undertaken, did not stampede to buy ITV aerials. Matters were not helped by a downturn in the economy and a series of industrial disputes. A–R lost over two million pounds during the waiting game. Networking came to provide a route out of this economic jungle. Each company was required to transmit 15 per cent of its own material, which usually took the form of regional magazine programmes. Such programmes could be supplemented relatively cheaply by using up the equally limited quota, roughly 14 per cent, for foreign filmed material. The bulk of the output could only be achieved, however, by horse-trading programmes with the other companies. A variation on the playground principle came into operation I'll show yours, if you'll show mine. It was difficult to hitch a ride on the network, in other words simply to provide openings for other companies' programmes, but it became essential to jog along with it. The 'opt in – opt out' system of networking which had originally been envisaged became unrealistic, as there were barely enough home grown programmes to go round in the early days. A–R and Granada even struck their own private deal whereby the former agreed to provide most of the programmes, if the latter coughed up most of its trading surplus. Free trade theory was once again translated into monopoly practice. This is not to say that the individual companies did not have their own specialities: Granada was strong on strong documentaries, ATV were the princes of light entertainment, ABC blazed the trail with television drama and A–R made a good start in current affairs. Such differences tended to be ironed out, however, by the need to fill schedules. After the big four had weathered the storm, networking became a fact of life since few of the newer companies were in a position to challenge the crude laws of supply and demand.

The clouds began to reveal golden linings towards the end of 1956. The barons had beaten the clock and could now settle down to doubling their money on the treasure trail. The bonanza was on and everybody wanted to climb aboard the wagon train. The admen now fell over each other to take their pick of the rich pickings. They thanked their lucky stars that none of the boxes seemed to contain a booby prize. The heavy losses, which had been sustained particularly by A–R and ATV, gave way to the gold rush. Klondyke fever reached epidemic proportions in 1958 when it was revealed that average profits were in the region of 130 per cent. Austerity was a bad memory and affluence a waking dream. Share prices rocketed. The barons were well placed to deliver their audience, bound with gags, since ITV transmitters now criss-crossed over most of the country. The size of the overall television audience doubled during the first three years of commercial television. The prophets of gloom wondered whether a form of thrombosis, known in America as television leg, was about to sweep the country off its feet. The chief executives of the new companies had had years of experience of nailing bums to seats, so it came as no real surprise when three-quarters of this enlarged audience voted with the fingers against the BBC. The companies never had it so good, since they were not really competing among themselves and the mighty BBC empire had not yet struck back.

BBC Television managed to hold on to some of its audiences, particularly for outside broadcasts, but it was beaten out of sight in many other programme areas. Morale was not helped by defections to the 'opposition' and the continued domination of radio within the hierarchy. The frightfully nice heroine of John Keir Cross's career novel, *Elizabeth in Broadcasting* (1957), pops over to the television studios to bone up on back projection. The main focus of attention, however, is still around Broadcasting House where hearty young things whack scripts into shape, sensitive poets nip out to the Swan and Cemetery, camp directors do it with feeling and secretaries, or seccies, pass round the marmite sandwiches. Television producers could not beat a hasty retreat to such a cosy world. They were in the front line of the broadcasting wars, despite twinges of conscientious objection to all forms of competition. Outlying territories such as light entertainment often fell without too many shots being fired, but the battle became deadly serious when news- and current affairs-based areas were threatened. The most dramatic example of this challenge came in 1958 when Granada changed the conventions of election broadcasting overnight through their coverage of the Rochdale by-election. News was also put under siege. The commercial companies had not been trusted to develop their own national and international news services in case the temptation to editorialize proved too much for them. They were all made to chip in to support Independent Television News instead. Although it took time for ITN to build up a stable production team, it was soon able to broadcast the news that news could no longer be regarded as the BBC's private patch. Daring innovations, such as newsreaders actually appearing in vision, were coupled with high journalistic standards. Even the most brutish ITV bashers were usually forced to concede that news coverage might be an exception to their narrow rules. The BBC's response took some time to come but when it came, with the appointment of Hugh Greene as boss of News and Current Affairs in 1958, it came with a vengeance. Greene, a trained journalist who went on to become the BBC's most innovative Director General a couple of years later, won some famous victories in these television battles. He probably even won the war itself.

THE FOURTEEN DAY RULE

BBC Television had established a reputation, albeit a coterie one, for discussion programmes such as *In the News* and *Press Conference* before commercial television was a ring on the till. Competition was nevertheless the spur which pricked the sides of its intent. The new-look *Panorama* was unveiled a couple of days before ITV was, although the competitive spirit was always a more popular tipple on *Tonight*. This legendary programme started to go out in 1957 to fill in the hole traditionally given over to the toddlers' truce, which was that early evening period when the parents had the broadcasters' permission to say goodnight to their children. American visitors were apparently always amazed that public service broadcasters should pay so much attention to audience figures and reactions. The *Tonight* team, which now reads like a who's who of broadcasting, nevertheless persisted in applying the Jean Brodie principle: if they hooked the audience early on then they might be the BBC's for the rest of the evening. The team built up average audiences of around seven million in the early days, as well as being successful pot-hunters when it came to television awards. They were thus never forced to judge the quality of the programme entirely by the width of the audience, even though they were always attuned to the verdict of the public voice. Such a concern was in keeping with the programme's house style, which made great play of the fact that established institutions and opinions would not be treated deferentially. The BBC itself did not escape unscathed, since the programme bent many of the groundrules traditionally associated with controversial broadcasting. It worked on the refreshing assumption that, as long as overall output was balanced, individual items did not have to be. This obviously suited a fast-moving, often improvised magazine programme. Its lack of deference usually took the form of hard-hitting interviews rather than attempts to satirize leading British statesmen in improper and undesirable ways. Members of the production team were nevertheless actively involved later on in *That Was The Week That Was*. Greene not only relished competition with the commercial barons, but he also helped to make sure that, for a time at least, competing views of the political world were on offer. The just beast was grazing in pastures new.

Tonight responded friskily to the spur of competition, although it was very fortunate that one of the rules which had frustrated earlier current affairs programmes had fallen into disrepute before it entered the starting stalls. Radio Reith had tried to improve its news coverage by introducing topical talks into the news bulletins. These often took the form of politicians explaining current legislation. They were eventually taken out of the news bulletin itself and put in the loose box or slot immediately afterwards. The war saw an increase in such programming with *Tonight's Talk* becoming a regular rather than just an occasional feature. Although the BBC jealously reserved the right to issue invitations to whom it chose, in practice it seems to have been quite prepared for a while to go along with what the government wanted. Such a policy could be justified as far as talks about war aims and objectives were concerned, but it became more problematic when politicians wanted to talk about domestic issues and legislation. The BBC was then very vulnerable to accusations that its programmes were barely disguised party politicals. It was therefore decided to try to back off from topical talks which smacked too much of the second reading speech. The politicians were not, however, prepared to take their feet out of the studio door without a struggle. The BBC objected to a proposed talk by R. A. Butler on education in the summer of 1943, but the War Cabinet insisted that it would have to be given at some point, preferably when the Education Bill was before parliament. Butler was therefore able to sing the praises of his own piece of legislation at the end of January 1944. The BBC Governors responded almost immediately by drafting what became known as a 'self-denying ordinance', in which it was stated that it was BBC policy that there should be no talks by politicians on issues that were either receiving attention in parliament or would be in the near future. This decision proved to be a wise one in the short term since it prevented the BBC from being explicitly used as an election platform when the Coalition government began to regroup along more traditional party lines. It was disastrous in the long term as it severely restricted the coverage of important issues. Once again, the BBC had preserved the right to issue invitations by limiting the range and scope of programmes. News and news-based pro grammes were not affected by the ordinance. The BBC could still, for instance, actually report parliamentary proceedings, as long as it did so in a proper and becoming manner. Yet its hands were tied when it came to discussion of these proceedings.

The ordinance, which originally had the status of a 'gentleman' agreement' rather than a formal requirement, came to be interpreted to mean that there had to be a blackout on subjects which were due to come before Parliament within a fortnight. As parliamentary business was usually only announced a week at a time on Thursdays, the politicians could play Hamlet with the BBC's forward planning sche dules. The 'Fourteen Day Rule' covered not only the anticipation of debates, but was also taken to apply to the whole of the parliamentary life of a particular piece of legislation. Private members' bills in parti cular were renowned for their senility. A fortnight really could be a very long time in politics. This ordinance would have placed severe restrictions on the BBC, if it had been required to comply with the letter rather than the spirit of the agreement. In practice, the rule was broken on a number of occasions when BBC executives decided that a particular subject was not important enough to justify a ban. The politicians had, nevertheless, snatched victory out of defeat. Minister were no longer able to sing the praises of their own pieces of legis lation, but by the same token a chorus of maverick backbenchers was not allowed to chant away about any vices. The rule thus tended to support the party leadership in cases where man and party machine were not in perfect harmony. The BBC was neatly caught in a trap of its own devising. The original objection had been to 'ex parte' state ments by ministers, but this was gradually extended to include othe politicians as well as unaffiliated commentators. Such extensions were usually worked out at the rather one-sided discussions which took place on a regular basis between the BBC and the major politica parties, often wrongly referred to as all-party discussions. The official reason why the major parties expressed themselves more than happy with the agreement was that it preserved the status and authority of Parliament by denying the BBC an opportunity to set itself up as a rival forum for debate. The unofficial reason was that, by holding both the BBC and the political maverick in check, two potentially dangerous birds were killed with one stone. Ministers did not really pass up the opportunity to broadcast over Britain since it was argued that party politicals, ministerials and budget programmes fell outside the terms of the agreement because they were not arranged by the BBC. The Fourteen Day Rule therefore had two important consequences for the presentation of current affairs: discussion was limited and the party machines could operate a closed shop.

Details of these arrangements were available to senior BBC producers through what were rather pompously known as *aides-mémoires*. They were made public in the 1950 *Yearbook*, although the conjecture must be that this was only done as Beveridge had decided to publish and damn them. There were definite signs before the Beveridge Committee considered the matter that the BBC found its position over the barrel an uncomfortable one, but concerted pressure for an end to the rule only began after the Report had highlighted the issue. Diplomatic overtures by the Governors failed, so it was decided in June 1955 to call the government's hand by asking for these informal rules to be written up formally. The BBC's bluff was itself called the following month when the 'gentleman's agreement' was codified. The summer recess prevented any debate, but the Commons turned their attention to the formal directive on 30 November when the Postmaster-General proposed that a select committee should be invited to consider the practice, but not the principle, of rules to prevent the anticipation of parliamentary debates. An amendment which sought to extend the terms of reference to principles was easily defeated on a free vote. The debate itself did little to establish the fact that Parliament was the most important forum for discussion in the country. Apart from some amusing exchanges between the honourable members for Lime Grove and the party hacks, it was a drab affair. The Select Committee, which reported back the following May, came to the conclusion that a Seven Day Rule would be more feasible. Although this sounds like a product of that gift for compromise given only to committees, the proposal did make sense given the way in which parliamentary business was announced. The Committee also recommended that a subject could be in season once it had been through a second reading. The BBC witnesses argued that all the rules should be abolished and strongly maintained that discretion had to be permitted even if there was a more limited regulation. The ITA had obviously not been a party to the original 'gentleman's agreement', but still found itself saddled with a formal directive in July 1955. It may be that the government's original intention to stand firm on this issue had something to do with a parental desire to make sure that its child behaved properly. The ITA witnesses reminded the Committee that broadcasting now resembled the free Press and so regulations were neither necessary nor enforceable. The two main political parties affirmed their commitment to some rule, but hinted that politics was about the art of the possible. The Liberals had already come out strongly against the rule before the Committee was set up.

The Committee also felt called upon to investigate some allegations made by Bob Boothby, both in the debate and in a written submission, about the way in which the original *In the News* team had been disbanded. Its investigations suggest that the Fourteen Day Rule was not the only weapon which could be trained against the BBC. *In the News* began in 1950 and quickly shook down into a weekly discussion session with a more or less regular panel consisting of Boothby himself, Bill Brown, Michael Foot and A. J. P. Taylor. Their forthright independence made good television, but it was bad news for the party machines. Lively broadcasters have seldom had impeccable party manners. Boothby told the Committee that this team had been broken up as a result of political pressure, although he was forced to admit that his evidence was only hearsay. It was still taken seriously enough for BBC staff and contract employees to be examined. Haley, who had been Director General at the time, was also made to jump through some hoops. Despite tenacious questioning by Dick Crossman and others, Boothby's case was not really proven. It appears that George Barnes, as befitted a former Director of the Spoken Word, had issued verbal rather than written instructions that the panel was to be placed on a strict rota. It was unfortunate for the BBC's reputation that these were given at a cocktail party in Richmond. The BBC had always distrusted the broadcasting 'personality': Priestley was seen as an over-mighty subject as well as a controversial politician. There was also a more immediate reason for Barnes's decision to ration the appearances of the gang of four. Michael Foot was no longer regarded as being representative of mainstream Labour opinion after the Bevanite revolt of April 1955. The received wisdom in the BBC was that a balance had to be maintained within the parties as well as between them. Boothby had therefore characteristically overstated the case by suggesting that there had been direct political pressure. Barnes was a reasonably honest, if cautious man. The attempt to unearth the news behind *In the News* is in fact much more revealing for what it says about attitudes and atmosphere than for any shocking facts. Barnes's world was one in which careful soundings were taken and rules of thumb gingerly applied. The atmosphere, which he probably played up a little for the Committee's benefit, reeked of cautious pessimism: 'pressure will be applied if we do something intentionally and deliberately controversial'. This attitude, which was perhaps inevitable for somebody who had been in the Talks Department throughout the war, meant that avoiding action would usually be taken before direct political pressure became a reality. Barnes and the other BBC witnesses did not relish the irony of being pressurized by politicians to reveal all about political pressure, but their answers suggest that the realities of political patronage made such explicit interventions unnecessary.

The Committee had to find in favour of some sort of restriction on the anticipation of parliamentary debates, although the unwritten report was against such rules and regulations on both theoretical and practical grounds. The government eventually decided to act on the unwritten rather than the written report. The formal directive was revoked on 18 December 1956 for an experimental period of six months. Sir Anthony Eden added the proviso during question time on the same day that the broadcasting organizations were still under an obligation 'not to derogate from the primacy of Parliament as a forum for debating the affairs of the nation'. The final evacuation of British troops from Suez took place four days later. The history of the BBC and ITV coverage of Suez still has to be written in detail. One of the questions that will need answering is how far the government's decision to keep the Fourteen Day Rule alive during the crisis minimized criticisms of their policy. *Press Conference* and *Panorama* certainly discussed the issues in ways which contravened the rule, although a reminder that it was still in force came when *Any Questions* was subjected to switch censorship during a live transmission. It was also during the Suez crisis that A. P. Herbert attempted to set fire to his Copyright Bill on *Press Conference* because the discussion of it was claimed to be an anticipation of a parliamentary debate. There has been a lot of speculation over whether the government actually prepared a plan for the complete take-over of the BBC. It may be that, once again, such explicit intervention was unnecessary given the kind of leverage which could have been exerted, if required, through the Fourteen Day Rule and other less tangible gentlemen's agreements.

EPILOGUE

It was unfortunately left to the Pilkington Committee, which reported in 1962, to sum up this second phase of post-war broadcasting. The BBC was a past master at watching out for these watchdogs and so devoted time and energy to the preparation of its case. The ITA and the commercial companies were new to the game and it showed. They made silly mistakes such as suggesting to this self-important bunch of worthies that television probably had little social effect. Golden rule number one was always to tell these committees what they wanted to hear rather than what you really thought. If television had little social effect, then their occupations would be gone. Remarks about the inevitability of trivialization because 'there is in life a great deal of triviality' did not go down a storm. The case for commercial television may not have been made particularly well, but it would have been clobbered even if it had been spoken with the tongues of men and of angels. The Committee, heavily under the influence of Richard Hoggart, was gunning for the trivial, tawdry, tatty and timid. Anything which lay outside Hoggart's own world of provincial puritanism was seen as belonging to this 'candy-floss' culture. The Pilkington principle held that popular culture was only vital when it was dead or dying. Commercial television was altogether too bright, brassy and brash to fit into this kind of homely nostalgia. The Committee doled out some praise for its administrative and engineering achievements, but this did not soften the blows that were inflicted on its programmes. It was argued that, if profit was the primary motive, then it was not surprising that no trouble was taken over audience reactions. Numbers were bound to be more important than opinions. Independent television was therefore in no position to cater for the minorities who were always trying to struggle out of every majority. According to the Committee, this contempt for audiences led naturally to programmes which ridiculed and humiliated ordinary folk. Perhaps the 'artificial good fellowship' of quiz inquisitors and gameshow hosts debased, even debauched, all these homely standards. If every programme had its own 'essential worth', then expensive prizes and other cheap gimmicks would not be necessary. Pilkington and company were definitely not game for a laugh. They believed that advertisements, like the giveaway shows, unfairly played upon the 'acquisitiveness, snobbery, fear, un-critical conformity' of decent folk. The Committee were guilty of pseudo-intellectualizing, but more fundamentally they were just guilty of being guilty. Good television could not exist unless it was weighted down with 'essential worth' and worthy purposes. Puritans have been known to close down theatres, although this time they acted with considerable restraint. They merely proposed a series of changes designed to give the ITA more control over the individual companies. No tawdry prizes for guessing that these changes had to be 'organic' ones. It was recommended that the Authority should be given total control over both scheduling and advertising. The companies were to be allowed to carry on making programmes on the understanding that they would have to sell them to the Authority, which would pay for them with the advertising revenue that had not been creamed off by the government. Most of the proposed 'organic' changes did not suit the politicians, although they were quick to grasp the advantages of levying large financial prizes from commercial television. The BBC was, by contrast, deemed to be in good organic nick. Its views were 'sound in principle' and any deviations in practice tended to be ex-plained in terms of the contamination of competition. Most of the evidence suggests that competition did not harm BBC Television at all. The Committee felt that the BBC should always be the major instru-ment of broadcasting in the country and, with this in mind, recom-mended the award of a second channel. The Pilkington Report was itself trivial, tawdry and tatty.

Much had changed since 1922 and much remained the same. Pilking-ton spoke the tongue that Reith spake. Much has changed since 1962 and much remains the same. Earnest puritans and vile politicians still claim the right divine to govern broadcasting wrong. Ironically, it was the BBC which felt the full force of a less intellectual variety of puritanism in the 1960s, whilst commercial television had to learn not to put its trust in politicians. New channels and other major developments are still regarded as pieces of political patronage: BBC 2 followed Pilkington's recommendation and Channel 4 eventually emerged out of the prolonged political dogfight over the Annan Report. There is little evidence at the moment to suggest that the public voice will have much of a say in determining the 'drama's laws' as far as the cable revolution is concerned. The third age of broadcasting may not be dramatically different. Politicians were sometimes ambivalent about broadcasting during its first forty years. They wanted to control it, but did not place it very high up on their list of priorities. The development since 1959 of the television general election, with its carefully staged media events and tastefully avoided questions, has unfortunately led to a more sustained interest. The Fourteen Day Rule itself may seem to be a historical curiosity, but the major parties still pack committees which try to make sure that improper and undesirable versions of politics are kept to a minimum or to a ghetto. The representation of the people is truly an act, which obeys the laws laid down for it by its political patrons. The televising of Parliament could be just around the corner, or the current attempt may join its predecessors in the dustbin of history. Whatever the result, the public voice will not be listened to. Although it is true that both the BBC and ITV have logged up some very impressive achievements in what used to be known as controversial broadcasting, the politicians can probably still regard both radio and television as friendly things. Leading British politicians are rarely held up for contempt in ways which may be both proper and desirable. This is because yesterday's men still control tomorrow's broadcasting.[2]

NOTES AND REFERENCES

1. 'Prologue at the Opening of Drury Lane' (1747). My thanks are due to Charles Barr, with whom I have discussed many of the themes of my essay, and to the BBC Written Archives Centre at Caversham for allowing me to consult their files, mainly on radio policy.
2. The best short account of the early days of radio is David Cardiff and Paddy Scannel's essay, 'Serving the Public: Public Service Broadcasting Before the War', in *Popular Culture: Past and Present*, eds. Bernard Waites et al., Croom Helm 1982, pp. 161–88. Andrew Boyle's biography of Lord Reith, *Only the Wind Will Listen: Reith of the BBC*, Hutchinson 1972, may now be supplemented by Roger Milner's account, *Reith: The BBC Years*, Mainstream Publishing 1983, which is based on his recent two-part dramatization for BBC TV. Charles Stuart's edition of *The Reith*

Diaries, Collins 1975, remains an important source for the inter-war period, as well as for the post-war period. The first two volumes of Asa Briggs's four-volume history of broadcasting in the United Kingdom, *The Birth of Broadcasting,* Oxford University Press 1961, and *The Golden Age of Wireless,* Oxford University Press 1962, are indispensable as far as the early history of the BBC is concerned. Michael Tracey's *The Production of Political Television,* Routledge and Kegan Paul 1978, contains a useful discussion on broadcasting and the General Strike of 1926. Briggs's third volume, *The War of Words,* Oxford University Press 1970, is the main secondary source for the war-time history of the BBC. Cardiff and Scannel have prepared an impressive Open University Course Unit on the subject, 'Radio in World War II', in *The Historical Development of Popular Culture in Britain,* Unit 2. The second chapter of K. R. M. Short's edition of *Film and Radio Propaganda in World War II,* Croom Helm 1983, may also be consulted. The fourth volume of Briggs's history of the BBC, *Sound and Vision,* Oxford University Press 1979, contains valuable discussions of post-war reconstruction, the Pilkington Committee and the development of television. Burton Paulu's *British Broadcasting in Transition,* Macmillan 1961, covers some of the same ground, as well as providing an analysis of the early days of commercial television. It is a pity that it is not more widely available. H. H. Wilson's *Pressure Group: The Campaign for Commercial Television,* Secker and Warburg 1961, remains the best book on the introduction of ITV, despite revisionist attempts to play down the 'conspiracy theory' interpretation. Peter Black's *The Mirror in the Corner: People's Television,* Hutchinson 1972, is also recommended. The first volume of Bernard Sendall's more official history of ITV, *Independent Television in Britain: Origin and Foundation 1946–1962,* Macmillan 1982, also needs to be consulted. The history of Granada is brought to life in the BFI's dossier, *Granada: The First 25 Years,* BFI 1981. Indeed, all the relevant BFI dossiers and monographs are very strongly recommended. Nicholas Garnham's *Structures of Television,* BFI 1973, remains one of the best introductory accounts of the politics of broadcasting. There is some discussion of the Fourteen Day Rule in Briggs's fourth volume and in Grace Wyndham Goldie's *Facing the Nation: Television and Politics 1936–1976,* Bodley Head 1977. Those requiring more detailed reading on the history of broadcasting ought to consult the excellent descriptive bibliography prepared for the IBA by Barrie MacDonald, *Broadcasting: A Selected Bibliography,* 1981.

Chapter 3

THE EVOLUTION OF CULTURAL STUDIES

TONY DUNN

I

Culture is now our nature. Nothing is pure, nobody is unmarked. Models for the description and analysis of culture include the model-maker. 'Subjects' are therefore decentred, issues and problems are tracked across academic boundaries, methods of study promote the exuberance of juxtaposition from information-abundance. Singular definitions – of courses and concepts – have to be resisted. Cultural studies is a whirling and quiescent and swaying mobile which continuously repositions any participating subject. Cultural studies is a project whose realization – absolute integrity through fragmentation and disassembly – is forever deferred. 'Composition is not there, it is going to be there and we are here.'[1]

Academic courses, however, have origins even if they refuse termini. Cultural studies began with the subjects it inherited. These are almost exclusively grouped under the humanities and social sciences, so any cultural studies degree bears both the traces and, often, the firm outlines of history, sociology, literature, psychology, linguistics, philosophy, anthropology and some elements of economics. The significant absence is science and technology. Not only were the academics constructing these courses technically ignorant of the sciences, they also endorsed received paradigms of a culture/nature divide. Subjectivity might be dissolved in the information-field, but objectivity still radiated its nineteenth-century aura of 'scientific truth'. Work by Thomas Kuhn,[2] Paul Feyerabend[3] and Margaret Jacob[4] has demonstrated how mistaken it is to separate any scientific project from its cultural and historical matrix, and how scientific breakthrough occurs through just that action of compositional abundance which should be the distinguishing method of cultural studies. The lack of any developed philosophy of science in British culture and a centuries' old ranking, as Martin Wiener documents,[5] of the arts-gentleman above the artisan-scientist in the country's power-structure also reinforced this absence. Apart from a few instances where the development of empiricism and the Royal

Society in the seventeenth century are covered, cultural studies courses have utilized an exclusively epistemological definition of science, deriving from Althusser's reading of Marx.

But two books, published in the late 1950s, did attempt some kind of trans-disciplinary investigation of culture. In *The Uses of Literacy* (1957) Richard Hoggart's proposition was that there existed several cultures simultaneously in Britain. His particular concern was with the characteristic, as he saw them, attitudes and relationships that made up the culture of the working class. Forms of mass entertainment, designed to promote a culturally classless society, were rapidly eroding and commercializing this distinctive culture, with its cycling clubs, music-hall songs, neighbourly support-system, decent scepticism and cheerful stoicism. Hoggart particularly focussed his literary analysis on mass publications – daily newspapers and family magazines – but he was aware that, in order to conceptualise his different cultures, he needed also the techniques of the anthropologist and the sociologist. His Preface disclaims professional expertise here but he does contend that this dual approach is necessary to bring into relief so intangible (and non-scholarly) a topic as popular culture.

From his Introduction to *Culture and Society* (1958), it is clear that Raymond Williams was proposing a very precise historical location of culture:

> The organising principle of this book is the discovery that the idea of culture, and the word itself in its general modern use, came into English thinking in the period which we commonly describe as that of the Industrial Revolution. . . . It thus becomes an account and an interpretation of our responses in thought and feeling to the changes in English society since the late eighteenth century.[6]

Some of the writers discussed – Arnold, Dickens, Lawrence, Eliot – would appear on any conventional literature course. Others – Burke, Cobbett, Tawney – would in some way be referred to on any conventional history course. Still others – Carlyle, Ruskin, Morris – had always been considered unclassifiable and it is perhaps Williams's positive revaluation of these great Victorian synthesizers that provides the best, early model of what a cultural studies degree should be. In contrast to Hoggart, Williams rejected the concept of purely class-directed cultures and was particularly sceptical of some distinct working-class culture: 'The traditional popular culture of England was, if not annihilated, at least fragmented and weakened by the dislocations of the Industrial Revolution. What is left, with what in the new conditions has been newly made, is small in quantity and narrow in range. It exacts respect but it is in no sense an alternative culture.'[7] He conceded that bourgeois culture was orientated towards 'the basic individualist idea' and working-class culture towards 'the basic collective idea' but, as a result of his historical analysis, concluded: 'In our culture as a whole, there is both constant inter-action between these ways of life and an area which can be properly described as common to or underlying both.'[8] His final call is for the development of a common culture, a subtle interplay between the old forms and a vision of a new socialist man. The act of culture-making must therefore be outward and exploratory. 'A culture while it is being lived is always in part unknown, in part unrealized.'[9]

Distinct traces of these two approaches are still visible in the cultural studies courses and degrees that have been developed from the 1960s onwards. The Centre for Contemporary Cultural Studies, which Hoggart founded along with Stuart Hall under the aegis of Birmingham University's English Department in 1964, has substantially carried on and particularized Hoggart's analysis, from a much more political stance. Where Hoggart was wistful about a culture which he felt was already fading, the Centre has been aggressively hopeful about its resistance and adaptation to the assault of mass commercialization. It has undertaken – and many cultural studies courses have followed its lead – a determined politicization of culture in the period. Their postgraduate work on, for example, youth culture in the mid-1970s introduced the mediating term 'subculture' to distinguish the culture of youth from that of their parents. But the whole thrust of *Resistance through Rituals* (the title suggests the symbolic as a mask for the political), published in 1976, was to distinguish a number of class-defined youth cultures, indeed to make class itself the determining category for any investigation of this field as against American-derived theories of youth as either a temporary 'generational' category or as a class in itself. So teds, mods, punks and rastas, as enclaves of costume-drama, have been proposed as oppositional alternatives. Recently, for the first time, the Centre (CCCS) offered an undergraduate course in communication and cultural studies, as part of a combined Honours degree. The preamble distinguishes between media versions of the world and the 'sense' that social groups continuously make of it. Different groups make different senses and the ground of these differences is social class. In the second year there are characteristic emphases on 'the theory and politics of culture' and 'the lived forms of culture in everyday experience of specific institutions, initially the school and the work-place.' By now gender and race have been added to class as determining concepts and it is these three socio-political categories that 'structure culture'. The cultural studies course at Middlesex Polytechnic, though less comprehensive since it is designed as a final-year Honours degree programme for students with a Diploma of Higher Education or equivalent qualification, shows similar emphases. Among the units of the course offered are: 'Working-class culture and its disintegration', where distinctions between low culture, high culture, popular culture and mass culture are investigated; 'Cultural process', where 'daily life', with specific reference to work, gender and race, is the site for the construction of cultural meaning; and 'Cultural production and consumption', which considers pop music, films and advertising and explicates cultural phenomena via the discourse, not of politics, but of its adjacent discipline, political economy. A cultural studies-type option on the humanities degree at Bristol Polytechnic – 'Culture, democracy and society' – investigates 'the politics of culture', and the career of Raymond Williams from his earlier concern for a democratic theory of culture to his engagement with Marxisms from the 1970s on and his consequent analysis of the political role of culture in class-divided societies. The three-year undergraduate course at Portsmouth Polytechnic, the first (1975) in the country, treats class rather as a sociological concept in the first year, and then traces its historical manifestations and permutations in a series of nineteenth-century historico-literary studies (called 'Culture and society') from 'The landed interest' in the early nineteenth century, through Chartism (the politics and the poetry) to the invention and uses of working-class leisure activities at the end of the century. As with the cultural studies degree at North East London Polytechnic, the Portsmouth degree locates culture historically right from the beginning of the course, through two seventeenth-century courses, one in 'Literature and thought', the other in the dominant themes and problems (a major one being the class-nature of the English Revolution) in the social history of the period. A mixture of say, Bacon, Christopher Hill, Rochester, Hobbes, Lawrence Stone, Keith Thomas and Locke is designed to train students in the different discourses that literature, history and philosophy have created for themselves for this decisive transitional period from the medieval to the modern world. In the second year each student chooses between one of two options which carries on to the end of the third year. The first is 'Popular fictional forms', an investigation of films, romances and thrillers. The second is 'Sociology of the mass media', theorized by content analysis and uses and gratifications models as well as models derived from semiotics. A third-year case-study, on youth culture, offers 'generational' and 'class' models and tests them against two historical moments, Russia in the early twentieth century and May–June 1986 in France.

II

The bulk of their work was done by Hoggart and Williams while teaching in the field of adult education. The freedom they had here from traditionally boundaried academic disciplines enabled them, through juxtaposition, to begin to make visible an otherwise invisible cultural environment. But it is in the 1960s and the 1970s that the field of cultural studies takes shape at the institutional levels of under-graduate and postgraduate work. Two moments are of particular importance. The first is the Wilson government of 1964–6, with its, comparatively, large expansion of places in first-degree education at university – continued by the creation of polytechnics from 1968 – where provision was made for growth in the humanities and social sciences as well as the pure and applied sciences. Jennie Lee's vigorous success, as Minister for the Arts, in extracting considerably increased public subsidies for the arts from the Treasury was an important complementary action in the area of Cabinet politics. In the year 1961–2 in England and Wales the number of undergraduate and post-graduate students at university was 113,000. In 1965–6 it was 169,000. In 1968–9 it was 211,000. In that decade the numbers had virtually doubled. The age-participation rate has not altered drastically in abso-lute terms. The percentage of school-leavers going straight into em-ployment in 1960–1 was 84 per cent, and 77.3 per cent in 1969. Overall student numbers were extremely low by comparison with France, Germany and Italy. But the increase was certainly large in relative terms. And from 1968 to the end of the 1970s have to be added the numbers engaged in degree-level courses in polytechnics and colleges of higher education, as well as a gentle upward curve in university numbers. By the end of the 1960s the 'student' had definitely replaced the 'undergraduate'. Labour rhetoric, as Conservative rhetoric later, expounded the need for an expansion in the numbers of those scienti-fically and technologically trained and that expansion certainly occurred. There was, however, a concomitant, if numerically less marked, expansion in the numbers of those on humanities and social sciences courses. The humanistic liberals within the ruling élite, plus the Leavisite *instituteurs* in the grammar schools and the prominent position of social scientists on Labour party policy-making committees (Abel Smith, Townsend, Titmuss) probably ensured this. The same phenomenon has been observable in polytechnic expansion from the late 1960s. But here new degree courses were often created at the same time as the departments or schools which administered them, within a context of much more restricted financial resources than the univer-sities. Inter-departmental teaching teams were and are encouraged and necessary in the polytechnics. Areas such as media and popular culture were envisaged as essential parts of the cultural studies field right from the start, not as occasional adjuncts to joint degrees centred on history and literature. Externally the CNAA's five-yearly scrutiny of the structure and content of all courses demanded a conceptual self-consciousness about academic aims and achievements which the universities have never been compelled to develop. Conceptual rigour was what many teachers on cultural studies courses had found lacking in their own education. The evolution of cultural studies courses has thus been marked by the assimilation of a wide range of social and cultural theory.

The second important moment is the challenge to the existing political order mounted by students, white-collar and blue-collar workers 'at the base' from 1968 to the early 1970s in Europe as a whole. It is in the course of these challenges that, as in the mid-Victorian England of Arnold, Ruskin and Carlyle, 'culture', as well as 'democracy', 'rights', 'classes' and 'the State', emerges as a concept for contestation. At the political level these movements, with slogans of *autogestion* and workers' control, and with the aim of transcending monopoly capitalist alienation, failed. The State in France, Italy, Germany and Britain remains, as do the Christian Democratic, Social Democratic and Communist parties, the trade union blocs, the inequalities of class structure, the alienation of most salaried and waged employment. The present Socialist administration in France incorporated *autogestion* into its vocabulary as an inheritance from 1968 via Michel Rocard's PSU (Parti Socialiste Unifié) but its attempts at modernizing reform seem to be blocked by much the same combination of internal and external financial forces as the first Wilson government encountered. What is a still-active inheritance of 1968 is the conjunction of a culturalist discourse with the conventional discourse of politics. With Hoggart there was still a gap between his account of working-class hobbies and customs and the structures of political and financial power which allow or endorse them. With a Marxist sociologist like Henri Lefebvre there is no disjunction. For him *'le quotidien'* (everyday life) is 'the domain of non-work relations in a milieu of alienation characterized by commodity fetishism and dissatisfaction'.[10] This is the thesis of Jean-Luc Godard's film *Deux ou trois choses que je sais d'elle* (1966). It is the concepts of the early Marx, so despised by Althusser, the chosen French intellectual for cultural studies courses in the 1970s, that Lefebvre finds the most powerful explanatory tools for a post-war France eagerly embracing American consumerism. Lefebvre was professor of sociology at Nanterre and so teacher of many of the students who made up the bulk of the March 22 Movement, the spearhead of the student confrontation in May–June 1968. Lefebvre had by then shifted from his virulent opposition to Sartrean existentialism in the 1940s. He supported the actions of Daniel Cohn-Bendit and his companions and saw their protest as not solely political (demands for better learning facilities, students to have their say in the dispersal of power within the institution, improved job prospects for a white-collar salariat). It was also, and primarily, cultural. 'Contestation is an all-inclusive total rejection of experienced or anticipated forms of alienation'.[11]

So alienation was the central, the dominating, concept to be materialized and overcome by 'freedom' in May–June 1968, as it was the central concept to be materialized and overcome in Marx's *Economic and Philosophical Manuscripts* (1844) and throughout the philosophical and artistic *oeuvre* of Sartre. It was Sartre the students occupying the Sorbonne and the Odéon wanted to hear, not Foucault or Lévi-Strauss. The anti-humanism of the structuralists had no purchase on ten million humans declaring their active presence in the world. The cultural primacy of '*les événements*' was further accentuated by the Situationists of Strasbourg, Nantes and Paris for whom liberated speech was the first act of cultural revolution against consumer society. Most of the witty slogans on the walls of Paris originated from the Situationist publications which had been circulating among students for several years. In structuralist terms they asserted the creativity of Saussure's *parole* over his *langue*. They were right. The conflict, as Allen Ginsberg recognized in another civil war situation, was as much over language as bodies:

Aiken Republican on the radio   60,000
        North Vietnamese troops now infiltrated but over 250,000
        South Vietnamese   armed men
                            our Enemy–
                            Not Hanoi our enemy
                            Not China our enemy
                            The Viet Cong!
                            MacNamara made a 'bad guess'

'Bad Guess' chorused the Reporters?
        Yes, no more than a Bad Guess, in 1962
                        '8000 American Troops handle the
                        Situation'. . . . .

Put it this way on the radio
Put it this way in television language
                        Use the words
                            language, language:
                                    'A bad guess'

Put it this way in headlines
        Omaha World Herald–   *Rusk Says Toughness
                                Essential For Peace*

Put it this way
        Lincoln Nebraska morning Star–

                        Vietnam War Brings Prosperity
Put it *this* way
        Declared MacNamara,   speaking language
                    Asserted Maxwell Taylor
                    General, Consultant to White House
        Vietcong losses leveling up three five zero zero

                                    per month . . . [12]

Situating the closure of political cliché within a poem of open-field structure is a powerful technique for exposing verbal tyranny. But, as Arthur Hirsch sums up, 'May was a revolution of consciousness without a revolution of structure, a cultural revolution without a political revolution'.[13] Without the support of the PCF (French Communist party), which attacked the students from the start, there was no hope for a successful cultural revolution. *L'Imagination au Pouvoir* was unimaginable for its Stalinist militants and the pendulum swung back to the anti-humanism of Althusser and the Maoists, for whom no act of liberation was conceivable outside the corral of the party.

III

In 1962 Perry Anderson was appointed editor of *New Left Review* and from then on that journal (and its later publishing enterprises New Left Books and Verso Books) became the chief bridgehead between English left intellectuals and European and Third World Marxism. When, in 1968, students in Britain too confronted university authorities with a series of political demands, their manifestos and commentaries were printed and publicized by the journal. To the editorial board events in France were about to be repeated in Britain. The high point of these hopes was the founding of the Revolutionary Socialist Students' Federation in May 1968 at the LSE after Cohn-Bendit and various student leaders from France, Italy and Germany had described their experiences. *New Left Review* printed the manifesto in full and supported the demands. They included: 'All power to the General Assembly' and support for 'Workers' power and the overthrow of capitalism and imperialism'. The most radical proposal was that universities should become Red Bases, islands of revolutionary praxis in a sea of bureaucratic control. It is notable that all these demands are primarily political. There are hints of the cultural alienation line – the contention that higher education is a basic industry for the manufacture of mental functionaries, or that Red Bases should be libertarian communes – but these are subsumed in the overall political nature of the demands. The RSSF manifesto is indeed an accurate summary of the majority student demands of the time, political first, cultural second. Only the documents culled from the sit-in at Hornsey College of Art (*The Hornsey Affair*, 1969) reverse that order. 'A student revolt is primarily a cultural revolt in physical form'. The artists, as usual, got it right. In retrospect it looks as if, much more than in France, the students' orientation was primarily political and that questions of culture were raised largely in the context of the counter-cultural hippies – another import from America. Certainly there is no evidence of a concern to preserve some working-class culture of football and 'chara' trips by means of Red Bases.

In the July–August number of *New Left Review* Anderson published a long essay entitled 'Components of the National Culture'. It is a blueprint for the cultural studies courses of the next decade. His thesis was that English intellectual life had suffered from the lack of a classical sociology and a developed Marxism. The necessary concepts were therefore not present to construct a revolutionary class-consciousness. They ordered these matters much better abroad. Radical critique of the culture had therefore devolved, not on departments of philosophy and sociology, but on English departments. This was due to the pioneering efforts of F. R. Leavis at Cambridge and the journal *Scrutiny* which he founded and co-edited for the twenty-one years 1932–53. Literature, and art in general, however, according to Anderson, 'deals with man and society, but does not provide us with their *concepts*'. [14] Leavis indeed, who had always refused to define his positions philosophically and politically, declared that concepts could not explicate a work of art and expressed a grinding contempt for the 'sociology of literature'. As for Marxism, its materialist base, in Leavis's view, both made it finally complicit with the capitalism it sought to transcend and reduced the art-work to a fictional representation of economic and social forces. Ideology was the least interesting aspect of the work and most easily discernible in second-rate literature, popular fiction. But Anderson had to admit that Leavis and his colleagues, alone, had challenged the culture of the ruling class and that in his writings on literature and society he had evinced a consistent and well-grounded hostility to those occupying the centres of metropolitan cultural power. His vision of a technologico-Benthamite society found undeniable confirmation in the rise of mass-media consumer society. It is also undeniable that the first tributary to cultural studies described above, the Hoggart/Williams/Hall line, descends from the Leavis fountainhead. All three have a first degree in English and by 1969 *The Uses of Literacy*, *Culture and Society* and *The Long Revolution* (1960), and the Birmingham CCCS represented the only new, sustained challenge to received notions of British culture in the educational world. What can be discerned throughout the 1970s is the gradual convergence of these two approaches – Leavisite and Marxist-structuralist – then the overcoming of the first by the second. The convolutions of Raymond Williams's *Marxism and Literature* (1977) neatly illustrate the process. He traces the rise of 'the aesthetic' as a distinct category at the end of the eighteenth century. Although it was mobilized to protest the increasing commodification of all products and relations in that society, it is finally a component of bourgeois society because it obscures the fact that art too is a species of labour. The beauty of art, Williams admits, induces effects of physical pleasure in the receiver but the aesthetic category is 'complicit with a deliberately dividing society'.[15] Aesthetics may well be describing 'certain invariant combinations of elements' elicited in the perceiving subject, but it will not describe 'the dulling, the lulling, the chiming, the overbearing'.[16] The overwrought alliterative rhetoric here betrays Williams's anger at trapping himself between the sociologist he is trying to turn himself into and the literary critic he was trained to be. The legitimate hesitancies and qualifications of *Culture and Society* seem, in this book, only a tactic to forestall criticism from any flank, aesthetic Right or sociological Left. Williams let himself be got at, and the inquisitorial interviews of *Politics and Letters* (1979) show who the terrorists were. *Marxism and Literature* is a bad book because it is a trimmer's book, but its equivocations are representative of a whole genre of writing on art and society, or cultural studies itself, since the early 1970s. It is as if Althusser, Gramsci and Lukács have had to be called over, either to reverse the refusals of Leavis and *Scrutiny* or to continue, at the level of theory, the battles lost at the end of the 1960s in political praxis. Régis Debray remarks in *Teachers, Writers, Celebrities*, 'The review is isomorphic with the separate fields of the aesthetic avant-garde, academic research and political action and welds them all together'.[17] *New Left Review* certainly promoted, and continues to promote, the first two. What it, and many of its readers lacked, in the aftermath of 1968, was any tangible connection with the third. The political battles of the 1970s were just that, political. They were conducted within the frameworks of traditional party and trade-union politics, whose dominant discourse was economic, not cultural. There was not even, as in France and Italy, a strong Communist party with its own fusion of the political and the cultural to agitate against from within and without. Even the most mechanical of Marxisms retains some notion of the dialectic and, by its very nature and history, pays some attention to consciousness and superstructure. British Trotskyite groups made some space for cultural politics – the sad death of Peter Sedgwick removes one of the best writers of this type – but they lacked a powerful political base. The anti-intellectualism of the Labour party and the trade unions resisted, and still resists, any contention that law, art, money and sexuality are nodal ganglia in the body politic.

IV

All these connections had been made, in writings and actions, from the late 1940s onwards, not in France, but in America. What is astonishing is the virtual absence of the USA as a crucial component of post-war

British culture in all the courses surveyed for this essay. The residual Cold War allegiances of early cultural studies practitioners and *New Left Review*'s campaign to orientate British culture towards European rationalism may be the prime causes. But it is in precisely those distinctive areas of cultural studies, the media and popular culture, that American models and practices have proven most influential in British culture. Post-war affluence obviously made the domestic arena a crucial site for media attention. The family that stays together pays HP together. Situation comedies and soap operas, where stresses on marriage and family from consumer affluence/poverty are dramatized and harmonized in solely interior locations, began on television in America in the early 1950s and were established in Britain by the end of the decade. *I Love Lucy* (1951), *Coronation Street* (1960) and *The Dick Van Dyck Show* (1964) have of course their specific cultural inflections, but they speak the same idiom. Recent reruns of the American shows on Channel 4 have demonstrated just how talented the script-writers were. Focussing domestic squabbles through the Gothic horror convention, as with *The Munsters* (1965), was a stroke of genius. Current debates on policies for the new technology of video, satellite and cable will take off from the experience of *laissez-faire* America, rather than the largely state-monopoly systems of continental Europe. The conformity of the Ike-Nixon years, the imperialism of the Kennedy and Johnson presidencies, bred their own internal cultural opposition, eagerly followed and adapted, first in Britain, then on the continent. The Beat writers, Elvis Presley, Hollywood epics, James Dean, MAD magazine, the Berkeley Free Speech Movement, the Civil Rights Movement, Bob Dylan, the Anti-Draft Movement – such genres, figures and events sometimes appealed to different social sectors in Britain, and sometimes (James Dean and country and western music are outstanding examples) a fierce partizan has grown up which quite transcends class cultures. And, in the 1950s, Britain's fading imperialism spawned its own indigenous parodies. The Union Jack is constantly ripped to shreds, colonial expeditions always lose their way, Bloodnok is always blown up by curry and sexual desire in Spike Milligan's *Goon Show* scripts. These, by any definition, were very popular radio shows. From the same source we can find the stoical working man of Hoggart's decent working-class culture undermined at the very moment of his elegiac celebration. Among the traditional songs that Hoggart's book wishes to preserve against American rock and roll is 'Any Old Iron'. Peter Sellers' version of the song was in the charts for eleven weeks in 1957, reaching number 17.[18] The miserable, quavering cockney voice that sings it is that of the 'old mate' in the *Goon Shows*, who is every snivelling caretaker who's ever refused help with keys and rooms. 'More than me job's worf'. Several studies from the Birmingham Centre have deplored the break-up of the working-class family and community in London's East End due to extensive redevelopment from the early 1960s. Harold Pinter is from the Jewish East End working class. What he has the murderer Goldberg say in *The Birthday Party* (1958) about respectability and deference: 'All my life I've said the same. Play up, play up, and play the game. Honour thy father and thy mother. All along the line. . . . What do you think, I'm a self-made man? No! I sat where I was told to sit. I kept my eye on the ball. School? Don't talk to me about school. Top in all subjects.'[19] – all this casts a malevolent shroud over the pieties of Hoggart and Wesker. And the nest of vipers which is the working-class family in *The Home-coming* (1965) only reminds us that the best-known example of an effective extended family system in the East End in the 1960s was the Kray brothers.

It was useless for Hoggart to deplore the juke-boxes and milk-bars of urban Britain. A large part of the new popular culture was there and the youth of the working class was spending cash on it. The first two number one records of 1958 were Jerry Lee Lewis's 'Great Balls of Fire' and Elvis Presley's 'Jailhouse Rock'.[20] Marie Lloyd and the music-hall, or workers listening to Ruskin on art and capitalism, could only be of archival interest in the face of hot gospelling and country music from the deep South. In fact, McDonald's, Jack Kerouac, jeans and Chuck Berry long ago zoomed across the frontier while exotic structuralist-Marxists are still being dragged to the customs by *New Left Review*. Britain, with its intensely urban and industrial capitalist history was far more receptive territory for mid-twentieth-century American culture than those continental societies with still-active peasant cultures. Rock music is a precise case in point. Its fusion of electronics and urban blues is indeed 'the sound of the city'[21] and it encountered no resistance when domesticated in Liverpool, London, and Newcastle. Continental groups, in contrast, sounded always muted and imitative. They had initially to compete against strong, indigenous systems of peasant- and folk-ballad on the one hand, and the pre-industrial musical forms of the artisanate and the urban poor on the other hand. Maurice Chevalier (who had his older following in England) is always threatening to drift across Euro-pop. Rock music is, of course, capitalist music, a Niagara of rubbish shot by rafts of excellence, Elvis Costello diving for pearl in the lagoons of Barry Manilow. Beauty from dirt seems the sequence appropriate to a culture of experience, not innocence. If, then, mass consumer society is the object of cultural analysis, it would be wise to attend to those who, like Norman Mailer, William Burroughs and Marshall McLuhan, have brilliantly probed its heartland for the last thirty years and given us reports fissured, like those of Carlyle and Ruskin, by precipitous discontinuities. More formal academic studies have appeared alongside such innovative writings. A list including David Riesman's *The Lonely Crowd* (1950), Wright Mills's *The Power Élite* (1955), William Whyte's *The Organisation Man* (1956), Vance Packard's *The Hidden*

Persuaders (1957) and Paul Goodman's *Growing Up Absurd* (1960) represents a most distinguished sociological investigation of new patterns of urban and suburban work, leisure and education.

Supermarkets, pop music and *Hawaii Five-O* form, by now, a large part of the cultural world that British students unproblematically know. 'The children of Marx and Coca-Cola' Godard called them back in the mid-1960s, and the trenchant exposés of popular consumer fetishes which are his films from 1962 to 1968 are as brilliant elisions of the cultural into the political and vice-versa as McLuhan's *The Mechanical Bride* (1951) and Mailer's *Why are we in Vietnam?* (1967). But Godard was not ashamed to go to school to Hollywood B-movies, as Sartre and Simone de Beauvoir went to school to Faulkner, Dos Passos and jazz in the late 1930s. American/French avant-garde connections have been established since the symbolists acknowledged that Poe's *Philosophy of Composition* (1846) had laid out the method for the modern poem, followed by Stein and Hemingway realizing that you learnt how to write modern prose fiction from cubism and Flaubert. No-one would want to minimize the basic methodological differences between the deductive dialectics of Sartre, Foucault, Roland Barthes or Jean Baudrillard, and the basically empirical approaches of Riesman, Mailer and McLuhan. But all these synthesizers have concentrated on the culturalization of the political in an epoch of consumer capitalism: 'the mutation from a political economy to a society of spectacle in which needs are no longer satisfied simply by objects but by the sign-systems they endorse or bring into play'.[22] Sartre's entire creative life was devoted to finding forms to express the historical interactions between the two. Foucault, with his emphases on surface and dispersion, maps the ley-lines of power across institutions and bodies since the Middle Ages. Barthes's writings begin with the double focus of the rigorously deductive procedure of *Writing Degree Zero* (1953) and *Elements of Semiology* (1964), and the playful casualness of *Mythologies* (essays written between 1954 and 1956). These are swift probes into the world of the consumer that McLuhan and Packard were shaping at the same time for America. His last works, particularly *A Lover's Discourse* (1977), use the open-field procedures that the work of Pound and William Carlos Williams exemplifies from 1910 onwards. Baudrillard provides perhaps the most pessimistic diagnosis. In 1973, in the still euphoric aftermath of 1968, he found in cultural activity the one area resistant to the inexorable laws of political economy (use value to exchange value to surplus to profit).[23] It was the one area where human activity might legitimize itself through pleasure, waste and loss. All other activity was codified by a self-referential system – 'the signified and the referent are now abolished to the sole play of signifiers' – and the end result was: 'the system comprises neither idealism nor materialism nor infrastructure nor superstructure. It proceeds according to its form and this form carries along all of them at the same time; production and representation, signs and commodities, language and labour power'.[24] In his latest works available to us in English, *Simulations* (1983) and *In the Shadow of the Silent Majorities* (1983), the margin has been absorbed by the centre, distinctions are hardly discernible between the real and the imaginary, it is only the traditionally fascistic states of banality and inertia that might give rise to revolutionary consciousness. The society of surveillance and spectacle, denounced in advance by the situationists in the 1960s, who themselves had absorbed the teaching of the phenomenologists on perception and the gaze in the 1940s, comes of age in Baudrillard. 'Every move you make/Every step you take/I'll be watching you' (The Police). Who, in the wake of the Thatcher media-victory of June 1983, can argue that Baudrillard's pessimism is over-determined? The masses once more desired their own repression. Baudrillard's rather abstract and dehistoricized formulations complement the detailed writings of Mailer on the particular forms of American consumer totalitarianism which begin with the articles collected for *Cannibals and Christians* (1966). It is therefore no surprise that what English translations we have of Baudrillard are all from American presses, the Telos Press and the press of the same name as Columbia University's magazine, *Semiotext(e)*. This has also been the source for translations of the documents and actions of the Italian *Autonomia* group. Unlike Baudrillard, it saw possibilities of subverting the media and a network of alternative radio stations in Italy in the 1970s, most famously Radio Alice in Bologna, provided genuine distinctions between the real and the imaginary. But their slogan 'inside and against' denies any objective, angelic overview of political praxis. The model-maker is always in his model. In an interview in *City Limits* (17–23 June 1983) Bifo, a prominent spokesman for the group, suggested cultural alternatives centred on narrative. Until recently: '. . . the only *story* we knew in Europe – at least in France, Italy and Germany – was the *political* story.' New narratives are needed which can propose alternative values for the new technics. 'How can we find the means to make the social time, freed by the introduction of microelectronics, truly *free* time? . . . We have to see *time* differently – otherwise we're left with emptiness, not freedom . . . The problem is to invent stories that connect electronics with liberation. It's a problem of imagination, and of language.' But time, freedom and narrative are themselves contested concepts, now as much by the political Right as the Left. The Tories have linked freedom with privacy to create a space into which their archaic narratives can electronically flow. To counter this monolith the phenomenological project, dominant in 1968, subordinated to Althusserianism and Maoism in the 1970s, returns.

V

It never arrived in Britain. A Left intelligentsia, which foresaw that culture would be the long-term terrain for political struggle, but with no purchase on the political process, directed its energies, throughout the 1970s, to the politicization of culture via journals, courses, books and conferences. The failure of 1968 and a defensiveness bred of isolation caused it to choose ideology and hegemony, whether applied to social structure or artistic creativity, as its central organizing concepts. These are both concepts of restraint and control. They both minimize the possibility of unexpected, radical human action. Likewise with structuralism and semiotics, those other components of the paradigmatic cultural studies course. A narrow version of the Saussurean view of language was adopted, *langue* rather than *parole*, so that it emerged as a pre-constituted system that most human beings unconsciously inherit and operate and that even its greatest practitioners can only minimally emend. Ideology, language and hegemony, as applied to art, social action or institutions, all operate *through* more or less passive human actants. The Sartrean project, to become human and therefore free, can have no place on this agenda. The creative use of language that his novels, philosophies, plays, essays and biographies demonstrate could only be egoistic flourishes at the margins of an impersonal language-structure. With hegemony, revolts and rebellions emerge finally as control-ruses by the élites.

Everything has its own dialectic. The élites, from the mid-1970s on, under the impact of the oil crisis and an intensified fight for markets due to increased American and European investment in Third World economies, have preached a very similar message at home. The discourse was, until recently, purely economic – wage restraint, balancing the budget, good housekeeping, sound money – and preached first by Labour and then by the Conservatives. Now it too embraces the cultural. Where Callaghan reduced theology to economics ('Inflation is the mother and father of all evil'), Thatcher proposes her own base/superstructure metaphor ('Economics are only the beginning; the object is to change the nation's soul'), which is the 'affirmative culture' of the nineteenth-century bourgeoisie and indeed forms part of 'Victorian values'. There is an important sense in which the concepts and metaphors dominating the cultural studies field to date are *in tandem with* rather than in opposition to political conservatism. There is now a conservative popular culture (*Old Tyme Music Hall*; Chas and Dave singing 'Mustn't Grumble' on their TV pub-show); a conservative spiritual culture, a conservative collectivism, a conservative privacy, blatantly conservative mass media and a proposed conservative history. The newly-formed History Workshop Centre for Social History has spotted the danger of this one and the intention to bring together history, music and the fine arts, cinema and television, linguistics and aesthetics within a loosely defined field is the most important new initiative for those engaged in cultural studies. There is also a conservative 'freedom', but here, as we have seen, the Left has offered no opposition. Burroughs's Re-write Department is still churning it out.

It is because of this unconscious complicity with the enemy that the strenuous efforts at the politicization of culture in Britain have had such limited success. The handling, in the majority of cases, of the literary component of culture is a representative instance. The categories of political economy have been substituted for those of aesthetics. The art-work is a 'product', the artist/critic a 'cultural worker', meaning is 'produced' from the art-work and enters the 'circulation' of meanings within the 'cultural economy'. The concept for elucidating these meanings is ideology. What are the motives for this revamped Zhdanovism? The first is democratic. The argument is that literature is an élitist category (with the artist as genius) which proposes itself over and above the dull and dreary grind of capitalist production and accumulation. Call it 'writing' and anchor it within that discourse of production and its mystificatory veil will be shredded. And indeed it would be foolish to omit from any account the money this artisan gets, the paper/oil/chisel/video he uses, and the space/time co-ordinates of his energy. But this discourse, because it is not designed for it, cannot answer questions of aesthetic discrimination and value, the stumbling-block for all sociologists of literature and art. The second motive is the guilty desire by Left intellectuals to participate somehow in the tough, material reality of the proletariat. Hence the incantatory repetition of such phrases as 'the materiality of language' or a 'materialist theory of discourse', terms which make no sense either in physics or linguistics. Intellectuals do not work on assembly lines, but this way they can claim that they too are engaged in assembly-line work. In the same way, investigation of popular culture offers a way for 'cultural workers' into working-class consciousness of the symbolic, denied as they are daily experience of the working-class community. The romances and thrillers, the Du Mauriers and Le Carrés are, of course, tosh, and their formulaic repetitions do qualify them for assembly-line status. So they are material only for a sociology of mass media where concepts of ideology and hegemony certainly apply. An article by Louis Menand in *The Nation* traces how the 1960s marked the breakdown of the categories 'high' and 'popular' culture. 'Before the 1960s criticism of popular culture was sociological and criticism of high culture was moral and aesthetic.' From then on popular culture was so all-pervading in the USA that cultural critics had to do something about it. The alternatives emerged as 'to treat all culture as commodity, or to treat all culture as art'.[25] The upshot of this is to hand the initiative to capitalism. Of course it will agree that artistic structures can only be evaluated as commodities. There's no such thing as a free read. Or it will agree that popular culture, which it manufactures anyway, is an equal alternative to the residual aristocratic culture which it subsidizes. What need to be created are forms of writing which mix the popular with scholarship and, by their newness of forms, oppose the linear discourses of the spectacular society. If language, as McLuhan demonstrates, is a technic which 'outers' all of the human senses simultaneously, and if literature is language charged with meaning to the highest possible degree, then for cultural studies to rob itself of this uniquely complex probe of personal and social relations is rank suicide. Verbal language, on television as well, is still the major mode of communication in our culture. We live in an epoch of endless public lying. Where else will resistance to Newspeak be found except in the painful integrity of literary artists? If new narratives are needed for Europe, why not look to those whose skill is narrating?

'. . . Scientific revolutions are inaugurated by a growing sense . . . that an existing paradigm has ceased to function adequately in the exploration of nature to which that paradigm had previously led the way.'[26] Substitute 'culture' for 'science/nature' and this is an accurate description of the state of cultural studies today. The field can be called explosively volatile due to the domination of it by concepts of restraint and boundary. Everything – clothes, buildings, food, the Scouts – should be present, for what is not cultural? But what should be random points in a field which are then temporarily positioned by a number of co-ordinates are in danger of becoming stone slabs on some dismal moor. A plethora of material bulks up against a conceptual frugality. The circuits become overloaded. The culture is moving very fast right now. High Technology + Conservative Ideology = Right Futurism. There are intimate links, for example, between increased nudity in public advertising, the efflorescence of dance studios, charity marathons and recycled *laissez-faire*. Their common factor is the body, their common concept is the possessive individualism of Locke, their common myth is Narcissus. 'Around the body, which is entirely positived as the capital of divine right, the subject of private property is about to be restored.'[27] By the time the syntax of our sociologist of literature has clanked round to get this collection in its sights, the target has fled, dissolved and reconstituted itself into some other foul ensemble. To merely hold a portion of the cultural field in view demands a dance of the intellect among words and concepts, what Pound called *logopoeia*. The revelatory writing on culture today, whose speed of syncopated information actually realigns the angles of the culture into diagrams that flash, is in a magazine like *Z/G,* not in that cladding of costly primers on deconstruction that armours one wall of every university bookshop. Barthes, McLuhan, Foucault, Burroughs, Deleuze and Guattari actually *do* the job, with speed, accuracy and wit. What Barthes dismantled was not 'literature', but a particularly continental bourgeois form of 'culture' – a massive weight of impenetrable material loaded on to the heads of student-bearers from an early age. His constant emphasis through semiology was on the *doubleness* of all phenomena under capitalism. But to lever open the gaps between appearance and reality, surface and depth, promise and betrayal, he had to fashion his own language-technic. The musing *essai*, fragmentary discourse, tonal shifts, wide range of subject matter, are all penetrative lightenings of the monolith.

VI

Literature, history and the media should probably still be the co-ordinates of the cultural studies field. The achievement of these disciplines so far in interpreting the country's culture to itself is of quite sufficient distinction. But the points in the field which they position could be defined as the 'recurring characteristics' in an area which is both open and closed, which has its frontiers, borrowings and refusals.[28] Are there, over a stretch of time, certain activities of British culture which display a recurrent patterning and whose demise, submergence or transformation can be pin-pointed? The favoured example is empiricism which, for Perry Anderson, becomes the philosophy of the British bourgeoisie and explains why it has had, for centuries, 'a deep, instinctive aversion to the very category of totality . . .'[29] The thesis needs to be complexified. Both Hobbes and Bentham are empiricists, yet they are both totalizers. Hobbes was vehemently rejected by the gentlemen-virtuosi of the Royal Society, Bentham embraced by the commercial and manufacturing middle class of Victorian England. Empiricism, like any other concept, must be historically positioned. A more promising 'recurrent' is the popularization of science from the sixteenth century to the present day. Such a course could begin with John Dee's Preface to the first translation of Euclid (1570), and work through the proposals of William Petty and Samuel Hartlib in the 1640s, the curricula of the dissenting academies at the end of the century, Sir Humphrey Davy's Royal Institute lectures in the 1820s, the degrees offered at the Normal School of Science in the 1880s, up to televisual presentations of science in *Tomorrow's World, Horizon* and *The Ascent of Man*. The content and the motives for the presentation of science in these epochs will, of course, differ, and here the language used, the structure of the receiving society and the media for presentation (book, pamphlet, sermon, poem, public lecture, correspondence course, television and radio) will act as controls upon any idealist concept of science. A booklist mixing Frances Yates's *Theatre of The World* (1969), S.

Toulmin and J. Goodfield's *The Architecture of Matter* (1962), M. C. Jacob's *The Radical Enlightenment* (1981), *The Science of Matter* edited by M. P. Crosland (1971), Marjorie Nicolson's *Newton demands the Muse* and *Science and Imagination* (1956), Brecht's *The Life of Galileo* (first produced 1943) and H. G. Wells's *Love and Mr Lewisham* (1901) only hints at the range of cross-disciplinary materials for such a course. Other recurrent points in the British cultural field could be parliamentary government, the law as image and practice (different theories of language are particularly pertinent here), banks and money. And clearly any such series of studies would gain immensely from comparisons with continental cultures. Students would thus be aware of the historical and national specificity of the material cited in such as Foucault and Gramsci.

Such an approach envisages a cultural field, not primarily thought by a set of super-concepts, but rather made visible by intersections of information. One of the strengths of a cultural studies degree has always been its refusal to grant cultural phenomena their face value. The binary emphasis of dialectical procedures has been of immense help here. What has almost been forgotten is that such procedures not only acknowledge stasis and blockage but also aim at overcoming them: 'if we do not distinguish the project, as transcendence, from circumstances, or conditions, we are left with nothing but inert objects and History vanishes.'[30] It is therefore important that students, right from the start, be trained, not in a single method, but in the practice of intersection and juxtaposition through historically valid instances. 'Creation of a *thing,* and creation plus full understanding of a *correct idea* of the thing, *are very often parts of one and the same indivisible process* and cannot be separated without bringing the process to a stop.'[31] Doing it generates its own liberatory excitement. As for the politics, that has to be a matter of setting up cultural studies groups within the Labour party, which feed into the party all that accumulation of analyses of consumer capitalism which are available from the last thirty years. The alternative scenario is conservative surrealism and futurism. McLuhan got it right when he entitled his last book *Culture is Our Business* (1972).

VII

Culture is our nature now. Every class is marked and each gender is scored. 'I have always found that Angels have the vanity to speak of themselves as the only wise; this they do with a confident insolence sprouting from systematic reasoning' (Blake).[32] New forms of writing about the culture need to be created. Models we have – McLuhan,

Barthes, Tom Wolfe – but British culture requires its own specific mixture of the erudite and the demotic. The best current example is the plays of Howard Barker. And since the country's collective dream is now figured forth by a thoroughly unhistorical nostalgia it is a new form of writing about the literature/history relationship (considering each as specific forms of language-use) which is the most urgent requirement. 'It is understood by this time that everything is the same except composition and time, composition and the time of the composition and the time in the composition.'[33]

NOTES AND REFERENCES

1. Gertrude Stein, 'Composition as Explanation' (1926), in *Look at Me Now and Here I Am: Writings and Lectures of Gertrude Stein, 1911–1945*, ed. P Meyerowitz, Penguin 1971, p. 24. Parts of my essay first appeared, in a somewhat different form, in *Journal of Area Studies*, No. 8 (Autumn 1983), and the editors' permission to reprint is hereby gratefully acknowledged.
2. T. S. Kuhn, *The Structure of Scientific Revolutions*, 2nd edn, University of Chicago Press, Chicago 1970.
3. Paul Feyerabend, *Against Method*, New Left Books 1975.
4. Margaret Jacob, *The Newtonians and the English Revolution, 1689–1720*, Cornell University Press, Ithaca, N.Y. 1976.
5. Martin J. Wiener, *English Culture and the Decline of the Industrial Spirit, 1850–1980*, Cambridge University Press 1981.
6. Raymond Williams, *Culture and Society*, Penguin 1971, p. 11.
7. Williams, p. 307.
8. Williams, p. 313.
9. Williams, p. 320.
10. Arthur Hirsch, *The French Left: A History and an Overview*, Black Rose Books, Montreal 1982, p. 101.
11. Quoted from Henri Lefebvre, *The Explosion* (1969), in Hirsch, p. 147.
12. Allen Ginsberg, 'Wichita Vortex Sutra' (1966), in *Planet News 1961–67*, City Lights Books, San Francisco 1968.
13. Hirsch, p. 148.
14. Perry Anderson, 'Components of the National Culture,' *New Left Review*, No. 50 (1968), pp. 5–6.
15. Williams, *Marxism and Literature*, Oxford University Press 1977, p. 156.
16. Williams, *Marxism and Literature*, p. 156.
17. Régis Debray, *Teachers, Writers, Celebrities* (1979), trans. D. Macey, Verso 1981, p. 72.
18. See Jo and Tim Rice, Paul Gambaccini, Mike Read, *Guiness Book of British Hit Singles 4*, 3rd edn., Guinness Superlatives 1981.
19. *The Birthday Party*, Act III, Methuen 1960.
20. See Rice *et al*.
21. Charlie Gillett, *The Sound of the City*, Souvenir Press and Sphere 1971.

2. John Roberts, review of *In the Shadow of The Silent Majorities*, *City Limits*, No. 108 (1983), p. 25.

3. The best selection of Marx's writings for the cultural studies student is *Selected Writings of Karl Marx on Sociology and Social Philosophy*, 2nd edn., eds. T. B. Bottomore and M. Rubel, Penguin 1963. David McLellan, *Marx*, Fontana 1975, places his ideas historically and philosophically with admirable clarity.

4. Jean Baudrillard, *The Mirror of Production*, trans. M. Poster, Telos Press, St Louis, Mo. 1975, p. 143.

5. Louis Menand, 'Glad Hearts at the Supermarket', *The Nation* (15 May 1982). My thanks to Eric Mottram for drawing my attention to this extremely astute article.

6. Kuhn, p. 92.

7. Baudrillard, *Fetishism and Ideology*, quoted in Jonathan Miles, 'The Naked, the Uniformed and the Dead', *Z/G*, No. 7 (n.d., probably 1982).

8. Fernand Braudel's formulation in 'The History of Civilizations' (1959), in Braudel, *On History*, trans. Sarah Matthews, University of Chicago Press, Chicago 1980.

9. Anderson, p. 13.

10. Sartre, *Critique of Dialectical Reason* (1960), trans. A. Sheridan Smith, Verso 1982, p. 97.

11. Feyerabend, p. 26.

12. *The Marriage of Heaven and Hell* (c. 1790–3), plate 21; see *The Poetry and Prose of William Blake*, ed. D. V. Erdman, Doubleday, Garden City, N.Y. 1970, p. 41.

13. Stein, pp. 27–8.

CULTURAL STUDIES AND METHODOLOGY

Chapter 4

METHODS FOR CULTURAL STUDIES STUDENTS

ANNE BEEZER, JEAN GRIMSHAW and MARTIN BARKER

INTRODUCTION

From its inception, cultural studies has been in the business of break-ing down traditions. Traditional conceptions of literature, for example, are criticized, refused or re-evaluated in the light of theories which connect them to questions of material production, class rela-tions and the ideological construction of subjectivity. Not only that, but the boundaries of what is considered appropriate for study have shifted dramatically. Theories of cultural production are now intended to account not just for the relationship between the nineteenth-century reading public and the novel, but also for the connections between twentieth-century mass publications and their readers. The *Sun* news-paper, a TV crime series or a full-colour advertisement are now subject to the same kind of close scrutiny which was once confined to a novel by Eliot or a painting by Goya.

Our problem, as teachers trying to devise and teach courses in cultural studies, has not been a lack of relevant books in the area. Any student will attest to the fact that these are all too numerous! The major difficulty we have faced is the accessibility of the research described therein. All too often what we have found is the juxtaposi-tion of 'grand theory' and apparently detailed empirical description, with little mediation between the two. This is unfortunate on two grounds; it obscures processes of analysis from students who may be seeking ways of approaching their chosen material for research and, by forcing incommensurate objects and processes into unwieldy and over-rigid theoretical frameworks, it can make close observation seem to be a redundant exercise. If all women's magazines are to be explained by their effect of 'constructing women in imaginary relations with the real relations of production and reproduction', then there seems little point in examining them in their particularity. Their differences are in danger of becoming lost from view. Women's magazines do address themselves to the serious issues facing women today at the same time as, in other features, they will be suggesting ways of 'pleasing the man in your life'. Teenage girls' magazines contain endless stories of 'girl meets boy' but also offer, in their advice columns, the suggestion that girls should not be over-serious about boyfriends. Are we just to see these contradictions or tensions as more subtle ways of presenting an 'ideological bloc' constructing the female reader, or are we to conceive methods of analysing magazines which do not predetermine the results to be obtained?

The problem of moving from theory to structured observation became an immediate problem for us while tutoring student project work. These projects are presented audiovisually and it may well be that the 'immediacy' of this form of tutor/student discourse particularly highlights methodological issues. Alongside the audiovisual presentation, students prepare a research file which documents the theoretical and technical problems they have encountered in producing the project, the analytic procedures they have used in the construction of their arguments, and provides suggestions as to where further research might usefully be undertaken. The project work develops from the basis of a project outline produced by members of staff. This contains a brief theoretical contextualization of the particular project topic together with suggestions as to the initial methods of analysis students should use. Our intention, in developing student project work, has been to develop ways of encouraging them to get 'close to the material' in a structured manner whilst still allowing for the possibility of the research producing its own 'surprises'.

We have borrowed the techniques or methods of analysis we use with students from a variety of sources, and they include methods of narrative analysis, commutation techniques, questions designed to probe the text/reader relation, discourse analysis and simple methods of content analysis. None of these are conceived of as watertight procedures which will yield inevitable results; rather our aim in using them is precisely to reveal the patterns, contradictions and tensions within students' research material. Questions are therefore designed to search out significant absences, to encourage substitutions which 'play' with empirical material, to draw up lists of words or phrases which appear to express similar, underlying assumptions or conceptions; in short, questions which try to reproduce the 'plasticity' that completed production often serves to obscure. Our hope is that by using these methods, students will be able to move from their own common-sense understanding to one which is, at the same time, theoretically informed and methodologically explicable. Without the necessary mediation of good methods, the danger is that the gulf between theory and empirical observation of materials will remain. Ironically, this can often show itself as the collapsing of materials into theory. The result is mutual impoverishment.

Rather than try to state in the abstract how our projects work, we have summarized the actual development of three. In each case, there was material of a kind which had been analysed in just the ways that worried us: women's magazines, advertisements and teenage girls' comics.

RECOGNIZING ADVERTISEMENTS

Most accounts and critiques of advertising start from the premise that advertisements are an easily identifiable category. Judith Williamson,[1] for example, suggests that they are 'a recognizable form' despite the fact that they occur within different technical media and have very varied 'contents' and styles. Her semiotic approach to advertisements, which treats them as 'enclosed texts', constructing the viewer in a chain of significance determined by the advertisements themselves, prevents her from enquiring into this paradox: that adverts are both easy to recognize yet infinitely varied as to style, context, content and mode of address.[2]

It was with the intention of further exploring this paradox that we devised the project described below. In the introduction to the project we made the point that many critiques of advertising, including that of Williamson, argue that advertisements are very powerful in their effects on our behaviour and attitudes, creating in us 'false needs', inducing us to become stupefied consumers or constructing us as 'ideo-logical subjects'. We suggested that this type of approach tended to concentrate on the analysis of particular images within advertise-ments, such as the 'image of femininity' or the 'image of the family', and we argued that these accounts either ignore, or exclude as an important area for analysis, the relationship between people's *prior* interests, purposes and knowledge and their reaction to or understand-ing of advertisements. These, we suggested, might well perform an essential mediating function between any one advertisement and its possible effects. A further problem of formalist interpretations of advertising is their extreme arbitrariness. For example, in her analysis of the Chanel No. 5 ad, which uses Catherine Deneuve's face as a selling point, Williamson argues that this advertisement completes its ideological work by making a transference of meaning between the product and the signifier, Catherine Deneuve, so that we understand the perfume as representing, and thus possessing, the glamour and beauty associated with Catherine Deneuve. But these are just two of potentially hundreds of associations that Catherine Deneuve's face may possess for us, and to isolate them in this arbitrary fashion is to commit what Trevor Pateman calls the Dictionary Fallacy,[3] that is, to assume that meaning is an inherent and immutable property of the text.

This project had two main objectives: firstly, to explore some of the conditions and contexts which work to limit the potential ambiguities of any one advertisement and secondly, to consider the circumstances which allow people to distinguish between advertisements and other forms of communication. Even prior to our recognition that Catherine Deneuve's face may be being used to represent glamour and beauty, we must first of all recognize that what we are seeing *is* an advertisement, which has the intention of selling us perfume, whatever the associations suggested. How do we 'recognize adverts' and what difference does this recognition make to our understanding of the 'information' they provide? It may well be that people have different kinds of predisposition toward different sorts of communication, attributing to some (news reports?) a greater degree of authority and veracity. Both of these questions cannot be answered by treating advertisements as formal organizations of signs which must then be deciphered and, therefore, they fall outside the theoretical framework established by semiology.

Initially, as a means of approaching these questions, we asked students to collect a number of advertisements, of as varied a type as possible, ranging from those which appeared in magazines and colour supplements to those found in newspaper classified columns. However, we realized that by doing this we were pre-empting the very question we wanted to explore, namely how they selected advertisements from other forms of communication. In order to tap this kind of ability, we asked them to make lists of those items of communication that they considered to be advertisements, and those which were not, providing reasons for each item's classification. One student did this on a journey from college to home and decided that such things as road signs, petrol and shop signs (excluding brand names) and other forms of 'street information' such as bus stops etc. did not *act* as advertisements whilst shop and petrol-station brand signs, cars (with make clearly visible) and hoardings fell clearly into the category of advertisement.[4] In discussion with the student it became clear that the principle of distinction operating was between information which was considered to be 'necessary' and that which was understood as being 'commercially motivated'.[5] Thus, it was argued that we do need to be able to distinguish between a greengrocer and a chemist, but the extra information that the chemist happens to be a branch of Boots is superfluous. What also emerged from discussion was that, apart from advertising particular products, many advertisements draw attention to their own status *as advertisements*, and are able to do this because of our *prior* familiarity with particular styles, logos and use of imagery. Even in those advertisements which offer least in the way of visual clues, our familiarity with a distinctive logo (as in Benson and Hedges adverts) can 'trigger' in us a recognition that we are, in fact, seeing an advertisement. (Ironically, the advertisers of cigarettes can use the legal requirement to display a 'Government Health Warning' precisely as such a trigger mechanism, thus allowing them to use 'artistic', 'surreal' and often very ambiguous images, whilst remaining confident that people will recognize the image as part of a cigarette advertisement.)

In order to explore further their reasoning for distinguishing between ads and non-ads, students were asked to modify their original ad category on the basis of the following questions:

1. From your original advert category, ask yourself what you would have to remove from them in order to make it unclear or ambiguous that they were advertisements.
2. Which ones can be made ambiguous? What else might they be (in their ambiguous state)?
3. Are there some advertisements which can't really be made ambiguous in this sort of way?

These questions were asked because in previous project work on themes within advertising we have developed what we term methods of 'deconstruction' as a means of analysing the particular construction in advertisements of location, setting, product, subject stance and subject gaze. Students are asked to remove, change or substitute these constituent parts of an advertised image, so that gaze may be altered, stance or setting changed or the product removed or substituted. This form of 'deconstruction' is obviously not to be confused with that developed in post-structuralist theories and is, in fact, much closer to the kinds of technique developed by Guy Gauthier in his *Semiology of the Image*.[6] The choice of what to use as a reasonable substitution derives from extratextual knowledge and, as our earlier remarks indicate, the value of this kind of exercise is not that some final, irreducible textual meaning can be achieved, but that by doing these substitutions one can have some means of testing the limits of the connotations on offer in any particular advertisement. Nor are we suggesting that one among the many connotations offered is 'preferred', since many advertisements precisely trade on the ambiguity of the images they use. The Benson and Hedges advert, which shows an hourglass in the bottom half of which is a dimly lit B and H logo, cannot easily be described as 'meaning' anything in particular other than 'this is yet another clever Benson and Hedges advertisement'. In other more 'realistic' advertisements these techniques can reveal that sporty cars, for example, are not the province of the 'working mum', just as family saloons, unless of the sleeker, hatchback variety, are not directed at the young, single man. Finer distinctions than these obviously very crude ones can be discerned when attention is directed at the beauty and cosmetic advertisements, and Trevor Millum[7] has convincingly shown the importance of gaze and stance, and the gender-based distinctions in these, in products directed at women or using the representation of women as a selling point.

In response to this exercise one student argued that in the large, glossy adverts as found in many magazines and on street hoardings almost all aspects of the advertisement would have to be removed in order to make its status as an advertisement in any way ambiguous. For many adverts, the removal of the product, lettering and brand name left only a neutral background or, in the case of numerous car advertisements, a photograph depicting some rural landscape. In fact, this student found the exercise difficult if not a little absurd, and this sense of absurdity seemed to stem from his inability to separate his expectation that adverts appeared in familiar settings and his attempt to 'defamiliarize' the category of advertisement. On the other hand, it was relatively easy to make the particular product being advertised ambiguous by simply removing the brand name, in many cases. The process of recognizing adverts appeared to occur in two stages, the first stage being the identification of a distinctive class of communication – advertisements, the second being the recognition of the particular product.[8] It seemed that it was the context in which an advertisement occurred which provided the vital clue as to its communication type, whether this context happened to be a magazine, a television programme or a street hoarding. This would suggest that people *expect* to see advertisements in these places and this expectation can be confirmed by very minimal visual or linguistic clues. Again, Benson and Hedges and Guinness ads 'trade' on this minimal cueing and, in a sense, 'share a joke' with the viewer about their status as advertisements, so much so that in Guinness ads the appearance of the brand name becomes a redundant piece of information.

The ideas emerging from our students' research into the processes whereby people assign communicative material into the category of advertisement are very close to Pateman's argument that 'advertisements are rarely identified in isolation or retrospectively, but rather are identified in a context where they have been anticipated'.[9] If expectation or anticipation does play an important part in our overall response to advertisements, facilitating our ability to decipher them, then it would seem that any ideological power that they may possess does not necessarily derive from 'their working behind our backs', nor does it seem appropriate to treat such ideologies as the function of the particular advert, since we recognize the single advertisement on the basis of our (prior) ability to distinguish them as a class.

Having established that the context in which an advertisement occurs provides the vital clue which allows people not only to recognize it as an advertisement, but to expect or anticipate that they will see an advert, students were asked to consider more precisely what they meant by the idea of context. It appeared to include different sorts of 'initiating conditions', ranging from location (as in the case of street hoardings) to a relationship that they perceived to exist between a commodity and a persuasion to buy, as in the case of shoes displayed outside a shoe shop. In the case of really well known and distinctive advertisements like those already referred to, it was argued that they had achieved such a familiar 'house style' that wherever they occurred, irrespective of context in magazines, on billboards etc., they would be recognized. They seemed to have achieved the emblematic character that previously was confined to popular works of art or national symbols. 'Context' was therefore subdivided into context (to refer to location only), relationship (where something *acted* as an advert only in conjunction with a recognized selling institution) and image. This last term was used to describe clever, 'arty' adverts which are recognizable 'at a glance', and it was thought that these adverts were often admired on aesthetic grounds and had become, in fact, a popular form of art. It is certainly true that in such adverts there is often a self-conscious use of either traditional 'painterly' or modern art styles.[10]

Obviously these distinctions are only the preliminary steps towards a more comprehensive account of the visual, linguistic and contextual clues which enable people to recognize advertisements. Using the methods outlined here, any theoretical distinction between advertising as a profit-making institution and publicity of various kinds becomes difficult if considered solely as an attribute of a 'text'. Particular categories of advertisement appear to be the product of a recognized intention to sell, of the format of the advertisement and of the way in which people's expectations about such formats are fulfilled. To isolate format, in the way that formalist approaches do, is to take only one element out of this complex interconnection, and treat it as the sole determinant of our reaction to advertisements. Differences, for example, between classified and magazine-type ads are not only the consequence of the use of different formats but also because these formats initiate quite separate sets of 'consumer' expectations, with the former often being considered as somehow less 'commercial' than the latter. Interestingly, classified advertisements have attracted little academic attention (although they are quite frequently the subject of consumer, 'watchdog' organizations' investigations); yet in terms of attention actually paid to advertisements, it is likely that it is this type that is most closely perused. This type of advertisement is treated as relatively harmless whilst the more colourful advertising display is treated with the utmost suspicion.

Raymond Williams[11] has called for a clarification of the concept of advertising, arguing that 'the real business of the historian of advertising . . . [is] to trace the development from processes of specific attention and information to an institutionalized system of commercial information and persuasion'. Clearly this distinction between information and commercial information or advertising is an important one which is as yet insufficiently theorized. Our student research into the processes whereby people recognize advertisements has pointed to the

101

crucial importance of context as the means by which 'correct' responses are cued. Large, colourful and glossy advertisements unambiguously proclaim their status *as advertisements* no matter how complex the particular image may be. Once this correct assignment of the information type is made, it seems that many people enjoy deciphering the visual puzzles displayed in advertisements in much the same way as they enjoy other forms of puzzle-solving activity.

Other sorts of advertisement, however, do appear to confuse the status of the information offered, and the type of advertisement our students picked out as an example of this kind of miscueing was the 'feature' variety as found in many women's magazines. Here, there seems to be a deliberate use of context to confound our expectations so that information on skin care and health, for example, will be presented in such a way as to imply that it is 'disinterested', with commercial considerations playing only a secondary or subsidiary role. The presence of a signal to the reader stating that 'it is an advertisement feature' may not necessarily dispel this ambiguity since, if expectation based on context is an important part of our ability to assign information status correctly, then, in a sense, we have *already misread* that information.

The way in which we learn to recognize the type of information offered to us, including that provided by advertisements, and the role played by different forms of context in facilitating or hindering this ability are issues that require further research. Our student project work did not pursue these questions, but we would argue that their achievements have established a possible basis for doing so by using methods of analysis which did not assume a unilinear and totally determined relationship between advertisements and viewers, but rather treated the prior knowledge and interests that people possess as a crucial element in the analysis of that relationship.

COSMOPOLITAN

Magazines for women have been a prominent feature of publishing for several decades, and maintain a large readership. They vary considerably in style and content, and whilst individual magazines may hit circulation problems or disappear altogether (for example, the magazine *Nova*), the market for them in general seems to remain very consistent. Nor are sales necessarily a good guide to readership, since many women borrow and lend the magazines, and read them without purchase when the opportunity arises (waiting rooms, hospitals, hairdressers etc.). The longevity and consistency of their appeal is itself of interest and invites the question how and why they appeal.

Women's magazines have also changed in significant ways over the past three or four decades, as the result both of additions to the market (such as *Cosmopolitan*) and of changes in magazines that have a longer history. Some of these changes are discussed by Marjorie Ferguson in her book *Forever Feminine*.[12] On the basis of a detailed content analysis, she identifies what she sees as significant shifts in the dominant themes of magazines such as *Woman* and *Woman's Own*. She also shows how women's magazines have sometimes responded to what they have seen as the most important changes in women's lives, and seen themselves as involved in the process of creating such changes.

There has been a fair amount of critical and feminist work on women's magazines. Some of it has been restricted to specific aspects of them, as, for example, Millum's work on images of women in magazine advertisements.[13] Other work has approached the question of what particular magazines, or women's magazines in general, offer to the female reader, and of what relationship we should see as existing between magazine and reader.

One particular approach to women's magazines which we have felt to be problematic is that which is underpinned by an Althusserian view of ideology as the construction of the subject. An example of this sort of approach is Janice Winship's article, 'Woman: an ideology of femininity',[14] Winship argues that the magazine negates or denies the real contradictions of women's lives. *Woman* magazine, she suggests, is determined by and constructed through an ideology of femininity, with subdomains of femininity, motherhood, sexuality and feminine individuality. It provides a false coherence by its elimination of contradictions. Winship accepts an Althusserian account of ideology as a 'level' relatively autonomous from the economic and political, and as representing not the system of real relations which govern the existence of individuals, but the imaginary relations of individuals to the real relations in which they live. The contents of the magazine are thus represented from particular standpoints which its women readers are constituted by and live within. The magazine therefore has a meaning for women in relation to the ideological representations which they live as their everyday lives. As a whole, she argues, it endorses femininity, which cannot be challenged from 'within'; hence, despite features such as the problem page, where women recognize and seek advice about, and implicitly recognize contradictions in, the problems they experience in their everyday lives, it cannot engage with these problems other than at the level of illusion, of ideology. Implied in this view is a theory about the relationship of the magazine both to 'reality' and to its readers. The relationship to the reader is one in which the reader is trapped within the specious coherence of femininity, and constituted by it in a way that makes any sort of critical dialogue between reader and magazine impossible, except from 'outside'. But, given the Althusserian account of ideology, it is not easy to determine where the resources from 'outside' are to come from. As a result of this view, Winship's attitude to *Woman* is almost entirely critical and dismissive; she regards it as patronizing women, and has not a good word to say for it.

This student project was in fact about *Cosmopolitan*. *Cosmopolitan* was chosen because, unlike some other women's magazines, especially the weekly ones, it is aimed primarily at the (indeterminately) young or youngish women who is normally assumed to be at work, financially independent, and anxious to evolve a lifestyle and sexual relationships of her own. *Cosmopolitan* has liked to see itself as catering for the progressive or independent woman who is out for success, and is no longer hidebound by the shackles of children, home, domesticity, etc. It is a very different magazine from *Woman,* and very much a product of post-1960s changes in sexual mores and conceptions of lifestyles possible for youngish single women, or women who live with men on bases other than those of monogamy or traditional marriage. Motherhood features very little in it. For these sorts of reason, apart from its intrinsic interest, it seemed to be a good testing-ground for the adequacy of the sort of theorization of the relationship of magazines to reality and to readers offered by Winship.

The starting point for the project was an analysis of the conception of 'work' offered by *Cosmopolitan*. There is a section in the magazine called 'Working Woman', and there are many articles and features on 'successful' women and on the problems encountered on the various routes they took to success. The student was asked to do an initial content analysis of about six to eight issues of the magazine, based on questions such as the following:

1. What sorts of job are seen as desirable, enviable, worth having and why? Where women are seen as successful, what criteria of success are being used?
2. How did successful women *become* successful? What conceptions are presented of possible routes to success?
3. What sorts of problem are women seen as encountering at work? What sorts of solution to these problems are recommended? What sorts of problem are never discussed?

In the course of undertaking the initial analysis, the student was struck by a number of things about the magazine which seemed significant in trying to understand it as a whole. She came to the project with an expectation that *Cosmopolitan* would be likely to contain mainly articles and features about fashion, glamour, famous personalities etc.; and she (and we) were surprised to find how large a proportion of the magazine was not just about these things, but tackled issues of central feminist concern. These included rape, domestic violence, abortion, sexual harassment, as well as general issues of sexual equality and equality of opportunity. There were also interviews with and features about well-known feminists such as Dale Spender. In addition, access to some publicity material, plus a study of editorial comment, made us realize the extent to which *Cosmopolitan did* see itself as dealing with 'serious' is ues of feminist concern.

The publicity material also suggested to us, however, that *Cosmopolitan* sees itself as making a distinction between its 'serious' and its more 'glamorous' aspect. (A letter from a correspondent described *Cosmopolitan* as '*Spare Rib* in *Vogue*'s clothing'.) The question we then faced was that of the relationship between the serious or feminist content and the glamorous image of *Cosmopolitan*. The student though that two things in particular seemed significant in helping to illuminate this.

1. *Titles*. A careful study was made of the titles of articles or features, and two things emerged:
   (a) It was often difficult to tell just from the title what the article was about.
   For example:
   'Frills or thrills' was the title given to an article about feminist books.
   'Women with a voice' was about women as singers and backing groups.'
   (b) The titles given to articles of feminist concern were all of the snappy, often ambiguous, alliterative or punning style given to article of fashion etc.
   For example:
   'What separates the girls from the boys?' was about sex discrimination.
   'Sock-it-to-you sense on marriage' was about marital violence and wife-beating.

2. *Juxtapositions*. These were of several sorts. For example:
   (a) The title page of an article about a serious topic would be opposite an advertisement portraying a typical glamorous image of woman, or conveying a message antithetical to that of the article. (An outstanding example was pointed out by another student who had seen in a previous *Cosmopolitan* an article discussing rape juxtaposed to a perfume ad whose caption read 'Bring out the beast in him').
   (b) The images and illustrations used in features about things such as domestic violence would often be indistinguishable from those used in features about fashion or 'lifestyle', or in the short stories included in the magazine.

There was a pronounced tendency for the general glamorous style of the magazine to infiltrate the serious articles. From editorial and publicity material, it was clear that there was awareness of a tension in the relationship between these two aspects of the magazine; but it tended to be dismissed by the argument that there is no reason why you cannot *both* be serious *and* enjoy yourself and have fun as well.

From the study of the magazine it seemed clear that *Cosmopolitan* cannot be understood as simply offering its readers any static conception of femininity, nor as confirming its readers in any such conception. Nor would it be correct to say that *Cosmopolitan* does not engage in any way with readers' 'real' problems. Discussions of problems of sexual harassment and domestic violence, for example, and the way they were portrayed cannot adequately be understood as mere ideological representation. A distinction between ideology and reality of the sort that Winship makes did not seem to help in understanding the magazine. *Cosmopolitan* explicitly recognizes the contested nature of notions of femininity, and in no way presents its readers with an entirely homogeneous conception.

Subsequently to the completion of the substance of the project, Ferguson's *Forever Feminine* was published. One of the main changes she identified between the 1940s and the 1980s was a shift in women's magazines away from the theme of 'getting and keeping your man' to the themes of 'self-creation' or 'self-production'. Furthermore, she argues, while it is still true, for example, that motherhood is a central theme in many magazines, some such as *Woman's Own* have played an important part both in recognizing the fact that women do and always have frequently worked outside the home, and in helping to remove *some* of the stigma and guilt previously attached to the idea of the 'working mother'.

The student making the project thought that the central theme of *Cosmopolitan* could be seen as that of *change*, and, especially, of changing yourself. The magazine was sensitive to many aspects of women's lives that had changed, and that needed changing, and it by no means failed entirely to discuss radical or collective solutions to women's problems. The dominant conception of change, however, was that it was something you could do for yourself. No woman, it suggests, need be stuck in any situation, whether it be dowdiness, a negative self-image, an unsuccessful love affair or a rotten job. There *were* references to sources of help such as Women's Aid, or to the particular problem of, say, low-paid working-class women, but the main emphasis was on individual effort, will-power and positive thinking, and the titles of many articles encapsulated this ('A day to change your life').

We thought also that there was a relationship between this conception of change, and the processes of juxtaposition and infiltration mentioned earlier. The 'serious' articles were glamorized by snappy titles and glossy images, and all aspects of change, despite the contrary implications of much of the text, seemed by this process to become rather similar. You can change your lipstick, your shape, your clothes, your style, your lover, your sexual behaviour, your attitudes, if only you have sufficient courage and zest and nerve. Furthermore, in many of the features on changing yourself, the conception of change was arguably a somewhat egoistic/narcissistic one. Tremendous stress was laid on the importance of being 'oneself'; on the way one feels about oneself, and on the validity of a quest for self-actualization. Other people sometimes appeared rather as a mere backdrop to this quest, or even as a means to it; and insufficient recognition was accorded to problems of social responsibility, the needs of others who might be affected by this quest for self-actualization, and the difficulty of postulating individual needs that are independent of the needs of others.

Cosmopolitan magazine was first published in 1972, and can be seen as part of the development of 'young women's' magazines in the 1960s and 1970s.[15] Its existence needs to be understood in the context of an increase in the spending power and independence of many young women, and of a challenge to conceptions of femininity that saw this as necessarily related to motherhood and family. The historical origins of the magazine, and its own insistence on the contested nature of femininity and the importance of change, suggest that it cannot be adequately understood as offering any single or coherent such conception, nor as trapping readers within this. Winship's view that women's magazines can only be challenged from 'outside' assumes a sharp demarcation between ideology and reality which does not help in understanding *Cosmopolitan*. It ignores the essentially contested nature of *conceptions* of femininity, and the way in which these are presented in the magazine. Nor can it be supposed that women readers are merely confirmed in some ideological misrepresentation of themselves. Such a view does not take account of the many different contexts in which, or purposes for which, the magazine may be read or used, and the way in which different experiences or interests may create different relationships with the magazine. There is no *one* way of reading *Cosmopolitan*, nor does it offer *one* coherent message to read.

In questioning an Althusserian approach to women's magazines like that of Winship, the alternative is not of course an uncritical acceptance of, or even liking for them. In the project, the student was extremely critical of what she saw as the frequent undermining of serious or feminist articles by a certain sort of glamorous presentation, and also of the concept of change presented in the magazine, in which there was insufficient stress on the possibility or necessity of social or collective meeting of women's needs. It is rather that an approach to women's magazines which starts from a theoretical premise that they are to be dismissed as mere ideology which simply demeans women fails to recognize their specificity and complexity and the tensions, changes and contradictions within them.

Such an approach is also bound to give an inadequate conception of the relationship between reader and magazine. In her book, Ferguson points out that women's magazines may well provide some women with one of the few sources they have of a really positive evaluation of themselves, and of a serious recognition of at least some of the day-by-day problems of being a woman. Understanding women's magazines must involve taking seriously the question why they have such a consistent appeal; and how, despite their frequent limitations and distortions, they have responded to changes in women's lives. An historical conception of them as mere ideology, to be dismissed some-what contemptuously, both fails to do justice to them as objects of investigation, and itself demeans women readers in presenting them as mere 'supports' for ideology.

TEENAGE GIRLS' MAGAZINES

Given the explosive rise of the women's movement alongside the continuing massive sales of teenage girls' magazines, it is hardly surprising that there should be a marked interest in questions about the influence of magazines such as *Jackie*. Their role in the socialization of young girls into forms of 'femininity' was bound to be questioned, and it has been.[16]

When we offered a project outline on them, it was with the specific purpose of finding ways of testing the kinds of claim that have been made about their influence. We felt it was important to remember just how accidental was the birth of this kind of girls' magazine. They arose in the 1960s because, to the publishers' surprise, their women's magazines were selling to a much younger audience than they had thought. Also, it is important to be able to keep a sense of their specificity; *Valentine* and *Marilyn*, early forerunners of our current crop, were markedly different, and these differences should not be lost in advance of considering their significance. We wanted this project to work, therefore, both to capture the particular nature of these magazines, but also to see if this could throw light on the way they might have an influence.

To be honest, we began from a point of considerable scepticism about the claimed power of these magazines. It was not only that arguments about girls being 'conditioned',[17] or 'imprisoned'[18] tend to be immediately qualified by admissions that not all are affected, that some girls resist the influence, or even make a subversive (e.g., anti-school) activity out of reading them. It was also that the concepts used to state the supposed mode of influence (for example, 'stereotype', 'identification', and 'ideological presence') had a superficial clarity that tended not to withstand analysis. And the theoretical approach adopted seems to make very little difference to the outcome. It is as though investigators knew in advance of looking what kinds of thing these magazines were. This situation is not unlike the similarities that have been noted between rejections by both left and right of 'mass culture'.[19]

Angela McRobbie's analysis is justly the best-known piece of work on *Jackie*, and an important piece of work by any accounts. It is an important case-study, because it is a thorough use, and therefore test, of a semiological approach. McRobbie argues that a semiological approach to *Jackie* reveals that it confronts girls with an 'ideological bloc of mammoth proportions', one that 'imprisons them' in a claustrophobic world of jealousy and competitiveness, 'the most unsisterly of emotions, to say the least'.[20] This is achieved because *Jackie* is a monolithic system, structured around a system of connoting codes: of romance, of personal life, of fashion and beauty, and of pop. In this system, everything is apparently organized to mobilize the effect. The layout, the language, title, colour and black and white printing, as well as the overt messages combine so that a single systematic message emerges. This message coheres exactly with the needs of consumerist capitalism. *Jackie is* a consumer product, it *sells* consumer products, and it embodies a powerful system of messages that sell leisure and romance, combining as consumerism, as the only relevant and desirable sphere of young girls' lives.

This is not a conspiracy, says McRobbie. D. C. Thomson create magazines, each with its own conventions, but 'within these conventions and through them a concerted effort is made nonetheless to win and shape the consent of the readers to a set of particular values'.[21] Or as she expressed it later in the article, through the magazines 'teenage girls are subjected to an explicit attempt to win consent to the dominant order – in terms of femininity, leisure and consumption, i.e., at the level of culture'.[22]

In worrying about these broad claims from McRobbie, we were not trying to neutralize *Jackie*, nor seeing it as merely 'giving girls what they want'. But it concerns us that her method creates an illusion of showing more than it actually is showing. When she argues that *Jackie* is organized through four main codes, what more is she saying than that there is an awful lot in it about fashion, romance, and so on? She certainly *seems* to be saying more, as the concept of a 'code' does hard labour in her argument. It transforms what is otherwise a quantitative content-analysis into a whole theory of ideology; and it does this by two key assumptions which are never argued for. The first is that what is in the magazine tends to reproduce itself in the heads of girls; the second is that what *isn't* in the magazine is being systematically shut out of girls' heads.

Regarding the first, she argues for example that, because in the stories girls frequently cannot trust their best friends, then jealousy is being taught. In such a view, a story-world is seen as wholly un-mediated, without any need to refer to what analysts have variously called the 'authorial stance', 'rhetoric', or 'presentational process'.[23] In other words, her approach does not see any need to consider the ways in which readers are put into particular relations with the world in the story, and the kind of narrative structure and process they use. Instead it 'reads off' that such stories are 'about' jealousy, in the same unproblematic way that other mass-media critics 'read off' that TV programmes are 'about' violence. Her assumptions here lead to plays on ambiguity of reference, as in the following: 'They [the stories] cancel out completely the possibility of any relationship other than the romantic one between girl and boy. They make it impossible for any girl to talk to, or think about a boy in terms other than those of romance.'[24] Is this the girls in the stories, or girl-readers? The distinction has entirely collapsed.

In this quote we also see the second assumption at work: what isn't in *Jackie* is being deliberately excluded from girls' lives. This means that such a magazine must somehow seek to embrace all the world, to define itself as everything. This is strange since no-one would ever say this of, for example, the *Radio Times,* or *HiFi Weekly.* If it is true of *Jackie,* we need to be told what in the magazine is doing it, and how.

This connects finally with a tendency in her account not to allow that there might be tensions within *Jackie.* All is terribly unified and unidirectional, even to the point where apparent tensions are con-cealed devices for preventing readers' escape. The differences between (idealized) stories and (real) problems turn into just another mobilizer:

> Comfortably apart from the more lighthearted articles, and set amidst the less flamboyant and colourful small advertisements, [the problem page] regenerates a flagging interest, and also sums up the ideological content of the magazine. It hammers home, in the last but one page, all those ideas and values prevalent in the other sections, but this time in unambiguous black and white.[25]

It is all extraordinarily homogeneous and successful, a unified mam-moth. Yet none of McRobbie's crucial transitions have been argued. It is as though semiology is a theory which permits us to know in advance what we will find, by which we could never be surprised.

In designing our project, we tried to suggest methods of looking at magazines such as *Jackie* which *would* be capable of surprising, and which would not make these kinds of assumption. Our emphasis had to be on students getting in close to them, to find out what relationship the magazine set up with readers, and what they ask of girls in the act of reading them. We also did not assume that all parts convey homogeneous messages.

Aware of the magnetic attraction of the standard view (be it put in terms of 'stereotypes' with which girls 'identify', or 'codes' by which they are 'imprisoned'), the first operation was to analyse Polly Toynbee's newspaper article on these magazines, asking: what clues does Toynbee leave as to her implicit assumptions about how girls are influenced by reading the magazines? and what view does she suppose as to why they read them, if they are as deleterious as she says? This, we hoped, would have the effect of distancing students from prejudgements about mechanisms of effect.

Our aim was not to put McRobbie's or anyone else's study to shame, but to understand magazines like *Jackie* better. So rather than attempt to rework her examples,[26] the project allowed students to look at recent editions of any such magazine.[27] And the student who took it on, in the end focussed on both *Jackie* and *My Guy*. She was asked, in the first place, to do a straightforward content-analysis of the kinds of material they contained. This proved significant. Contents are fairly stable over time and magazines, with about a quarter given over to stories (both written and photostrip), the rest divided between problem pages, quizzes and other 'fun' material, pop news and pinups, fashion, and advertisements (with occasional more informative pieces, for example on jobs for women). All this seemed no different from McRobbie's picture.

But it was discovered that these classifications easily became arbitrary. First, the magazines would often mix together kinds of materials, and formats of presentation. Adverts would use strip-formats, like the stories, fashion articles would be an open confusion of advice and adverts. But the more important reason turned out to be that virtually every page was integrated into the magazine as a whole by headlines, jokey bits, references to the staff of the magazine and the like. Often, issues would have a theme which would take over and organize all the main contents (for example, Valentine's Day).[28] These linking elements were part of what could be called the magazines' 'persona', that is, their way of conveying a conception of themselves and of how readers should involve themselves.[29]

The next task, therefore, for the student was to investigate this 'persona'. Questions were asked such as: what kinds of language are used in 'editorial' comments? What kinds of information are we offered, about the magazine and its editorial staff? What relationships appear to exist among the staff, and between staff and the 'stars' whom they interview or present to readers?

It emerged from these that the 'unity' of the magazine is more complex than at first appeared. Overall, the 'persona' of the magazines was of a bright, fun-loving, bantering family, full of foibles and silly games. But two parts of the magazines differed significantly from this: the stories, and the readers' problem pages.

The latter, our student discovered, do not have to suffer the bantering the 'staff' otherwise inflict on each other – indeed, the 'people' (Cathy and Claire in *Jackie* or Chris in *My Guy*) who answer readers' worries hardly appear in the rest of the magazines. The pages are, as it were, insulated. The student then looked at a sample of readers' letters and tried to write her own answers to them, in order to try to get a grasp of the principles that inform the magazines' answers. To her horror, she found that she was saying things remarkably similar to the magazines. Analysing the principles which guided the kind of answers both were giving, it emerged that they were guided by a kind of 'practical common sense', a pragmatism which did not sit easily with the rest of the contents.

At the other extreme, the stories did not overtly reveal a 'persona'. In order to find out, therefore, what their narrative stance was, the student decomposed the stories into three elements: the narrative guide (the parts, usually outside the boxes, that tell how the story is developing), action and speech (the overt story), and the thought-balloons (which, strangely, had been called by McRobbie marks of a 'higher level' of discourse, an 'intellectual' pursuit[30]). This simple deconstruction turned up some suggestive items.

First, there was usually a tension in the stories between what the characters say and what they are thinking. They don't seem able to express their thoughts. This tension becomes a powerful factor in progressing the stories, but never resolves them. Secondly, when the crucial transition was to be made (usually to a 'clinch' between girl and boy), it almost always happened by accident or surprise. The narrative guide would intervene, saying things like 'Then, before we knew what was happening . . .', or 'Suddenly, without either of us meaning to . . . .' This device recurred endlessly. It was as though a special kind of cause had come into operation, as a necessary part of the formula of the stories. There *had* to be success in the relationship, so a kind of Fate stepped in. Our student dubbed the intervening force the God of Romance. She found that this was not a hidden god, though, but one whose interventions were plain to see.

The narrative guide was of a very particular kind. It varied (often within the same story) between being the voice of the main female character, and being a magazine-voice. Always chatty and informal, this voice presented the stories as if they had recently ended. Lessons had just been learnt, and were now being passed on – a point which confirms McRobbie's comment that the magazines have an older-sister feel, giving advice to the younger ones.

But what these discoveries suggested to us, and which bore on our original worries about McRobbie's global analysis, was that these magazines are far more particular than she realizes. The stories always ended, not with a commitment to an everlasting relationship which fulfilled the woman or realized her essence (or anything like that). They ended, rather, with what might be called the *achievement of a passage*. The goal which was achieved was the breakdown of a communication barrier between girl and boy. And only at this point could speech and thought come together without tension.

If this is right, it suggests that such fiction is addressing a narrow range of felt problems, of how to cope with the inherited girls' role of having to wait for sexual advances. But the stories address these needs ritualistically. The student who did the project described this as like a dance, whose steps can be formally analysed. Typically, boy and girl will meet by accident and be attracted. Misunderstanding will ensue, and the girl will retreat. The boy will wait. They will meet again by accident or design, and great tensions between thought and speech will occur. 'Then, as if by accident . . .' the barrier of misunderstanding will be breached, and they will move to each other.

There are, of course, all sorts of variation on this theme, and it would be a worthwhile exercise in itself to gather the range of such formulae. What is important is that the dance-like quality is not hidden from the reader, and that, also, the ritual feel sits uneasily with the very real problem pages where ritual answers are not offered and do not apply. And there, of course, the 'persona' was different and demarcated.

There was much more work than one student could do, just on these aspects of such magazines. The point we are making is that even a preliminary analysis, using quite simple methods, but ones which do not presume what they will find, undercuts the more global but amorphous claims of a semiological approach. It also offered exciting possibilities for a student to discover for herself the very specified nature of some of these magazines.

CONCLUSION

These three projects were typical of what we have managed so far, in respect of methods, and of new insights gained by students. But the range has gone much wider than these more obvious materials. Our students have also analysed TV quiz shows, Superhero comics, local radio phone-ins, *Questiontime,* and the Scarman Report, using equivalent methods. Not all, of course, have been wild successes, the reasons being a mixture of differences among students, and differences in our own capacity to stimulate and point possible directions.

One question we now often find ourselves asking is what kind of theory and assumption is our approach premised on. To be frank, we are not at all sure of the answer. To some extent, we should justify the approach by its results. This way of working with students offers them an openness, such that genuinely new discoveries are there to be made. And in the course of making discoveries, many cannot help making connections with their own beliefs and attitudes. This is obviously partly a function of the kinds of material, and of the way they choose their topic. If they were constrained into studying nineteenth-century advertisements, for example, they would be less likely to feel personally challenged by their findings than they can be from studying, say, the presentation of forms of family life in modern advertisements. But partly also, it is the ability of these kinds of method to enable students to burrow inside the materials they are studying, to get at their patterns and structures, which alters their perceptions. This is particularly so because, so often, what they are burrowing into is a sample of what passes as the 'taken-for-granted' and 'commonsense' at present.

Inasmuch as we can identify a structuring theory behind our development of these approaches (and we neither fully agree on this, nor are able to state it very clearly), the following seems to emerge. First, we believe that there is a kind of politics contained in approaches such as semiology which we do not accept. For example, there is more than an accidental connection between the analysis McRobbie offers of *Jackie* and the attempt to create the 'feminist alternative', *Shocking Pink*. The connection comes through semiology attributing enormous power, theoretically, to such magazines to 'construct subjectivities'. We were very struck by the development of this in the more recent *Feminism for Girls*,[31] in which it is suggested that feminism is like an alternative *germ*, which hopefully will be *caught* by more girls and will thus make them immune to traditional definitions of femininity. This is very much in tune with the approach we are criticizing, in (a) giving enormous power to images and conceptions to 'catch' people, and thus (b) minimizing any role for conscious evaluation and critical understanding of possibilities. (This connects, incidentally, with the much more general and very common view that McRobbie takes of the nature of 'consumerist capitalism' and its virtually limitless power to reproduce us ideologically in the right shape for its 'needs'.)

Second, and as a consequence of questioning this idea of 'construction of subjectivities' as perhaps philosophically meaningless, we would draw on those approaches which view the relationship between media and audiences as more like a *social* relationship, between preexistent social personalities. This means we would emphasize the conversation-like quality of the media, their form of address, the 'persona' with which they address us, and in particular the prior understanding needed for this 'conversation' to be possible at all. From this perspective, we cannot accept the 'behind-our-backs' view of the influence of ideology which is current. We prefer to see it rather as a struggle for forms of understanding in which the resources people can call on are crucial factors.[32]

An illustration will help explain the last point we would want to make about our theoretical premises. It is not uncommon for feminists to abstract a difference in presentation of gender across a wide range of materials, ranging through comics, advertisements, birthday cards, novels and news photographs. Because differences can be found, they are declared to be evidence for, and functions of, an underlying common ideology which is exerting itself through each example. This has the effect of flattening differences. So, a shortage of girl characters in the *Beano*[33] has a significance directly related to the separation of sex roles found in birthday cards.[34] They are both expressions of the same 'stereotype' of women, and are working hard to reproduce that stereotype. Our worry is not only that this makes such ideologies and stereotypes curiously Platonic, essences which hang in the air deter-mining particular instances. It is also that it negates the possibility of distinguishing celebratory, mythological, jokey and even subversive uses of sex distinctions.[35] Instead we believe that our approach en-courages students to look at particular objects for their internal pattern of relations and the specific ways these fit together. In this way, it is possible to see the nature of the unique object as a basis for then considering the historical placing of, and influences on, its nature. Theoretically, this means making a distinction between contingent relations and necessary structuring relations among aspects of objects. It also means that the determination of the particular character of the object has to precede the full consideration of its social and historical situation.[36]

We would not claim to be doing anything unique, and in fact a great deal of the best work currently available in cultural studies shows evidence of using similar approaches.[37] But this is not always the work which is given the greatest public attention, perhaps partly because – like our own work – it does not seem to profess a developed theoretical base. It would in fact be good if it were possible for other people who share our worries about the predominant semiological paradigm, and are working to develop approaches parallel with those we have attempted in our project work, to collaborate and work together to strengthen the theoretical underpinnings of such research.

NOTES AND REFERENCES

1. Judith Williamson, *Decoding Advertisements,* Marion Boyars 1978.
2. In *The Reader's Construction of the Narrative,* Routledge and Kegan Paul 1981, Horst Ruthrof analyses the various types of presentational process found in fictional works, by means of which a narrator/implied reader

relationship is constructed. He suggests that this can vary from the extremely authoritarian (Ruthrof cites the example of Genesis), where the implied reader relationship is one of childlike dependence on an acceptance of the fiction-making process, to the democratic/egalitarian in which the relationship between narrator and implied reader gets close to an equal partnership. It may be that a similar range of narrator/implied reader relations are on offer in advertisements, in which case the question of the construction of the subject becomes much more open and, therefore, problematic.

3. See Trevor Pateman's article, 'How is understanding an advertisement possible?', in *Language, Image, Media,* eds. H. Davis and P. Walton, Blackwell 1983.

4. We need to emphasize that this was only an initial method of prompting students to think about the communicative status of advertisements, taken as a whole. We are not of course suggesting that an adequate theory of advertising, as a distinct form of communication, can be developed solely on the basis of these kinds of discrimination.

5. In many ways this is a very problematic kind of distinction to make. It could easily lead to the argument that advertising and other forms of commercial information create 'artificial needs', which are then distinguished from 'real, human needs'. (See, for example, Denys Thompson's Introduction to *Discrimination and Popular Culture,* Penguin 1973, where just such a distinction is proposed.) We would oppose this kind of thinking since it implies that 'real needs' are somehow less socially constructed, a product of human biology or psychology, whereas we would argue that, in this sense, all human 'needs' are irrevocably social in their origin, and that the point of analysis must be the elaboration and critique of historically particular forms of social determination.

6. Guy Gauthier, *The Semiology of The Image,* trans. D. Matias, Educational Advisory Service, British Film Institute 1976.

7. Trevor Millum, *Images of Woman: Advertising in Women's Magazines,* Chatto 1975.

8. This sequencing or staging in the process of recognizing advertisements can be confirmed by anyone who has observed children's viewing of TV advertisements. Very often they 'play a game' with them, trying to identify the particular product being advertised from amongst a range that use similar filmic conventions, narrative structure, etc.; that, in fact, come close to being an identifiable genre.

9. Pateman, p. 188.

10. John Berger (*Ways of Seeing,* Penguin 1972) illustrates the way that some advertisements quite overtly mimic themes and subjects taken from classical paintings. Our point, however, goes beyond this fairly conscious copying and draws attention to the ways in which many advertisements highlight the construction of images in general by their use of unusual juxtapositions, highly stylized figures and careful colour composition.

In *Art in the Age of Mass Media,* Pluto 1983, John Walker also draws attention to the way in which advertisements aspire to the condition of fine art, as he puts it. Walker acknowledges that the best advertisements use 'increasingly self-reflexive and formal devices derived from avant-garde art', but argues that this leads to a 'disturbing discrepancy between their formal innovations and their trivial content, between the artistry of the means employed and the commercialism of the ends served'. Advertisements, says Walker, are 'conservative or reactionary in their values' no matter how entertaining they may be.

This kind of argument worries us for two reasons: firstly, it implies that 'values' can be assessed apart from the formal devices employed to express them, an argument which, if applied, say, to the 'television and violence' debate would be seen as precisely pre-empting that which requires investigation; and secondly, the radical disjunction between high and mass culture is unquestioningly reaffirmed. The social relationships within which *both* are produced and received is a matter for investigation, and little advance can be made if the relations between the arts and commercialism are assumed to be different from those existing between fine advertisements and commercial interests. We would argue that research into the 'politics of pleasure' and the critique of ideology cannot usefully be considered to be separate intellectual concerns.

11. Raymond Williams, 'Advertising: The Magic System' (1960), in *Problems in Materialism and Culture*, Verso 1980.
12. Marjorie Ferguson, *Forever Feminine*, Heinemann 1983.
13. See Millum.
14. Janice Winship, 'A woman's world: *Woman* – an ideology of femininity', in CCCS Women's Studies Group, *Women Take Issue*, Hutchinson 1978.
15. Ferguson, p. 34.
16. Among the main analyses of their influence have been Connie Alderson, *Magazines Teenagers Read*, Pergamon 1968; Angela McRobbie, '*Jackie:* an Ideology of Adolescent Femininity', CCCS Stencilled Occasional Paper No. 53, 1978; Sue Sharpe, *Just Like a Girl*, Penguin 1976; Myra Connell, *Reading Romance*, unpublished MA thesis, University of Birmingham, 1981; and most recently Jacqueline Sarsby, *Romantic Love and Society*, Penguin 1983. In among these have been a host of occasional articles, particularly in the magazines of the women's movement.
17. See, for example, Polly Toynbee's article in *The Guardian* (30 October 1978).
18. McRobbie, p. 3.
19. A related point has been made in a useful article by Steve Neale on the concept of 'stereotype', 'The Same Old Story: Stereotypes and Difference', *Screen Education*, Nos. 32/33 (1970–80), pp. 33–37.
20. McRobbie, p. 3.
21. McRobbie, p. 2.
22. McRobbie, p. 7.
23. See, for example, Wayne Booth, *The Rhetoric of Fiction*, University of Chicago Press, Chicago 1961; and Ruthrof.
24. McRobbie, p. 20.
25. McRobbie, p. 29.
26. This would anyway be a problem, since – in common with most other writers on popular culture – she does not give references to the editions of the magazine she used. This is surely poor practice, since it makes any form of re-analysis very difficult. We do not see why referencing in studies of popular culture should be any less exact than in academic arguments. In fact, given the fleeting nature of much of the material, it ought to be stricter.

27. If we were re-evaluating McRobbie's analysis, it would have been necessary to go back to her own examples, since the introduction of the photostrip story in the mid-1970s occasioned quite a change in the style and shape of the stories. We are not sure, though, that the nature and significance of the change would have shown up on her semiological approach.
28. This could even lead, on occasion, to issues being given over to the theme of breaking the format and being a rebel!
29. We borrow this term from an article which we find students feel to be very useful for initiating ideas on this issue: Donald Horton and Richard Wohl, 'Mass Communication and Parasocial Interaction', *Journal of Psychiatry*, XIX (1956), 215–29. Grant Noble makes interesting use of their ideas in his *Children in Front of the Small Screen*, Constable 1975.
30. McRobbie, p. 16.
31. See *Feminism for Girls*, eds. McRobbie and Trish MacCabe, Routledge and Kegan Paul 1981.
32. On this, see the reply article by Anne Beezer, 'Response to Alison Assiter', *Radical Philosophy*, No. 36 (1984), pp. 16–19. The article is a response to a debate on the meaning of 'sexist language'.
33. See Judith O'Connell, *Sexist Images in Children's Comics and Television Programmes*, BA dissertation, University of Sheffield, 1982. This was abstracted in *Sheffield Educational Research: Current Highlights*, No. 4 (1982).
34. We take this example from a talk given by representatives of the British Film Institute, in introducing a teachers' pack on the idea of stereotypes.
35. It can be argued, in fact, that this abstracting of characteristics can be just plain misleading. In the case of the *Beano*, we would want to argue thatwe should not be counting boys versus girls, but children versus adults, since the significant opposition is the power-relations between these. This is important, since O'Connell interprets the low level of readers of the *Beano* among girls as a consequence of the small number of girl characters with whom they can 'identify'. This misleads dangerously, since until recently there was in fact a virtual fifty/fifty split between boy and girl readers. The decline in female readership has to be read differently, we would argue, as a function of a reduced willingness of girls to see themselves through the *Beano's* mildly subversive child versus adult game. The reasons for this have little or nothing to do with the *Beano* itself.
36. An article in a recent edition of *Radical Philosophy* makes stimulating proposals for a theorization of this attempt. John Allen, 'In Search of a Method: Hegel, Marx and Realism', *Radical Philosophy*, No. 35 (1983), pp. 26–33, presents an account of a Marxist method of doing empirical research which makes just such distinctions between contingent and necessary relations, enabling subsequent investigation of the social and historical context.
37. We have been very struck by Andrew Bethell's *Eye Openers* series, for example, a quite brilliant series of analyses of photographs and their meanings.

Chapter 5

CRITIQUES OF CULTURE: A COURSE

JON COOK

A course in cultural studies, called Critiques of Culture, has been taught for the past eight years in the School of English and American Studies at the University of East Anglia. The initial form of the course reflected the intellectual interests of the four or five teachers who first debated its possibility. These can be given in a summary fashion through the names of writers and associated themes: Marcuse and the critique of domination; Freud's enquiry into the unconscious and its manifestations in language; Marx's concern with ideology; the linguistics of Edward Sapir and Benjamin Lee Whorf issuing, as it did, in questions about language, perception, and the relativity of cultures. These disparate intellectual forces were all at work on a tenuous but common basis in the study of literature – the 'first' subject of all the teachers concerned with the course. Because of this, and because we all worked in England, Leavis's cultural criticism and its subsequent transformation by Raymond Williams played a formative role with its stress upon the difficult relation between individual or collective creativity on the one hand and, on the other, culture as the medium which either enabled creativity or caused it to wither at the root.[1]

Such a summary brings out some of the elements in play during the discussions which preceded the teaching of the course. It emphasizes, too, the heterogeneous and eclectic character of the material we wanted to define as cultural studies. Alongside this heterogeneity, there was a bold attempt at synthesis: to analyse the surface forms of culture, in spoken utterance or literary text, as the often unconscious articulation of class conflict and domination. The problem, one that required a good deal of intellectual and administrative labour, was to get this ambitious project into a shape which could be taught to undergraduates. We felt, quite properly, that the success or failure of the project was as much to be decided in the response and participation of students. It was this fact perhaps which gave a partial intimation of the difference of cultural studies from existing academic disciplines. The unification and the definition of the subject was to be discovered in the manner of its teaching and this, in turn, would entail a protracted negotiation of authority between teachers and students about what was to count as culture and its study. At the outset, then, there was the sense of a possible modification of the established hierarchy of an academic discipline, in which the boundaries of a subject are decided by the research of experts, whose findings are then transmitted down-ward for information, debate and limited redefinition. This did not at all imply the abandonment of research as a constitutive activity of cultural studies; but it did indicate an additional location for it, the seminar group, and not least because the choices made there about working relations could themselves become potential evidence about the distribution of authority and initiative in contemporary culture. This, in its turn, connected to anxieties about the nature and possibility of practice within the culture at large: 'Interest in the active process of making is suppressed in favour of the more negotiable activity of responding to an object . . . I believe that the emphasis on practice is now crucial and that neglect of practice is a contributory factor to our cultural crisis.'[2] The difficult question and the working challenge was to create the conditions in which cultural studies might join an 'active process of making'.

I doubt that we got far with meeting this challenge in our first attempt at teaching the course. Our advertisement of the course to students was written in a ponderous, impersonal and intimidating language: 'The aim of the course is to introduce students to some major issues in the area of cultural studies. The main strategy for the course will be to locate moments in particular debates about culture, taking these as concrete instances to be studied in their historical and social particularity.' Such language evidences an anxiety it seeks to deny: the invocation of the jargon term, 'concrete instances', bespeaks a fear of the labyrinth of abstraction that cultural studies might become. The selection of debate as an organizational principle carried with it a connotation of openness, of issues as yet unresolved, but our manner of presenting these debates was as an alien intellectual theatre which the students could come to as an audience: 'Week Four. 1) Seminar on culture, alienation, and labour. The central issue here will be work: Marx, Freud, and Marcuse all advance different versions of the relation of work to culture, and before comparing them it is necessary to be clear about Marx's view of mental and material labour, which depend in turn on his analysis of alienation.'[3] One problem with this formulation, taken from an early course plan, is in the logic it implicitly proposes for cultural studies. The 'central issue' is caught up in an infinite regress which seeks to explain one concept by appeal to another. Such a procedure trades on what were then at least glamorous terms – 'mental and material labour', 'alienation' – and it proposes a model of cultural studies as a subversive dictionary which our students might learn to consult. The serious question was whether in undertaking such a procedure we were explaining the concepts in any relevant sense. What we needed was some reference to the forms of life, captured either in a moment of intuition or of historical reconstruction, which would connect concepts to behaviour and action in a way that would break out of the conceptual regress. The students were not slow to see this. Their early criticism of the course included a comment on the lack of historical context for the thinkers we addressed. We were clearly failing to deliver our promise of 'historical and social particularity'. A related criticism mentioned 'students' innocence', as though they lacked the experience to make the concepts meaningful, an experience which their teachers had, but were somehow withholding.

From the beginning then the course was caught up in the task of mediating the abstract with the particular, of making connections between objective and subjective knowledge. It is simple enough to see our early mistakes with the vantage of hindsight, and self-criticism is easy when it is criticism of a past self. We were conscious at an early stage of the difficulty of our material and of the importance of teaching method. Our first response to this was to intersperse the exposition of theoretical concepts with the practical criticism of literary texts. This had an ostensible function. The detailed analysis of extracts from literary works was a means of surfacing the culturally conditioned assumptions which were brought to bear in making sense of a piece of literature. The exercise could form an initial demonstration of the relations between literature and ideology. But there was an implicit function, too, that had to do with the coherence of the seminar group itself. If the exposition of theory had the effect of dividing silent students from articulate teachers, the recourse to practical criticism of a literary work could recombine the group as students brought their own interpretative abilities to bear. The danger of this was that the seminar course lost its distinctiveness: in practice if not in intention cultural studies became an odd way of studying literature. The point was made a number of times by students who pressed us to define the specific nature of cultural studies. The problem was that we had contributed to the division which led them to press the question in the first place. Our exposition of theory had been conducted in the terms of a traditional didactic mode. The authority of esoteric texts was transmitted by initiated teachers to uninitiated students. I suspect this made us appear to be harbouring a secret about the subject of cultural studies which we did not in fact possess. Moreover, our procedures risked a humiliating contradiction: our earnest offer to give access to the major concepts within an ambitious project of human liberation served to reinforce the very modes of domination it sought to criticize.

Various circumstances gave rise to this dilemma, each one indicative of the historical matrix which bound together the intellectual project and the institutional conditions of the course. Some features of the intellectual project have already been mentioned but these need to be supplemented by a more detailed definition. One important focus here was Perry Anderson's essay, 'Components of the National Culture'. Its value lay precisely in its structuralism, in its dialectical analysis of the intellectual disciplines that were variously included or excluded by the dominant cultural formation. Our own institutional context, closely connected to literary study, was itself in a problematic relation to Anderson's central thesis that English intellectual life was characterized by an 'absent centre', one that should be filled by Marxism and classical sociology as the constituents of a science of the whole social formation. Literary studies was, of course, a topic of Anderson's analysis: in the absence of the 'proper' centre of Marxism and a theoretically informed sociology, literary studies, particularly that form of it which had originated in Cambridge after the First World War, had become a surrogate totalizing discipline, addressing itself to questions about the quality of life across a whole society but in such a way that the development of radical critique was inhibited by the enigmatic appeal to literary works within a national tradition as the definition and embodiment of goodness. Thus the very centrality of literary study in English culture was, according to Anderson, a symptom of a wider poverty. Yet Anderson's own essay carried an historical echo of the self-same literary formation which he sought to criticize. There was a genealogical connection which Anderson's own attempt at parricide could not obscure. Certainly the writer who paralleled and preceded Anderson in the vigour of his denunciation of the dominant academic culture was Leavis, and Leavis himself was only one figure in the larger resonant episode, the formation of Cambridge English.[4] For those of us trained within literary studies Anderson's essay served to reactivate an institutional memory, one which had been obscured by subsequent developments, but could still be recaptured, partially in the work of Leavis, but also in the writings of I. A. Richards and William Empson where the study of literature had been grounded in questions of communication, class and culture. Their work was a partial prefiguration of Anderson's in its concern with an enfeebled and intellectually stunted dominant culture. There were, of course, evident differences between this earlier intervention and Anderson's critique. Cambridge English had attempted a transformation of the classical study of language, literature and thought in the crisis of cultural definition that followed the First World War. It was an odd and unstable alliance of various elements: Arnold's cultural criticism, behavioural psychology, utilitarianism, and Freud. Anderson's argument emerged from the social sciences and proposed a triple injection of Marx, Weber, and Durkheim as the necessary theoretical accompaniment to a revolutionary student movement. But the reminder of difference recalled similarity: the claim, in both cases, to the founding of a rigorous mode of enquiry within the humanis-

disciplines which would then direct the attention of an English intellectual élite toward an analysis of the cultural crisis which surrounded their work.

'Components of the National Culture' renewed a question about the direction of English intellectual life which had been posed earlier within the context of literary studies, and at a founding moment in the history of the discipline. However, reading Anderson's essay in relation to this earlier context had the effect of unsettling both his diagnosis and his prescription. 'Components' projected the national culture as a stifling and comatose weight upon radical enquiry. Redemption lay in filling the 'absent centre', but that could only be achieved by importing strength from abroad in the form of European Marxism and social theory. Working from an institutional base within literature posed the problem in a different form. It was not so much a matter of filling the absent centre as of reactivating dormant or suppressed energies. There was, moreover, a line of radical enquiry in the work of Williams and Hoggart which was connected to the formation of Cambridge English.[5] Their work in the 1950s and early 1960s kept open the question of the character of a socialist culture, although in a way that bore a highly defensive or critical relation to Marxist concepts. Our work was to renew the dialogue between literary studies, on the one hand, and Marxism and psychoanalysis on the other, but not in a way that simply assumed that literary criticism was an otiose or surrogate discipline. The mix was volatile and the outcome of putting the different discourses together was unpredictable. But at least the history of literary studies supplied a precedent for an educational experiment of this kind, a point insufficiently recognized in Anderson's account.

From the outset, then, the agenda of the Critiques of Culture course was set in terms of an unresolved question about the relation between English and European resources. This question was made explicit in the course in our attempt to assess the debate between E. P. Thompson, Anderson, and Tom Nairn on the state of the national culture.[6] Presenting this debate to the students was complicated by the difficulties of position and identity in teaching the material. Nairn's essay, in particular, analysed the literary culture of modern England as the ideological integument of a conservative nation, and, by implication, called into question our own training within that culture. It became impossible to accept as an axiom that the English literary tradition was there to be read and reread as a source of unqualified semantic and moral richness. Our teaching of literature passed under the sign of Walter Benjamin's aphorism: 'There is no document of civilization which is not at the same time a document of barbarism'.[7] It became a part of what is by now a considerable body of work concerned with the research of literature's limits and weaknesses rather than with the celebration of its strengths. But, alongside the conscious position, the statement of the limitations of this or that critical procedure, the discovery that George Eliot's moral insight was implicated in her role as bourgeois ideologue, there was a less conscious, more intractable, and ambivalent process: the effort to move beyond our formative education in reading, discussing and writing about literature, one which had been centred on the close reading of texts. Hence another meaning can be discerned in the alternation between the exposition of concepts and the close reading of texts which characterized our early teaching of the course. In addition to its pragmatic function in securing fragile group coherence, there was a nostalgic element in close reading: the moment when we returned to the security of our place as trained readers of literature after the exposed and difficult task of expounding theory.

Our selection of course materials reflected the conscious and unconscious work required to redefine ourselves as teachers of cultural studies. Baldly put, this meant a double relation with the subject of literature: on the one hand, a departure from the celebration of a literary tradition as an enduring defensive strength within the national culture; on the other, an effort to recover and develop a project within literary studies which had been dispersed. But this is just one respect in which our development of cultural studies was overdetermined, an effect of the simultaneous operation of manifold causes. Again the debate between Anderson, Nairn, and Thompson can serve as an example. In the relevant essays these three writers address themselves explicitly to a crisis in the national culture. In taking their explicit disagreement about the character of this crisis as one topic for discussion in the course, other meanings became impacted in the material. To expound the argument was to create the possibility of its displacement. 'Origins of the Present Crisis', 'The Peculiarities of the English', 'The English Literary Intelligentsia', essays which were symptomatic readings of the culture, became themselves symptoms of other conflicts, whether over Britain's entry into the EEC, the relation between national and racial identity, or problems of productivity. Our discussions of Anderson, Nairn, and Thompson became the marginal reflection of a larger struggle which manifested itself now in a parliamentary debate about immigration law, now in racist brutality, and now in strike to defend jobs. In one sense this indicates little more than the fact that a particular argument over the national culture necessarily took its place within a much larger field of discourse and action. In another, it was the particular excitement of cultural studies that it was open to the historically charged nature of its materials, and at a point where history did not consist in the retelling of a story about a threatened past but in a demand and pressure upon the activity of discussion itself.

If this openness to historical demand served as an ideal project for the seminar, which would consist precisely in the displacement of its materials into the immediacy of struggle, it also created, both among teachers and students, an anxiety about the boundaries of the subject. The historically loaded character of the materials for study, and their implication in contemporary conflict produced a sense that whatever cultural studies was, it always exceeded any particular example of its operation. This could produce paranoia and despondency or a nervous pursuit of new theory. Cultural studies was really something that went on elsewhere, in Birmingham, perhaps, where somehow all these things had been got right. In practice, such responses were little more than an evasion of the dynamism and novelty of the subject.

The conservatism of our initial teaching practice can now be seen in a clearer light. From literary studies we inherited an established teaching routine, close reading or practical criticism, which could produce co-operative work or an isolating competition of individual sensibilities. Anderson's 'Components of the National Culture' mediated in an urgent and polemical form the requirement of theory but left entirely unresolved how theory was to be taught. In practice such irresolution could and did lead to a duplication of an authoritarian teaching mode: the works of Freud and Marx replaced those of Shakespeare and Joyce as esoteric texts whose meanings were to be transmitted to a passive student audience by initiated teachers. Then there was the unconscious development of the course itself and the multivalent meanings of the materials of cultural studies, both of which produced anxieties about the limits of the subject and the place of students and teachers within it. One way of defending against the anxiety of formlessness in the subject was to rely on established teaching procedures, whatever our innovative intentions.

Within the pattern of determinations which shaped the course, one further element needs to be noted: the immediate institutional context. The Critiques of Culture course emerged from a 'new' university and was lodged in a faculty whose founding principle had been the interdisciplinary study of history and literature. This principle had initially been interpreted as a matter of training students in the separate disciplines and then permitting them in their final year of study one term in which the two subjects could be studied in combination. In the early 1970s this practice was debated within the faculty and an alternative model proposed whereby the two subjects could be studied in a more continuous combination. The hope was to create a new third subject out of the synthesis of history and literature in a way that would establish an area in the School which could respond to the major work of writers such as Williams, Lucien Goldmann, Lukács and Thompson. Within this particular project. The Critiques of Culture course was to be the theoretical and critical adjunct to more historically specific courses.

These proposals for a different relation between the established disciplines within the School brought with it a sense of disturbance in the established order of things. Something more was happening than just the usual round of academic politics. A minor skirmish had been joined in the more general struggle for symbolic power, given the definition of that latter term by the social theorist, Pierre Bourdieu:

> Symbolic power – the power to constitute the given by stating it, to show forth and gain credence, to confirm or transform the world view and, through it, action on the world, and hence the world itself, the quasi-magical power which makes it possible to obtain the equivalent of what is obtained by (physical or economic) force, thanks to its specific mobilisation effect – is only exerted insofar as it is *recognised* (i.e., insofar as its arbitrariness is misrecognised).[9]

The debate was, centrally, over recognition. What had been understood as a necessary and sufficient practice of interdisciplinary study was dislodged, made arbitrary, by an alternative proposal which was implicitly a bid for the 'power to constitute the given by stating it'. The outcome of the debate was a compromise whose terms were permitted by the decision to increase the size of the School of English and American Studies as part of a general policy of university expansion. The central fiefdoms of literature and history remained intact while the proposal for the more integrated form of interdisciplinary study found its institutional expression in the creation of a new degree programme, English studies, whose students were to be recruited from the increased number entering the School.

The administrative and bureaucratic dimension of this compromise needs to be kept in view. It was the condition for a temporary and partial resolution to an argument about the nature and organization of the humanist disciplines. A potential conflict was managed by an increase in financial resources and student numbers and, as such, cultural studies became an episode in the evolution of a particular institution. But its integration into the intellectual work of the School left the central disciplines of literature and history largely unaffected. The Critiques of Culture course was so placed as to be available as an optional subject to the small numbers of students taking the new interdisciplinary English studies programme. Other students might take the course but not as a central component of their study and without the prospect of taking an examination connected to the course. Despite our conviction that the work we proposed was of central importance, our location was on the margins of the School.

But, whatever its marginal status, cultural studies was recognized as a subject which could be taught and examined. This recognition was not, however, equivalent to a passive adoption. In order to exist as an accredited subject, cultural studies had to be defined according to a grid of academic regulations. To teach it at all meant to teach it according to certain norms: it was to be taught in the form of a term-long seminar course; students taking the course should, as a result, be prepared for a three-hour examination paper in their final year of study; given the priority of literature and history, the course could command only a small teaching resource. Nor were these constraints simply external to the work of teaching the course. They informed our activity by apportioning our time. They enforced a pedagogic goal in so far as one of our tasks was to prepare students for an examination. They supplied a visibility to the course: it was advertised as one among a range of courses on offer to students in a given term and it had to be advertised according to the same rules as other courses. Cultural studies had to be fitted out administratively and this was one indication of the fact that it had to take its place within an established distribution of knowledge and power. This pervasive and seemingly anonymous administrative definition no doubt produced an unreflecting conformity. Institutional conventions made decisions for us in areas where it seemed there was no decision to be made. Thus our early definitions of cultural studies took a group of authoritative texts as their starting point and their point of return. We used these texts to establish the concepts of the subject – class, language, the different meanings of culture – and to define the significant debates. The procedure was justified by inertia because it repeated what went on in the study of literature and history – the same reading and adjudication of authoritative texts. What was study if not just that activity? What was cultural studies if not an activity of that kind?

It is difficult to describe a model for the subsequent development of the course. This is not surprising given the complexity of determinations – institutional, political and intellectual – which marked its beginning. Our first efforts at teaching cultural studies can be seen as a script that had to omit a great deal in order to get written at all. Its development can then be understood as an effort to fill in the blank spaces, to make good what was left out at the beginning. If, at the outset, cultural studies included the activities of close reading and theoretical exposition, it became clear that working out the distinctiveness of the subject depended upon their transformation. In the former case this meant changing what was read and how it was read; in the latter, it meant separating out from the intimidating character of theoretical systems those analytic methods which would prove most useful to the students. The utilitarian character of the proof meant that the issue could not be decided *a priori*. Useful methods were those that furthered the work of the seminar group and it was, therefore, in the activity of the group that the matter was decided.

An important change in what we read and how we read it occurred after four years of teaching the course. We decided to take a study of advertisement as our starting point. There were various reasons for this. One was, certainly, to engage in a direct analysis of a powerful medium in contemporary culture. Secondly we felt sufficiently confident to declare the distance of cultural studies from one influential conception which had found in advertisements not a starting point for the study of culture but a sign of its terminal degradation. The intention was not simply to dismiss that conception but to find a method of analysis such that critique would not founder in denunciation, whether from a left-wing or a right-wing position. This meant working with a model of economic base and cultural superstructure in the sense that what enabled the activity of advertisement was the peculiar freneticism of the late-capitalist world and the effects this had upon the making of values. But it also meant the development of a mode of reading which would account for the ubiquity and the fascination of advertisements for the ways in which they offered verbal and visual pleasure for either a distracted or an attentive gaze.

This is not the place for a detailed resumé of our work on particular advertisements. We drew on various models for analysis in the works of John Berger, Judith Williamson, and Barthes.[9] In turn, these last two writers worked from a basis in semiological theory and we tried to incorporate this into the range of cultural theories taught on the course. But the analysis of advertisements was not simply a route to theory. In the history of the course it marked a shift in the organization of authority which was evidenced in a variety of ways. Our starting point was no longer in the theory of culture or in debates about definition. Advertisements emanated from a contemporary phase of capitalist culture but they were obviously not analyses of it. Whereas in the early phase of the course our sense of culture had been derived from the study of various kinds of theoretical reflection, all more or less judicious and restrained, advertisements confronted us with a different language, garish and enigmatic, mixing together verbal and visual codes. The claim for permanence which resides, however forlornly, within the book was replaced by a form evanescent by design to be consumed for pleasure rather than studied for knowledge. Whatever the power of advertisement it did not reside in an academic institution centred on writings whose authority was enhanced by the accretion of scholarly interpretation and debate. The character of advertisements, at once extra-mural and immersed in contemporary events, meant that they were more evenly shared between staff and students as a cultural experience.

Starting with quotidian and non-academic material allowed us to reorganize the introductory work for the course. Instead of asking students to write brief essays defining key terms and to read the work of selected cultural theorists, they compiled a dossier of advertisements and analysed them, drawing on the books by Barthes, Berger and Williamson as they saw fit. This work, done individually during the vacation, became the basis for collaborative presentations on advertisement during the opening sessions of the course. Given that the meaning of an action is in part determined by its place within a structure, the students took on more of the work of initiating the course and, by virtue of that fact, accrued a little more power and confidence in their interpretative abilities. Nor was their initiative that of a solitary voice, giving a discussion paper to a silent group of fellow students and staff. The students worked as teams who came prepared to share the work of beginning together. Nervousness and confidence alike could be communicated. The result was a perceptible shift in the atmosphere of the early meeetings of the course: more discussion, more participants in the discussion, and the release of an excitement about beginning something new and different.

We had effectively reversed our conception of how to begin a course in cultural studies. Instead of trying to make strange theory familiar, we now attempted to make the familiarity of advertisements strange through their analysis as a sign system. As a result two interrelated facts became evident. One was the assumption of semiology as a method of cultural analysis. Semiology provided the concepts necessary to an analysis of the ubiquity and the importance of advertisements. Moreover, when semiology became 'semioclasm', when understanding the mechanisms of signification joined a critical enquiry into the historical context of the sign system, we discovered the beginnings of an adequate mediation between an analysis of particular phenomena and general questions of class dominance and control. There was a juncture between the knowledge of a practice, advertisement, the development of a method, semiological analysis, and the critical recognition of an historical order, consumer capitalism. But the juncture was also a knot and here the second fact emerged, one that had already been anticipated by Barthes in the concluding essay of *Mythologies*: '. . . myth essentially aims at causing an immediate impression – it does not matter if one is later allowed to see through the myth, its action is assumed to be stronger than the rational explanations which may later belie it.'[1] Barthes's statement presumes a 'poison dart' theory of culture: withdrawing the dart is no cure because the poison is already in the system. Rational analysis affords a knowledge of how cultural practices organize attention and perception, and yet is unable to develop a moment when critical reason might open the route to freedom. It may be, as Jean Baudrillard has suggested, that the peculiar character of contemporary culture is to replace that rational pursuit of freedom by a logic of spectacle and fascination which denies political goals.[77] In the seminar meetings this was experienced as an alternation between excitement as we discovered how the language of advertisements worked and a baffled anger as we recognized the power of such a language to infiltrate and structure consciousness.

From one perspective, our experience reflected a classical problem in the relations between knowledge, agency, and selfhood. Ernest Gellner provides a useful summary:

> It is perhaps regrettably inherent in the advancement of knowledge that the more we understand and control, the more we see how we ourselves can be

understood and controlled. . . . It was irritating enough for the poet when the scientists explained the sunset. It is considerably more upsetting for all of us when they begin to explain us. There is a kind of duality between the man who believes or knows, chooses and values, and the mere phenomenon who is explained. In modern thought, there is a kind of pursuit of the former by the latter. Once, we were all self, not nature – indeed nature herself was self-like. Now it is the self proper that shrinks and disappears. [7]/

But Gellner's formulation keeps the startling nature of the pheno-menon he describes at a safe distance. In our seminar meetings the problem was, on occasion, felt more intensely. It was as though in the pursuit of the knowing subject by the instruments of knowledge, the latter had indeed overtaken the former. The self might shrink and disappear, but only to reappear on the other side of the looking glass. We discovered the vertiginous possibility that the self was an effect of the phenomena that it sought to describe, that what we assumed unquestioningly, the privilege of subjectivity, was the product of ex-ternal forces: our inner lives were created and displayed on advertising billboards.

More than the hangover of enlightenment was at issue. If one aspect of the problem was the ironic reversal of the intellectual project which linked knowledge of the world to the realization, not the disappear-ance, of the self, another had to do with the historical character of advertisements themselves, the fact that they were drawn from the contemporary culture of capitalism, and bore the imprint of a subtle, tolerant domination. Jürgen Habermas has given some account of this phenomenon:

> Theoretical attention is directed not so much to the conflict-engendering mechanisms of the economic system as to the defensive mechanisms following in the wake of crisis, to the ways the state deals with conflicts, and to cultural integration. In consequence of this displacement of conflicts, warded off at the institutional level, to the periphery, to the geographical, social and psychological margins, the groups in which conflict potentials accumulate need not be identical with the bearers of politically enlightened and organised action. [7][9]

Habermas's statement refers to a set of problems parallel to those experienced and debated in our investigation of contemporary culture. Advertisements were themselves an example of 'cultural integration' and the 'displacement of conflict'. Their effect upon subjectivity has already been described. But, beyond that, there was a possible identity of function between the material studied on the course and the course itself. Critiques of Culture, as one aspect of the emergence of cultural studies, was itself a phenomenon of contemporary capitalism and might therefore bear the imprint of its integrative power. Might not cultural studies itself be a mode of displacing conflict, a convenient slot for puppet radicals to play out their fantasies of dissent and social critique while the larger power held sway unhindered? Indeed, the very indeterminacy of the subject might prove a crucial part of its ideological effect, a licence permitting us to attend to these margins where, in Habermas's fastidious phrase, 'conflict potentials accumulate', only then to rework these into the conformist phrases of academic language.

These gloomy possibilities indicated two problems: that of a method which seemed to deliver up a determined world with ever diminishing scope for human action and that of a subject, contemporary culture, whose conforming power overrode the effort of analysis. A familiar kind of Marxist analysis would have it that these problems were little more than the symptoms of privilege. The course was after all housed in a privileged institution and its existence had been secured as a result of what must now seem a relatively generous phase of educational provision. Removed from any experience of significant struggle, we rehearsed our ideological collusion by describing a social world impervious to radical change. The subjective aspect of this collusion was defined by ambivalence: statements of radical intent were undermined by a secret and impermissible wish that forged an unchangeable world as a result of our desire not to change it.

The image of the course as an instrument of pacification and conformity was too strongly felt to deny. But the image itself needs to be analysed and connected to other, alternative images. It evidences a structure which seems familiar to groups on the Left, one that combines megalomania, paranoia and self-hatred, often with bewildering variety and speed. Megalomania is the effect of an assumption about theory, that it delivers the theoretician from the realm of 'false' or 'complicit' consciousness and permits him to rise above the world of which he is a part. This tendency is compounded by the belief that complex and withering analyses of the bourgeois world are an equivalent for the political action needed to change it. Paranoia is, then, the reverse effect of theory: social life as represented by theory appears as a system so effective that it can absorb any intention to change it. Existence becomes a conspiratorial power set over against the individual or collective will. Self-hatred is a consequence of both megalomania and paranoia, and marks the point at which the thwarted expectation of power over the world is explained as a deficiency of political will or as the product of ideological complicity.

Work done in the course, however, was not simply confined by this structure. In the seminar group and in the increasing participation of the students in it there was a model, however precarious, of co-operative activity whose direction could not be read of in advance as little more than a repetition of the dominant order. Moreover, discovering the limits of theory as well as its potentiality, and, more particularly, discovering the absence of any substantial connection between contemporary theory and a practice other than the replication of intellectual work, was itself a complex education. In part, this meant sloughing off the expectation that cultural studies would provide what Habermas has called 'revolutionary self-confidence and theoretical self-certainty'.[14] It meant, too, the difficult recognition that our knowledge of culture was to be derived as much from the resources of the seminar group as from reference to external authorities. And then, subtending both these recognitions, was a third: the knowledge that in the elaborate order of theory there was a promise of paternal power, manifested alike in the craving for order and certainty, in the assumption of an objective knowledge set over against the vagaries of an ideologically bounded subjectivity, and in the disavowal of responsibility for a world of which the theorist was nonetheless a part.

What I am trying to describe is not a position for cultural studies that is secured beyond theory. Each time we teach the course the process of learning the potentialities and the limits of theory has to be undertaken. Nor is it the case that this process is simply the result of a dynamic internal to the course. It evidenced the relation of our work to developments outside it, developments that were not exclusively academic. Three of these in particular have had important effects: the 'poverty of theory' debate, feminism, and the repeated defeats of the political Left since 1979. I have already commented in some detail upon the first of these, but one more point needs to be made.[15] However much events outside the course and our own work within it revealed the limits of theory, this did not result in a simple reaffirmation of the value of individual experience or in a sense that culture was to be understood as the aggregate of such experiences. A commitment to methodological individualism seemed untenable in relation to the anonymous or collective phenomena we sought to understand. It became evident that the meaning of an advertisement could not be grasped in the description of a sequence of individual actions and intentions, if only because the very structures of address in advertisements called into question the capacity of individual consciousness to determine meaning. Our task was to overcome a sterile siege of contraries, whether it appeared in the opposition between theory and experience or in the attribution of methodological priority to individual actions over collective forms of agency. One model for a work which overcame these oppositions was Barthes's *Mythologies*, which moves from individual acts of response and description towards a theoretical refinement of their meaning.

But the model of Barthes's work did not have an unlimited application. *Mythologies* offered a mediation between experience, theory and the disclosure of knowledge *vis-à-vis* the language of objects and images in contemporary culture. It reminded us that no detail was without cultural significance. But the relation between the three terms of experience, theory and knowledge was not a constant across the whole range of cultural activity and was therefore not subject to a single working method. The course became the proving ground for this insight, not least in the effects of feminism within it. Stuart Hall, in his account of work at the Birmingham Centre, has argued that feminism was not another cultural theory to be added to the existing range but a whole restructuring of the field of study and the same holds true for the development of our own course.[16] How this occurred is difficult to describe. Feminism entered the course not as a theory like semiology nor as a cultural practice like advertisement, but with all the effects, either diffuse or focussed in anger, of a major political movement. This meant a reworking of the terms of experience and of knowledge. Feminism created a language which redescribed culture and, in so doing, produced the possibility of a new experience of culture. A theoretical discourse was no longer a prerequisite for a knowledge of the power that worked its way through the pleasures of a society given over to commodity consumption. The truth of feminism was disclosed in a language which could move close to the grain and texture of everyday experience. It was there, with embarrassing immediacy, in the composition of the course itself: three teachers, all men, and, each year, a group of students, the majority of whom were women. A fact which had previously passed unmentioned now became significant as, amongst other things, one more item in the oppression of women. Feminism repeated a pattern of earlier work: the engagement with theory and politics had the effect of producing knowledge about culture as a subject to be studied but this had its reflexive moment. What was studied and how it was studied shifted the pattern of working relations in the seminar group itself.

Feminism produced other effects and other formations in the work of the seminar. As the relation between theory and practice in Marxism waned, feminism renewed the militancy of cultural critique upon a different conceptual terrain. But the innovatory power of feminism did not rest on its explicit political basis alone. It spoke from various places: in the semiological analysis of advertisements as a new kind of semioclasm which sought to break the relation between signifier and signified in the cultural representation of women; in the context of psychoanalytic accounts of culture through our enquiry into the sources of gendered subjectivity.[17] Here our thinking revisited the problems of determinism, this time in a reading of Jacques Lacan which seemed to fix the division of gender in the forms of language itself. Again we were confronted with the pursuit of a seemingly unobtainable position: how could new accounts of gender identity and relation be formed in a language whose structure was founded on patriarchy. One answer was to hand in the advocacy of a revolution in language found in the work of Julia Kristeva and other French feminists.[18] But I want to stay for the moment not with a possible answer but with the dilemma itself, because it reveals a characteristic fix in the discourses that enter into cultural studies, one that has been already indicated in the earlier discussion of determinism. It was as though work in cultural studies was subject to the law of Jekyll and Hyde: each analysis of culture which discerned a pattern of domination from a revolutionary perspective was confronted by another which argued the impossibility of revolutionary change. Our experience of feminism marked this dilemma with particular intensity, and not simply because of the evident depression that followed from our discussion of Lacanian thought. Something more was at stake than an acknowledgement of the truth of determinism. It was as though we had pressed our thinking far enough to reach a point where the available concepts were insufficient to the nature of the problem, that we had come to a place where discourses faded and died and where there was no available theory to point the way forward. One hypothesis might be that we had reached a deconstructive turn, a point where ostensibly opposed concepts, freedom and determinism, and their political correlatives, militancy and resignation, were shown to be mutually complicit partners in the episteme of cultural studies. A more forceful and historically rooted account of the genesis of such problems comes from Marx, in his description of the rhythms of bourgeois revolutions:

> Bourgeois revolutions, like those of the eighteenth century, storm swiftly from success to success, their dramatic effects outdo each other, men and things seem set in sparkling brilliants, ecstacy is the everyday spirit, but they are short lived, soon they have attained their zenith, and a long crapulent depression seizes society before it learns soberly to assimilate the results of the storm-and-stress period.[19]

Marx locates the manic-depressive cycle in the historical character of bourgeois society. The trumpeting of innovation is followed by the depressed assimilation of its results. A similar pattern could be detected in the rhythm of our learning and development in cultural studies. The problem then became, and still is, to discover a different periodicity, the equivalent in intellectual work of the form of the proletarian revolution which Marx opposes to the rhythms of bourgeois life: 'On the other hand, proletarian revolutions . . . criticise themselves constantly, interrupt themselves continually in their own course, come back to the apparently accomplished in order to begin it afresh, deride with unmerciful thoroughness, the inadequacies, weaknesses and paltriness of their first attempts . . . until a situation has been created which makes all turning back impossible.'[20] Such a description is as much at odds with the current stereotypes of 'revolutionary self-confidence and theoretical self-certainty' as it is with the advocacy of utopian imagination. Alongside the aggressive and self-hating fantasy which informs this and other passages from *The Eighteenth Brumaire of Louis Bonaparte* (1852), Marx gives us a rare account of what the lived connection between theory and practice might be, a process characterized by co-operation, self-criticism, interruption, recursiveness, a sense of failure. This reflexive mode has a subjective aspect: the willingness to continue work in the absence of the triumphalist fantasies that Marx sees as a characteristic of bourgeois existence. Most recently, the intellectual and political development of groups in the Critiques of Culture course has hinged on a willingness to go beyond the oscillations of militancy and resignation to the more substantial definitions of task indicated by Marx.

But the survival and consolidation of the course has depended on more than the negotiation of a complex intellectual and emotional dynamic. Since the course started the institutional surround has altered in ways that have consolidated its strength. Within the School of English and American Studies these changes have included the development of a linguistics focussed upon the operations of power within language and the growth of film studies.[21] More generally, there was a greater willingness to develop a central subject, literature, in its relation to other cultural media. It is tempting, then, to see the early history of the course in terms of a metaphor of movement from periphery to centre. This would be at once to overestimate its success and misperceive its direction. Rather the kind of work done in the course has been relayed and developed elsewhere in ways that make cultural studies a less obviously eccentric activity within the School. This in its turn has reopened an argument about the organization of the humanist disciplines that is as much characterized by refusal and denial as by dialogue, but one that will nonetheless have an important effect upon the future shape of the institution, if the institution is to have a future.

The institutional consolidation of cultural studies permitted another change: in the last two years we have extended the teaching of the Critiques of Culture course across two terms. In the second term work is focussed upon the study of contemporary British culture and this follows a first term concerned with introducing students to a range of methods for the analysis of culture. The simple fact of having more time has created the basis for new kinds of work, notably the organization of student research projects. Within a broad constraint that these projects should be on some aspect of contemporary culture, the students have decided what that particular aspect should be. They have so far chosen various topics: youth sub-cultures, images of gender, the local Press, a history of women's institutions in post-war Britain, a study of television. Through this variety a definition of cultural studies has emerged from the students' work. This can be crudely stated as a concern with the nature of popular culture, but this concern takes on cogency only if the popular itself is extensively redescribed. In effect, the students' work in cultural studies transformed the relation between élite and popular formations disclosed in one of its originating subjects, literary criticism. In the latter two strategies for defining popular culture emerge: one in denunciation and nostalgia, in the polemical division between mass civilization and minority culture and the nostalgia for an organic culture; the other in the more subtle and fascinating manoeuvres of pastoral where the literary work resolves class contradiction and conflict in the imaginary realm of art.[22] By contrast, the students' work offered a different account: popular practice was conceived in its relation to hegemony and thereby implicated in a negotiation or an acquiescence, a subversion or a redefinition of the terms of power.[23] But this mode of attention to the popular dissolved the boundaries set around it by either denunciation or pastoral. In the clear direction they gave to their work, the students effected both a disjunction and a redefinition of the relations implicit in the study of culture. What was being contested was the relation between a social élite, the minority of students in higher education, and an élitist consciousness which defined its speciality by contrast to popular culture. In studying popular culture the students were studying their culture and in doing that they were attempting to construct a common culture.

Writing in the past tense, however indefinite, can make this seem like an achievement. In reality it is more like a work undertaken than a secure ground: self-criticism, interruption, hesitation and guilt are as much a characteristic of the work as a sense of progress. What we are reaching for is a mode of work which will acknowledge a complex situation that can be simply stated: cultural studies is a reflection of the fact that the culture we study is our own and, because of that, we are responsible for making it as well as analysing it. To create the conditions for that reflection in an institution historically devoted to its denial has been the emergent task of our work in cultural studies. At least we have gone some way along the road.

NOTES AND REFERENCES

1. The basic theoretical texts at this early stage of the course were Freud, *Civilisation and its Discontents*; Marcuse, *Eros and Civilisation*, Beacon Press, Boston, Mass. 1964, and *One Dimensional Man*; Marx and Engels, *The German Ideology*, ed. C. J. Arthur, Lawrence and Wishart 1970; Benjamin Lee Whorf, *Language, Thought and Reality*, MIT Press, Cambridge, Mass. 1964; Williams, *The Long Revolution*, Penguin 1965.
2. Williams, 'Literature in Society', in *Contemporary Approaches to English Studies,* ed. H. Schiff, Heinemann 1977, p. 102.
3. This quotation and the preceding one come from documents written by the staff to introduce students to the Critiques of Culture course.
4. For a detailed account of the formation of Cambridge English see Francis Mulhern, *The Moment of Scrutiny,* New Left Books 1979.
5. Among the relevant work here is Hoggart, *The Uses of Literacy*, Chatto 1957, and Williams, *Culture and Society*.
6. The three texts we drew on were Anderson, 'The Origins of the Present

Crisis', *New Left Review*, No. 23 (1964), pp. 26–53; Tom Nairn, 'The English Literary Intelligentsia', *Bananas*, No. 3 (1976), pp. 17–22; Thompson, 'The Peculiarities of the English'.

7. Walter Benjamin, 'Theses on the Philosophy of History', in *Illuminations*, ed. Hannah Arendt, Fontana 1973, p. 258.

8. Pierre Bourdieu, 'Symbolic Power', in *Two Bourdieu Texts*, trans. R. Nice, CCCS Stencilled Occasional Paper No. 46, p. 6.

9. The relevant texts are Barthes, *Mythologies*, trans. A. Lavers, Cape 1973; Berger, *Ways of Seeing*; Williamson, *Decoding Advertisements*.

10. Barthes, p. 130.

11. A relevant text is Baudrillard, *In the Shadow of the Silent Majorities . . . Or the End of the Social*, trans. P. Foss, P. Patton and J. Johnston, Semiotext(e), New York 1983.

12. Ernest Gellner, *Thought and Change*, Weidenfeld 1964, pp. 213–14.

13. Jürgen Habermas, 'A Reply to my Critics', in *Habermas: Critical Debates*, eds J. B. Thompson and D. Held, Macmillan 1982, p. 222.

14. Habermas, p. 222.

15. For more on the 'poverty of theory' debate see the essays grouped under 'Culturalism: Debates Around The Poverty of Theory', in *People's History and Socialist Theory*, ed. R. Samuel, Routledge and Kegan Paul 1981, pp. 375–409.

16. See Hall, 'Cultural Studies and the Centre: some problematics and problems', in *Culture, Media, Language*, eds Stuart Hall, Dorothy Hobson, Andrew Lowe, Paul Willis, Hutchinson 1980, pp. 15–48.

17. See here Williamson, pp. 60–7, and for some of the theoretical background Jacques Lacan, 'The Mirror Phase', trans. J. Roussel, *New Left Review*, No. 51 (1968), pp. 71–7.

18. See Julia Kristeva, *Desire in Language*, ed. L. S. Roudiez, Blackwell 1980; and *New French Feminisms*, eds. E. Marks and I. de Courtivron, Harvester 1981.

19. Marx, 'The Eighteenth Brumaire of Louis Bonaparte', in Marx and Engels, *Collected Works*, Lawrence and Wishart, 1975– , Vol. XI, p. 106.

20. Marx, pp. 106–7.

21. For an indication of some of the relevant work see Roger Fowler, Bob Hodge, Gunther Kress, Tony Trew, *Language and Control*, Routledge and Kegan Paul 1979.

22. For an example of denunciation and nostalgia see Leavis, 'Mass Civilization and Minority Culture', in *Education and the University*, Chatto 1948, pp. 141–71; and for pastoral see William Empson, *Some Versions of Pastoral*, Penguin 1966.

23. For the concept of hegemony see Gramsci, *The Prison Notebooks*, eds Q. Hoare and G. Nowell Smith, Lawrence and Wishart 1971.

Chapter 6

COMMUNICATION STUDIES: DEFINITIONS AND PROBLEMS

DEREK LONGHURST

> Because of the importance the institutions of communication now have in
> our society, we should include the teaching of certain basic facts about them
> in all our education. This should include something of their history and
> current social organisation. [7]

WHAT IS COMMUNICATION STUDIES?

One of the problems with communication studies is that its development has been largely restricted to the higher education sector with
few schools and colleges of further education able to provide the
resources and staff to teach such an interdisciplinary 'subject' on any
extensive scale. It is for this reason that the question 'What is communication studies?' is frequently posed, at careers conventions for instance, by parents, teachers and students alike. The most common
misconception – or at least half-truth – is that it is 'something to do with
the media'. As a result, many students apply for places on communication studies degrees in the hope that they will be provided with an
illuminated pathway to exciting, 'creative' jobs in the 'glamorous' and
mystified professions of journalism, advertising and the media.

This is ironical for two reasons. Firstly, communication studies, like
cultural studies, arose out of a radical educational movement of the
1960s and 1970s which sought to break down discipline boundaries and
open up to question commonly-accepted and institutionally-defined
'knowledges'. Such objectives put into practice, it was suggested,
would provide a progressive alternative to 'subjects' studied through
discrete disciplines and, further, would register not only the rapid
technological development of modern communication systems but
also the crucial importance of communication generally in the *construction* rather than the transparent reflection of social meanings.
Secondly, communication studies degrees are differentiated from
many film studies degrees in that they primarily offer *critical* and

analytical perspectives on the media rather than a vocational training in 'how to make films for Channel 4'.

Thus, some students feel cheated or hostile when they are faced with theoretical problems raised by a sociological or political-economy approach to the analysis of the media rather than extensive practical work or the 'easy' and more familiar procedures of a literary-critical approach of watching a television or film 'text' and then discussing it in a seminar. Of course, all communication studies degrees contain elements of both theoretical analysis *and* textual criticism – but practical work tends to be present for pedagogic reasons as an 'aid' to the analysis of televisual or cinematic codes and conventions as well as a gesture towards the fact that some students may get pleasure (!) and satisfaction from this kind of activity and learn a great deal in the process. No matter how willing course teams may be to meet these important demands, two problems emerge.

1. In a period of unemployment there is increasing pressure to mould degree courses towards more directly vocational training, no matter how cosmetic in some instances. At the same time, staff and resources are not being made available in order to satisfy this 'social need' effectively. A great deal depends, of course, on how this social need is to be defined.
2. If practical work in video, film and radio is introduced, how can it be integrated into degrees which are structured around theoretical concepts and empirical instances of communication (e.g., gender stereotypes in advertising) and which set themselves to provide a range of conceptual frameworks through which they may be analysed?

A central aim of all communication studies degrees is to stimulate students to evaluate and critically assess approaches which may have points of contact and mutual illuminations as well as contradiction and conflict. And this is perhaps the crucial point to make. Communication studies is, by its very nature:

(1) An interdisciplinary field of research and debate, *not* an academic discipline.
(2) A self-conscious set of intellectual and educational practices in that degrees in communication studies attempt to lay bare the theoretical and ideological assumptions contained within a variety of approaches to the analysis of communicative acts, processes and contexts.

Thus, two central questions addressed by communication studies are:

1. How are linguistic, psychological, social and cultural meanings constructed, negotiated, exchanged or, indeed, suppressed? Hence

139

knowledges of the world/reality are seen to be problematic, not simply there to be observed and described by the interpretation of facts or experiences through the application of 'common-sense' approaches. Indeed, language in itself is seen to be mediating rather than transparently 'reflecting' reality.

2. What assumptions are employed in the act of interpreting such meanings and phenomena?

In confronting such complex issues there are two basic models around which a degree can be structured:

1. An integrated programme based on a central theory of communication which operates as a controlling rationale for the study of material traditionally examined through the perspective of different disciplines. The great danger inherent in this model is simplistic crudity – how useful is any definition which is broad enough to account adequately for a speech act *and* the televised representation of a sporting event? – and, in relation to this framework, which areas of debate and enquiry are potentially excluded because they do not 'fit' the controlling definition.
2. More commonly, communication studies degrees are structured around a pluralist philosophy which presents students with a range of complementary and even conflicting methodologies in the analysis of mass communication, linguistic communication, interpersonal and intrapersonal relations, the social construction of individuals, groups, gender and cultural relations, popular culture and cultural transmission, film, visual art, advertising, popular fiction and literature. Therefore, the majority of communication studies degrees are differentiated from cultural studies in that they draw on the disciplines of linguistics and psychology as well as sociology, history and the analysis of cultural production and processes.

Because students arrive at higher education from widely divergent educational backgrounds and with a variety of A-level experience, it is important to provide a foundation year which will introduce them to the central disciplines, concepts and problems involved in the study of communication in society. The two subsequent years tend to introduce 'strands', sometimes with 'core' compulsory units (e.g., mass communications, sociolinguistics, social psychology) and a variety of optional modules predominantly in cultural studies (film, advertising, popular and 'literary' fiction). Generally, the intention exists to guard against the danger of students 'learning a little about a lot' by introducing the opportunity of educational choice so that they may specialize in areas of particular interest to them while also increasing the movement towards greater interdisciplinarity in the third year.

To summarize, then, communication studies is focussed around the study of languages and codes, institutions and practices through which the individual and groups produce and represent meanings, understand and construct the society in which they live. Hence, the media are examined as institutions through which cultural meanings are produced and reproduced; language as a system of conventions which influence its use not as a simple, transparent medium of communication; various conceptual models are offered in the study of the capacity of the human mind to perceive, process and represent information; together with the social contexts and pressures which govern such acts of communicative exchange or negotiation. It is important to stress, however, that such concerns cannot be examined in purely theoretical terms and need to be explored through a blend of theory *and* empirical study to allow students the opportunity to concretize concepts through specific examples or case studies.

FUTURE DEVELOPMENT OF COMMUNICATION STUDIES

In common with every other sector of education, many of the problems currently restricting developments in communication studies have to be seen in the context of government-imposed cutbacks in educational expenditure. The institutional history of the area seems relevant here. While the universities constructed important and influential research centres during the 1960s (most notably the Birmingham Centre), it was the polytechnic sector which proved most open to the formation of interdisciplinary undergraduate degrees during the mid–1970s. Largely, of course, these were staffed by a generation who had themselves been educated during the period of expansion and innovation of the 1960s and early 1970s.

The difficulties affecting communication studies in the current context are those caused by the necessity and desire for expansion in a period of crisis and increasing cutbacks in resources especially in public sector higher education. It is an area of rapid development in research, new approaches and ideas, a field of study which attracts everincreasing applications from students. Hence, with no expansion in resources, in common with the rest of the education system staff are being pressed to teach more hours, thereby reducing their capacity to continue research and publication. The possibility of sabbaticals and study leave is severely restricted; there are few opportunities to employ new staff and thereby inject 'new blood' into the system. Clearly, such constrictions are not peculiar to communication studies alone but there are, perhaps, particular difficulties associated with the development of a new and expanding field of enquiry such as communication studies. Because of its *inter*disciplinarity (*not*, I would argue, multidisciplinarity), communication studies makes intellectual demands on staff which perhaps they do not have to face in quite the same way when they teach their specialisms on single-discipline degrees. The result is a process of constant reappraisal of the *relation* between the different elements of the degree together with the necessity of engaging with – and adapting to – each other's approaches and disciplines. This requires an educational context which allows staff the time and intellectual freedom to involve themselves effectively in this kind of practice.

With regard to resources, communication studies possibly falls between two stools. On the one hand, it shares the need for books, research periodicals and library facilities associated with the traditional, 'literate' humanities disciplines while, on the other, making demands for 'plant' (such as cameras, studios, sound equipment, video recorders, etc.) which makes the area comparable with the sciences. Because the traditional knowledges are longer-established they share the advantage of that history while communication studies is faced with the problem of expanding in a period of crisis and contraction. This issue is exacerbated when we take into consideration the rapid developments in new technology currently affecting our society (information technology, cable and satellite television etc.) and which communication studies has a responsibility to register in what is offered to students.

Taking all this into account, it would be unfortunate if the picture drawn here were to seem totally bleak and pessimistic. Indeed, the point is that communication studies, against all the odds, remains a vibrant area which attracts staff who are enthusiastic and committed teachers, who continue to engage in research and publication and who are often very active in the struggle to preserve educational opportunities, conditions and standards within their institutions. The problems I have outlined exist because short-sighted government policies on education have led to widespread frustration that the full potentialities of the area cannot be explored.

Even so, there are many positive features to have arisen out of communication and cultural studies degrees. At a very early stage students are faced with the necessity of examining a variety of methodologies and concepts which tends to preclude the privileging of any single discipline or 'body of knowledge' as 'natural' rather than produced. Thus, simplistic discussion of the 'meaning' of the 'text' as in, let us say, much literary criticism is displaced by analysis of the processes of signification (the ways in which a 'text' *makes* 'sense' what it connotes in relation to ideology – the social practice of constructing meanings through institutional discourses).[2] This serves to raise questions about the relation between knowledge and power relations in society as well as drawing attention to the key issue of subjectivity where assumptions concerning the notion of the unified individual-subject (the 'I' which sees and interprets 'the world' in a direct and transparent manner) are questioned by the analysis of *subjectivities* (of gender, class, race, age, family etc.) which are socially and culturally constructed and *through* which humans interpret 'the world'. An important contribution, then, of communication studies is to problematize the 'natural', the 'universal' and 'commonsense' methodologies.

COMPUTING AND INFORMATION TECHNOLOGY

Typically, in the present political context, the one area in which resources are expanding is computing and information technology with special government funding available to institutions to encourage the development of courses in IT.

Clearly there will be increasing pressure on communication studies degrees to incorporate information technology into their structures for pragmatic and vocational reasons (i.e., employment prospects for graduates). I do not have the space here to do more than outline the parameters of a very complex debate but it is a matter of some importance for the future of communication studies that *debate* about the introduction of IT does take place.[3]

WHAT IS INFORMATION TECHNOLOGY?

Broadly, it is the development of technological systems for collecting 'information', processing and interpreting it, together with the development of systems for communicating and distributing 'information' with speed and accuracy. It is often argued that this will make our society more 'efficient' as those in control of the various political, industrial and social institutions of the nation will be better placed to reach more accurate evaluations and implement decisions and policies more effectively. The debate tends to polarize, then, around those who see IT as 'a good thing' and those who are more suspicious of the possible social and political consequences.

So far as communication studies is concerned there are, of course, numerous areas of crucial interest: the influence of IT on mass communication systems, film making, journalism; the development of word-processors and more rapid international commercial systems of communication; analysis of the most effective means of ensuring communication between users and technology (often referred to, revealingly, as the *man*–machine interface). And, finally, the concept of artificial intelligence has drawn together philosophers (logic), linguists and cognitive psychologists as well as computer scientists in their common concern with systems which can learn and reason, analyse human experience and even assess the capacities and expertise of their users in order to adjust the processes of communication between machine and human.

If, to some, this sounds Orwellian there is the added populist political sloganizing of 'IT good ('skills', jobs, use-value); social science bad'. There are, in this context, two dangers. On the one hand, institutions will react cynically and pragmatically 'tacking on' IT wherever there is a space; or, on the other, there is the equal educational danger of refusing to meet the challenge offered by IT – uncritical acceptance and total rejection are two sides of the same coin. So how, then, can progress be made?

One of the important contributions communication studies can make is to place 'new' (?) technology in the context of methodologies which investigate the social origins and consequences of technological development and which question the notion of the 'neutrality' of technology. Issues which must be integrated into the study of IT can be suggested as follows:

Are the electronic knowledges a form of cultural production? Does the technology determine the knowledge? What commercial and industrial pressures have shaped research? Space, military, surveillance industries? What forms of ownership and control of technology are in operation? Debate concerning the potential forms of political and social control or resistance which may ensue? Secrecy, confidentiality and availability of information.

Impact on definitions of 'skills', labour, sexual division of labour.

Influence of new technology on the entertainment industry, on definitions of leisure/pleasure, the video industry, home computers, computer magazines. Gender division a crucial concern here.

Representations of 'new' technology generally in political discourse; science fiction etc.

Does information technology necessarily operate in favour of bureaucratic control?

Are there alternative forms available for the organization and operation of information technology? How can these be defined and implemented?

Clearly, all of these questions demand extensive debate and analysis and I am able here only to suggest some of the concerns which should shape the introduction of IT into communication studies degrees. The exciting and hopeful prospect is that communication studies is particularly suited to this crucial educational task.

NOTES AND REFERENCES

1. Raymond Williams, *Communications*, Penguin 1962, p. 132.
2. For further explanation of some of these terms see Tim O'Sullivan *et al.*, *Key Concepts in Communications*, Methuen 1983.
3. This debate has been greatly stimulated within the CNAA Board for Communication and Cultural Studies by valuable, informal papers produced by George Rzevski and Richard Johnson. I would like therefore to acknowledge their influence on my argument.

QUOTES AND REFERENCES

TOPICS IN CONTEMPORARY CULTURE

Chapter 7

TELEVISION SITUATION COMEDY

TERRY LOVELL

STUDYING TELEVISION

A relatively new medium, television tends not to be studied in the ways which seem 'obvious' for other media, as a brief comparison with film shows. Much writing on film is devoted to the analysis of single works. Then, once the idea gained ground that the director was the person responsible for the film's most distinctive qualities, its 'author', 'auteur' studies which looked at the whole output of a single director proliferated. Thirdly, film may be studied according to type or genre (western, thriller, romantic melodrama, musical, etc.). And finally, it may be examined in its institutional context, the film industry.

The institutional approach is the one which appears to be most 'natural' for television, and this type of study dominates work on television. There is relatively little work of a substantial kind written about individual television programmes, or about the work of television 'auteurs'. It is only 'art television' which invites and receives attention in such terms, but then usually as *art* rather than something specific to television, produced as it were against the odds.

One reason for this difference in the way television is studied is its heterogeneity. It is a medium which appears to be a neutral relay for other forms and materials – journalism, drama, sport, film, variety shows, etc. – with nothing distinctively its own, so that it becomes interesting chiefly for its social function and effects in an advanced industrial capitalist society.

Graham Murdock and Peter Golding have written extensively about television. They argue that television must be understood primarily as a commercial organization which produces and distributes commodities. For them, it is the commodity form itself – television as a product which must be sold to the broadest possible audience – which determines the nature and shape of its programmes. This, they argue, gives television a certain homogeneity behind the surface diversity, which is essentially ideological. The need to reach a mass audience leads to television which caters to the 'lowest common denominator' of public taste and prejudice. There is, they claim, 'a constant tendency to avoid the unpopular and tendentious, and to draw instead on the values and assumptions which are most familiar and most widely legitimated'.[1] Hence they believe television to have an inbuilt conservatism which can only be evaded at the margins, in programmes with minority appeal, inevitably slotted into off-peak viewing hours. The consequence of this view is that popular television such as crime series, soap operas, quizzes, variety acts, are largely ignored, and it is only recently that this type of television has gained serious attention in terms which do not take it for granted that it is aesthetically worthless, ideologically pernicious, or both.[2]

Raymond Williams gives an account of the history of television broadcasting which suggests a possible reason why television presents itself as it does. He argues that radio and television transmission *processes* preceded the development and definition of *content*, and as a result, television was inevitably parasitical upon 'existing events – a coronation, a major sporting event, theatres'.[3] Its novelty consists in its ability to bring the public world into the increasingly privatized home; again an emphasis on social function rather than form. He does recognize however that television, over time, developed forms peculiarly its own, in the dramatic series and serial, and in the drama-documentary. But what he considers unique to television, the characteristic which defines it, is the viewing experience it affords. This he identifies in terms of 'sequence or flow'. Television is typically not switched on for a single programme, but for a period of time, frequently a whole evening. He argues that advertising breaks and other interruptions such as trailers all become part of a continuous flow of discontinuous and unconnected items. The effects of television are mediated by this experience of flow, which overrides the effects an individual programme might have if it were watched *as* a discrete item.

Williams's concept of flow draws attention to television's mode of consumption – the viewing situation at home. Edward Buscombe and Manuel Alvarado develop a similar argument from the point of view of production rather than consumption.[4] They share Murdock and Golding's definition of television as commodity production, and like any other such, its product must, they argue, be standardized and reproducible. Hence the tendency noted by Williams, to produce series and serials. The process of scheduling generates a uniformity which also favours the series/serial format. The schedule creates a grid of programme slots, or units of time, classified according to the size and composition of the audience who will be watching at that time. These pre-given slots must be filled with material deemed suitable to that audience and that time of day. The length and format of a programme is therefore determined not by anything intrinsic to its form or content, but by the demands of the schedule.

The extent to which new developments such as video recording, cable and pay television will break and alter the programme planners' control of flow, and the conditions under which television is viewed, is debatable. In part it may depend on how far scheduled flow is predicated on existing patterns of family organization, and how far the 'flow' of family life has adapted itself to the rhythms established by the television schedule.

While recognizing the need to identify the industrial and commercial constraints of television's mode of production and consumption, Ian Connell offers a salutary warning against the assumption that these constraints are entirely negative in their effects. The danger is that we reintroduce into television studies old and not very helpful distinctions between 'art' which is individually produced and 'serious', and homogenised commercial entertainment. Commercial production may have positive, innovative effects. Benjamin believed the resulting destruction of the 'aura' of the work of art was something to be welcomed.[5] Connell challenges in addition the identification of production for the masses with conservatism; far from excluding the tendentious as Golding and Murdock claim, 'the multifaceted imperative to maximize audiences frequently leads on to what many would regard as wayward paths; the tendentious and controversial are not confined to minority slots in the schedules, it frequently is a constitutive element of mainstream fictional productions and as such is one of the generative sources of "drama" '.[6]

If Connell is correct, and I believe he is, then it follows that we cannot anticipate the aesthetic or ideological effects of a given form of television on the basis of its type, or its place in the schedules. It also follows that institutional studies of television, valuable as they have proved to be, cannot tell us much about the effects of particular types of programme. We need to analyse popular forms with the same care that is given to 'serious' programmes – news, current affairs, documentaries and drama. And we need to develop better methods of monitoring the effects and significance of television for specific audiences.[7] The line between 'conservative' and 'progressive' or innovative television is not easy to draw, and perhaps these are in any case not the most useful categories of analysis. But it is certainly wrongly drawn when it separates 'mere entertainment' from 'serious' programmes.

In this essay I will be looking at situation comedy, a form which is more or less specific to television – one of its innovations. It is a form which is widely denigrated, but which enjoys great popularity. It has received almost no critical or theoretical attention. While I take many of Williams's points about flow, my decision to look at a *genre* of television precludes the type of analysis he favours. But in any case I am not entirely convinced that the flow is as pervasive as he suggests. Television may well be switched on all evening, in the only living room of the family home; but different members of the family unit will control the flow at different points in time, will pass through at different points during the evening, and will pay more or less attention to different programmes.

SITUATION COMEDY: COMIC NARRATIVE

Situation comedy comes under the category of 'light entertainment' and is produced by a department of that name within both BBC and commercial channels. In addition to situation comedy, light entertainment comprises variety shows, quizzes and games, and general entertainment. As a percentage of total viewing time on both BBC and ITV, light entertainment including sitcom may seem small, at about 7 per cent of BBC 1's output, and rather more of the commercial companies'. But sitcom almost invariably goes out during peak viewing hours, and in a recent survey of attitudes to broadcast output carried out for the BBC by NOP, comedy ranked second only to the national news. In an average year the sitcom buff may expect to be offered some 36 new programmes, 25 repeats, and about 15 new series of old favourites.

Sitcom is defined most simply as a comic narrative in series format. It shares with other types of comedy on television, such as *The Morecombe and Wise Show*, the intention to produce laughter, while its telling of a story places it with other non-comic series such as *The Sweeney, Angels,* etc. Most sitcoms are series rather than serials, but a hard-and-fast distinction is difficult to sustain. Serials are dramatized narratives, like series, but they are split into episodes so that the story is told piecemeal. (In the special case of the long-running serial such as *Coronation Street*, there are parallel and interlocking stories rather than a single narrative, and in principle the story has no ending.) The serial has narrative continuity from one episode to the next, while the series has only continuity of character and situation. The events of one episode have no narrative consequences for the next. Each episode is complete in itself. Some classic examples are *Dad's Army, Porridge, Fawlty Towers, Steptoe and Son.* However, there are some sitcom series which *do* have some minimal narrative continuity over a block of episodes, for instance *Solo, Butterflies,* and *Agony.*

Something should be said at this point about writers and producers of sitcom, since I am not organizing my discussion around either, but rather in terms of different types of sitcom. A recent study remarked on 'the very enclosed nature of most sitcom production – a very small number of men are in charge . . . it is rare for new writers to break into the field. . . .'[8] This situation suggests that it would be fruitful to trace out connections between different teams of writers and producers, and the emergence of different types of sitcom. The team of Jimmy Perry and David Croft, for instance, has produced distinctive departures from the usual sitcom.[9] Other writers with a string of successes to their name include Carla Lane, Eric Chappell, Dick Clement and Ian La Frenais, Johnny Mortimer and Brian Cooke, and Peter Tilbury. But while such a study would overlap analysis of sitcom by types, it would have a different emphasis. Here I am primarily interested in the ideological parameters of different types of sitcom; hence the interest in sitcom genres.

There are a number of major theories of narrative structure and process, and (fewer) of jokes and the comedic. But we run into problems when the two resources are explored jointly in the hope of making them yield up a viable approach to comic narratives. If we ask what it is that makes sitcom funny, the narrative element has a habit of receding; if we begin to analyse the narrative structures of sitcoms we find ourselves describing them in ways which lose from sight the fact that they are funny. This problem is not new. Freud found that a joke evaporated when it was transcribed into what he termed 'the joke thought'.[10] In his work on film comedy, Gerald Mast identified eight types of comic plot, but was forced to acknowledge that most of them generated non-comic as well as comic narratives.[11] Mick Eaton ends his analysis of the dénouement of *Carry on Cabby* (1963) with the comment that 'it would be ludicrous to argue for a comic specificity of the structure of this plot'.[12] In the face of this difficulty it is tempting to separate narrative structure from comedy, and to identify the source of the comic in elements independent of the narrative with which they are articulated. Eaton takes this line of argument when he finds the source of comedy not in the narrative itself, but in 'those excesses – gags, verbal wit, performance skills – which momentarily suspend the narrative'.[13] While these are unquestionably some of the elements which produce laughter in sitcoms, I do not accept that comedy in comic narratives can be reduced to a series of jokes, gags, etc., strung out along a facilitating narrative which is not in itself funny. There are *stories* which are comic, or whose 'funny side' we may be invited to see through the telling, whether or not these stories are interlarded with jokes and witticisms by the teller. A plot synopsis of any episode of *Porridge*, which would leave it without its jokes, gags verbal and visual, reaction shots, and Ronnie Barker's superb timing – all of which are highly important in the production of laughter – would nevertheless remain clearly recognizable as a *funny* story.

Freud distinguished between jokes, comedy and humour, and argued that while jokes are made, the comic is 'found'. It is 'an unintended discovery derived from human social relations'.[14] But why are some aspects of 'human social relations' funny? Are they in themselves comic, or are they only so if looked at in a certain way, or from a certain distance? Are there some situations which are always per-

ceived as funny, and any which cannot be? The situation of the child
Tristram Shandy when accidentally circumcised as a result of an accident with a window pane would certainly not have been seen as funny
by the victim if it had happened in real life, although he might have
come to see 'the funny side' when the pain had diminished and no
permanent damage ensued. Neither is it funny as told by Sterne simply
as a function of the telling. It is a funny *story*, not a joke.

The notion of the comic being found and not made does not help
very much in the case of sitcom. Here, we are not considering anything
'found' in real life which is unintentionally funny, but an artifact
constructed for the very purpose of making us laugh. The comic
intention of sitcom is clearly signalled, just as clearly as the comedian
telling a joke. Apart from their actual content, sitcoms signal comic
intention through their credits, and through the creation of a comic
climate by having the drama enacted before a studio audience, unseen
by the audience at home, but whose infectious laughter punctuates
what we see.

Sitcoms, then, share in common the intention to produce laughter
through the telling of a series of funny stories about characters tied
together in some ongoing 'situation'. The intention to produce
laughter may be organized around a number of elements. Firstly, the
situation. The situations of sitcom are usually defined quite broadly
and are rarely in themselves inherently funny. Consider some of the
more famous sitcom situations: imprisonment, marriage, family life,
shopwork, the Home Guard. All of these might serve just as readily to
generate melodrama, adventure, or some other non-comic fictional
form. What the 'situation' provides is a setting for comedy, rather than
a comic setting.

Laughter may be solicited through the dramatization of *funny
stories,* although it is possible to create comedy through a story that is
not funny (e.g., *The Cat and the Canary* (1927, 1978)); finally, through
the creation of comic characters, through jokes and verbal/visual gags,
comic performance, etc. In the majority of sitcoms, all of these
elements are in play, but they are relied on differentially. The Carla
Lane comedies do not require very funny stories, while *Porridge*
starring a well-known comedian, draws heavily on jokes, wisecrack-
ing, etc.

SITUATION COMEDY: NARRATIVE STRUCTURE

If it is granted that there is such a thing as a comic narrative, then do
comic narratives have a distinctive type of narrative structure? I
believe not. It is no accident that attempts to classify comic narrative

such as Mast's have produced descriptions that are not exclusive to comedy. Funny narratives occur in almost all types of narrative structure.

Steve Neale, writing about genre, defines narrative in terms derived from Tzvetan Todorov.[15] 'Narrative', he says, 'is always a process of transformation of the balance of elements that constitute its pretext: the interruption of an initial equilibrium and the tracing of the dispersal and refiguration of its components.'[16] Todorov developed his theory of narrative through work on non-realist genres, especially the fantastic. In fact many of the formalists whose work on narrative structure has been so influential have studied non-realist forms – fairy-tales, myth, folk stories, etc.

The most common basis of narrative connection is a chain of cause and effect which links the action. Todorov classifies narratives according to the type of causality the narrative recognizes, and I shall utilize a rather crude version here, as follows.

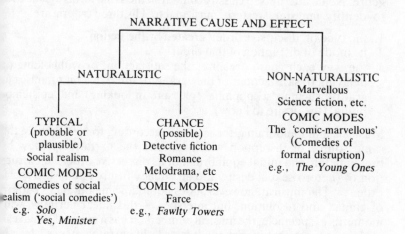

NARRATIVE CAUSE AND EFFECT

NATURALISTIC

TYPICAL
(probable or plausible)
Social realism
COMIC MODES
Comedies of social realism ('social comedies')
e.g. *Solo*
Yes, Minister

CHANCE
(possible)
Detective fiction
Romance
Melodrama, etc
COMIC MODES
Farce
e.g., *Fawlty Towers*

NON-NATURALISTIC
Marvellous
Science fiction, etc.
COMIC MODES
The 'comic-marvellous'
(Comedies of formal disruption)
e.g., *The Young Ones*

To speak of 'naturalistic causality' is misleading here, since the fictional worlds of sitcom are social worlds, and the concept of social causation does not necessarily coincide with natural causality. Different theories of society generate different conventions of social realism, and would displace our classification of what is probable, possible or plausible.[17] The dominant view, which informs the conventions of most social realist comedies, is one which traces events and actions back to earlier events and actions, to the motives and intentions of individuals, and also the unintended consequences of those actions. A typical narrative chain will consist of actions, interactions and their consequences. Fictions which obey the conventions of social realism are limited in the characters they create, the situations they place them in, and the chain of cause and effect, to what is deemed

155

probable or at least plausible. The realist goal of 'showing things as they really are' determines a narrative strategy based on natural causality, typical events and characters which are everyday and unexceptional.

Those genres where causality is governed by chance are often labelled escapist. Like social realism, they recognize the boundaries of possibility of the real social world. Nothing is allowed to happen which might not happen in reality. They produce tales of what might just conceivably occur in a given social world, a given situation. But since their primary goal is not to 'show' that reality, but to entertain, they emphasize the surprising, the unexpected, the unusual and the exceptional. While social realism remains as close as possible to the probable, these forms are limited only by the possible.

Non-naturalistic genres whose narrative chains do not recognize normal laws of cause and effect create their own connecting principles. Comedy does not fit into this schema, because in my view it is not a genre. Neale attempts to classify comedy in the same terms that he uses to identify gangster, western, musical, etc. His three criteria are:

1. the type of 'discursive order' created by the fiction
2. its mode of disruption of that order
3. the way each genre organizes the satisfaction, or withholding or delaying of satisfaction, of the various desires which it promises to gratify, such as 'scopophilia' (pleasure in looking) and 'epistemophilia' (the desire to know).

Musicals and melodrama, for instance, according to Neale, share the same source of disruption which initiates the narrative process by breaking into the initial equilibrium of its discursive order, 'the irruption of (hetero)sexual desire into an already firmly established social order'.[18] The musical, however, does not follow melodrama's pattern of climax and resolution, but intersperses this linear narrative with moments of spectacle, the musical numbers. It has a series of climaxes.

Neale argues that in comedy it is orderly narrative *per se* which is disrupted, and that the disruption takes the form of jokes, gags and other excesses which temporarily suspend the narrative flow. This description fits to some extent those comedies which consist of narratives interspersed with jokes. But it fails to account for funny narratives as such. Moreover Todorov's categories are here stretched to their limit. In his schema, as adapted by Neale, the typical narrative structure opens on an order which is in equilibrium, and a condition of narrative *process* is that this order must be disrupted. Disruption is necessary to narrative process, not something to which it is opposed.

The importance of intentionality to the comic has already been mentioned. Unless we recognize the intention to produce laughter we would not classify a fiction as comedy, even though we may now *find* some fictions comic (for instance, some early Gothic novels) which produce effects which we may now find comic quite unintentionally.

The classification of genres according to the type of causality recognized can be used to identify the constraints of similar genres in comic mode. Todorov discusses the way in which the boundaries between word and thing break down in certain forms of the marvellous. He instances, in William Beckford's *Vathek* (1786), the rotund Indian who, when kicked by the enraged Caliph, 'huddles into a ball', and provokes a riot of fantastic football across the countryside, in which everyone compulsively joins. When we turn to the comic it is not difficult to recognize an equivalent in what John Ellis terms 'comedies of formal disruption'.[19] Eaton adapts this category which he defines as those comedies which, 'aware of language, work by deconstructing and recombining it'.[20] In this type of comedy the characters occupy a fictional world which defies the laws of nature and society. A recent example is *The Young Ones*. The world of this sitcom is not without a certain anarchic order, and part of the fun is in recognizing its crazy logic or, better still, anticipating it. But the point I want to make is that *The Young Ones* is not comedy *because* of its play with language, logic, and causality. The marvellous does this too, but is *not* comic. The difference between them is that stories like *Vathek* produce, and intend to produce, wonder, while *The Young Ones* creates funny stories which produce, and intend to produce, laughter.

COMEDIES AND THE SOCIAL WORLD

The Young Ones is exceptional among television sitcoms. Most are set in recognizable social situations which bring together a small number of characters in regular social interaction. They therefore create fictional worlds in which nothing may happen except those things which might happen in reality. But they are not all comedies of social realism. Ellis's distinction between comedies of formal disruption and comedies of social disruption needs to be extended to take account of the different ways in which sitcoms relate to and reference social reality. It has been argued[21] that comedy and realism are opposed, because comedy's signalling of its intention to produce laughter has the effect of highlighting the *telling,* while realism, it is argued, privileges the told, disguises the telling. Yet much realist fiction uses comedy extensively, and there are 'comedies of social realism'. But just as the marvellous in comic mode licenses certain types of comic strategy, so comedies of social realism license different forms of comedy. Clearly the sequence of visual/verbal jokes which runs through one episode of *The Young Ones* in which characters bring into the house successively, phlegm, a bottle of yellow liquid, and a coatful of puppies and kittens, as measures of the deteriorating state of the weather, would be out of court in a comedy of social realism! Since realism, in comic or non-comic mode, must restrict its action to the plausible, its comedy tends to be naturalized. It appears as a property of the world depicted, not as something constructed in the telling. It 'brings out' what is inherent in 'the human condition'. One common strategy for doing this is to create a character with a sense of humour who registers and comments on or reacts to the unintentional comedy s/he sees around her. 'Follies and whims divert me, I own, and I laugh at them whenever I can', says Elizabeth Bennett in *Pride and Prejudice* (1813). This *finding* of comedy in the social world depicted draws attention away from the manner in which it is *produced* in the text, in a way quite commensurable with the goals of realism.

Sometimes the character who draws attention to the comedy is him/herself a comic character. More usually in comedies of social realism, this role is played straight. Fletch in *Porridge* is an example of the former, but Fletch's persona as comic – in fact as Ronnie Barker thinly fictionalized – would be out of place in a work of realism. In *Beryl's Lot* the titular character, Beryl, plays this role, and appropriately, is studying sociology and psychology at evening classes.

Comedies of social realism, then, reference the social world through notions of what is typical. At the other end of the spectrum we find those comedies which, like the non-comic forms they resemble, remain governed by naturalistic cause and effect, but their characters and action may be deeply implausible. There is far greater scope here for stereotyping and caricature. Like detective fiction, romance etc., this type may be escapist, because it openly acknowledges its primary goal of entertainment. Farce is one type of comedy which has this characteristic. Unlike comedies of formal disruption, nothing happens which might not happen. Unlike comedies of social realism, what happens is extraordinary rather than typical, as are the characters that we meet. In farce, John Lahr tells us, 'where characterization is minimized and action emphasized, mischief is fate'.[22] Like its non-comic equivalents farce links its action through chance encounters, coincidences, mistaken identities, etc. It all remains within the bounds of the possible, but such fictional worlds are bounded only by Murphy's Law – if it can happen, then sooner or later it will.

There is an element of truth in the view which finds comedy opposed to realism. While it is possible to laugh at 'the human condition', comedies of social realism usually have a prominent sober side. The 'human condition' is at best tragicomic. It is probably also true that comedies which can openly strike out for entertainment value have a headstart. But this is partly a matter of taste. The sitcoms which seem to me to be closest to comedies of social realism are rather subdued in tone, producing a rueful smile rather than a good belly laugh. *Sol* establishes this tone right from the beginning with a credit sequence that signals regret and melancholy, rather than comedy.

THE TYPICAL

Before anyone has time to object that *Solo* and *Butterflies* are no closer to social reality than, say, *Porridge* or *Fawlty Towers*, let me explain what I mean by this claim. In talking of 'social reality' in connection with sitcom, I am not speaking of sociological definitions, but of prevailing *social* definitions – what generally passes for social reality. In other words, what will be widely *recognized* as true to life. If this did not at times diverge very considerably from sociologists' accounts, then the sociologist would be redundant. The recognized social order which sitcom references comprises two levels: a normative or ideal order – what things ought to be like – and a 'real' order which comprises what usually and typically happens. Crime has no place in the normative order which it violates but has a recognized place in the 'real-typical'. People will have ideas and beliefs about crime, probably stereotyped, and certainly not always drawn from knowledge or experience.

Because people's ideas of 'the typical' are, precisely, *typed,* there is a possibility of some convergence between the requirements of social realism and the necessity, dictated by the constraints of the fictional series, to produce recognizable situations and characters quickly, through stereotyping, even caricature. Yet there is still a clear distinction between those characters in sitcom who are meant to pass as socially typical and those who are not. Only in the former case will the objection be raised that the character is not 'true to life'. Felicity Kendal's Gemma, Wendy Craig's Ria, Nigel Hawthorne's Humphrey, are intended to carry some representative value and the reaction they tend to produce among afficionados is 'Yes, that's *just* like . . .' John Cleese's Basil Fawlty and Ronnie Barker's Fletch represent nothing but themselves. They must be true only to their series-constructed selves, and not to anything outside the series that they are supposed to resemble.

Sitcoms which come closest to social realism often generate their comedy through the exposure of contradictions and contrasts between these two orders – the ideal-normative and the real-typical. In *Solo* and *Butterflies*, the highly charged ideal of romantic love is subject to comic deflation against the series' construction of the real-typical of marriage and personal relations, and vice versa. We laugh at the ideal, because the 'reality' we are shown falls so far short. We also laugh because we recognize its impossibility, and we laugh at ourselves and at the characters for nevertheless wanting and insisting on it. It depends on our assent to both levels presented, and the comedy will fail if we refuse the validity of the ideal, or refuse to recognize the series construction of the 'real-typical'. This 'real-typical' will inevitably draw upon what Gramsci termed 'common sense' – platitudes, popular truisms, common experiences, observations, prejudices. In this genre we laugh at the familiar. In *Yes, Minister* the solemnity and self-importance of the apparatus of state and politics is undercut by comic exposure of 'what everyone knows', or rather believes, goes on 'behind the scenes'. Yet as Giles Oakley has pointed out, this 'reality' is patently constructed out of common-sense lore, right and left criticism of bureaucracy and red tape etc.[23]

The conventions which govern character and action in comedies of social realism, then, are bounded, and in part determined, by those comedies' reference to a real social world. But they are also constrained by a whole range of other determinations. These have begun to be explored in work on other popular television forms, especially on series and the long-running serial.[24] Because of its series format, this work has some application to sitcom. Eaton argues that the limited range of 'situations' used in sitcoms is determined not so much by their relevance to social reality, but by the constraints of format: 'the "situation", to fill the demands of the time-slot, the demands of constant repetition of/in the series, needs to be one whose parameters are easily recognisable and which are returned to week after week. Nothing that has happened in the narrative of the previous week must destroy or even complicate the way the situation is grounded.'[25] This is as true of *Porridge, Fawlty Towers* and *Steptoe and Son* as it is of *Solo, Yes, Minister* and *Butterflies*. But sitcom's generic subordination to the requirements of the repeated series does not obliterate the differences between them in terms of the relationship of their conventions to prevailing views of the real-typical.

A different determination which does have the effect of closing the distance between different types of sitcom has to do with audience expectations and knowledge of the character-types played by leading sitcom performers. Comedies of social realism will be assessed not only in terms of their 'truth to reality' but also 'truth to character'. Dorothy Hobson found that both types of assessment were made by the women with whom she watched *Butterflies*, who distinguished between what was believable for the social type that Ria stood for in the series – the well-heeled middle-class housewife with grown-up family – and what was believable for a character played by Wendy Craig.[26] Even in comedies of social realism *series* expectations are gradually built up in a manner that allows a gap to open up between these expectations and the demands of social realism. Marion Jordan describes this process in *Coronation Street*.[27] We begin to refer what we see to the knowledge we have built up over time of Hacker, Humphrey, Ria, Bet, etc., rather than to the 'typical' politician, civil servant, middle-class housewife or working-class barmaid.

THE NON-TYPICAL: A BRIEF LOOK AT 'GEORGE AND MILDRED' AND 'PORRIDGE'

The Murphy's Law end of sitcom is entirely free from the constraints of plausibility. Governed only by the possible, they are from the start a law unto themselves. What Basil Fawlty may do, and what may happen as a result, is limited only by our series knowledge of Fawlty and our extra-series knowledge of Cleese. We expect the unexpected. Disorder rules.

In between these two extremes we find the bulk of television sitcom. Fletch/Ronnie Barker's social world is predictable, and he acts within it in character, but we are not asked to relate behaviour, character, or situation, to any 'real-typical'. However, the real-typical may still play an important part in relation to sitcoms which place themselves outside the conventions of social realism. In *George and Mildred,* the real-typical is referenced through comic reversal, based on sex and gender. George and Mildred, like Basil Fawlty and Fletch, do not have to stand for anything except themselves. They belong to a possible rather than a plausible world, which takes its point of departure from the audience's knowledge of the social conventions of the real world. Role-reversal is only funny in relation to 'the normal'. In one episode of *George and Mildred* there is a dream sequence very similar to the one in the film *Take it Like a Man, Ma'am* (1975). In this sequence sex/gender roles are reversed, men have babies and behave in heavily stereotyped 'feminine' ways, while women are loud, overbearing, beerswilling breadwinners. But in *George and Mildred* there is comic pleasure over and above that which stems from imaginary role-reversal, for in this upside-down world both George and Mildred can go on acting in character. Mildred continues to make sexual demands of George which he continues to avoid by pleading a headache.

But the social norms which are reversed in comedies like *George and Mildred* are present, subtly, in the narrative development. Class is represented through lifestyle, and all the characters marked by self-conscious class identity are stereotyped. George is the seaside postcard working-class male of the credits, Mildred the nouveau-riche social climber. Their neighbours, the Fourmiles, belong on the slightly up-market middle-class estate in a way that George and Mildred clearly do not. Richard Fourmile, characterized (or caricatured) as 'young executive class' snobbery, is full of humourless self-importance and pretensions, and intolerant equally of George's grossness and Mildred's vulgarity. Mildred's emulation of middle-class norms is comically undermined by her failure to understand them, and by George's refusal/inability to play the game. But the position from which the audience is invited to laugh is one which denies the validity of class distinctions – 'ordinariness', 'normal' common-sense *human*

values. We laugh *at* not only George and Mildred but also the Fourmiles, for their distance from this position of 'the ordinary' which no
one character holds. However these values are affirmed at moments in
the series, often at points of resolution, but also in moments shared
between the two women when the pretensions of class and social
climbing can be forgotten.

This pulling of the audience, through laughter, to an endorsement of
'common-sense normality' brings the ideological operations of *George
and Mildred* close to those of many realist comedies. *Porridge* is
structured around contest rather than role-reversal. On the one side is
the penal system backed by the full weight of legitimate authority and a
battery of penal sanctions; on the other Fletch/Ronnie Barker armed
only with his native wit. He gains informal authority over the men by
usurping the prison welfare service. In an exchange with Barraclough
in the episode *Men Without Women* (1974), he explains why the men
prefer to bring their problems to him than to the welfare officer –
'welfare officers, they're a bit like the padre, ain't they. Can't be
trusted,' and in any case the men prefer him because he 'speaks their
language'. The prison system of *Porridge* is constructed round the
contrary poles of reform/welfare and punishment. In this same
episode, Fletch manipulates the welfare system to gain an illicit weekend off on parole. In another, he manipulates the punitive system to
stage-manage a riot and get rid of a new oppressive warden. At stake in
the weekly contest is Fletch's 'cockiness'. It is threatened by both poles
of the system. He may 'have the cockiness knocked out of him' as
Mackay so charmingly puts it by punishment or by kindness, if he lets
either get to him.

Most of the characters in *Porridge* are comic – people whom we are
invited to laugh at or with. Because this is not a comedy of social
realism – we are not required to believe that Slade Prison or any of its
inmates are 'typical' – there is room for heavy stereotyping, even
caricature, as in *George and Mildred*. The prisoners are presented as
lumpen and stupid. Fletch's wit passes them by. Like the kindly
warden, Barraclough, they can only register that he *is* clever. They are
slow-witted but good-natured. The gay prisoner, Lukewarm, and his
lover, Trevor, are interesting in that they are presented partly against
stereotype. We laugh in part because we expect homosexuality to be
coded through camp.[28] In one scene, Lukewarm is unobtrusively knit-
ting.

The wardens are also characterized either with or against stereo-
typical expectations. Mackay is the archetypal vindictive screw, a
disciplinarian with a proud record in the Argyll and Sutherland High-
landers. Barraclough is weak, deferential to Fletch, cowed by Mackay.
He is identified with the prisoners both by being slow-witted (like
Warren, he fails to understand Fletch's jokes, and like Heslop, he is
given to inane *non sequiturs*, which earn him exasperated reactions

from the prison governor). Finally, like the prisoners he brings his marital problems to Fletch's counselling service.

Fletch is not developed either with or against stereotype, but neither is he the 'rounded individual' of social realism. He *is* highly individualized, through his persona as comic. In a sense, Fletch plays Ronnie Barker. Like Barker as comedian, Fletch is self-consciously funny in a way that the other characters are not. He is funny *for us* since his jokes and wit are wasted on *them,* a highlighting of audience collusion which *Porridge's* freedom from the constraints of realism permits. The comic performance of prisoners and wardens is 'innocent'. Fletch stands in for us, in finding them funny. So, unlike *George and Mildred,* we are positioned for laughter *with* a character, with whom we collude. The collusion is particularly marked in *Men Without Women,* where we, the audience, are party to Fletch's parole trick before either the other prisoners or the wardens. Our interest in the narrative once we are 'in the know' is limited to witnessing Fletch's triumph and their dismay when they successively find out.

Although we are positioned for laughter with Fletch, we don't have to identify with him, and our laughter does not in this case place us with the social norm, because the series is so distant from the real-typical. Despite its setting, it has no relevance to the 'law and order' motif, which structures police series such as *The Sweeney. Porridge* places itself outside this concern by offering us prisoners who are manifestly (with the exception of the prison mafia), not real 'villains' and are inconceivable as a threat to law and order. The ideological motif to which it does belong is 'the individual against the system'. It draws on traditions of low comedy, and in Fletch we have an addition to the gallery of working-class rogues who have entertained us within this tradition for centuries. *Porridge* offers the pleasure of seeing authority and power flouted without cost, but his persona as comic entertainer means that we don't have to take any of it too seriously. Our laughter does not imply or require recognition that 'that's the way things are'. *Porridge* is closer in this respect to *Fawlty Towers* and Murphy's Law, as *George and Mildred* is to *Solo* and the 'real-typical'.

COMEDY AND IDEOLOGY

This final question is the one which causes most hesitation. It is not too difficult to show that Les Dawson's jokes are sexist; that *Porridge*'s fictional world is one in which women are firmly subordinated, and that its metaphor of 'cockiness' reinforces the link between male sexuality and dominance, domination and castration. But is there any more fundamental connection between say, sexism, or generally reactionary ideologies, and either comedy in general or sitcom in particular? That we cannot produce an example of a 'subversive' sitcom is neither here nor there if we want to establish some *necessary* link between ideology and comic form. Indeed it would be most surprising were we to find unequivocally 'subversive' entertainment going out at peak viewing time. And recent work which has attempted to rescue popular forms from the charge that they always and necessarily function to reinforce and reproduce the dominant ideology has not been based on strongly assertive counterclaims for progressive status. It is rather a matter of establishing that such works are not, or not always, completely hegemonic. But like Gramsci's 'common sense', they pull two ways. It is a matter also of establishing that entertainment is of interest in its own right, *before* we bring it to be arraigned at the bar of ideology.[29] In fact the question might be reversed, so that instead of asking comic forms for their ideological credentials, we might ask which ideological systems have generated good comedy.

The Ellis/Neale distinction beween comedies of formal disruption and social comedies is usually invoked to favour the radical potential of the former at the expense of the latter. I have argued that there is a range of types of comic narrative which have differential relationships to the 'real-typical' of social life, from 'comedies of social realism' to farce, with most sitcoms falling somewhere in between. Comedies of social realism share the realist goal of 'showing things as they really are', adapted for purposes of comedy to 'showing the funny side of life'. Non-realist comedy is still set in recognizable social situations, and like realism stays within the bounds of the possible, but within these broad limits it provides pleasurable escape from social reality. The former invites laughter at what we recognize as 'typical'; the latter takes what we recognize only as its point of departure. It can then play all kinds of games with that recognized reality, but we are not expected to take it seriously. All these forms of comedy offer different possibilities for ideological mobilization.

COMEDIES OF SOCIAL REALISM

I have argued that these comedies reference a recognized social world. But what is recognized is not entirely constructed in and through the 'dominant ideology', and is moreover contradictory. For both these reasons comedies of social realism can have a critical cutting edge. Television sitcoms of this type, such as *Solo,* work on the whole to produce tolerant acceptance of an imperfect but after all 'human' world. They produce a wry smile and at best the wish that things might be different, rather than any urgent sense that they can and should be. But if comedies of this type on television are as a matter of fact conciliatory, it does not follow that they are so inevitably. The argument that finds ideological conformity inherent to this form may be made on the grounds that truly radical work must challenge the mode of telling as well as what is told; or on the grounds that realism requires recognition, but that what is recognized is what the dominant ideology has naturalized. My own view is that comedies which expose the inconsistencies and contradictions of the social world to laughter may extend 'recognition' beyond its usual boundaries; or, they may strengthen the sense that that order, flawed as it is, is normal and inevitable. On the other hand, I am sceptical of claims made for the greater subversive potential of comedies of formal disruption, which can easily degenerate into the rather tiresome frolics of the Pythons.

NON-REALIST SOCIAL COMEDY

Those sitcoms which depend on role-reversal again cannot be assessed in abstraction. Comic reversal may be a distant relative of the spirit of carnival – those practices in some cultures in which licence is granted, in privileged time and space, for the upending of normal social relations. Social anthropologists have usually interpreted such institutions in functionalist terms, claiming they act as safety valves and reinforce the order which is in temporary suspension. However, comedies which dissolve social and sexual boundaries even for a time may in some circumstances have different effects. The carnival may escape control. It has to be said that in television sitcom as it manifests itself today, the danger is slight.

In conclusion, I would argue, tentatively, that if we string sitcoms out on a continuum from social realism to Murphy's Law, then *de facto* the relationship to the 'dominant ideology' seems to work as follows: the closer the referencing of social reality, the less 'subversive' the sitcom tends to be. This is not because this form of comedy is inherently conservative, but because the conventions of realism invite the audience to take the fiction seriously, even when it is a comedy, because it is to be seen as social comment. Radical criticism in a form that claims representational value is potentially damaging, and this is why it is realist forms which have most frequently provoked controversy and censorship. At the other end of the spectrum, precisely *because* the conventions in play invite us to see characters and action as exceptional, there can be greater licence. Paradoxically, unless the audience can be brought to see the relevance to politics and social reality of non-realist forms, they will remain innocuous. And where they succeed in doing this, they will no longer retain the privileges of comic licence. The fact that many of us prefer to occupy this licensed space, and find the comedies generated there more inventive and funny, should not mislead us into a mistaken rationalisation of this preference on political grounds.

NOTES AND REFERENCES

1. Peter Golding and Graham Murdock, 'Capitalism, Communications and Class Relations', in *Mass Communication and Society,* ed. James Curran *et al.*, Edward Arnold 1977, p. 39. The present essay owes its existence to the Sitcom Study Group which was set up after the British Film Institute Summer School on Television Fictions of 1981. The group continued to meet for some eighteen months, and its work resulted in a day event on sitcom at the National Film Theatre in December 1982, and a dossier published by the British Film Institute which accompanied it. I would like to thank the group, especially its convenor, Jim Cook, for the help and intellectual stimulation it provided. Many of the sitcoms mentioned in this paper are available for hire from the British Film Institute Film and Video Library.

2. See Richard Dyer *et al.*, *Coronation Street,* British Film Institute 1981; Dorothy Hobson, *Crossroads,* Methuen 1982.

3. Raymond Williams, *Television: Technology and Cultural Form,* Fontana 1974, p. 24.

4. Manuel Alvarado and Edward Buscombe, *Hazell: The Making of a TV Series,* British Film Institute 1978.

5. See Benjamin, 'The Work of Art in the Age of Mechanical Reproduction' (1936), in *Illuminations.*

6. See Ian Connell, 'Restructuring Popular Television', unpublished paper.

7. See *The Effects of Television,* ed. J. D. Halloran, Panther 1975; David Morley, *The Nationwide Audience,* British Film Institute 1980; G. J. Goodhart *et al.*, *The Television Audience,* Saxon House 1975.

8. Jim Cook *et al.*, *Television Situation Comedy,* British Film Institute Dossier 1982, p. 99.

9. See Susan Boyd-Bowman, 'Back to Camp', in Cook *et al.*, pp. 56–65.

10. See Freud, *Jokes and their Relation to the Unconscious* (1905), in *Standard Edition,* VIII.

11. See Gerald Mast, *The Comic Mind,* University of Chicago Press, Chicago 1973.

12. Mick Eaton, 'Laughter in the Dark', *Screen,* XXII, 2 (1981), 23.

13. Eaton, p. 22.

14. Freud, *Jokes,* p. 189.

15. See Todorov, *The Fantastic: A Structural Approach to a Literary Genre,* trans. Richard Howard, Case Western Reserve University Press, Cleveland, Ohio 1973.

16. Steve Neale, *Genre*, British Film Institute 1980, p. 20.

17. See Lovell, *Pictures of Reality,* British Film Institute 1981.

18. Neale, p. 22.

19. See John Ellis, 'Made in Ealing', *Screen,* XVI, 1 (1975), 78–127.

20. Eaton, p. 22.

21. See Cook, 'Narrative, Comedy, Character and Performance', in Cook *et al.*, pp. 13–18.

22. John Lahr, *Prick up your Ears,* Penguin 1980, p. 225.

23. Giles Oakley, 'Yes Minister', in Cook et al., pp. 66–79.

24. See Dyer *et al.*; Hobson; Alvarado and Buscombe.

25. Eaton, 'Comedy', *Screen,* XIX, 4 (1978/9), 69.
26. See Hobson.
27. Marion Jordan, 'Character Types and the Individual', in Dyer *et al.*, pp. 67–80.
28. See Andy Medhurst and Lucy Tuck, 'The Gender Game', in Cook *et al.*, pp. 43–55.
29. See Dyer, *Light Entertainment,* British Film Institute 1973.

Chapter 8

'SCIENCE FICTION' AND THE 'LITERARY' MIND

LOUIS JAMES

I

Rick Deckard is a bounty-hunter in the twenty-first century.[1] Mankind has created androids that perfectly resemble human beings in all but slight differences in emotive reactions. Stronger than humans, the androids have now become a danger. Rick's task is to identify and then eliminate them. To discover an android, Rick poses a set of questions to which there were established humanoid reactions on the Voigt-Kampff scale. If the subject fails to give the right reactions, he or she has to be 'retired'.

In preparation for writing this article, I devised my own simple Voigt-Kampff scale to test the reactions of teachers of English litera-ture to science fiction. Having taught the subject in the United States I had a model of reactions to expect. My questions were simple: How much, if any, science fiction have you read? What is your reaction to science fiction? Would you consider *Gulliver's Travels* to be science fiction? Explain your reaction to this question. I then told three anecdotal stories from a science fiction anthology and measured the subject's reaction. Finally, there were questions about whether the subject enjoyed the Western or detective fiction.

The responses were much stronger than I had expected. Some 90 per cent were antipathetic to science fiction. Where one or two writers were excepted (the most common being Ursula le Guin, one subject opting for Ian Watson) it was often with the qualification, 'Well, "X" is not *really* a science fiction writer anyway'. There was unfavourable reaction to the three mini-stories. *Gulliver's Travels* was *not* science fiction, one explanation being that 'it was too good to be science fiction'. The result of the 'control' question concerning the Western and detective genres was interesting – a majority enjoyed at least one of these. This suggested that reactions were not against forms of popular literature as such.

Yet, whatever the reaction of my sample group, science fiction studies are rapidly expanding in universities and schools. The first two SF university courses on record started in 1961: by 1976 there were

over 2,000 in the United States alone.[2] One of them was started by
myself at the University of Colorado at Denver. At that moment an
out-of-work academic, I was temporarily hired with the suggestion
that I should draw the largest possible quota of fee-paying students.
The class enrolled over 120 students, who stayed the course un-
deterred by my warning that I had read few science fiction novels and
was no expert in the field. That year Prentice-Hall published a *Science
Fiction* volume in its series 'Twentieth Century Views', declaring that
SF 'is one of the most popular forms of contemporary literature . . . a
fully-fledged, critically acknowledged genre'.[3] Eight of the twelve
contributing scholars were academics. There is a flourishing Science
Fiction Research Association in America, and a Science Fiction Foundation in London, while the Modern Language Association has a
seminar devoted to the genre. Academic journals on the subject
include *Extrapolation* (1959–) and *Science Fiction Studies* (1973–),
and there are all the other indications of an established form such as
annual conventions, newsletters, and annual awards.

There is only one problem. What is 'science fiction'? The victims of
my Voigt-Kampff scale test did not have a clear definition, but neither
does the authoritative *Encyclopaedia of Science Fiction* (1979).[4] One
approach is to note the diversity and the sub-genres associated with the
subject. The excellent course taught at the Boulder campus of the
University of Colorado by Dr Marty Bickman (which I plundered)
distinguished six categories. These were time and space travel;
Frankenstein, androids and robots; the exploration of outer and inner
space; satire and social criticism; encounters with the alien; the multiple dimensions of reality. To these one might wish to add utopias and
dystopias and, more recently, feminist science fiction.

This does not provide a definition of the genre. The most persuasive
(and influential) definition is by Darko Suvin. For Suvin, it is 'a literary
genre whose necessary and sufficient conditions are the presence and
interaction of estrangement and cognition, and whose main formal
device is an imaginative framework alternative to the author's empirical environment'.[5] Whereas conventional fiction creates imagined
worlds based on experienced reality, and fantasy achieves its mode by
undermining that 'truth', science fiction stands in between, creating a
world logical and consistent with the one we know, yet altered in a
significant element. H. G. Wells himself, as Suvin notes,[6] suggested an
aesthetic of science fiction based on the success with which a work
achieves this consistency within an area of alienation, and gives as an
example an account of human society where sexual differences no
longer operate in the way we know them. In fact at least one science
fiction story does just this – le Guin's *The Left Hand of Darkness*
(1969). Another example could be Isaac Asimov's story 'Robbie'[7]
which explores the process of bringing up a girl in a perfectly normal
American middle-class family, except that the 'nannie' is a purpose-

bought robot. What happens when the girl begins to grow up, and has to recognize her most intimate relationship is with a machine?

The value of Suvin's theory – for the complexities of which the reader must turn to the original essay – is undeniable. It is also true that it is an academic exercise which does not give an adequate sense of what the reader is likely to encounter in the science fiction section of bookshop or library. Here the variety is immense, not only of theme, as I have suggested, but of style and quality, ranging from the intellectual conundrums of Ian Watson's highly intelligent fantasies to the tits-and-biceps space swashbuckling of Robert E. Howard's Conan epics. To say that the former are the 'good' science fiction books is to let the definition wag the mongrel. And, indeed, there are other approaches which also need to be explored.

II

A Reader's Guide to Science Fiction (1979), by Baird Searles, Martin Last, Beth Meacham and Michael Franklin is an Avon paperback written by the staff of the Science Fiction Shop, New York. The views expressed are therefore practical rather than academic. After paying respects to Mary Shelley and Jules Verne (but rejecting Poe), Searles focusses on Rider Haggard. Haggard 'was *not* dubbed "the father of science fiction" by anybody . . . [but] he may well have been the biggest influence of all on the soon-to-emerge American school, as we shall see'.[8] For Haggard's exotic accounts of extraordinary adventures within the *mapped* world of Africa (we are, as yet, not far from Suvin's approach) set the scene for the emergence of science fiction in the pulp magazines. Edgar Rice Burroughs's first contribution to *All Story* magazine was 'Under the Moons of Mars' rather than within the kingdoms of King Solomon, but the hero John Carter, the beautiful Dejah Thoris (Princess of Mars), and the world of 'ancient cities, lost cultures, and startling flora and fauna'[9] were not far from the scenes of Rider Haggard's *She* (1887). If this would seem to be an American evaluation, one may turn to Brian Aldiss whose *Penguin Science Fiction* (1961) was to go through six reprintings in as many years. 'Science fiction – the fact needs emphasizing – is no more written for scientists and technologists than ghost stories are written for ghosts. . . . SF owes a greater debt to Lewis Carroll than H. G. Wells'.[10]

The development of the 'science fiction' industry is credited to Hugo Gernsback (1884–1967) who has given his name to the annual Hugo Awards offered, since 1963, to the best short science fiction work at the annual World Science Fiction Convention. From the appearance of *Amazing Stories* (1926), Gernsback edited a series of pulps that were to provide a rough model for the genre, and which from 1929 he called 'science fiction'. The form drew together a closely-knit group of devotees, both writers and readers. 'Science fiction writers are a gregarious lot – nearly everyone knows nearly everyone else – so it was only natural that they should get together and form a professional writers' organization',[11] wrote Don Thompson about the early attempt to form an association based in Milford, Pennsylvania in the early 1950s. Most of the writers were young – detractors might say, juvenile. Frank Herbert, who went on to write the hugely successful *Dune* books, began when he was eight, and by his teens was being published in the pulps. Asimov, the most prolific and arguably the most influential writer in the genre, wrote 'Robbie', his first robot story, when nineteen; by twenty-one he had not only begun his *Foundation* trilogy, but published his best-known short story, 'Nightfall'. Howard, a writer of a different aspect of science fiction, began publishing his popular work at nineteen, and by the age of twenty-four was dead. One is, of course, reminded that the most significant science fiction story of all, *Frankenstein* (1818), was written by a young woman of eighteen.

The readers were likewise an in-group, generally without much formal education, especially in English literature (Asimov's education had come from omnivorous reading in his parents' candy-shop in Brooklyn.) They were almost exclusively male, and with a science orientation. John Campbell, who is credited with raising the standard of writing in his magazines (he required 'real science *and* real story', wrote Asimov),[12] claimed that his research revealed his readers had above-average education, with a large proportion of 'decision-influencing executives in major manufacturing industries'.[13] However, examination of issues of Campbell's *Astounding Science Fiction* suggests that this was true of the readers' dreams rather than their actual situations. There are advertisements for Charles Atlas and for correspondence courses to 'make your dreams come true – ACT NOW'. A typical issue included, alongside science fiction, an article by Asimov on 'The Micropsychiatric Applications of Thiotimoline' and another on 'The Mystery of the Blue Mist of Mars' by R. S. Richardson.[14] These are at the level of competent populist science, and the long terminology serves exoticism as much as scientific complexity. It would be wrong, however, to be patronizing about the seriousness of the overall tone, or the response shown in the correspondence section. Howard W. Martin, Castleton, Indiana, who was encouraged by *Astounding Science Fiction* into reading on nuclear physics, colloid chemistry, astronomy, mathematics, logic, psychology, neurology, cybernetics, semantics and dianetics ('until Hubbard changed trains'), embarks on a long debate concerning Korzybski's concepts of syllogism, intense in its earnestness. John Buddhue of Pasadena picks up 'author Ashby' for a point in 'Commencement Night', a tale which described a burning meteorite striking the earth, whereas, for reasons

Buddhue explains, a meteorite falls below glowing heat some ten miles up in space. 'I know it isn't important', he concludes apologetically, 'but I thought you, and he, might like to know.'[15] The audience would appear to fall largely in an intelligent, largely self-educated lower-middle-class group on both sides of the Atlantic, for Campbell's magazine and its ilk were syndicated in England, together with English examples such as *New Worlds of Science Fiction* and *Science Fantasy*.

But by 1959, when Kingsley Amis gave his lectures on science fiction at Princeton, later to be published as *New Maps of Hell* (1960), the academic world was beginning to weigh in. That year saw the first issues of an academic journal devoted to the genre, *Extrapolations*. The science fiction writers' clan was also becoming more self-aware, and in 1965 they formed the first major association of 'SF' authors, the Science Fiction Writers of America. This included writers published in the States, though citizens of England and the Commonwelath. In 1967 Harlan Ellison published the first of the influential *Dangerous Visions* collections of specially commissioned stories, the emphasis being laid on experimentation and the extraordinary. They did achieve much of the old-style elation, but within a framework of sometimes feverishly 'literary' effort. This is shown in many of the titles – 'The Flies', 'Riders of the Purple Wage', 'Lord Randy My Son', 'Go, Go, Go, Said the Bird'. The stories are deliberately too diverse in selection to make any generalizations useful, but one might at random take Fritz Leiber's 'Gonna Roll Dem Bones' – Kafka out of Tolkien with dashes of Hawthorne, Poe and Walt Disney. The oafish Joe Slattermill, bored with his gin-sodden wife, amorphous mother and predatory cat (Mr Guts) bunks out of his cottage to 'roll the bones' in fantastic Night Town's surrealist gambling den, and finds himself pitching the dice on a bottomless table against the Big Gambler who is Death himself. To explain how he wins would spoil the story, which is told with some panache.

But 'science fiction'? Ellison's explanation, that it shows a 'Leiberesque conception of the universe being unified by magic and science and superstition', in keeping with 'Jungian explanation for the personal madness of our times', may seem a desperate attempt to justify including a lively tale in an SF volume. Nevertheless, it has a certain logic in the context of Campbell's extended article in *Astounding Science Fiction* called 'The Scientist'.[16] He details the consequences of scientific awareness on the modern man – the universe is an absolute system to which the scientist must submit, yet within which, as it is known by experiment and proof, the scientist must be a courageous initiator; the scientist's best friend is the machine, for it is more honest than man. He then goes on to declare, 'The scientist looks at the Ptolemaic theory of the universe, and the modern theory of the cosmos, and says: "They are not very different; each yields the same predicted observations to the first decimal point." ' This is confusing to the non-scientist, he admits, but the scientist is concerned with the process of discovering truth by using logical structures which may appear 'non-scientific to the lay reader'. (Campbell might have quoted, for instance, the example of Newton discovering the laws of gravity within Biblical fundamentalism.) On this reading, the 'fantastic' element is a concomitant of the 'scientific' attitude, which is open to the 'new', and the shifting perspectives the 'new' involves. Thus although Mary Shelley's *Frankenstein* is in fact 'anti-science anti-progress', notes Baird Searles, it involves 'speculation' on biology and chemistry; however unscientific Haggard's African fantasies may appear, they are the product of 'speculation in anthropology, geography and archaeology'.[17] Imagination is a scientific faculty. Pressing through galactic nightmares of aliens and exotic spaceships and Martian jungles as remote as Burroughs's Congo we find ourselves face to face with a contemporary version of Wordsworth on poetry: 'The remotest discoveries of the chemist, the botanist, or mineralogist will be as proper to the poet's art as any upon which it can be employed'.[18]

This is to some extent borne out by the most influential collection of science fiction of all, *The Science Fiction Hall of Fame*, in which the Science Fiction Writers of America chose the 'best' science fiction stories to be published up to 1964. The collection was subtitled (on reflection, pessimistically) 'The Greatest Science Fiction Stories of All Time'. It was reprinted fifteen times in five years and with its sequels formed, more than any other work, the basis for the sudden academic expansion of SF studies. The second most popular story in the first volume was Stanley G. Weinbaum's 'A Martian Odyssey', an early pulp story that appeared in 1934.[19] Jarvis is one of the crew of the early spaceship Ares, challenging the void and 'an absolutely unknown world' in 'the tiny rocket driven by the cranky reaction motors of the twenty-first century'. He lands on Mars and is befriended by an ostrich-like alien he calls 'Tweel' whom he saves from a carnivorous plant-creature. Tweel's method of propulsion is leaping 150 feet through the air to land on his beak. The two build up a relationship – Tweel can count and recognize diagrams – and they travel across a landscape where beings based on silicon build coral-like pyramids and the plant-things trap their prey (and nearly Jarvis) by creating an illusion of whatever their victim wants most – in the case of Jarvis, it is a buxom blonde called Fancy Long. The final escape is from barrel-shaped creatures who appear purely mechanical until Jarvis and Tweel find themselves surrounded in a tunnel and Tweel shows his true nature by risking his life to defend the humanoid. Jarvis himself is only rescued by the last-minute appearance of the Ares, and the story ends by his producing, as the proof of his story, the magic curative stone he had stolen from the barrel-people. The story would seem to reinforce the claim by Aldiss that science fiction has more relationship to *Alice in*

Wonderland than Wells. But the story also shows throughout quite a different curiosity to that of Carroll's work – it imagines a world where living creatures are constructed from silicon rather than carbon; where hallucination has been harnessed by biological evolution; where a creature-society is organized on the principles of an ant-hill. To press these issues is to destroy the delightful unself-conscious *brio* of the story, but they operate.

The difficulty was that the 'innocent' pulp stories were subjected to exactly this academic investigation as the 2,000 plus university science fiction programmes ground under way (including my own). The first choice of the collection was Asimov's 'Nightfall', written when he was nineteen and published in 1941. Asimov recounts attending a lecture at the Cambridge Center for Adult Education when the teacher spent the time discussing his short story. Asimov identified himself and noted that 'everything he had said about my purpose in writing "Nightfall" was wrong – gloriously wrong – majestically wrong'. The speaker was unperturbed. 'And just because you wrote that story', he said, 'what makes you think you know anything at all about it?'[20]

The problem is not the lecturer's reply, which can be perfectly well justified, and the story is, in fact, written with a built-in ambiguity that invites speculation. More ominous is Asimov's reaction, 'Dr Gunther was right. I may be very ignorant about many things, but I learn quickly. A writer is not the best judge of his own work . . .' Asimov went on 'to learn quickly' and never wrote work again with the immediacy of 'Robbie' or 'Nightfall'. The 'golden age' of science fiction, as Kingsley Amis, who himself helped inaugurate the academic development of science fiction, has lamented, was over. *Astounding Science Fiction* has been succeeded by *Omni,* whose sales dwarf those of the early pulps. The composition is significantly similar to the earlier serials, a mixture of popular science, correspondence columns, science fiction, and popular superstition upgraded from advertisements for 'the Queen of the Lucky Cornish Piskeys, Joan the Wad' to a section on 'Antimatter' (UFOs and the like), and invitations to join the Rosicrucians. It is large, glossy, successful, and imaginatively aseptic. Tweel would not have got a look-in.

III

Elmer D. Goodbody does not notice the jolting of the number 78 bus taking him to Santa Monica this 25 November 1954. He does not look up to notice the greying, bearded figure, curiously dressed, sitting in the seat beside him and peering with indecent curiosity across at the copy of *Galaxy Science Fiction* he is reading. I wish Elmer had a different name, for it fits too well with a certain class of male American readers in the inter-war years (Elmer worked in the science laboratories as a lab assistant at UCLA), but there it is, 'Elmer D. Goodbody' stamped on his battered Sears Roebuck briefcase, and if I changed his name I would have to lie.

Elmer is in fact racing across space between the galaxies. He is a pinlighter. A pinlighter, as you will know if you have read the story Elmer was engrossed in ('The Game of Rat and Dragon', by Cordwainer Smith),[21] is a telepath. When the first spaceships ventured between the galaxies they met the terror of some dark force, terrible beyond terrestrial understanding of evil. When the spaceships were recovered those still alive were reduced to human vegetables, their staring eyes unable to focus on anything but the force that had cauterized their reason. Then scientists discovered that those with a telepathic gift could sense these dark forces. By themselves humans could not hope to react fast enough to the power and speed of these dragons, but their minute perceptions could be magnified by pinlighter machines, and their reactions coupled to those of beings immeasurably faster, more sensitive, more predatory. Cats. Through years of experimentation and training scientists found ways of linking man and animal until now man and cat were paired in a deadly, unthinkably dangerous duel between Life and the Other.

Elmer is coupled to Lady May, a perfect pedigree Persian whose relaxed good breeding disguised the amused condescension towards the clumsy, poorly-groomed humanoid by her side. Perhaps condescension is the wrong word. For all his awkwardness she rather *likes* him. If only he would not put that smelly smoking thing in his mouth. And if he would only clean his nails. But then all such thoughts vanished. In milliseconds, the dragon/rat crosses the space between the galaxies. A sudden fear and exhilaration bond man and cat. The spaceship flashes from planoform to planoform. Faster than Elmer's mind can follow, Lady May darts the light-bombs at the inconceivably fast shadows. A terrifying pain shrivels his right arm and side, he fights to keep his concentration . . .

But the bus is coming up to Acacia Avenue. Impatiently, Elmer pulls the communication chain over his head and registers that the driver nods his head. Elmer is waking up in hospital. The attractive nurse is taking the napkin off the goblet of orange juice. As she looks round he sees in her eyes that he is a hero. He looks into her dark pupils, feels the touch of her hand on his forehead, catches the woman-scent beneath the smell of hospital and perfume – and fights down his nausea. Why cannot humans be more like *cats*? The bus jolts to a stop. Pushing the pulp magazine into his bag Elmer struggles out of the bus. I (for you knew who the stranger was, didn't you?) get out too and follow him as he walks up the wet street towards No. 23. I do not need my Voigt-Kampff scale to test Elmer. Here is the real thing. My questions here are different. 'Elmer, do you think the story suggests that each age shapes evil in its own way? The story notes that the old Earth had, incomprehensibly, been destroyed by its inhabitants. Does the writer indicate that the purely exploitative relationship between man and cats in the new world will meet a similar fate? Elmer, the only women in the story are a giggling girl of six, a cat and a nurse who makes you feel sick. Would you say, Elmer, that the story is *sexist*? Or do you see the story as alienated in a wider sense? Isn't the final position of the narrator the same as Gulliver at the end of Book Four . . .' But Elmer does not answer, not only because he is in Los Angeles in 1954, and I am at my desk in Canterbury, England, thirty years later.

IV

I do not want to spoil my point by overemphasizing it. If it can be misleading to study early science fiction stories out of context, this does not mean that they are no longer accessible, even to an academic audience. The danger is not to realize that we may be seeing aspects of Cordwainer Smith's story interesting that would have bored Elmer, and that we may find elements that Cordwainer Smith did not intend to be there. (Equally, aspects of the story that excited Elmer a good deal I am likely to find trite.)

But, you may say, this is true of all past literature read today, and by readers necessarily taking a different social and intellectual perspective from that of the first audience: the point is too obvious to be worth making. The way in which a direct and imaginative genre has been rarefied into an intellectual study, however, indicates that however trite it may seem, it is indeed a point that needs saying. It also leads on to the perpetually challenging issue of the relation between a 'high' cultural form and a 'low' one.

Arguably every major development in British literature – including those identified with Chaucer, Shakespeare, Richardson, Wordsworth or Dickens – came about to some extent through one stream of class culture sparking off against another. This process seems to follow a recognizable course. At a time of poverty in English opera, Gay drew on popular ballads to create *The Beggar's Opera* (1728). This changed the course of the 'high' culture, and had some impact on the 'low' culture, which however continued and developed in its own right. The full impact of popular melodrama on 'high' culture in the nineteenth century came, not with the Covent Garden performance of Pixérécourt and Thomas Holcroft's *A Tale of Mystery* (1802), for this was an 'artistic' French import, but when, in 1826, Drury Lane and later

Covent Garden were saved from financial ruin by importing the 'popular' *Black-Ey'd Susan*, complete with nautical star T. P. Cooke, over the river from the working-class Surrey Theatre. Melodrama, mediated in particular through the fiction of Dickens, became a central element in Victorian culture; yet by mid-century it was already easy to distinguish between two strands. The 'low' was to continue, partly incorporated into music-hall ballads, into early film, while the 'high' strand continued, as in *Lady Audley's Secret* (novel 1862, drama 1863) and Irving's performance of *The Bells* (1871) to the work of Hardy and Shaw – indeed, Peter Brooks has suggested in *The Melodramatic Imagination* (1976), to Henry James. To return to science fiction: 'SF', after its heady heyday in the 1950s, evolved a recognizably 'intellectual' strand, illustrated by such talented writers as Watson and le Guin. These react *against* the very marvels and wonders and horrors that drew Elmer to *Astounding Science Fiction*, and explore the speculative possibilities opened up by the genre. Meanwhile the 'low' genre has turned largely from literature and emerged in comic book, television and film – not *Star Wars* or *E.T.*, which relate more to *Peter Pan* than science fiction, but *Alien* or *Blade Runner* with their red-blooded celebration of excess.

But what, then, has happened? Few, I believe, would deny that Ursula le Guin is a writer of 'science fiction', yet she has specifically denied that she writes about science, or about the future, two of the basic assumptions about the genre. 'Prediction is the business of prophets, clairvoyants, and futurologists. It is not the business of novelists. A novelist's business is lying.'[22] Her own definition, a 'thought-experiment', is itself too narrow and too broad to help us pin down a concept of the genre as a whole. Interestingly, the same problem occurs when we try to identify other popular 'genres' in their impact on 'high' culture – the popular ballad, for instance, or melodrama. Earlier in this paper I noted that no satisfactory comprehensive definition for 'science fiction' has yet been found. Perhaps this is the point to invoke the stories I used in my Voigt-Kampff test.

V

Mr Thoresby received a rejection slip. It said, 'Thank you for your ms *The Last Man on Earth* . . . Unfortunately we are overstocked with non-fiction'.

The boatload of white men approached the savages encircled on the beach. They brought with them presents and many marvels. They carried small brown boxes which, when they were by them, made a curious noise like a cricket. They made friends with the savages, and, to show they had become their brothers, they left behind a brown box. For when the savages came near it, now it clicked for them, too.

He came to the end of the universe. And there, stretched out in flaming letters, were the words,

THIS WAY UP

These stories come from Asimov's anthology of *Short, Short Science Fiction* (1978). Most readers would recognize that they are appropriate there, but it is difficult to say why. The first and last presume a future setting, though the second story, alas, does not necessarily do so. However, with a little adaptation, the stories except possibly the last would fit into other categories. The first resembles the children's story, 'The last man alive in the world sat all alone in his house. Suddenly the front door bell rang'. This, as Aldiss has remarked, was once a ghost story; now it is a science fiction story.[23] Substitute for the geiger counter in the second an infected blanket and one has a story that could be told, with the Swiftian device of the 'innocent' point of view, since the sixteenth century. Science fiction, then, can be seen as *an ambience which gives a specific perspective* on a range of fiction that has come down to us as, say, in earlier periods the Gothic, utopias, fantastic travel or social satire.

Raymond Williams has written that each age has its 'structure of feeling'.[24] This is at once broader and more finely focussed than ideology, 'currents of thought' or 'spirit of the age'. It permeates the nuances, the balance of meaning, the weight and value of word and sentence. Williams has written that it includes 'elements of impulse, restraint and tone; specifically affective elements of consciousness and relationship; not feeling against thought, but thought as feeling and feeling as thought; practical consciousness of a present kind, in a linking and interrelated continuity'. Because it is part of a structure of reality conditioning all that is perceived within it, it directs the complicated interactions of social process, from scientfic and political ideology to journalism and the arts. It has been argued, for instance, that there is more than a coincidental relationship between the balance and order in the physics of Newton, the development of the symphony, and the landscape gardening of Capability Brown; that the melodramatic impulse towards the dialectic of Good versus Evil shaped the political thought of Marx and Engels and the evolutionary theories of Darwin.[25]

As a theory this overview has the problem that it is too easy, too neat. Society does not work in a monolithic way; it holds within itself contradictions, time lapses, and processes of communication that are more complex than a direct relationship between thought and cultural expression. On the other hand there are points of crisis – the French

Revolution, the popularization of Darwin, the dropping of the atom bomb on Hiroshima – which focus and direct patterns of perception in ineluctable ways. It is not arbitrary to look for a scientific moment which assumes a symbolic dimension beyond its actual innovation: Darwin's *Origin of Species* (1859) was a culmination of earlier work popularized by Charles Lyell and Robert Chambers in the 1830s and 1840s. Einstein's first popular and authorized version of his theory of relativity, published in 1920, was appropriately *prophetic* rather than retroactive, opening the way for a galaxy of scientific developments: splitting the atom (Rutherford's atomic theory was formulated in 1921); the beginnings of space travel; the computer revolution; the formulation of quantum physics; and the construction of DNA with its implications for genetic engineering. If Darwin is the scientist of 'melodrama', Einstein is the symbolic father of modern 'science fiction'.

Einstein's 'theory' and the impact of his ideas have as little relationship to actual readership of his work as in the case with Marx or Freud. He questioned time, space and the supremacy of human empiricism. It shifted the cognitive basis for knowledge from consolidation to speculation. Darwin's importance was that he consolidated with immense research ideas that were already in currency; Einstein offered mathematical concepts for progressive evaluation. This distinction can be reinforced by a wider perspective. Thus the Victorian age, in its literature, its architecture, its political and economic thought, looked backwards. Its ideal was in the country-based society it had lost and, behind this, the medieval society that gave images to the Gothic and pre-Raphaelitism. Its major fiction, notoriously, tends to be set in the past: Eliot's *Middlemarch* (1871–72) examines the mid-Victorian crisis in terms of the 1830s. The 'science fiction' age reverses this. The social concept of reality is always one step ahead of fact: before robots become an integral part of society we speculate on their impact and nod at each manifestation of their growing importance; politics are dominated by the idea of the prosperity (or disaster) about to come; fiction, film and documentation fill our minds with images of the coming holocaust. This is not a unique phenomenon. In the crisis of the seventeenth century, for instance, when England was convulsed by changes of belief and order, the dominant literary form became not the newspaper but the prophetic almanack. Towards the end of the era, it has been estimated, some 400,000 were published each year.[26]

Science fiction evolved within a similar perspective. Frank Herbert's *Dune* novels recognizably explore contemporary ecological problems in terms of an unknown future world; Asimov's *Foundation* trilogy and Arthur C. Clarke's *Childhood's End* (1953) are futuristic ways of exploring the problems of contemporary survival in a totalitarian state. This attitude not only creates a different form of fiction, it recreates that of the past. *Frankenstein* has been generally taken as a seminal

179

science fiction novel. Yet as originally written, it is a novel of ideas and nightmares, closer to *Faustus, Paradise Lost* and (as the subtitle reminds us) *Prometheus,* than to Wells's fiction or Asimov's *I, Robot. Frankenstein* as we know it was created by James Whale and Boris Karloff in 1930 in Universal Studios, Hollywood, USA.

The ambience of science fiction changes the way we perceive the objects, themes and relationships within it. Melodrama, the modality of paradoxical doubt and faith, is preoccupied with eternal values – good, evil, virtue – but does so within images of the here and now. It finds significance in the pitch of felt emotion, in stylized speech and gesture, the iconography of human types and the tableau. Investing the commonest domestic items with sentimentalized meaning, it finds its purest form in the closed room. There are no closed rooms in science fiction. Its landscapes are shifting and galaxies-broad. It searches not for the touch of the familiar but the *frisson* of the strange. In Ray Bradbury's 'Mars is Heaven!',[27] the crew of the spaceship are astonished to find themselves, not in an alien landscape, but in the nostalgic world of their childhoods. 'In the living room of the old house it was cool and a grandfather clock ticked high and long and bronzed in one corner.' It is all warm recognition, relatives, friends, young pleasures. Then through the night the truth begins to break in. The next morning, as the village buries the bodies of the seventeen space-men in the homely old churchyard, the faces of the mourners were 'shifting like wax, shivering as a thing does in waves of heat on a summer day'.

This fits with Suvin's aesthetic of science fiction. However, para-doxically, the 'English literature' tradition is likely to quarrel with science fiction because it is not estranged enough. *Frankenstein,* in Mary Shelley's version, is acceptable because it expresses horror at the monster; the modern version makes the monster the hero. There are many destructive robots, androids and computer brains in SF, but there are, equally, evil humanoids. SF has no inherent grudge against the machine; indeed, as Campbell told the readers of *Astounding Science Fiction,* the scientist (that is, the reader of his magazine) 'likes to work with machines'.[28] So in Lester Del Rey's story Helen of Troy becomes 'Helen O'Loy',[29] a robot programmed to the point where she becomes the perfect woman who captivates the lifelong affection of her two lovers and whose perfection has to be disguised by secret adjustments bringing lines to her face and grey to her hair. And not a succubus in sight.

One of the commonest complaints of victims who failed my Voigt-Kampff test lay just in this area. Science fiction has no depth of characterization; it is mechanical and so humanly speaking superficial. This, I would suggest, is rationalization of a sense that science fiction is not 'good' literature. Science fiction can be 'good' or 'bad' (whatever the terms mean), as with any form of fiction. But 'characterization' can have many different strategies and perspectives. Before Dickens came to be acceptable, the same charge was levelled against his characters, but Pickwick, Oliver Twist or Krook are fictionally effective in spite of lacking psychological depth or moral complexity. Indeed, it is in exploring the interface between man as psychologically complex, and man as conditioned, that SF can react to contemporary issues with specific immediacy. Lecturing to a small group of humans on androids in fiction I noticed a certain unease developing. Pressing the issue I established that two had heart pacemakers, one a kidney transplant, another was on a kidney machine, while two admitted being on drugs for chronic conditions. I await with interest teaching my first 'test-tube' human within the next two decades.

The real complaint, I suggest, was not that SF did not explore areas of profound human concern, but that it did; this at a time when the conventional forms of humanist creative fiction were themselves increasingly unable to cope with their traditional terrain. Concerns with religion, cataclysmic suffering, eschatology, the meaning of human endeavour, had been refined out. Human relationships in society had been narrowed to sexual preoccupations, and sex itself reduced to attempts to romanticize glandular functions. Against the history of literature as a whole, let alone the actual world situation, the position of the literary critic appeared increasingly irrelevant.

At this point I may appear poised to hail 'science fiction' as the only relevant literature for today. This has already been done, and done when it was no longer important or meaningful to do so. Literary critics began to move in on SF when, with the impact of the Second World War and radical social changes on both sides of the Atlantic – notably to do with the development of television and changing standards of living – the genre as it was encouraged by Gernsback and Campbell was already becoming safely anaesthetized and so ready for the 'lit. crit.' dissecting table. It was taken up, not so much as a genre (we have seen it largely defies classification) but as a focus for the study of alternative culture. William Golding's *The Inheritors* (1955) can well be defined as a work of science fiction, as Amis has noted.[30] Golding was of the literary establishment, and so a 'straight' writer. (*The Science Fiction Hall of Fame,* however, has claimed E. M. Forster.)[31] The division between 'literature' and 'SF' in fiction is itself becoming modified. As universities and colleges relax their nervous suspicion of the genre, a range of modern fiction, from Anthony Burgess's *Earthly Powers* to Salman Rushdie's *Midnight's Children,* bridges the gap – the United States, with writers such as Vonnegut, Pynchon and Barth, were again ahead of England in this. The 'non-academic status' of science fiction is becoming academic.

VI

Under all this ticks yet another time bomb. In 1946 Denis Gabor invented the hologram, and although his discovery was rewarded with the Nobel Prize in 1971, the implications of the breakthrough have been barely tapped.[32] Gabor photographed an object using a laser beam. The beam was split, one half being reflected on to a photographic plate off the object, the other half hitting the plate direct. The result was a grey wavy pattern which, when re-illuminated by the laser, created a three-dimensional image of the object standing in space. The startling visual effect was perhaps its least importance. The image embodied an infinite number of perspectives, and a single cubic centimetre of photographic plate is estimated to contain the equivalent of some billion bytes of information. It presaged the outdating of the semiconductor, not only in terms of storage capacity, but in the kind of information it can hold. The computer works through the process of coding information into binary units: the hologram directly stores information in the three-dimensional form we know it. Previously, the brain was thought to work on lines similar to a gigantic chemical computer, with glia and synapses serving the function of semiconductors. Now a more convincing analogue is the process of the hologram.

But if the brain records and stores information by a process analagous to holography, what does this tell us about the nature of the reality we are observing? Developments in quantum physics suggest that we are decoding structures that operate on parallel principles – the hologram of 'the universe'. Except that while we decode 'reality' within our conditioned sense of time and space, we are limited from 'reading' a further dimension which would enable us to look through the barrier of time. This would in turn enable us to see the true nature of matter. For if mass is energy, and energy is movement, to solve the problem of time would allow us to see the pattern that lies the other side of movement. It is an exploration that would have delighted Campbell. For it involves not only subnuclear physics, mathematics, and the exercise of the imagination, it has equal relevance for research in telepathy and even psychokinesis. If this theory is true (and it is at least as likely as space travel seemed in 1930), how will this be reflected in fiction, and how will the developments in fiction occur? I do not know. I am an academic literary critic, not a writer of science fiction.

NOTES AND REFERENCES

1. See Philip K. Dick, *Do Androids Dream of Electric Sheep?*, Rapp and Whiting 1969; reprinted as *Blade Runner*, Granada 1972.
2. Patrick Parrinder, *Science Fiction: its Criticism and Teaching*, Methuen 1980, p. 131.
3. Mark Rose, *Science Fiction*, Spectrum Books, Englewood Cliffs, N.J. 1976.
4. *The Encyclopaedia of Science Fiction*, ed. P. Nicholls, Doubleday, New York 1979.
5. Darko Suvin, 'Narrative Logic, Ideology and the Range of SF', *Science Fiction Studies*, IX (1982), 4.
6. Suvin, p. 5.
7. Isaac Asimov, *I, Robot*, Doubleday, New York 1950; Fawcett Crest, New York 1970, pp. 11–29.
8. Baird Searles, Martin Last, Beth Meachum and Michael Franklin, *A Reader's Guide to Science Fiction*, Avon Books, New York 1980, p. 249.
9. Searles *et al.*, p. 251.
10. *Penguin Science Fiction*, ed. Brian Aldiss, Penguin 1961, pp. 9–11.
11. Don Thompson, 'SFWA: The Thing that Spawned Nebulas', *Unknown Worlds of Science Fiction*, I, 3 (1973), 48.
12. Asimov, 'Forward', in *Dangerous Visions*, ed. Harlan Ellison, Doubleday, Garden City, N.Y. 1967, p. x.
13. Quoted in Parrinder, p. 35.
14. *Astounding Science Fiction* (British Edition), No. 3 (1954), pp. 87, 95.
15. *Astounding Science Fiction*, No. 3, p. 128.
16. *Astounding Science Fiction*, No. 5 (May 1954), pp. 2–3.
17. Searles *et al.*, pp. 246, 249.
18. Wordsworth, *Preface to the Second Edition of Lyrical Ballads* (1800); one accessible reprinting is in Ernest Bernbaum, *Anthology of Romanticism*, Ronald Press, New York 1948, p. 306.
19. See *The Science Fiction Hall of Fame*, ed. R. Silverberg, Doubleday, Garden City, N.Y. 1970– , Vol. I, pp. 13–39.
20. *Asimov*, eds J. D. Olander and M. J. K. Greenberg, Taplinger, New York 1977, pp. 203–4.
21. Reprinted in *The Golden Age of Science Fiction*, ed. Kingsley Amis, Hutchinson 1983, pp. 223–38.
22. Ursula le Guin, 'Preface' to *The Left Hand of Darkness*, Ace Books, New York 1976, p. xii.
23. Aldiss, p. 9.
24. Williams, *Marxism and Literature*, Ch. 9.
25. Wylie Sypher, 'The Aesthetic of Revolution: the Marxist Melodrama', *Kenyon Review*, x (1948), 431–44.
26. See Bernard Capp, *Astrology and the Popular Press*, Faber 1979.
27. Reprinted in ed. Silverberg, pp. 391–409.
28. Campbell, p. 3.
29. Ed. Silverberg, pp. 62–73.
30. Amis, 'Starting Point', reprinted in Rose, p. 11.
31. Forster, 'The Machine Stops', in ed. Silverberg, Vol. II B, pp. 248–79.

32. For a popular version of holographic theory, see, e.g., Peter Russell, *The Brain Book,* Routledge and Kegan Paul 1979, pp. 151–61.

Chapter 9

THOUGHTS OUT OF SEASON ON COUNTER CULTURE

ALEC GORDON

> All concepts in which an entire process is semiotically concentrated elude
> definition; only that which has no history is definable.
>
> (Nietzsche)[1]

> Everything that was directly lived has moved away into representation.
> (Guy Debord)[2]

As a continuing topic of interest and research for cultural studies in
Britain today, 'counter culture' has come to be firmly identified with
working-class youth culture and 'counter-school culture'.[3] The historical moment of the late 1960s and early 1970s when middle-class
youth cultures were interpreted as 'counter cultures' has passed into
the popular memory of the period or it has become objectified in the
historically abstracted gaze of academic discourse. In official sociology
counter culture is subsumed under the heading of 'youth culture'.[4]
Outside the intellectual (re)constructions of the 'non-dissenting
academy'[5] echoes of the structure of feeling labelled counter culture
persist in the nostalgic form of personal witness. What was once
charismatically lived has lost its spectacular aura only to end up in the
reified forms of an official cluster of images or a marginal ghetto of
fugitive representations. Would that what Aldous Huxley said about
the magnetism of the medieval age, in an essay published at the turn of
the 1930s entitled 'On the Charms of History and the Future of the
Past', was applicable to the images, constructions and interpretations
of counter culture as a now erstwhile and significant past: 'Only in a
confused and complicated present could a piece of the past simultaneously mean so many different things.'[6] Would that cultural studies
and sociological intellectuals with academic tenure were bothered
about and by the question: 'Were we no more than idle children of
affluence condemned to restore the revolutionary dramas of the past in
terms, merely, of colourful slogans and rhetoric, or did our escapades

185

point to some, as yet, unknowable seed-plot of the future?'[7]

To be sure, this question might seem of no special existential rele-vance to anyone who has been intellectually and politically formed since the period in question. But the choice expressed here bears a force precisely insofar as the historical moment of counter culture ha become one of radical, dramatic reference manifest in slogans and rhetoric of rejection and resentment as well as of unfulfilled poten tialities. In this situation the choice before cultural studies is betweer either continuing to cut itself off from the contaminations – the utopiar ideals and idealist ideologies – of the period of the late 1960s and earl 1970s, or taking upon itself the task of discerning and intellectuall legitimating in the present the objective possibilities for praxis and organic critical thought which emerged during the charismatic his torical moment of counter culture. Like any historian the protagonis of cultural studies has to adopt and stand by a definite 'subjective point of view in order to achieve an 'objective relativity'. In the word of Henri Lefebvre:

> *The past becomes present (or is renewed) as a function of the realization of the possibilities objectively implied in this past.* It is revealed with them. The introduction of the category of the *possible* into historical methodology permits us to conceive the objectivity – while yielding its due to the rela-tivity, novelty and inexhaustibility – of history, without collapsing into pure relativism. It restores historical actions and personages to the effective movement of history, without falling into subjectivism.[8]

Cultural studies has contributed to revealing the real historical *con tents* of counter culture in its own terms – namely the social clas determination of the 'styles' of middle- and working-class youth sub culture interpreted as counter cultures. But this perspective does no exhaust the historical complexity of the phenomenon. According t the three types of reduction introduced by the late John O'Malley i his *Sociology of Meaning* – the ideological, the factual and the tran cendental[9] – the approach of cultural studies to counter culture i ironically for its self-understanding as a form of neo-Marxist ideolog critique, an *ideological* reduction. That is, it has naively accepted th synonymic association of the term counter culture with youth sub culture without enquiring into the historicity, the constructed nature c counter culture as an ideological form. The question of critical defin tion, bearing in mind the provenance of counter culture as an eman cipatory idea (straight away to be reduced to a media label), has bee bypassed for an immediate ostensive identification of the term with th social referent of youth sub-culture. Surprisingly, in the face of th power and depth of its theoretical critiques, this approach is positivist in that it accepts the empirical existence of counter culture as a soci fact independent of its character as an ideological form. The effect this naturalistic attitude is to reify the constructed nature of counter culture.[10]

The conventionalizing of the identity between the given term counter culture and youth sub-culture has led to its acceptance in the field of cultural studies as summing up the historical content of counter culture. A perfect example of the uncritical acceptance of this identity is to be found under the entry on 'counterculture' in *Key Concepts in Communication*.[11] This is a telescoped historical overview of counter culture written from the standpoint of the now orthodox interpretation which proposes that the historical identity of the phenomenon resides in the class determination of sub-cultural style. As such this construction falls a long way short of O'Malley's second *factual* reduction which shows itself in a critical consciousness of theoretical, methodological, ontological (the nature of social reality and of the realities a critical practice constructs, including a self-critical consciousness of its own reality) and axiological (value-accepting, value-constituting and value-realizing) assumptions. A critical practice which achieves a factual reduction is concerned with the phenomenality and objectivity of the phenomena it endeavours to understand and the objectivity of the phenomena it theoretically constructs, as it is more deeply concerned with the phenomenality and objectivity of its own reflection. Now one of the themes paramount in counter culture criticism has been the search for and the making of 'alternative realities' so it is proper that any enquiry into the facts of its history and its interpretation should foreground these aspects of counter culture as a topic of continuing interest for cultural studies.

There are no innocent beginnings or introductions to a topic. We all more or less consciously commit ourselves to a definite starting-point which involves decisions on matters of theory, method, selection of material to be discussed, mode of exposition, arguments for and against already constituted arguments, value and perhaps explicit political commitments and possibly suggestions for future study and research. For my part, because of the availability of adequate documentation on youth sub-cultures *qua* counter cultures in Britain and owing to the complete absence to my knowledge of any detailed piece of research into the historical origins of counter culture (in contrast to theoretical constructions of the determinants of youth subcultural styles in capitalist Britain), I propose to discuss certain aspects of the genealogical origin of counter culture.

The French Marxist historian Pierre Vilar has said that the study of the incubation and emergence of unexpected events is the most difficult task for the historian. 'It is not easy to name what makes the new emerge out of the old . . . It must be admitted that we have no theory of the articulation between the global functioning of societies and the incubation of events.'[12] Insofar as all cultural studies research involves at some stage historical considerations, we are all called upon to focus our attention on and apply our intellectual curiosity to the study of the historical origins of the phenomena we elect to enquire into or which force us to consider them because of some current urgency. Adorno remarked that the history of philosophy is the history of forgetting. If this is so then how much more must disciplines which interface with philosophy be prone to amnesia.[13] The fate of counter culture as a utopian-ideological idea has been one of forgetting in the form of its reduction to a reified sociological concept. Perhaps it is precisely because it was a utopian idea that it was unable to be realized as a lived form of cultural praxis in other than a marginal and fugitive way. Precisely because of the subordinate, repressed, invisible or maverick situation of the 'romantic' infrastructure of social science it is not surprising that the genealogy of counter culture has been of its appropriation by intellectuals who have as their theoretical paradigm or cultural unconscious the 'classical' infrastructure of social science.[14]

As a counter to the absence in contemporary cultural studies in Britain of a perspective on counter culture which recuperates and continues the inaugural romantic critique which was at the origin of this emancipative, utopian project, the rest of this essay will be devoted to a reading of Theodore Roszak's *The Making of a Counter Culture*[15] which situates it in the historical moment of its making, using certain social theory which I consider relevant to its interpretation. Raymond Williams's conceptualization of cultural hegemony and certain sociological work on generations. My overall aim is 'historicist' in the sense that I consider that counter culture as romantic critique is needed today as a genuine form of cultural praxis. Fredric Jameson says that the term historicism 'cannot today be pronounced without furtively turning up one's lapels and glancing over one's shoulder'.[16] Who knows, perhaps one needs to be something of a stealthy private investigator to carry out a historicist cultural enquiry in view of the implications of Althusser's critique of conceptions of Marxism as a historicism.[17] We need an image of ourselves as critics over our own shoulders and, where and when necessary, also as critics over the shoulders of those intellectuals who we think are responsible for reductionist and distorting interpretations of a piece of the past which, in Jameson's words, 'speaks to us about our own virtual and unrealized "human potentialities" '.[18] My interpretation of Roszak's romantic critique is historicist in that, in critically reading over the shoulder of the ideological reduction of counter culture to a reified sociological category in the discourse of cultural studies, it seeks to call attention to the need for such a critique as part of the struggle for the making of counter-hegemonic culture in Britain. The specificity of this project is captured by Williams:

It is significant that much of the most accessible and influential work of the counter-hegemony is historical: the recovery of discarded areas, or the redress of selective and reductive interpretations. But this in turn has little effect unless the lines to the present, in the actual process of the selective tradition, are clearly and actively traced. Otherwise any recovery can be simply residual or marginal. It is at the vital points of *connection*, where a version of the past is used to ratify the present and to indicate directions for the future, that a selective tradition is at once powerful and vulnerable.[19]

Counter culture as romantic critique is not active in the present situation as the lived appropriation of an alternative tradition. Of course a variety of romanticisms exist in contemporary British culture, ranging from popular socialist forms to a continuing English literary romantic *mentality*. The manneristic pseudo-romanticism of youth culture should also be mentioned, motivated, as it is, by sartorial, libidinal, egoistic, narcissistic and status-seeking interests and drives. But the species of romanticism I am referring to is expressed in the phrase 'the return of the sacred' and in a sacramental world-view as part of a poetics of personal being linked to a philosophical ecology of the person, the conditions for which have to be properly cultural on a collective scale. At the present moment in the history of Western culture such a romantic cultural praxis is confined to a utopian existence. This absent profile on the political horizon does not, however, refute its anthropological truth concerning the repressed or unfulfilled potentialities of and for being human. It is in this philosophical light that I now turn to consider Roszak's *The Making of a Counter Culture* needful of the caveat: 'Artlessly reconstruct the 1960s, I doom you.'[20]

We have littered contemporary American history with a hundred aspiring preludes whose aggregate current meaning is precisely the fight for the last word about their meaning, but whose future dénouement is not yet revealed to us.' So wrote a past President of the American SDS (Students for a Democratic Society), Carl Oglesby, at the end of the 1960s in an article symptomatically entitled 'Notes on a Decade Ready for the Dustbin'.[21] The aspiring prelude in question, which was first heard during the climactic moment of the late 1960s in North America especially, but also in Britain, was that of 'counter culture'. This emancipative idea became popular with the publication and influence of Roszak's *The Making of a Counter Culture*.[22] Roszak, a visionary-idealist intellectual of the American New Left believed, at the time of writing (1967–68), that a strict minority of the young and a 'handful of their adult mentors' were the bearers of a new 'cultural constellation' against 'the technocracy' and its legitimating scientific ideology. The alternative to this citadel advocated by Roszak was a romantic-mystical project founded on the cultivation of the 'non-intellective levels of the personality' and the development of a visionary-communitarian cultural praxis. In Roszak's own rendering:

> It strikes me as obvious beyond dispute that the interests of our college-age
> and adolescent young in the psychology of alienation, oriental mysticism,
> psychedelic drugs and communitarian experiments comprise a cultural
> constellation that radically diverges from values and assumptions that have
> been in the mainstream of our society at least since the Scientific Revolution
> of the seventeenth century.[23]

Roszak appropriated, applied and productively constituted the term
counter culture at a moment in the history of Western capitalist societies when radical students and youth were variously considered by
enthusiastic fellow-travellers outside or on the margin of this social
base, or by spokesmen internal to them, to constitute a 'new historical
agent' in one form or another. The paramount feature of the political
conjuncture of the time was that the respective working classes in
Western capitalist societies were perceived by New Left intellectuals
as being apparently incorporated into the bread and circuses of newly
emerged consumer capitalism; thus they were no longer considered by
these very same intellectuals to constitute – or even represent – the
necessary revolutionary force to overthrow capitalism. In this political
situation, on the basis of antagonistic contradictions affecting students
and youth – which they included – sections of this social base were
hailed by ascendant New Left intellectuals as a new 'revolutionary
vanguard' or as a new 'subjective factor' on the road to socialist
revolution. But, wrote Marcuse in his influential *An Essay on Liberation:*

> Such a revolution is not on the agenda. In the domain of corporate capi-
> talism, the two historical factors of transformation, the subjective and
> objective, do not coincide: they are prevalent in different and even anta-
> gonistic gropus. The objective factor, i.e. the human base of the process of
> production which reproduces the established society, exists in the industrial
> working class, the human source and reservoir of exploitation; the subjec-
> tive factor, i.e. the political consciousness exists among the nonconformist
> young intelligentsia . . . The two historical factors do not coincide . . .
> The constellation which prevails in the metropoles of capitalism, namely,
> the objective necessity of radical change, and the paralysis of the masses,
> seems typical of a non-revolutionary but pre-revolutionary situation.[24]

It was in this political situation that Roszak, like many other New Left
intellectuals, considered a section of white, American middle-class
youth an unprecedented force for radical social change. However
without the leadership of adult social forces he deemed that they had
no chance of overturning the established order. He wholeheartedly
subscribed to the interpretation that the industrial working class was
atomized and incorporated into capitalism and, in consequence, that
the last thing they constituted was a revolutionary force. He thus
viewed the position of the radical adult intellectual *vis-à-vis* the
alienated young as resembling that of the renegade bourgeois intellectual face to face with the immiserated working class in nineteenth

century Europe. The problem, as he saw it, was how to enlighten the radical young; how to galvanize them into concerted action along with their already enlightened mentors. Tom Bottomore contextualizes this predicament of the radical intellectual with reference to the historical vicissitudes of radical thought in North America in his *Critics and Society*. His general thesis is that 'intellectual critics in the United States have only intermittently found a political movement with which they could identify themselves'.[25] As well as the absence of any organized and enduring movement of political protest and opposition receptive to radical ideas, an indigenous anti-intellectualism has always militated against the forming of organic bonds between radical intellectuals and social movements. One of the chief characteristics of a strain of the New Left and youth culture during the 1960s was its more or less vehement revolt against rationalism on behalf of a romantic alternative to the scientific intellect and the bureaucratic rationality which supported it and which, in the form of a social-behaviourist ideology, it legitimates.

Roszak's *The Making* finds its cultural meaning in this historical context offering to the protesting young, as it did, a diagnosis of their situation, along with a critique of American/Western culture at the level of scientific rationality and the intellectual legitimation of a visionary-mystical praxis. The American New Left and the widespread youth culture inspired Roszak's critique but, in turn, members of the latter were animated by and received direction from *The Making* at a key moment in the transformation of the whole protest movement. This was the liberatory moment of the late 1960s when the trajectories of the New Left/student movement and the white middle-class sub-cultural movement, the hippies, converged and interpenetrated, so raising the whole movement to what appeared then a new stage of historical action and personal expression. Employing selected concepts from Williams's analysis of culture in class-divided societies, the historical moment of the appearance of counter culture can be interpreted as having occurred when the two wings of the white American movement interacted with each other and when this mediation was perceived, labelled, defined and given intellectual legitimation under the sign of 'counter culture' by a New Left intellectual. In Williams's terms, the moment of the appearance of counter culture in America can be understood as the moment of the historical emergence of an unincorporated alternative and opposi-tional culture.[26]

It could be hypothesized that two conditions are necessary for the origin of a counter culture in the light of the provenance of the American counter culture: (1) the emergence of an unincorporated alternative and oppositional culture within and against a specific cultural-ideological hegemony, in a particular society in a situation of cultural disjuncture and political struggle between the group who constitute this disaffiliated culture and the established society, as manifest in 'the clash of irreconcilable conceptions of life'[27]; and (2) the perception, labelling and interpretation of this emergent, unincorporated alternative/oppositional culture as a 'counter culture' from within or without its social base by a perspicacious fellow-travelling intellectual who identifies with the virtually realized potentialities for new modes of social and personal being of such a new metamorphic culture-in-formation. Given the meaning Roszak assigns to counter culture in *The Making* – 'a culture so radically disaffiliated from the mainstream assumptions of our society that it scarcely looks to many as a culture at all, but takes on the appearance of a barbaric intrusion'[28] – condition (2) becomes the necessary practice of the intellectual legitimation as 'cultural' of an apparently non-cultural radical challenge to a particular status quo. Such intellectual legitimation constitutes the definitional recognition of an alternative/oppositional culture in the face of the delegitimation, containment by or incorporation into a specific hegemony.

What, in turn, are the conditions for the first condition for the origin of a counter culture to occur, given the American case as our historical reference? That is, what are the conditions for the historical possibility of the emergence of an unincorporated alternative/oppositional culture? I will answer this question theoretically with reference to Williams's analysis of cultural hegemony in class-divided societies and historically with respect to the concept of generational struggle as it occurs in *The Making*.

Williams proposes three concepts as necessary in order to distinguish the different cultural elements which make up any plural cultural system in a class-divided social formation: *effective dominant*, *residual* and *emergent*. Such a discrimination is necessary in order to carry out a differential understanding of the complexity of hegemony and, in particular, the dynamic and adaptive qualities of any hegemonic culture proper. This is because hegemony is not singular but has internal structures which require constantly to be renewed, recreated and defended in the face of challenges to its continual reproduction. In Williams's theoretical model the *effective dominant* culture is the central system of practices, meanings and values in any society in a given historical period.

The key to understanding the modes of operation of the effective dominant culture lies in comprehending the mechanisms of *incorporation* by which hegemony is reproduced. In a capitalist society the primary agents of the transmission of the effective dominant culture are the educational institutions. Precisely because of this crucial role in the reproduction of hegemony the educational institutions in a capitalist society are now a major economic as well as cultural moment. But, more generally, the reproduction of hegemony is continually carried out at the level of particular ideological practices, including what Williams refers to as a philosophical level or 'true level of theory', in the complex process which he calls the *selective tradition:*

> that which, within the terms of an effective dominant culture, is always passed off as 'the tradition', 'the significant past'. But always the selectivity is the point; the way in which from a whole possible area of past and present, certain meanings and practices are chosen for emphasis, certain other meanings and practices are neglected and excluded. Even more crucially, some of these meanings and practices are reinterpreted, diluted, or put into forms which support or at least do not contradict other elements within the effective dominant culture. The processes of education; the processes of a much wider social training within institutions like the family; the practical definitions and organisations of work; the selective tradition at an intellectual level: all these forces are involved in a continual making and remaking of an effective dominant culture, and on them, as experienced, as built into our living, its reality depends.[29]

The selective tradition is continually active and adjusting in its toleration of alternative opinions and attitudes, and even alternative senses of the world. This process of negotiation, adaptation and accommodation is present in different forms in all the institutions of civil society, but it is particularly noticeable at the level of political practice. The limits of the circulation and effectivity of alternative incorporated ideology are the limits of the variation of internal controversy in all practices. However, in class-divided societies there are practices, experiences, meanings and values which are not integrally part of the effective dominant culture. Williams conceptualises these as *alternative* and *oppositional*. The nature of adversary cultural forms is directly dependent on the complex internal relations within the effective and dominant culture and thus they are subject to historical variation in real circumstances. The mutations of alternative and oppositional cultural forms are dialectically related to the vicissitudes of the effective dominant culture. To understand the complexities of this ongoing dialectical interaction Williams introduces the important distinction between *residual* and *emergent* forms of both alternative and oppositional culture. By 'residual' he means 'that some experiences, meanings and values which cannot be verified or cannot be expressed in terms of the dominant culture, are nevertheless lived and practised on the basis of the residue – cultural, as well as social – of some previous social formation.'[30] The obvious case of a residual cultural form lies in the realm of religious practices and values. Another significant example is rural-pastoralism.[31] A residual cultural form is a survival from a previous social formation or a current practice with reference in a past historical period. Consequently it is at some distance from the effective dominant culture. However, the spiral of incorporation continually operates to absorb these survivals because of the necessity for the dominant culture to make sense of them. There is also the possibility of a residual cultural form gaining an effectivity which contests the effectivity of the dominant culture. The leading role of the Catholic Church in the political struggle of the Polish masses and dissenting intelligentsia is a contemporary example.

Encapsulated in the definition of *emergent* forms of alternative and oppositional culture is the emphasis on the continual production of new meanings and values. Owing to their adversary and antagonistic nature, attempts at incorporation are launched immediately the signs of emergent cultural forms appear in a new historical moment. To grasp the complexity of the dialectical interactions between dominant/residual, dominant/emergent, residual/emergent and alternative and oppositional forms of the latter and their continual variations over short historical periods and phases Williams formulates concepts for precise analysis and so distinguishes between *residual-incorporated* and *residual not-incorporated* and between *emergent-incorporated* and *emergent not-incorporated*. For Williams the difference between alternative and oppositional cultural forms is the difference

> between someone who finds a different way to live and wishes to be left alone with it, and someone who finds a different way to live and wants to change the society in its light. This is usually the difference between individual and small group solutions to social crisis and those solutions which properly belong to political and ultimately revolutionary practice.[32]

Williams's analysis of cultural hegemony enables us to respond theoretically to the question of what the conditions might be for the historical emergence of an unincorporated alternative/oppositional culture. No dominant culture is totally and absolutely effective. There are always alternative if not oppositional forms as part of a real hegemony because no effective dominant culture exhausts the capacity to create counter-meanings and values. Being composite, a selective tradition has already incorporated what were past residual and adversary meanings. The question why particular social bases emerge as alternative and/or oppositional forms has to be answered by historical and empirical analyses. A complete analysis would have to consider all the levels of a real hegemony in the more global context of a total social analysis. In the case of the American counter culture of the late 1960s the relevant constellation of facts are: an economic moment of overproduction and surplus; a political moment of an incorporated working class and a radical protest movement; a social-ideological moment of a relative failure of family, school and college as positive socialization agencies; a cultural moment of unprecedented possibilities for the creation of alternative and subversive meanings and values; and an intellectual moment of widespread social critique and the proposing of utopian alternatives by a radical and disaffiliated intelligentsia.

This constellation of facts and forces acted together to produce a situation in which an emergent and oppositional culture was generated during a moment of cultural disjuncture whose surface expression took the form of a profound generational antagonism. This was not a fiction of social scientists. Generational struggle was the social form which the crisis of social reproduction took in all the advanced capitalist countries during the disjunctive moment of the late 1960s. Roszak traces the genesis of youth as a significant force for social change to the irruption of acute generational conflict in American society. He cites the authority of José Ortega y Gasset to support his commitment to the importance of convulsions in generational transition as often the key factor in accounting for sudden moments of rapid and radical social change. 'In the "today", in every "today", various generations coexist and the relations which are established between them, according to the different conditions of their ages, represent the dynamic system of attractions and repulsions, of agreement and controversy which at any given moment make up the reality of historic life.'[33] However, the actual significance of generations in the historical process has to be investigated for each particular society at a given historical moment in the context of a total social analysis. Karl Mannheim's work on generations enables detailed discriminations between the vertical and horizontal dimensions of generations to be discerned in any practice of historical analysis.[34] He distinguishes between generational location, generation as actuality and generation units. *Generational location* ascribes to individuals belonging to the same age group a common experiential location in a society. *Generational actuality* refers to the possibilities of a common project among individuals sharing a similar generational location. And a *generation unit* comprises individuals who share common attitudes, intellectual identifications, interpretations of the social world and who express these in similar social action. Thus homogenous 'youth', representing an apparently specific generational actuality, is divisible into several generational units which may well be – and more often than not are – in conflict with each other because the structural bases of generation units are class factors – that is, specific economic, political, ideological and cultural determinants.

The importance of Mannheim's distinctions for the present discussion is that they afford the possibility of extending the interpretation of the origin of counter culture being developed. Mannheim claims that new generational units only realize the potentialities inherent in a generational location under conditions of accelerated social change. Too rapid change ruptures the process of cultural transmission and a generation gap ensues. In turn, this hiatus motivates a new generation unit to create a novel 'generation style' which sharply differentiates it not only from the older generation(s) but also from its other peer generation units. It was just such a leading generation unit which Roszak perceived and positively labelled a 'counter culture'.

As for Roszak's role *vis-à-vis* this leading generation unit: Mannheim recognizes that radical intellectuals of an older generation, to which they are marginal, may act as 'forerunners' of a new, younger generational style. Roszak perceived that the 'adolescentization' of dissent posed a dilemma as perplexing as the proletarianization of dissent did for left-wing intellectuals whose elected historical agent in the revolutionary process is the industrial working class. He analysed that 'with the present situation we are perhaps at a stage comparable with the Chartist phase of trade unionism in Great Britain, when the ideals and spirit of a labour movement had been formulated but had not reached anything like class-wide dimensions. Similarly, it is still a small minority of the young who now define the generational conflict.'[35] Roszak's impressionistic, unsystematic social analysis of counter cultural youth in *The Making* lends itself to analytic clarification and thus to a superior historical understanding (*pace* Lefebvre) if it is reinterpreted using Mannheim's terms. A number of Roszak's statements can be non-reductively related to Mannheim's key concepts for generational analysis. For instance, at the outset of his book Roszak distinguished the 'strict minority of the young and a handful of their adult mentors'[36], who constituted the counter culture he perceived/labelled, from other contemporary generation units: the socially conservative young, liberal youth, old-line Marxist youth groups and the militant black young whose political project he viewed as being too limited by virtue of its nationalistic and ethnic concerns. Throughout the early chapters of *The Making* Roszak refers on numerous occasions to the quantitative aspect of the common generational location of the counter cultural young. However, their common project and self-conscious sense of a group solidarity is precisely what Mannheim calls a generation actuality.

When it came to further discriminations between the varieties of the 'technocracy's children' Roszak divided the young into the socially conformist and the 'incorrigibles' who either turned political or dropped out.[37] Some of the latter became 'ne'er-do-well dependents' whilst others 'simply bolted'. When discussing the role of the university campus in helping to crystallize the group identity of the young Roszak discerned an alliance between a leading group of 'campus elders' (radical graduates), younger intellectual students, non-students ('campus roustabouts'), discontented junior faculty and the 'dissenting academy'. For Roszak the campus 'community' was a radical alliance of all these elements in the orbit of 'youth'. What gave them a sense of solidarity was the gravitational effect of a pervasive generational actuality founded on a personalistic ethic. Despite the tensions between the beat-hip and the student-New Left varieties of dissent Roszak perceived a positive similarity of sensibility at the deep humanistic level of a beneficent and altruistic concern for the person. This sense of a widespread and profound generational actuality was encapsulated in the SDS motto 'One man, one soul'.

The deliberate absence of any systematic sociological base to hi impressionistic analysis notwithstanding, Roszak's sense of the crucial importance of generational analysis for an understanding of the cultural crisis of his – and our – time is captured with gravity in a diagnostic statement of undeniable relevance and poignancy for any contemporary reading of the signs of the time, for any deep understanding of the continuing cultural crisis in our current historical moment.

> The counter culture takes its stand against the background of this absolute evil (the shadow of thermonuclear annihilation beneath which we cower), an evil which is not defined by the sheer *fact* of the bomb, but by the total ethos of the bomb, in which our politics, our public morality, our economic life, our intellectual endeavour are now embedded with a wealth of ingenious rationalization. We are a civilization sunk in an unshakable commitment to genocide, gambling madly with the universal extermination of our species. . . .

> If the counter culture is . . . that healthy instinct which refuses both at the personal and the political levels to practise such a cold-blooded rape of our human sensibilities, then it should be clear why the conflict between young and adult in our time reaches so peculiarly and painfully deep. In an historical emergency of unprecedented proportions, we are that strange culture-bound animal whose biological drive for survival expresses itself generationally.[38]

As the possibility of nuclear war is, quantitatively speaking, even more threatening today than it was in the late 1960s, we have an experiential basis in the present to appreciate that it is an ideological reduction in the extreme to consider the counter culture of the 1960s solely as a manipulative act of media-hype – as has been done.[39] To be sure, once the *label* counter culture was circulating in the American media it was inevitable that the reality it referred to would be equated with the more spectacular signs of youth style. But the historical reality of the alternative and oppositional culture which Roszak not only labelled but productively analysed and interpreted as a counter culture emerged out of a situation of generational antagonism and cultural disjuncture. The war in Vietnam especially brought home the biological, generation-based revulsion against the hypocritical atrocities of the American military-industrial complex.

This raises an important point for cultural studies analysis: generation-based conflict is a crisis in the transmission of culture; that is, a crisis of socialization and acculturation – of the passing on from one generation to another, through the mediating institutions of family and education, of a whole institutionalized way of life, as manifest in the patterning of social behaviour and forms of social character. Disjunctures in cultural transmission are thus ruptures in historically protean 'structures of feeling' – the lived, experienced expression of a particular generational actuality based on a specific generational location, realized in the social behaviour and the 'style' of distinct generation units. Discussing his concept of 'structure of feeling' in the context of developing a perspective for historical cultural analysis, Williams writes:

> One generation may train its successor, with reasonable success, in the social character or the general social pattern, but the new generation will have its own structure of feeling, which will not appear to have come 'from' anywhere. For here, most distinctly, the changing organization is enacted in the organism: the new generation responds in its own ways to the unique world it is inheriting, taking up many continuities, that can be traced, and reproducing many aspects of the organization, which can be separately described, yet feeling its whole life in certain ways differently, and shaping its creative responses into a new structure of feeling.[40]

What is missing from this theoretical account of generational transmission, sophisticated though it is, is a sociological conceptualisation of the *horizontal* divisions of an apparent singular generation into more or less distinct generation units. A definite structure of feeling is then more properly applicable to a well-formed generation unit rather than to an undifferentiated generation.

From this theoretical model it can be hypothesized that, during a climactic moment of cultural disjuncture, as manifest in acute generational conflict, radical structures of feeling both more rapidly emerge and pass away into historical representation. The genealogy of the American counter culture provides ample evidence for this thesis. During the inchoate phase of the rapid emergence of the counter culture we find various statements of bamboozlement and surprise on the part of 'observers', 'commentators' on 'the youth scene', as we also find academic sociologists admitting their perplexity faced with the sudden appearance of a 'youth counter culture'.[41] Charles Reich rhetorically captures this state of dumbfoundedness in his *The Greening of America:*

> Beginning with a few individuals in the mid 1960s, and gathering number ever more rapidly thereafter, Consciousness III has sprouted up, astonishingly and miraculously out of the stony soil of the American corporate State. So spontaneous was its appearance that no one, not the most astute or the most radical, foresaw what was coming or recognized it when it began. It is not surprising that many people think it a conspiracy, for it was spread, here and abroad, by means invisible. Hardly anybody of the older generation, even the FBI or the sociologists, knew much about it, for its language and thought are so different from Consciousness II as to make it virtually an undecipherable secret code. Consciousness III is, as of this writing, the greatest secret in America, although its members have shouted as loudly as they could to be heard.[42]

Ironically, both Reich and Roszak have been referred to as 'sociologists' when, by training, Reich was a lawyer and Roszak a cultural historian who was totally opposed to mainstream positivist sociology.[43] Neither Reich nor, especially, Roszak was committed to the structural-functional orthodoxy that obtained in American sociology during the 1960s.

Reich divides American history into the succession of three forms of consciousness labelled Consciousness I, II and III respectively.

> These three types predominate in America today. One was formed in the nineteenth century, the second in the first half of this century, the third is just emerging. Consciousness I is the traditional outlook of the American farmer, small businessman and worker who is trying to get ahead. Consciousness II represents the values of an organizational society. Consciousness III is the new generation. The three categories are, of course, highly impressionistic and arbitrary; they make no pretence to be scientific. And, since each type of consciousness is a construct, we would not expect any actual individual to exhibit in symmetrical perfection all the characteristics of one type of consciousness.[44]

Reich constructs a singular homogenous consciousness which he attributes to a single homogenous generation. Now although Roszak did not, as I've said, carry out a sociologically informed analysis of the horizontal and vertical generational divisions which he discerned cutting across American youth, at least he made distinctions between empirically observable groups. To have attempted a formal sociological analysis, however, would have meant succumbing to the myth of objective consciousness and its underlying scientific reality principle. With this qualification in mind, I intend to proceed to a reinterpretation of Roszak's impressionistic social analysis of the American counter culture using the research findings of an American sociologist in the theoretical context of Mannheim's concepts for generational analysis and Williams's analysis of cultural hegemony.

In *The Long Revolution* Williams says that in any historical period there are at least three generations.[45] Reich's model concurs with this view in proposing that the three types of consciousness he constructs exist simultaneously in American society. But what about vertical age divisions *within* one generation? Clifford Adelman in his *Generations: A Collage on Youthcult* (1973) confronts this question with particular reference to the American counter culture. Acknowledging the qualitative but confusing dichotomy between 'counter-culture' and 'counter-politics', he introduces three terms which govern his quantitative analysis: 'core', 'hard core' and 'gravitational field'. In the spring of 1971 Adelman conducted a questionnaire-based study of a random sample of college-educated young people between the ages of seventeen and thirty-two. He distributed a seven-page questionnaire to a corpus of 530 respondents. It was divided into three sections. Section A consisted of questions designed to determine social and geographical movements, media habits and attitudes, degrees of counter-cultural and counter-political involvement and political attitudes. Section B consisted of an examination of the respondent's knowledge of both popular and general and counter and mainstream culture; whereas Section C sought to elicit more specific attitudes.

What were Adelman's results? Most significantly, three distinct vertical sub-generations emerged. Within the 17–32 range divisions occurred at 21 (born 1950) and at 26 (born 1945). The older group aged 2–32 he called the 'elder juniors' and the age group 17–20 the 'juniors'. The age group in between he called the 'centre group'. Theoretically Adelman referred to these divisions as psycho-cultural generation groups. His overall general conclusion was that, despite these vertical divisions, there was a 'community of spiritual interest that *dominates* the entire age spectrum, encompassing affairs and attitudes both political and cultural'.[46] That is, in Mannheim's terms, a generational actuality was manifest inclusive of all three vertical sub-generations. Adelman also found that the leading sub-generation was the 'elder juniors', which correlates with Roszak's 'campus elders'. Adelman discovered that the members of the oldest sub-generation were the political leaders at the same time as being the most articulate about their political ideas and cultural values. He also found more or less definite correlations between the elder juniors/hard core group, between the centre group/core grouping and between the juniors/the gravitational field. These were not exactly strict correlations; they were tendencies interpreted from the results of the questionnaire.

In Mannheim's terms the three-tiered American counter-cultural generation-as-actuality was divided horizontally into two fairly distinct generation units. However, the respective counter-cultural and counter-political vanguards drew from all three vertical sub-generations. In the late 1960s in America these phenomena became socially visible, so much so that radical, fellow-travelling older intellectuals could not but have been affected by the dominant community of interest in the generational actuality of 'youth'. It is among the numerous affirmative interpretations of this emerging structure of feeling that Roszak's cultural interpretation finds its place. One American commentator on Mannheim's work sums up, using Mannheim's concepts, Roszak's role in the developing of the intellectual legitimation of the emergent structure of feeling of counter culture youth.

> Mannheim . . . recognized that older people who are marginal to their own generation may act as forerunners of a new generational style. Just as renegade bourgeois intellectuals contributed to the evolving class ideology of the proletariat, so older individuals, we may argue, first shaped and practised the attitudinal nucleus upon which configurations such as the youthful 'counter culture' are based. On a more general level Mannheim maintained that individuals belonging to earlier or later age groups may be attracted to an 'alien' generation unit, especially if these are favoured by the trend of the times.[47]

In a letter to me dated 21 April 1975 Roszak spelled out his attraction to counter-cultural youth in America in the late 1960s.

I hope you won't misread my work the way so many others have. The important word is 'culture', by which I mean consciousness of self and world: a complex of values and perceptions. *'MCC' was about 'youth' primarily as an audience for a cultural revision which I had always accredited to more mature thinkers,* and indeed to a tradition in our society that runs back (at least) to the Romantic movement. Counter culture means Blake to me . . . and Goethe, and Wordsworth, and Shelley, and Emerson, and Thoreau . . . And (to distinguish the line of descent more critically) Tolstoy rather than Marx, Jung rather than Freud, Norman Brown rather than Herbert Marcuse. *College kids became interesting to me when they began to vibrate audibly to that cultural current and began to broadcast its style to the society at large. MCC* explains why I think the campuses came to play this special role in the early and mid-60s. Now, the style has moved off the campuses . . . as one would expect. (my emphases)

It would be difficult indeed to write about William Blake's utopian and, in a symbolic mode, socially critical poetry or the orphic politics Roszak opts for in the same discourse that has constituted this essay. I fully admit that poetry – and especially romantic poetry – defies sociological writing; and no amount of positive reference to the 'socio-logical imagination' or a 'poetics' for sociology will convince me other-wise.[48] In my view consideration of the 'poetics' of counter culture requires a different mode of writing from a reductionist sociological one. A non-reductive study of *romantic* counter culture still awaits to be written. It certainly won't happen in Britain as long as counter culture is identified with the study of the class determinants of youth sub-cultural styles to the exclusion of the recognition of the con-structed nature of counter culture as a cultural interpretation.

To find a theoretical point of view responsive to contemporary forms of romanticism considered as a counter culture within the intellectual field of cultural studies, we can refer again to the writings of Williams. At the end of the short chapter on 'hegemony' in his *Marxism and Literature* (1977) he says that the major problem for cultural theory is to be able to distinguish between alternative and oppositional projects generated from within a specific hegemony, which then limits and operates to incorporate them, and projects which are irreducible to the terms of the original or adaptive hege-mony. Williams suggests that a case can be made that almost all adversary projects are, in practice, limited by the effective dominant culture: 'the dominant culture . . . at once produces and limits its own forms of counter-culture. There is more evidence for this view (for example in the case of the romantic critique of industrial civilization) than we usually admit.'[49]

I would argue that a genuine alternative or oppositional project is not produced by a dominant culture, unless by some ruse of dialectical thinking we say that the reaction of an adversary culture to a dominant culture is tantamount to 'production'. But determination does not equal production. Counter cultures do not have their origin in a simple, mechanically conceived reversal of values. They come about through acts of more or less conscious historical agency as an attempt to resolve specific contradictions in a situation of cultural disjuncture. In the case of the romantic critique of industrial civilization, even Roszak, in his letter cited above, refers to a counter-tradition with a lineage traceable back to the European romantic movement.[50] The intellectual domestication of romanticism since the early nineteenth century has not exhausted its essential adversary nature. The 'discrimination' of romanticisms is a site of intellectual struggle; it is not an academically administered practice of classification. The general point about tradition being an area of contestation is made by Williams: 'tradition is in practice the most evident expression of the dominant and hegemonic pressures and limits. It is always more than an inert historicized segment; indeed it is the most powerful means of incorporation.'[51] This is why, to reiterate, much of the most accessible and influential work of (a) counter-hegemony is historical: the recovery of discarded areas, or the redress of selective and reductive interpretations. Thus Roszak's appropriation of the tradition of European romanticism is not historically regressive. On the contrary, given that the struggle for and against selective traditions is a crucial part of contemporary cultural struggle, he sets the romantic critique against the scientific reality principle. The elaborated version of Roszak's critique is to be found in *Where the Wasteland Ends: Politics and Transcendence in Postindustrial Society* (1973) where he defines romanticism as 'the struggle to save the reality of experience from evaporating into theoretical abstraction or disintegrating into the chaos of bare, empirical fact'.[52] For Roszak, it is by way of the critique of the 'single vision' of Newton, Bacon and Descartes that the romantics become our contemporaries.

On the level of intellectual legitimation the making of the American counter culture, in Roszak's productive cultural interpretation, has to be understood for what it is: an appropriation, reactivation and continuing of the romantic critique of the scientific world-view. This project has not to be dismissed as an outmoded act of mere romantic conservatism. Mannheim included the latter in his developmental view of the stages through which the configurations of the four forms of utopian mentality have passed in modern times: the orgiastic chiliasm of the anabaptists, the liberal-humanist idea, the conservative idea and the socialist-communist utopia.[53] Writing in the 1930s, Mannheim distinguished three alternatives open to intellectuals thrown up by the social process: affiliation with the radical wing of the socialist-communist proletariat; the destructive critique of the ideological elements in science by liberal-humanist intellectuals who have become sceptical of or have abandoned belief in the possibility of a secular utopia; and the retreat from the world and conscious renouncing of direct participation in the historical process by chiliastically-inclined intellectuals. Mannheim writes of the romanticists: 'The third group takes refuge in the past and attempts to find there an epoch of society in which an extinct form of reality-transcendence dominated the world, and through this romantic reconstruction it seeks to spiritualize the present. The same function, from this point of view, is fulfilled by attempts to revive religious feeling, idealism, symbols, and myths.'[54]

But Roszak is no conservationist intellectual seeking refuge in the cultural milieu of past romanticism. His project is the reactivation of selected romantic critiques (Blake, Goethe and Wordsworth) with the aim of intellectually legitimating visionary experience as the true nucleus of our personal being. He is not advocating a sequestered subjective idealism or the solitudinous enactment of private epiphanies for he is well aware that the conditions for visionary ex-perience are cultural and historical and therefore need to be struggled for socially. To understand Roszak's project then it is no use placing his adoption and productive interpretation of counter culture at the beginning of a chronology which culminates with the current use-in-power of counter culture within cultural studies. In his eighteenth thesis on the philosophy of history Walter Benjamin says of the historian who understands that not every historical moment or event is 'historical' (chronological) that he '. . . stops telling the sequence of events like the beads of a rosary. Instead he grasps the constellation which his own era has formed with an earlier one. Thus he established a conception of the present as the "time of the now" which is shot through with the chips of Messianic time.'[55]

The historical origin of counter culture was, as I have argued in this essay, a critical practice of intellectual legitimation (of visionary experience) and attendant delegitimation (of scientific rationality in its reductionist positivist form) in a situation of cultural disjuncture. But the possibility of this critical practice was founded on the forming of a 'fusion of horizons', to use a hermeneutic phrase,[56] between a still active residual tradition (romanticism) and an emergent alternative cultural praxis in Western society in the late 1960s. Jameson lucidly grasps the kind of understanding needed to do justice to this project. We need to be able 'to convey the sense of a hermeneutic relationship to the past which is able to grasp its own present history only on condition it manages to keep the idea of the future, and of a radical and utopian transformation, alive'.[57] Cultural studies in Britain – including mainstream academic sociology – has miserably failed to convey any such sense of the origin and radical character of counter culture as the revitalization of the romantic critique of industrial civilization. In his sixth thesis Benjamin writes: 'In every era the attempt must be made to wrest tradition away from a conformism that is about to overpower it.'[58] We can add that in every historical situation – in which a certain past reactivated in a definite present fuse together to propose a utopian image of the future – the attempt must be made to redress reductive or indifferent interpretations of cultural acts which reveal the potentialities of a certain tradition for the present; that is, that we are made aware through a historical hermeneutic reflection of our repressed and unrealized human potentialities.

In cultural studies there has been a carelessness and a casualness about discriminating the different structures of sense which have been constructed around counter culture as a radical utopian idea. Research shows that this now taken-for-granted descriptive label has been a charged ideological term accruing around it a complex of philosophical, theological, social scientific, political, aesthetic and ethical thought. It is this field of intellectual construction which has not been recognized in Britain. The shift from counter culture as label/term to the class nature of youth sub-cultural style has meant an effective goodbye to consideration of the intellectual field of counter culture. How can we account for the historical blindness of cultural studies on this score? To hazard an interpretation: during the historical moment of the emergence of counter culture as itself a cultural interpretation the problem of intellectual legitimation was foregrounded for New Left intellectuals in America. With the passing of this historical moment of emergence, which was characterized by charismatic and kerygmatic philosophizing, a phase of immediate non-recognition of this utopian thought and the reification of counter culture as emancipative idea ensued. The formalization and scientization of counter culture was an expression of the very objectivist rationality which Roszak had made his adversary. The incorporation of counter culture into cultural studies has continued this process of reification *vis-à-vis* its utopian character.

Perhaps to comprehend the visionary, kerygmatic nature of counter culture as a socially symbolic act which aims to transcend the historical conditions of its determination, a viewpoint at odds with the desacralizing sociological attitude is called for. How, overburdened with so much cultural theory and (post)modernist consciousness, can we be unashamedly 'hailed' by a form of consciousness and cultural action which aims to create a re-enchanted, sacramental view of person, body, community, whole earth and transcendence? Here we may reflect on how, in our own existential situations, we are at odds (if we are) with the society we live in, so much so that we are spurred to 'thoughts out of season' – the quintessential example in modern critical thought being Nietzsche's 'untimely meditations'. At the end of the Foreword to his essay 'On the uses and disadvantages of history for life' he sums up the significance of being a classical scholar for his self-understanding of his own historical identity:

it is only to the extent that I am a pupil of earlier times, especially the Hellenic, that though a child of the present time I was able to acquire . . . . untimely experiences. That much, however, I must concede to myself on account of my profession as a classicist: for I do not know what meaning classical studies could have for our time if they were not untimely – that is to say, acting counter to our time and, let us hope, for the benefit of a time to come.[59]

Counter culture, as romantic critique, is currently 'untimely' in late capitalism and it will probably remain so because, as a form of utopian criticism, its attempted politicization can only make it an ideology in Mannheim's sense. As presently constituted in Britain, cultural studies, whose dominant perspective is the development of a 'cultural materialism', cannot but construct an account of the socially deter-mined nature of the phenomena it studies. As the conduit mediating European theoretical modernism into British left intellectual culture – at the interface with the historical reconstruction of indigenous popular, intellectual and political traditions and institutions – cultural studies is dominated by a surfeit of what Nietzsche called the 'historical sense': 'or the capacity for divining quickly the order of rank of the evaluations according to which a people, a society, a human being has lived, the 'divinatory instinct' for the relationships of these evalua-tions, for the relation of the authority of these evaluations to the authority of effective forces.'[60] For cultural studies everything is always and already 'historical'. Everything is situated, has a position in the 'social formation', is 'constructed' in ideology and language. The devaluation which this historicizing entails is what Nietzsche means by 'historicism'. The historical sense, the sixth, ignoble sense is inexor-ably nihilistic in that it devalorizes what is of the greatest and highest value while indulging in what Nietzsche calls 'obsequious plebeian curiosity'. Theoretically, then, cultural studies is limited to the ideo-logical and factual reductions in O'Malley's meta-theoretical critique. The third reduction in O'Malley's scheme, the *transcendental* reduc-tion, is excluded from the discourse of cultural studies. To talk of 'transcendental subjectivity', 'transcendental objectivity', 'transcen-dental reflection' and 'transcendental mediation' is to introduce phenomenological philosophical terms into a mode of theoretical speech which eschews such difficult language from the perspective of cultural materialism whose political aim is transformation rather than trans-signification, which it would class as contemplative and philoso-phically idealist. The neo-positivist rationality of cultural studies is such that the vertical, rhapsodic mentation of the visionary intellect is foreign to it. In a word, it is characterized by a poverty of metaphor and an absence of poetic heart. Thus counter culture in its visionary form is anthropologically strange to it. 'The sheer surprise of a living culture is a slap to reverie . . . Real events can save us much philosophy.'[61] This is the rub: cultural studies has abrogated any attempt to 'rejoice . . . to construct something/Upon which to rejoice'.[62] Its endeavour is 'timely' in dwelling on the history of the present. Its relativist historical horizon is oblivious to what Benjamin calls 'Messianic time'. Is the latter only a heuristic theological image with no real historical content because our social and personal being has become so concrete and anti-transcendental?[63]

Nietzsche's aphorism which heads this essay is introduced in the context of discussing the genealogy of 'punishment', which he affirms has not one but many meanings: 'The whole history of punishment and of its adaptation to the most various uses has finally crystallized into a kind of complex which is difficult to break down and quite impossible to define.'[64] The same understanding applies to the concept of history, to the history of mankind and to deep thinking about the nature of historical time. In his eighteenth thesis Benjamin wrote: 'The present, which, as a model of Messianic time, comprises the entire history of mankind in an enormous abridgement, coincides exactly with the stature which the history of mankind has in the universe.'[65] The 'constellations' we form as part of the making of hermeneutically-conscious historical relationships are twofold: diachronic with a certain elected past whose reference is a potential future pregnant with the unrealized potentialities of this past; and synchronic – of a vertical, totalizing form. The two interrelated constellations of counter culture in its romantic form are the diachronic reactivation of romantic criticism as the synchronic humus of visionary experience.

The imperative always to historicize, always to situate, always to seek the historical and social determinations of a phenomenon means that the approach of cultural studies to visionary, epiphanous experience is itself pre-determined. The drive is to describe, reduce, explain through causes, through genesis or through function. The American literary-philosophical critic Geoffrey Hartman formulates the dilemma between historical situating and the genuine transcendental nature of visionary trans-signifying experience:

> With so much historical knowledge, how can we avoid historicism, or the staging of history as a drama in which epiphanic raptures are replaced by epistemic ruptures, *coupures* as decisive as Hellene and Hebrew, or Hegel and Marx. Can a history be written that does not turn into something monumental and preemptive? In *The Unmediated Vision* I described Romantic and post-Romantic poets in their struggle against mediatedness, in their desire for the kind of vision denounced by Althusser and deconstructed by Derrida, but I was unable to formulate a theory of reading that would be historical rather than historicist.[66]

As a philosophical topic, 'counter culture' raises the issue of the locus of reality. I have found the key dilemma nowhere better stated than by Barthes at the end of his essay 'Myth Today':

> . . . there is as yet only one possible choice, and this choice can bear on two extreme methods: either to posit a reality which is entirely permeable to history, and ideologize; or, conversely, to posit a reality which is *ultimately*

impenetrable, irreducible, and in this case, poeticize. In a word, I do not yet see a synthesis between ideology and poetry (by poetry I understand, in a very general way, the search for the inalienable meaning of things).[67]

The absence of a synthesis between ideology and poetry so characterized and, I would juxtapose, between historical situatedness and visionary, trans-signifying experience means, according to Barthes, that, where we have the will, we are condemned always to speak *excessively* about reality.

NOTES AND REFERENCES

1. Nietzsche, *On the Genealogy of Morals* (1887), in *On the Genealogy of Morals and Ecce Homo*, ed. W. Kaufmann, Vintage Books, New York 1967, p. 80.
2. Guy Debord, *La Societé du Spectacle*, Buchet/Chastel, Paris 1967, p. 9.
3. See John Clarke *et al.*, 'Subcultures, Cultures and Class', in *Resistance Through Rituals: Youth Subcultures in Post-War Britain*, eds. Stuart Hall and Tony Jefferson, Hutchinson 1976, p. 57 ff.; *Working Class Youth Culture*, eds Geoff Mungham and Geoff Pearson, Routledge and Kegan Paul 1976, pp. 7, 22 ff., 111–12, 115, 119; Paul Willis, *Learning to Labour: How Working-Class Kids get Working-Class Jobs*, Saxon House 1977; Mike Brake, *The Sociology of Youth Cultures and Youth Subcultures*, Routledge and Kegan Paul 1980; Richard Middleton and John Muncie, 'Pop Culture, Pop Music and Post-War Youth: Countercultures', *Open University Popular Culture Course*, Unit 20, Block 5; Paul Willis, 'Male School Counterculture', *OU Popular Culture Course*, Unit 30, Block 7; O'Sullivan *et al.*, *Key Concepts in Communication*, p. 55.
4. See Jane Thompson, *Sociology Made Simple*, Heinemann 1982, p. 124 ff. For other sociological studies of 'counter culture' in Britain during the 1970s see Frank Musgrove, *Ecstasy and Holiness: Counter Culture and the Open Society*, Methuen 1974; Kenneth Leech, *Youthquake: Spirituality and the Growth of a Counter-Culture*, Sphere/Abacus 1976; Frank Musgrove, with Roger Middleton and Pat Hawes, *Margins of the Mind*, Methuen 1977; David Martin, *The Dilemmas of Contemporary Religion*, Blackwell 1978; and Bernice Martin, *A Sociology of Contemporary Cultural Change*, Blackwell 1981.
5. See *The Dissenting Academy: Essays Criticizing the Teaching of the Humanities in American Universities*, ed. Theodore Roszak, Penguin 1969. For a collection of bizarre, iconoclastic and perverse countercultural writings see Jo Berke *et al.*, *Counter Culture: The Creation of an Alternative Society*, Peter Owen 1969.
6. Aldous Huxley, 'On the Charms of History and the Future of the Past' (1931), in *Music at Night and Other Essays*, Penguin 1950, p. 95.
7. Robert Wistrich, 'Viewpoint', *The Times Literary Supplement* (4 April 1980), p. 387.
8. Lefebvre, 'What is the Historical Past?', *New Left Review*, No. 90 (1975),

p. 34. For the view which proposes that the duties of the radical historian are (1) to suggest to the protagonists of the present new alternatives for action and (2) to project alternative futures on the basis of the richness of past experience see Staughton Lynd, 'Historical Present and Existential Past', in ed. Roszak, pp. 87–101.

9. John O'Malley, *Sociology of Meaning,* Human Context Books 1972, p. 41. These three reductions roughly correspond to Edmund Husserl's 'philosophic', 'phenomenological' and 'transcendental' reductions respectively.

10. For the perspective on reification which informs this essay see Burke C. Thomason, *Making Sense of Reification: Alfred Schutz and Constructionist Theory,* Foreword by Tom Bottomore, Macmillan 1982.

11. O'Sullivan *et al.*, p. 55.

12. Pierre Vilar, 'Marxist History, a History in the Making: Towards a Dialogue with Althusser', *New Left Review*, No. 80 (1973), pp. 84 and 103.

13. For a perspective on the historical obsolescence of ideas which deploys the 'negative dialectics' of critical theory see Russell Jacoby, *Social Amnesia: A Critique of Conformist Psychology,* Harvester 1977.

14. The distinction between the 'romantic' and 'classical' infrastructures of social science is developed by Alvin Gouldner in his essay 'Romanticism and Classicism: Deep Structures in Social Science', in *For Sociology: Renewal and Critique in Sociology Today,* Penguin 1975, pp. 323–66.

15. Roszak, *The Making of a Counter Culture: Reflections on the Technocratic Society and its Youthful Opposition,* Faber 1970.

16. Fredric Jameson, 'Marxism and Historicism', *New Literary History,* XI (1979/80), 43.

17. See Althusser, 'Marxism is not a Historicism', in *Reading Capital,* trans. Ben Brewster, New Left Books 1970, pp. 119–44.

18. Jameson, p. 70.

19. Williams, *Marxism and Literature*, p. 116.

20. Clifford Adelman, *Generations: A Collage on Youthcult,* Penguin 1973, p. 55.

21. Carl Oglesby, 'Notes for a Decade Ready for the Dustbin', in *The Movement Toward a New America: The Beginnings of a Long Revolution (A Collage) A What?* assembled by Mitchell Goodman, A Charter Member of the Great Conspiracy on behalf of the Movement, Pilgrim Press, Philadelphia Pa., Knopf, New York 1970, p. 738.

22. Parts of chapters I, II, IV, V and VI of *The Making of a Counter Culture* first appeared in a series of four articles published in the liberal-left weekly *The Nation* in March and April 1968. These four *Nation* articles were completed in November 1967 but *The Making* was not published until September 1969. The facts of chronology are important for an accurate interpretation of the *raison d'être* of *The Making* and its historical moment of writing. Less than a month after the final *Nation* article appeared the events of May 1968 in France occurred. Roszak subsequently included reference to these in his book (pp. 2–5, 68). Between November 1967 and September 1969 the shift from the historical moment when students/ middle-class youth were considered an emergent unincorporated alternative and/or oppositional culture to its incorporation and fragmentation had started to take place. The escalation of political and cultural events during this climactic moment led to oppression by the American state. The

inflammatory attempts to meet this oppression with violence by both the white and black movements led to the break-up of the official nationwide students' organization SDS (Students for a Democratic Society), the emergence of the Weather People, the forced fusion of macho-theatre politics with hippie ideology (the 'yippies'), the gradual emergence of the women's movement as a new social base for alternative and oppositional cultural and political projects and the retreat into the communes.

23. Roszak, *The Making*, p. xii.
24. Marcuse, *An Essay on Liberation*, Allen Lane 1969, pp. 56–7.
25. Bottomore, *Critics of Society: Radical Thought in North America*, Allen and Unwin 1969, p. 122.
26. Williams, 'Base and Superstructure in Marxist Cultural Theory' (1973) in *Problems in Materialism and Culture*, pp. 31–49.
27. Roszak, *The Making*, p. 43.
28. Roszak, *The Making*, p. 42.
29. Williams, 'Base and Superstructure', p. 39.
30. Williams, 'Base and Superstructure', p. 40.
31. On the topic of pastoral and counter-pastoral see Williams, *The Country and the City*, Chatto 1973, pp. 12–34; and Julian Moynahan, 'Pastoralism as Culture and Counter-Culture in English Fiction, 1800–1928 – From a View to Death', in *Towards a Poetics of Fiction*, ed. M. Spilka, Indiana University Press, Bloomington, Indiana 1977, pp. 239–54.
32. Williams, 'Base and Superstructure', pp. 41–2.
33. Roszak, *The Making*, p. 42.
34. Karl Mannheim, 'The Problem of Generations', in *Essays in the Sociology of Knowledge*, ed. P. Kecskemeti, Routledge and Kegan Paul 1952.
35. Roszak, *The Making*, p. 40.
36. Roszak, *The Making*, p. xii.
37. Roszak, *The Making*, p. 33.
38. Roszak, *The Making*, p. 47.
39. For the interpretation that the commercialization of 'counter culture' was incompatible with the very property system on which the commercial media were themselves grounded, see Alvin Gouldner, *The Dialectic of Ideology and Technology: The Origins, Grammar and Future of Ideology*, Macmillan 1976, pp. 110–11, 157; and Irwin Silber, *The Culture Revolution: A Marxist Analysis*, Times Change Press, New York 1970.
40. Williams, *The Long Revolution*, p. 65.
41. For an explanation of the failure of sociologists to foresee the emergence of radical youth culture *qua* counter culture see David Schichor, 'The Counter-Culture: Why was Sociology Taken by Surprise?', in *Youth Unrest*, ed. G. Shohan, Jerusalem Academic Press, Jerusalem 1976, pp. 182–97.
42. Charles Reich, *The Greening of America*, Allen Lane 1971, p. 160.
43. For a brief comparative note on Roszak and Reich see R. Serge Denisoff and M. D. Pugh, 'Roszak and Reich Return to the Garden: A Note', in *Theories and Paradigms in Contemporary Sociology*, eds. M. H. Levine and O. Callahan, Peacock, Itasca, Illinois 1974, pp. 426–30; and for an empirical test of their respective characterizations of youth culture which found that neither conceptual schema was verifiable see Denisoff and Pugh, 'Consciousness III or Counter-culture: A Preliminary Study', *Youth*

and Society, V, 4 (1974), 397–410. Their conclusion is that Mannheim's generational analysis is more appropriate to the understanding of the phenomenon of 'counter culture'/'Consciousness III' than impressionistic ideal-type images. For the immediate reception of Reich in America see *The Con III Controversy: The Critics Look at the Greening of America,* ed. P. Nobile, Pocket Books, New York 1971. A Soviet critic of New Left ideology, Eduard Batalov, referred to both Roszak and Reich as sociologists and to Roszak as a 'left bourgeois ideologist': see *The Philosophy of Revolt: Criticism of Left Radical Ideology,* trans. K. Judelson, Progress Publishers, Moscow 1973, pp. 55–56, 212.

44. Reich, p. 11.
45. Williams, *Long Revolution,* p. 67.
46. Adelman, p. 45.
47. Gunter Remmling, *The Sociology of Karl Mannheim,* Routledge and Kegan Paul 1975, p. 43.
48. For the thesis that there is a fundamental opposition between poetry and sociology see J. P. Ward, *Poetry and the Sociological Idea,* Harvester 1981; and for a positive attempt to formulate a 'cognitive aesthetics' for social inquiry see R. H. Brown, *A Poetic for Sociology: Towards a Logic of Discovery for the Human Sciences,* Cambridge University Press 1974.
49. The struggle to establish a counter-selective tradition is a crucial part of the intellectual delegitimation of a dominant selective tradition. In the case of the American counter culture see *Counter-Tradition: A Reader in the Literature of Dissent and Alternatives,* ed. S. Delaney, Basic Books, New York 1971; and Michael Horovitz, *A Freak's Anthology: Being Golden Hits from Buddha to Kubrick,* Sherbourne Press, Los Angeles 1972.
50. For his part, Roszak was responsible for two anthologies as contributions to the formation of a counter-selective tradition: *Masculine/Feminine: Readings in Sexual Mythology and the Liberation of Man,* ed. with Betty Roszak, Harper and Row, New York 1969; and *Sources: An anthology of contemporary materials for preserving personal sanity while braving the great technological wilderness,* ed., Harper and Row, New York 1972.
51. Williams, *Long Revolution,* p. 115.
52. Roszak, *Where the Wasteland Ends: Politics and Transcendence in Post-industrial Society,* Faber 1973, p. 278.
53. Mannheim, *Ideology and Utopia: An Introduction to the Sociology of Knowledge,* Routledge and Kegan Paul 1960, p. 190 ff. For an application of Mannheim's categories of 'ideology' and 'utopia' to the vicissitudes of European student movements see Gianni Statera, *Death of Utopia: The Development and Decline of Student Movements in Europe,* Oxford University Press 1975. For an analysis of chiliasm as a counter cultural theme see Michael Y. Bodeman, 'Mystical, Satanic and Chiliastic Forces in Countercultural Movements: Changing the World or Reconciling it'. *Youth and Society,* V, 4 (1974), 433–47; and for an interpretation of chiliasm in the context of the anarchistic protest of youth see James Joll. 'Anarchism – a Living Tradition', in *Anarchism Today,* eds. D. E. Apter and Joll, Macmillan 1971, p. 224. For socialism in its utopian mode considered as a counter culture see Zygmunt Bauman, *Socialism The Active Utopia,* Allen and Unwin 1976, p. 47 and ch. 8; and for intellectual opposition to the oppressive *status quo* in Russian society interpreted as

counter culture see Howard L. Biddulph, 'Soviet Intellectual Dissent as a Political Counter-Culture', *Western Political Quarterly*, XXV, 3 (1972), 522–33.

54. Mannheim, *Ideology and Utopia*, p. 233.
55. Benjamin, 'Theses on the Philosophy of History', in *Illuminations*, p. 265.
56. 'Fusion of horizon' (*Horizonverschmelzung*): 'it is part of real understanding that the concepts of a historical past are regained in such a way that they include, at the same time, our own' (Hans Georg Gadamer quoted in Joseph Bleicher, *Contemporary Hermeneutics: Hermeneutics as Method, Philosophy and Critique*, Routledge and Kegan Paul 1980, p. 267).
57. Jameson, p. 72.
58. Benjamin, p. 257.
59. Nietzsche, *Untimely Meditations*, trans. R. J. Hollingdale, Cambridge University Press 1983, p. 60.
60. Nietzsche, *Untimely Meditations*, p. 133.
61. Willis, *Profane Culture*, Routledge and Kegan Paul 1978, p. 1.
62. T. S. Eliot, 'Ash Wednesday', in *Selected Poems*, Faber 1954, p. 83.
63. For discussions on the topic of counter culture and transcendence see Jackson W. Carrol, 'Transcendence and Mystery in the Counter Culture', *Religion in Life*, XLII (1973), 361–75; Robert A. Evans, *Belief and the Counter Culture: A Guide to Constructive Confrontation*, The Westminster Press, Philadelphia, Pa. 1971, ch. 6; Roszak, *The Making*, p. 137 ff. and ch. 10; and F. X. Shea, 'Reason and Religion of the Counter-Culture', *Harvard Theological Review*, No. 66 (1973), pp. 95–111. For a contribution relevant to the kind of 'historicist' approach advocated in this essay see Martin Schiff, 'Neo-transcendentalism in the New Left Counter-Culture: A Vision of the Future Looking Back', *Comparative Studies in Society and History*, XV, 2 (1973), 130–42.
64. Nietzsche, *Genealogy of Morals*, p. 212.
65. Benjamin, p. 265.
66. Geoffrey H. Hartman, *Saving the Text: Literature/Derrida/Philosophy*, Johns Hopkins University Press, Baltimore, Md. 1981, p. xx.
67. Barthes, 'Myth Today', in *Mythologies*, pp. 158–59.

Chapter 10

GENDER, EDUCATION AND CHANGE

EILEEN AIRD

It has been convincingly demonstrated by now that girls are seriously and systematically disadvantaged within education from their earliest years in playgroups to their entry into the more rarefied atmosphere of university courses.[1] This disadvantage manifests itself in a number of ways, some of which are only too obvious, others subtler and often unrecognized both by the majority of teachers, even women teachers, and the majority of pupils. Curriculum content and design epitomize the more overt forms of discrimination in their forcing of sexist choices of subject. The debate about this issue should not focus on whether all girls do a little token woodwork and all boys try their hand at cookery, but on the more important question of the criteria governing the selection of O- and A-level subject clusters. Girls still concentrate on the humanities and social sciences and boys still elect to study mathematics and the sciences with all the attendant career implications of such choices. In a society which is apparently choosing to narrow its higher educational opportunities at a point in time when applications from girls are still not equalling those from boys, unless girls choose to enter non-traditional degree courses such as engineering, technology and the applied sciences, the number of places open to them in higher education will remain static or even contract.

The structuring and organization of school life both inside and outside the classroom also disadvantages girls by constantly re-inforcing the gender differentiations which characterize wider social structures. The infant school which groups boys' lockers on one side of the room, girls' on the other and which gives each child a pictorial symbol from a range which includes cars, trains and aeroplanes for boys and flowers, ballet dancers and fairy tale queens for girls, is underlining, not only that girls must be grouped separately from their four-year-old male counterparts, but is also stressing that different assumptions and expectations are relevant to each group. Such a school, and there are many of them, will almost certainly still be using a reading scheme which emphasizes activity, adventure and variety as integral to male experience, and passivity, domesticity and rootedness as integral to female experience. In many of the more old-fashioned reading schemes still in use in infant and junior schools girls are presented with images of women considerably more limited than those available to them in actuality. What are they to make of the contradictions in a world where mother works full time, their woman teacher drives away from school in her own car and they see a female school doctor, yet they are learning to read, one of the most significant skills of cultural signposting, from material which offers no reflection of this reality? It seems unlikely that at five or six they will rationalize the contradiction by recognizing that their reading material is out of date. It is much more likely that they will begin to learn that assumptions about gender identity are disturbingly unrelated to their own feelings, needs and expectations; that there is little correspondence between their experiences as women and the cultural definitions of femininity available. This split is widened in secondary schools where the arts and social science curriculum is likely to concentrate on works by and about men. So that in literature lessons if women writers are studied, Jane Austen and Charlotte Brontë being obvious examples, there is no emphasis on their concerns as women writers within a male tradition. It is much more likely that in enlightened schools there will be a class rather than a gender analysis allowing the trivialization of Jane Austen because she dealt only with the middle classes, and her appropriation into the ranks of moral ironists, with no attention paid to her insights into the class and gender circumscriptions of female identity.

There are more serious and fundamental reinforcements of gender differentiation taking place daily in our classrooms in less obvious but potentially even more damaging ways. Evidence is accumulating which indicates that for numerous reasons teachers of either sex are likely to give more attention to boys than girls.[2] Boys are often livelier and more persistently demanding of attention: they have learnt the lesson of active engagement since birth. It is assumed that they need to do as well as possible in the educational system in order to get a job and earn enough money to support a family. It is also and wrongly often assumed that they are brighter and will automatically achieve higher grades in academic work than girls. Conversely girls are expected to be better-behaved and quieter than boys. It is hoped that they will be more helpful and compliant than most boys and therefore can be safely left to get on with work on their own. Because it is assumed that girls always have the possibility of marriage and motherhood as a central vocational choice less emphasis is often placed on their academic and career aspirations. Michelle Stanworth has pointed out that both men and women teachers consistently underestimate girls' abilities and also have lower expectations of their future careers than they have of boys' futures.[3] This means, she argues, that teachers 'will always be reluctant to make girls prime candidates for attention in the classroom'. So the subtle and hidden differentiations of attention, verbal nuance and facial expression reinforce gender distinctions, and girls have to learn how to cope with both overt and insidious prejudice.

Carol Buswell's work reveals that this mechanism of selective attention may function particularly forcefully in the crucial stage of early adolescence when it is further complicated by class factors.[4] Teachers have even lower expectations of working-class than of middle-class girls. Girls between thirteen and sixteen are in the main struggling with the physiological, psychological and emotional changes implicated in the adolescent rite of passage from girlhood to womanhood in a patriarchal society. Their desire to be the subject of their own lives, a desire which initially belongs to all infancies however severely restricted, will have already encountered frustrations and deflections in their earlier school experiences. They now meet serious educational disadvantage at a time when they are also learning what it is to be sexually objectified. To the inequalities involved in gender are now added the complexities of an adult sexual identity, and it is small wonder that at this stage many girls simply give up and stop trying to claim attention from teachers whose energies, both positive and negative, are directed elsewhere. Girls' ambitions and aspirations for their own futures may now be deflected into interest in their boyfriends' futures. The prophecy that girls will not do as well as boys because their energy is directed towards marriage and motherhood becomes self-fulfilling.

Disadvantage accumulates and as Eileen Byrne has demonstrated working-class girls from a rural background are statistically much less likely to reach the sixth form or enter higher education than are middle-class boys from a city school.[5] There is simply too much for those girls to contend with unless they are particularly well supported by family, friends and teachers. Support in the educational system tends, though, to be extended to children at either end of a spectrum: to those who are already advantaged by ability, personality or aspiration and to those who have severe learning difficulties or are seen as disruptive. In under-staffed, over-crowded schools without an educational policy of positive discrimination on the grounds of gender, class and race the only girls likely to receive active and systematic emotional sustenance are either those who are both unusually able and unusually confident – the combination is important as ability in girls so often goes unrecognized – or those who are equally distinctive by virtue of their difficulties, either academic or behavioural. While this is also true of boys it is obviously the case, for all the reasons already outlined, that it will apply more extremely to girls. To recognize these factors is only the first step in the drive to change them and we need now to turn our attention to a definition and implementation of change.

Although changes in the school system are only coming about slowly there has been faster progress in the development of women's courses in adult education. Work has been building up during the last decade to the point where most Workers' Educational Association districts, many extramural departments and increasingly some local education authorities offer women's studies courses. The format, design and aims of these courses are many and varied and include theoretical courses which develop an analysis of women's oppression from an interdisciplinary perspective; courses of the 'New Opportunities for Women' type which combine several aims; and very informally structured groups which explore the lives of women as they are experienced daily. The great strengths of the adult education system are its ability functionally to respond rapidly to real demands and its philosophical commitment to developing new areas of work. It is no accident that the expansion of women's studies in adult education has taken place during the decade which has seen the growth of the women's movement in Britain. The changes which have taken place in this work have reflected some of the changing debates within the women's movement.

Broadly speaking there has been a change from liberal and utilitarian aims to radical ones. The first adult education women's studies courses in this country began in the first years of the 1970s and were represented by two different types of course: the theoretical women's studies course which developed a critique of existing social and political structures and the 'Fresh Horizons'/'NOW' type of course which combined a number of elements in a longer course. The NOW courses in their first manifestation were primarily concerned with access and confidence. The assumption was that if women gained access to educational and vocational opportunities usually assumed to be more accessible to men then previous educational and occupational disadvantage would be transcended and women would take their rightful place in a man's world. To achieve this end it was recognized that women needed to gain greater confidence in their abilities. NOW courses consequently combined a number of elements which might include intellectual and academic work, career and educational advice and information, and some work designed to boost women's self-confidence.

This body of work was radical when compared to the typical liberal adult education class, which is subject based, assumes academic neutrality as not only achievable but actually desirable, and eschews personal disclosure in favour of a formal insistence on the development of logical and ordered insights into knowledge. Knowledge is felt to be external to the lives and experiences of students. Many of the early women's studies courses were viewed with great suspicion and even hostility from within the entrenchments of conservative adult education, gaining credence and respectability only when it was discovered that they attracted large new audiences of younger students into classes. As they were originally envisaged, though, these courses still belonged to a liberal or even a utilitarian educational tradition for they were based on a theory of disadvantage which sought to equalize rather than to change. Success in such courses was judged either by the usual criteria of student numbers and staying power or in quantifiable terms such as entry to higher education or to jobs.

The intentions of the courses were innovative in that they sought to draw into adult education groups of students who, in terms of age, education and class, would not usually seek adult education provision. The structuring of the courses also indicated a departure from established practice in the combination of academic work with elements of advice, information and counselling about future directions. These future directions were conceptualised however within the existing *status quo*. The courses were informed by a desire to help women to gain advantages not easily available to them but without necessarily developing a critique of the reasons for this disadvantage. They were extremely important courses from which women gained a great deal and which led directly to change for individuals. They offered women the possibility of studying in a context directly tailored to their needs in terms of hours, teaching style and content. The prime motivation of the courses though was still that of the liberal educational system in placing the emphasis on the individual and developing no analysis which would have given a context for individual experience. Towards the end of the decade it became clear that a shift in theoretical understanding was taking place from the establishment of access to an insistence on the need for change.

The earlier courses did offer a theory of change but it was seen as reformist rather than fundamental and it did not question the wider social institutions or the psychological structures within which women live. This theory assumed that women have not had equal access to educational and job opportunities by accident rather than design, it expected that most women would be married mothers who would place their roles as wife and mother high on their list of vocational priorities and so it did not seriously question the theories of female identity available to women. Nevertheless these courses established a groundwork for choice in women's lives and eradicated most of the gross inequalities of structure and attitude at work in the school system. Since many of the courses were only open to women students and were mostly taught by women tutors, students had the experience of being in a purposive all-female group. Women, of course, particularly if they are at home with children, spend a good deal of time in all-female groupings but may not necessarily recognize the strength of such relationships for they fall into the interstices of family life which is seen to take place when mother, father and children are together and to be somehow held in abeyance during the daytime when men are at work outside the home and women wait within it. Such is the prevailing ideology although the actuality is that many women are also at work outside the home, either through choice or necessity. The NOW courses offer women an exit from the home to an environment where they could concentrate on themselves rather than others. They also and very significantly give the opportunity for recognition of the similarities in women's lives across class, educational and occupational differences.

It is clear from reading the accounts women have written about the impact of such courses on their lives that their effects are far-reaching and include personal changes as well as educational and vocational choices. The following statement is typical of those made by women at the end of the course: 'I feel that it has enabled me to look at my life from a different perspective and has given me courage and confidence to be me. I feel that I have gone through some sort of metamorphosis. I like the new me better.' The change this woman describes as having taken place concerns identity and autonomy. To understand how and why such change can come about we need to look to psychoanalytic accounts of personality development as well as to the sociology of education.

Freud's theory of Oedipal development is asymmetrical in its conceptualisation of the processes at work in the acquisition of gender identity. Boys, he argued, make a relatively straightforward transition from love of the mother, who is the primary attachment figure for both boys and girls, to the love of other women. This transference from one woman, the mother, to other women, particularly the wife, is effected by way of the castration complex. The boy fears that he has entered into an unequal rivalry with his father for his mother's affection which, unless he renounces his claim to his mother's attention, will result in punitive mutilation at the hands of his father. This will reduce the boy to the inferior status of his mother whom he already understands to be a castrated man. The implications of this theory involve not only men's emotional dependence on women but also their fearful distrust of men, although these are features which are rarely highlighted in discussions of Oedipal theory. Men are left in an uneasy identification, with other men fixed as potential rivals and judges and an ambivalent reliance on women which includes emotional dependence, sexual desire and a sense of moral superiority – in Freudian psychology men are considered to have more developed superegos than women. The acquisition of both male and female gender identity necessitates, in classical psychoanalytic theory, the knowledge of inequality and is always tainted with an ambivalence of feeling and attitude which is culturally manifested as well as personally experienced.

The acquisition of female gender identity is not understood by Freud to involve the same degree of ambivalence towards the opposite sex but instead includes hostility from girls to mothers, women to women. Escape from what is seen as the early claustrophobic intensity of the girl's infantile dependence on her mother is achieved through the transference of attachment from the mother to the father and thence to other men. Oedipal theory becomes very confused though when we try to ascertain the processes of this transference. Freud describes the pre-Oedipal phase in girls as being masculine in character because it involves active libidinal seeking and object-love of the mother. This must be relinquished in favour of a biological destiny of passivity symbolized by the replacement of the clitoris as the main erotogenic zone by 'the truly feminine vagina' and by attachment to the father as the main object. Freud saw but, because of the overwhelming burden of his own cultural prejudices, failed to understand the significance of the girl's relationship with her mother: 'we get an impression that we cannot understand women unless we appreciate this phase of their pre-Oedipal attachment to their mother'.

In his essay on 'Femininity',[6] the last and most important discussion of female identity he formulated, Freud doesn't offer a clear conceptualisation of the movement from pre-Oedipal to Oedipal affection in girls but simply states that it is observed to happen and to be accompanied not only by renunciation of the initial attachment to the mother but also by the development of hostility. This remains a part of the girl's relationship to her mother from then on, and by extension is assumed to be a part of all relationships between women. He considers but rejects, because they are not specific to girls but refer generally to inevitable infantile frustrations, various possible passages from pre-Oedipal to Oedipal stages, but finally develops a theory of the castration complex. This is complementary but not analogous to the male castration complex. The latter is brought about by the boy's perception of his mother's body as castrated and his fear that he will suffer the same ignominious fate. In a girl, Freud argues, the castration complex is initiated by penis envy, 'which will leave ineradicable traces on her development and the formation of their character and which will not be surmounted in even the most favourable cases without a severe expenditure of psychical energy'. Indeed he argues later in the essay that penis envy is rarely completely resolved. A sense of her own clitoral inferiority leads the girl to renounce the clitoris in favour of the vagina and to hate her mother, who like all women is now seen as castrated, for not conferring on her the longed-for penis. The girl now turns from the mother who has deprived her of a penis to the father who may supply one, and this transition is accompanied by a turning away from the activity of the phallic phase into the resolution into feminine passivity. Freud sees the Oedipus stage as a moment of peace for girls in their passage from the misleading activity of infancy to the achieved passivity of mature femininity: 'the girl is driven out of her attachment to her mother through the influence of her envy for the penis and she enters the Oedipus situation as into a haven of refuge'. The Oedipal phase in girls lasts longer than in boys and according to Freud may never be completely resolved, even with the birth of a son who is the only legitimate provider of the penis the woman has envied.

The whole shaky edifice of this argument relies on the theory of penis envy and clitoral inferiority and it is hardly surprising that so revolutionary a thinker as Freud undoubtedly was ended on a more acceptable note of doubt and uncertainty:

> That is all I had to say to you about femininity. It is certainly incomplete fragmentary and does not always sound friendly. But do not forget that I have only been describing women in so far as their nature is determined by their sexual function. It is true that that influence extends very far; but we do not overlook the fact that an individual woman may be a human being in other respects as well. If you want to know more about femininity, inquire from your own experiences of life, or turn to the poets, or wait until science can give you deeper and more coherent information.

This deeper and more coherent information is now available. Melanie Klein and the object-relations school of psychology reinstated the mother as the important attachment figure in the lives of both boys and girls. The practical work of W. H. Masters and Virginia Johnson established the clitoris as the main erotogenic zone in women. The theorizing of recent feminist therapists such as Nancy Chodhorow[7] and Luise Eichenbaum and Susie Orbach[8] has emphasized the extent to which Freud's theories of femininity never broke free from the patriarchal straitjacket of their cultural context, which denied women's autonomy. A much more fruitful way of considering the development of female identity might be to see that pre-Oedipal attachments are not given up in favour of Oedipal attachments but remain alongside them. This means that women are psychologically attuned to both men and women, although their nurturing capacities are culturally channelled in the direction of men and children rather than towards each other.

Chodhorow develops a socio-psychological theory of the acquisition of gender identity which shows women to be more capable of relationship with others within our culture than are men. She argues that this system is self-perpetuating because of the emphasis placed on women's mothering: 'Because women are themselves mothered by women, they grow up with the relational capacities and needs and psychological definition of self-in-relationship, which commits them to mothering. Men, because they are mothered by women, do not. Women mother daughters who, when they become women, mother.' Women's greater capacity for relationship is directed towards the perpetuation of a system which guarantees male economic independence and female economic dependence. It also involves men's emotional dependence on women, whose own dependency needs are frequently unmet.

I want now to take this point of Chodhorow's about women's greater capacity for relationship and particularly for nurturing relationships and apply it to the processes of a NOW course. The relationship between tutor and students in a women's studies course is a complex one. Tutors are rôle models for students, providing a living example of the possibility of activity for women and epitomizing self-direction as it is described by Adrienne Rich in 'Claiming an Education'[9]: 'The difference between a life lived actively, and a life of passive drifting and dispersal of energies, is an immense difference. Once we begin to feel committed to our lives, responsible to ourselves, we can never again be satisfied with the old, passive way.' The relationship also includes identification and dependency. Although the tutor has educational and career advantages that most of her students do not have and is seen to be acting autonomously as teacher, organizer, counsellor, this is in some senses illusory for like her students she is a woman living in a patriarchal society. Her life is constrained by the same pressures which constrain her students' lives and will often be bound by the same dilemmas of multiple commitments. The identification between tutor and students is of a different order from the them-us relationship which characterizes most tutor-student exchanges. Instead tutor and student are linked together by the same experience and self-knowledge and the identificatory process is one of mutuality. This is a major strength of women's studies courses in demystifying the relationship between tutor and student. This is as central an aspect of the learning generated by such courses as that which takes place through the demystifying of academic processes.

The third and most important aspect of the relationship between tutor and student is one of dependency and this needs particularly careful handling as it is in danger of blurring into identification. Chodorow has argued that the mother in a patriarchal culture produces daughters who mother and sons who don't. This makes the relationship between mother and daughter one fraught with particular pressures and distortions. It is the mother who mediates to her daughter rôle of denial, self-constraint and service which she knows has limited her own life and which will equally limit her daughter's life. It is this ambivalence of nurturing and yet curbing which excludes positive identification between mother and daughter, rather than penis envy or castration complex. The lesson which girls progressively learn from other women is that their own dependency needs may remain largely unmet because of their role as nurturer of men and children. The main identification between women can then become that of mutual nurturers of others and the support and caring which women offer each other in daily actuality is culturally devalued, because it is always seen as secondary and coincidental to the real tasks of a woman's life.

When women come to a women's studies course they become members of an all-female group offering nurturing of women as the primary objective. The intention of this nurturing is importantly different from the intentions of mothers who mediate to their daughters the gender roles of patriarchy. Dependency in a women's studies group is likely, initially, to be operating at an intense level because of the accumulation of unmet needs which fifteen women bring with them. The strategy by which these needs are met is one of mutual nurturing, for balancing the dependency in the group is a reservoir of caring skills built up among a group of women over a number of years of adult life. Initially it is likely that the tutor will have to hold the dependency of the whole group and of individuals. As the weeks go by and trust grows among the women a network of responsive caring will be established which diffuses and meets individual needs. The process is internal to the group, and is not primarily focussed on shaping women to external roles but on an equal recognition of need, ability, self-image and aspiration. The movement is from the dependency of the early weeks of the course, when many women are frightened of committing themselves to exploration and perhaps change, to the independency of the final weeks of the course when choice becomes possible. This widening of horizons is achieved not just through the acquisition of intellectual skills and a theoretical perspective, important though these are, not through the confidence which allows women to claim access to a man's world, but rather it comes about through women's nurturing of women.

Women's studies courses seek to reverse the deprivations which mothering of women by women inevitably entails in a society which does not give equal value to men's and women's aspirations and needs. Change comes about through a complicated process of identification and the acceptance of mutual dependencies which involves the whole group of women. The group objective is the growth of autonomy in individual members and the dynamic is one of support and commitment directed towards independence. The self-image which is generated is one of positive identification with the strengths and power of other women. This transcends the more negative bonding in inferiority which can characterize women's groupings which are not overtly defined as women-centred. Students often recognize this positive identification as the greatest gain of the course and the following statements by NOW students at the end of their course reveal not only an acceptance of the similarity of the problems encountered by all women, but also a confident knowledge that the nurturing of women by women leads to change:

> I was feeling rather depressed at the beginning of September but as a result largely of getting to know and converse with others on the course, I now have a much more positive attitude to life and the future.

> When I started the NOW course I had been on my own as a single parent for almost 12 months and was still floundering around thinking how empty life was. Coming to the course and sharing my and other women's experiences of life has helped me to see myself through a different pair of eyes.

The different pair of eyes offers a solider image of self but also scans a world which may now seem open to definition, shaping and choice. The agency of this movement towards autonomy is the experience of being supported by other women in establishing oneself at the centre of one's own life and supporting other women in achieving this for themselves. The feelings of neediness, emptiness and loss which many women experience are replaced by a confident sense of self as valuable and valued because each woman in the group has at some point in the course benefited from the nurturing skills of the other women. The ambivalent relationship with the mother, which sought both to protect the daughter from the inequalities of patriarchy and to bend her to sustain them, is replaced by the encouragement of women by women to grow into their own strength.

NOTES AND REFERENCES

1. See Eileen Byrne, *Women and Education*, Tavistock 1978; *Learning to Lose*, eds Dale Spender and Elizabeth Sarah, The Women's Press 1980; Michelle Stanworth, *Gender and Schooling*, Hutchinson in association with the Explorations in Feminism Collective 1983.
2. Stanworth, pp. 25–33; and eds Spender and Sarah.
3. Stanworth, p. 28.
4. Carol Buswell, 'Sexism in School Routines and Classroom Practice' *Durham and Newcastle Research Review*, IX (1981), 195–200.
5. Byrne, pp. 53–54.
6. Freud, *New Introductory Lectures on Psychoanalysis* (1933), in *Standard Edition* XXII, 112–35.
7. Nancy Chodorow, *The Reproduction of Mothering: Psychoanalysis and the Sociology of Gender*, University of California Press, Berkeley 1978.
8. Luise Eichenbaum and Susie Orbach, *Outside In Inside Out*, Penguin 1982.
9. Adrienne Rich, *On Lies, Secrets, Silence*, Virago 1980.

Chapter 11

RACISM IN SCHOOL TEXTBOOKS

DAVID WRIGHT

Activity in schools is difficult to analyse: every classroom is different, and many classrooms are private places, where an outsider alters the atmosphere. However, the analysis of published materials for schools is an activity open to anyone, and, if carefully handled, it can provide insight. It is also a surprisingly neglected field; yet analysis of this type is of considerable value for understanding contemporary culture. The authors of textbooks are both transmitting the material they feel is worthwhile for students, and also – consciously or unconsciously – they are transmitting attitudes and values. These attitudes and values reflect the authors' view of the world, and also – consciously or unconsciously – they shape the attitudes and values of the pupils. And, while discovering these two elements in a study of school resources, you will also discover something of how your own attitudes were shaped when you were a pupil at school. The examples which follow suggest some possible approaches to individual studies.

The study of geography textbooks can be particularly rewarding for several reasons. Firstly, large numbers of textbooks are published, since almost all pupils study geography at some stage; by contrast, sociology is a minority option in schools. Secondly, most authors of geography books are not as self-consciously aware of the problems of bias, or of class-bound attitudes, as are the authors of sociology texts. Thirdly, topics tackled include items such as race, which are highly significant for the study of contemporary culture. Although the examples developed here are critical of the books studied, the comments are not meant as destructive criticism: the books in question are in most respects good books, by good authors. The authors are not being deliberately racist: the racism in the books is accidental, even if alarming. The books are used to illustrate how authors' attitudes shape their books, and hence help to shape pupils' attitudes.

Textbook analysis, I should add, is in its infancy. Although there is an International Textbook Research Institute at Brunswick, West Germany, with its own journal (*Internationale Schulbuchforschung*), the research articles in that journal are dominated by the description of errors of fact. Elsewhere, much of the criticism of textbooks has been by individuals strongly committed to a particular political viewpoint, who select sentences from old or out-of-date books to 'prove' how wrong the textbooks are. The examples which follow can therefore also be seen as attempts to move textbook analysis away from domination by factual accuracy on one hand, or domination by an ideological viewpoint on the other hand. This essay thus invites you, the reader, not to read the 'authoritative' findings of an expert, but to engage in thinking about how to analyse textbooks for their hidden significance in both describing and shaping contemporary cultural attitudes.

The two examples here use different methods. Both seek to be fair, but neither seeks objectivity: the personality and viewpoint of the author are not suppressed, but are expressed in different ways. The first example concerns race *per se*, and raises the following topics:

1. the mere lip-service paid to UN declarations that are signed by the UK government
2. the contrast between the high ideals expressed in authors' prefaces and publishers' blurbs and the actual content of the books
3. the authors' fascination with the minor physical differences in *homo sapiens*
4. the lack of sensitivity to the UK's multicultural society
5. the unchanging nature of some statements presented in school
6. the relative lack of criticism of school textbooks, and of the values they convey. Pupils, teachers, and parents seem surprisingly unaware of bias in textbooks.

If it is accepted that attitudes to race are a vital element of today's society, it follows that what pupils learn about race is a vital issue for today's schools and teachers, and it is worth citing the UNESCO resolution on Education for International Understanding which was signed by the UK government in 1974: 'Member states should promote appropriate measures to ensure that educational aids, especially textbooks, are free from elements liable to give rise to misunderstanding, mistrust, racialist reactions, contempt or hatred with regard to other groups or peoples.'[1]

Two particular textbooks have been chosen to avoid the pitfalls of some other critical studies of textbooks, which have focussed on old and out-of-date books or little-known books. These two books are modern and up to date. They both have over 200 large-format pages, so there is plenty of room for accurate information and thorough discussion. They are designed for older and higher-ability pupils, so it cannot be claimed that over-simplification is because the pupils need it. They are both very popular books. They are both by respected authors, who are active teachers themselves. The publishers are among the foremost names in British educational publishing. And both books have received good reviews.

My purpose is not to criticize these particular books. Rather, by focussing on books that are in every way above average, the article seeks to raise important general points. If there are problems in *these* books, there are likely to be bigger problems in many other books.

Man and his World (1975) had been reprinted six times by 1982.[2] The book is by two university academics: J. A. Dawson, a senior lecturer, and David Thomas, a professor. The 1982 Nelson catalogue describes the book as 'this highly acclaimed basic text'. It states that the book 'reflects a thorough reappraisal of human geography as a subject, in the light of the latest developments in geography teaching. While providing a solid factual basis it moves beyond the facts to an interpretation of geographical patterns and processes'. These are high claims for quality and accuracy.

Elements of Human Geography (1979), by Charles Whynne-Hammond, is a more recent book.[3] The author is a graduate of London University, and a lecturer at Southgate Technical College in North London. This book, too, has high claims made for it by the publishers. On the back cover of the book, it is described as 'thoroughly researched, comprehensive in scope, with comprehensive coverage of topics'.

These high claims will be tested against the parts of the books that discuss race. The two books represent extreme ends of a spectrum of authorship. *Man and his World* should represent academic excellence, in that the authors are two senior university academics. If this book has academic weaknesses, other books are likely to have even greater weaknesses. *Elements of Human Geography* represents the chalkface in a high-density multicultural area. The author writes in his preface: 'I have spent many pleasurable and interesting hours teaching my students at Southgate Technical College, have learnt a great deal from them in return, and have written this book with the aim of catering for the needs of their successors'. One might expect a book that is ideally suited to students, and very conscious of our multicultural society. The origin of most other school books is likely to fall within these extremes. If both these books are unacceptable in their attitude to race, it is likely that many other books will also be unacceptable.

It seems reasonable to suggest that the starting-point for any study of race would be *The essential genetic unity of the human species* – a phrase from a statement on 'Race Relations and the Secondary School Curriculum' from Ealing Community Relations Council, and distributed by the Commission for Racial Equality. In other words, *unity* is the key feature of *homo sapiens*: members of mankind are biologically more similar to each other than – for example – a blackbird and a thrush.

But this key concept is totally absent from both books. In *Man and his World,* Chapter 1 is called 'The Diversity of Man' – not the unity of man. After a quick study of the history of mankind, we plunge directly into an account of the difference between races, without first considering the unity of mankind. *Elements of Human Geography* also omits the key concept of mankind's genetic unity. The chapter on 'Population Distribution' starts uncompromisingly with the sub-heading 'Race and Races'. The first sentence of the chapter states bluntly, 'Everyone knows that human beings are not the same the world over'. Clearly, it is only the differences that matter to the author, not the similarities. He continues: 'Of all the methods used in identifying human groups, the most common is by *race.*' There is no evidence given for this assertion; nor is the reader invited to question whether division by continent, or by country, or by faith, or by age, or by wealth, or by occupation, or by interests might be more common, let alone more useful or more important.

The Ealing Community Relations Council leaflet also recommends that 'the nature of the minor physical differences between peoples' should be studied by all secondary pupils. Both books are strong on differences – but nowhere do they stress that the differences are minor. Two pages on the different widths of heads, noses, chins, lips, etc. take on the role of major contrasts, since the similarities are never mentioned. *Man and his World* tells us that 'the Negroid head form has a strong inclination towards prognathism (a jutting chin)'. Both books state that negroid people have 'everted lips'; one book explains this as 'turned outwards'. Are such pseudo-scientific and obscure words really necessary? And might it be true that whites have lips that are turned inwards (inverted?) by comparison with black people? Why are other people described by comparison with whites, with the assumption that whites are normal and others are odd, rather than described in their own right? 'The lips are thick' is a statement about 'negroid people' in both books. But 'thick' does not just mean 'broad' to pupils: 'thick' is also used as an adjective to imply low intelligence.

Dawson and Thomas write, 'head hair is coarse-textured and curly or woolly'. Whynne-Hammond renders this, 'Coarse hair, usually curly or woolly'. The authors agree closely with each other. But 'thick' and 'coarse' have numerous meanings – mostly uncomplimentary or worse. The contrast is 'fine' for 'caucasoid peoples'. A fine contrast! 'Woolly hair' may not seem insulting at first sight – until it is misinterpreted as 'woolly-headed' and applied to minds and thinking. The contrast is 'straight or wavy' for 'caucasoid' people (in both books): these words have many positive connotations in contrast to the negative connotations for the words applied to 'negroids'.

The 'mongoloid' group – another word with negative meanings – have 'broad faces' (Dawson) or 'flat faces' (Whynne-Hammond), 'flat noses' (both books), and 'coarse hair' (both books). They have 'the epicanthic fold' (both books): this is explained as 'with skin drooping over the eyelids'. 'Drooping' is not an attractive term.

The ultimate in negative terminology comes from Dawson and Thomas's description of 'capoids' (Bushmen and Hottentots): 'Females exhibit a pronounced physical peculiarity named steatopygy (that is, an excessive development of the fatty tissue on the buttocks).' Notice the negative words: *'pronounced peculiarity'* and *'excessive* development'. Why do these authors describe other people as 'peculiar' with 'excessive' development? Might we not be equally peculiar in *their* sight? Would the authors welcome a comment such as this, if a 'capoid' wrote a geography book: 'Britons have a pronounced physical peculiarity named ossopygy (that is, inadequate fatty tissue on the buttocks)'? And, if not, why do they write in such terms about other people? If invited, pupils – accustomed to long sedentary hours on hard wooden seats – might see this so-called 'excessive development' as meeting their needs. Perhaps it is we who are the people who are not adapted to our environment? But the authors do not invite pupils' reactions.

Both books offer very negative descriptions of non-whites, and very positive descriptions of whites. This may only be accidentally racist – but it is certainly ethnocentric. It seems as if the authors have not considered their role in education for a multiracial society. In summary, where familiar words are used, the words used for whites have positive connotations (fine, straight, fair), and the words for non-whites have negative connotations (coarse, woolly, flat, drooping, thick). Where unfamiliar words are used (epicanthic, everted, prognathism, steatopygy) it is the non-whites who have these odd and unfamiliar words applied to them; the whites appear 'normal'.

It is not only the similarities of *homo sapiens* that are missing. Neither book emphasizes that several differences are greater *within* racial groups than *between* racial groups. The concept of the mean being less significant than the standard deviation from the mean is important in other parts of both books. But the authors ignore their own wisdom when tackling race – why?

Only Whynne-Hammond discusses differences within races in any detail – but this becomes a discussion of differences between the means of sub-groups: Nordic, Mediterranean and Alpine peoples are contrasted. Once again, his own group (Nordic) comes out rather well: 'fair-haired, blue-eyed, fair complexion'. How different from the 'olive complexion' of 'Mediterranean people' and the 'sallow complexion' of the Alpine people.

What is the origin of such statements? My first hypothesis was that the original material might be from the inter-war period. *Gill's Oxford and Cambridge Geography*, completely revised and edited by L. Dudley Stamp in 1933[4] did indeed contain the same phrases: 'Indo-European (Caucasian or Aryan) race: fair skins; silky hair. Negro Race: black woolly hair; flat noses; thick lips. American Indian Race:

coarse black hair; sharp intelligent features.' But, despite Stamp's reputation of being one of the greatest geographers of all time, his 'complete revision' was markedly less than thorough in this instance. Forty years earlier, in the 1893 edition of *Gill's Imperial Geography* exactly the same phrases are present.[5] Could it be pure Darwinism, I wondered?

To my amazement, I then found exactly the same phrases in Rev. J. Goldsmith's *Grammar of Geography* (1827)[6]: 'the jet black negroes and other Africans of various shades of black, having woolly hair, thick lips, flat noses, prominent chins and downy skins'. These phrases are thus over 150 years old, and predate by more than a generation Darwin's *Origin of Species*. The phrases in an elementary book, designed for rote-learning by young pupils, have apparently been copied and recopied over the years until they now appear in new books for senior pupils of high intelligence, one of which is written by a professor of geography! In fact, there is one way in which the Rev. J. Goldsmith is *less* ethnocentric than today's authors: he writes about 'the white and brownish nations of Europe, Western Asia, and the North Coast of Africa; who, according to our notions of beauty, are the handsomest and best formed of the human race . . .' It is only '*our* notions of beauty' that he is commenting on, and he leaves scope for recognizing other criteria of beauty. And Gill's *Geography* claimed that it is the Amerindians, not the whites, who have 'intelligent features'!

But these descriptions of physical characteristics are *not* the most alarming elements in the books. Whynne-Hammond moves beyond the description of physical characteristics to mental characteristics. He states: 'Some psychologists believe that certain mental attributes can also be an aspect of race – factors like nature and intelligence.' These anonymous psychologists seem to carry his approval because he does not mention that most psychologists do not agree with them. And he makes sweeping statements without providing any evidence. Of Nordic people, he writes: 'Mentally they are apt to be inventive and energetic, and have the ability to plan. Found in Britain and Northern Europe'. The author is, of course, in this group. No-one would deny that he is inventive and energetic and has the ability to plan. Text-book authors have to have such characteristics. *But* by stating these things he seems to imply that the other groups are different. He does not describe the mental state of non-whites, but the implication of inferiority is there. This is blatant racism – yet the book was first published as recently as 1979. Of the Mediterranean people he asserts 'mentally they may be poetic, musical, artistic and hot-tempered'. I too, would be hot-tempered if I were described in that way by an author who had just described himself as 'inventive and energetic'. How fortunate that this author lives in London, not in Wales, for he states, 'in Britain this type can be found in Scotland, Ireland and Wales'.

Why is this unsubstantiated gossip allowed to appear in print? The author starts his book by saying, 'The subject (geography) is becoming less descriptive and qualitative, and more scientific and quantitative'. Yet by page twenty-two he is becoming totally unscientific. And he is leaving both white and black pupils to wonder what black people are like 'mentally' by comparison with 'Nordic' whites. This is dangerous nonsense. Small wonder that by page fifty, he is asserting, 'Many countries can no longer absorb large numbers of aliens . . . some countries are highly selective indeed in their acceptance of foreigners'. With 'facts' like these, one might expect the statement 'Only Nordic caucasoids need apply'.

Dawson and Thomas, who avoid statements about the mentality of racial groups, write 'often . . . in-migration is perceived as the introduction of alien and unwanted groups which upset the economic well-being and social homogeneity of the existing society . . . ' There is no discussion of whether this *perception* may be wrong. It is statements like this, in respected books by respected authors, that reinforce lies, half-truths and misconceptions about the causes of immigration to Britain. By describing people's alleged perception, are they not encouraging the perception they describe? With exams in sight few teachers or pupils will have the time or inclination to question the textbook – most pupils will grasp it as *the* means to that coveted certificate.

What can teachers do about it? They could leave out these sections from their teaching – but sections that are omitted often prove to be the most interesting for pupils. They could *use* them in discussions on race – but it's a brave teacher who submits chapters like these to intensive analysis. If these sections are wrong, what about the rest of the book? Why did the school waste money on the books in the first place? Why should pupils believe the teacher rather than the textbook?

There are other questions which arise from material of this type:

1. If teachers with sufficient expertise to be authors of standard textbooks write this insensitive material, what hope is there that other books – and other lessons – are less bad?
2. If no-one is willing or bothered enough to criticize – or even notice – such material, things will not improve. *Man and his World* has been in print for a decade; why has no-one queried its content?
3. At a conservative estimate, 100,000 pupils have studied *Man and his World*. Some of them are now policemen, teachers, social workers. Others will soon qualify in these fields. What will their attitudes to race be?
4. The newer book seems to be worse than the older book. Could it be

that the assumptions that 'things are getting better' and that the problem is 'old books' are *wrong*?

My second example for analysis is also concerned with race, but in this case the author's main concern is not race *per se*. Here, British pupils look at other countries; and in the process their attitudes towards their own country are being shaped by frequent allusions to the superiority of white people. My approach is via the simulated responses of pupils. It is an approach also used in an article in the impeccably academic *Journal of Curriculum Studies*,[7] set in an American context. The three authors suggest various ways in which a chapter of an American high-school text about North Africa might be understood or misunderstood by a twelve-year-old student. The authors make numerous suggestions on how a student might recognize bias and distortion. The UK study which follows adopts a similar approach, but focusses specifically on black British pupils. The textbook in question is used widely in both all-white and multiracial classrooms.

This 'simulated responses' approach is somewhat unfamiliar, but it has several advantages. It encourages reflection and discussion, rather than providing data which may merely provoke questions about the validity of the sampling methods used. Equally important, it avoids treating pupils merely as 'research fodder' in this way. There are also major ethical questions involved in asking black pupils their reactions to insensitive textbooks. Blacks are 'picked on' too often, in too many school playgrounds, and I would not wish to add to this process in school classrooms.

There are, of course, problems with this approach. In particular, there is no way of proving that the simulated responses are valid ones. In fact, an exercise with real pupils produced numerous comments on interest and dullness, and on level of difficulty, of a variety of texts, but no comments on bias.[8] But this is not conclusive evidence: the pupils were all white, and they were handling unfamiliar textbooks. At the very least, the 'simulated response' approach will produce reactions and discussion; more refined approaches may then be developed in the light of criticism.

The case-study focusses on 'Class 2D': a class of thirty twelve- and thirteen-year-olds, who like geography lessons, are of average intelligence but above-average motivation. Two of the pupils (John and Mary) are British-born black pupils, whose parents came from the West Indies. The class is fortunate both in having a keen, hardworking and popular geography teacher, and also in possessing a complete set of thirty textbooks with attractive presentation and full colour. Because the books are so much more up to date than most other resources in the geography department, their teacher is willing to base most of the year's work on this book. The book is *Patterns in Geography – Two* by W. Farleigh Rice.[9] First published in 1975, the book had reached its fifth (unaltered) edition by 1980, and is probably the best-selling textbook for geography classes of twelve-year-olds. Exact figures cannot be obtained, but very few other geography textbooks are reprinted every year.

The book studies aspects of Australia, West and South Africa, and the Middle East. The pupils are pleased to find that they will be studying exciting overseas places; Mary and John are particularly pleased that West Africa has been included. The teacher, too, is happy both with the topics and with the book. As well as an attractive and colourful presentation – vital to sustain 2D's interest – he finds the book's stated philosophy to be in line with his own view of an appropriate type of geography syllabus for his pupils: '*Patterns in Geography* presents factual material to encourage reasoned discussion . . . It is not intended as a comprehensive regional geography, but it does present the broad patterns of regional distinctiveness.' The publishers would therefore seem to be claiming both balance and objectivity in its treatment of topics. The omission of large areas (e.g., all tropical Africa except West Africa) permits much more thorough treatment of the areas selected. But beneath the attractive appearance of the book lies a set of assumptions and omissions that deserve analysis. There are subtle differences in the treatment of Australia (an area with a white majority), West Africa (a Third World area) and South Africa (a white minority area), but in all three areas the study is made from a white man's point of view. It is a matter of concern that there has been virtually no written criticism of the assumptions in the book, other than a brief paragraph concerning the South African section.[10]

2D starts work in September on the first chapter of the book, 'The People of Australia'. The first sentence states, 'During the last hundred years many families have migrated from Britain to live in Australia'. 2D is interested . . . perhaps it is a land of opportunity? There is no mention of who may be accepted by Australia; no-one seems to know that most blacks are excluded. The next sentence, '. . . the continent . . . was almost empty when the first European settlers arrived', also passes without comment. Mary happens to know that the continent was not empty, and that the inhabitants had black skins. She notices that the aborigines are not mentioned, and she wonders whether the original inhabitants are not relevant to geography . . . perhaps the means whereby the white men acquired black land is to be tackled in history? (She will be disappointed.) But surely the present-day existence of black people in Australia deserves a mention? Once again, Mary will be disappointed: not a single one of the forty-seven colour photographs on Australia shows a black person, nor is there a single mention of them in the thirty-six pages on Australia.

On page six, the tasks become more specific: 'State what help the Australian government offers to immigrants'. Once again, there is no mention of who is acceptable. The next task begins, 'Explain why Australia wants immigrants . . .' This is the homework for the class. John shows the work to his parents, who had enquired about emigration to Australia and had discovered that black people are rarely accepted. They tell John, who feels cheated that the book glosses over this policy: clearly the book is written for white children. The task continues, ' . . . and then explain why Britain does not want immigrants'. John knows that his father was recruited by a British firm while he was still living in Barbados, in the 1950s, and that he was wanted in Britain to help solve a labour shortage. The whole family feels angry at the implication that immigrants have always been unwelcome, and they feel that this book is turning the rest of the class against them: the seeds of racial misunderstanding are being sown. But there is nothing they can do about it.

The next part of the book studies West Africa. This is an area which has fascinated John and Mary ever since they saw *Roots* on television. The area is introduced with three pictures of jungle, and a close-up photograph of a man's head. The man is black and is frowning. The task reads: '3.1 Heading: *People and cultivation in the forest zone of West Africa*. This man is one of the inhabitants of the forest areas. Accurately describe his features. Perhaps make a drawing, adding labels to indicate those features which are distinctive'. The teacher is sensitive enough to omit all reference to the picture and to the exercise, but it is prominent on the page, and the pupils cannot help noticing it. When one of the white pupils loudly asks John, 'Is that your dad?', he means it as a joke, but John feels that some of the sniggers are less than friendly.

The impact of this exercise – not only on John and Mary, but on the rest of the class – can be best judged by imagining a self-portrait in a textbook about Britain in a West African school, with an identical task: 'This person is one of the inhabitants of the urban areas of Britain. Accurately describe her features . . .' We are not told the purpose of this exercise, but it seems likely that pupils in 2D will construe it as an attempt to emphasise racial *differences*, rather than the similarities of *homo sapiens*. Odious comparisons are likely to be drawn by pupils.

The next part of the book studies South Africa. After the West Africa section, in which the Africans are regarded at a distance, the section on South Africa seems to start positively with close-up photographs of a teenage girl from each of the four main racial groups. Three of the girls are smiling, and their eyes seem to shine; but 2D quickly notices that the African girl is not looking at them, and not smiling. This may seem a trivial detail to adults, but pupils relate to a smiling face much more readily than to an unsmiling one. The effect on 2D is very important. It seems particularly unfortunate that both the West African and the South African chapters begin with an apparently unfriendly black face.

South Africa is studied in a completely different manner from West Africa. As with West Africa, there are two chapters, with nineteen photographs (excluding six small close-up photographs of types of rocks and minerals). But, this time, both chapters are concerned almost entirely with urban themes: 'Settlement and Mining in South Africa' and 'Johannesburg and its Influence'.

Certainly, there is a higher proportion of South Africans than of West Africans who live in towns or work in mines – but it is only a difference of degree. The *total* urban population of West Africa is in fact much bigger than that of South Africa – yet pupils will have received no image of any towns in tropical Africa other than the mud-brick section of Kano.

John glanced through the pictures of South Africa. Apart from the four small portraits, and six close-ups of minerals, there are fifteen photographs. Black people are only shown in four of them:

1. Drilling in a (white-owned) gold mine;
2. Picking oranges on a (white-owned) farm;
3. Feeding maize to (white-owned) dairy cattle;
4. Ploughing by oxen (caption: 'Bantu subsistence farming').

There are also views of a Bantu village (without people visible) and of a gold mine with a 'compound for Bantu workers'. And that is all; the other nine photographs have no reference to black people.

Mary had questioned, but ultimately accepted, the absence of mention of black people in Australia: perhaps minorities did not matter in geography. But she expected to find plenty of detail about black people in South Africa. She was pleased to find statistics and a map which showed that there were more black people than white, at the start of the section on South Africa. But when the class was allowed a double lesson (when the regular teacher was away on fieldwork) to choose any South African topic they wished to write about, Mary chose 'Black South Africans', only to find that a thorough hunt through the fourteen pages only offered her six sentences:

After crossing the Orange River they (the Afrikaners) met African natives – the Bantu – who were migrating slowly southwards (p. 57).
Unskilled Bantu came to work in the mines; they were housed in areas set aside by the mining companies (p. 58).
It is essential that the labour for the mines is both plentiful and cheap: such labour is provided by the Bantu who work usually for nine months of a year. Then they return to their tribes to help grow crops and keep cattle (p. 63).
Most Bantu are subsistence farmers, producing food for themselves. They have no need of transport for their products and so they can farm in areas at an even greater distance from the market (p. 66).

All six sentences can be questioned in terms of fact and implications, but Mary did not notice most of these. She did, however, realize that there is no suggestion in the text or the photographs that Africans live in towns: towns are presumably for white people? There is no discussion of justice or injustice; or of government control. Africans work on farms and in mines; their labour is cheap: that is all that needs to be said. Six sentences are sufficient; all the other pages concern the people who really matter: the whites. The teacher's comment on Mary's work when it was marked? 'Rather brief. Try to write more'!

John had heard his father say that almost all the land in South Africa is for whites; he tried to find a map which showed whether this was true. But not one of the eight maps gave any hint of this fact. He did not mention this to the teacher because he did not want to draw attention to himself, but he began to wonder why such a map was not there.

After various exercises based on these eight maps, the teacher sensed that 2D were getting bored. He therefore moved on to study an excellent air photograph of Johannesburg with an accompanying 1:50,000 map extract. The pupils had to study a map in their worksheets which showed five urban zones. The two residential zones are labelled: 'Older residential: high density'. 'Newer residential: low density.' This time, John was not satisfied. 'Where are the African townships? Aren't they new *and* high density?' The teacher tried to explain that the map only showed the land inside the city boundary – but John still could not understand why this should be so. The textbook picture was of a prosperous, trouble-free urban area, with booming industry and a contented populace. As if to emphasize the point, the book lists *thirty-six* multinational corporations with factories in South Africa. Soweto was in the news, but not in this book. Mary said nothing, but she too was puzzled by this map and exercise: did people who looked like her in South African towns only exist on television? Perhaps fortunately, she and John did not notice the other distortions in the maps and statistics.

Finally, 2D were asked to choose one of the six activities that the book offers to encourage imaginative involvement with the people of South Africa. Only Mary and John seemed to notice that *all six* exercises concerned imaginative involvement with the white minority only:

1. Writing as though you were one of the pioneer Afrikaners seeking new farm land, state why you chose to move eastwards . . . (p. 56).
2. Imagine you are one of the Voortrekkers arriving at the Orange River in your ox wagon. Write the diary entry for this day . . . Write [about] the thought that you will be in a free land tomorrow (p. 57).
3. Describe [the minerals] as if you were a farmer trying to memorize

them, in the hope that you would discover some rich mineral on the land you intend to farm (p. 57).
4. Imagine you owned one of the claims [at the Kimberley diamond mines] . . . (p. 58).
5. Imagine the dismay of the first miners [in Johannesburg] who arrived with just picks and shovels, believing that they would make their fortunes on the new goldfields . . . (p. 60).
6. Imagine you have been asked to choose the site for a new factory . . . (p. 66).

John received the comment on this work, 'Could do better'. But he no longer wanted to do better.

These examples have focussed on race, but textbook analysis can be used on any other topic of significance to the study of contemporary culture, for example sexism, and also class structure – and the tacit alliance between many textbook authors and rich capitalists, whereby industry is studied almost entirely from a managerial viewpoint, seeking least-cost location and maximum profits. This essay has discussed some of the opportunities of studying published data designed for use in schools. It is an underdeveloped area, where method is uncertain and workers are few. The bias of the analyst is often as marked as the bias of the resources. But school textbooks clearly shape attitudes, and this field has been neglected for too long.

NOTES AND REFERENCES

1. UNESCO Resolution on Education for International Understanding, para. 39.
2. J. A. Dawson and David Thomas, *Man and his World*, Nelson 1975.
3. Charles Whynne-Hammond, *Elements of Human Geography*, Allen and Unwin 1979.
4. *Gill's Oxford and Cambridge Geography*, 126th edn., ed. L. Dudley Stamp, George Gill 1933.
5. *Gill's Imperial Geography*, rev. edn., George Gill 1893.
6. J. Goldsmith (pseud.), *Grammar of Geography*, Longmans 1827.
7. R. N. Kantor *et al.*, 'How Inconsiderate are Children's Textbooks?', *Journal of Curriculum Studies*, XV, 1 (1983), 61–72.
8. See David Wright, 'Evaluating Resources: Why not ask the Pupils?', *Multicultural Teaching* (1983).
9. W. Farleigh Rice, *Patterns in Geography – Two*, Longmans 1975.
10. David Hicks, 'Bias in Books', *World Studies Journal*, 1, 3 (1980), 14–22.
11. In this rapidly growing and rapidly changing field, journals are probably more useful sources than books. The following journals may be useful: *Education Journal* (Free news-sheet published by Commission for Racial Equality)

Multiracial Education (Journal of NAME: National Association for Multiracial Education)
Multicultural Teaching (published by Trentham Books)
World Studies Journal (published by World Studies Teacher Training Centre, at York University)
Times Educational Supplement

Chapter 12

TEXTUALITY/SEXUALITY

SUSAN BASSNETT and KEITH HOSKIN

Hélène Cixous has written, 'there has not yet been any writing that inscribes femininity'[1]: despite the fact of women writing, and despite the gradual establishment of woman's right to write over some 200 years. Women may have appropriated textual, as they have appropriated sexual rights, but the problems which both textuality and sexuality pose do not thereby appear to have dissolved.

We want to argue that the fact that we can talk of a writing which could inscribe femininity is a sign that textuality has already changed, that it has become systematically different and expresses already a new power in writing that is multiple and multiform. Yet this new textuality is constantly compromised, and it is as yet unclear how femininity can be inscribed, because writing has been historically male, and writing of all kinds – visual as well as verbal, and including this writing – bears the marks of that history still.

There are power relations inscribed in texts: it is presumed for instance that the Text, as a trace which endures through time and space, is memorable; it is presumed, generally, that it is neutral and asexual: its Author is classically the 'one who writes', its Reader the 'one who reads'. That apparently asexual 'one' is male: his neutral voice hides the fact that there is an inherent sexuality in texts (and textuality about the sexual); that voice is a framing device by which readers, male and female, are 'framed', so as to ignore the text's sexuality (and how their sexuality is textual). There are two things which are in fact one here: the one history of the Logos – which Derrida has called logocentrism, but which has also been phallocentrism.[2] Cixous again: 'Nearly the entire history of writing is confounded with the history of reason, of which it is at once the effect, the support and one of the privileged alibis. It has been one with the phallocentric tradition. It is indeed that same self-admiring, self-stimulating, self-congratulatory phallocentrism.'[3] Neutrality centres. The classic Author/Reader, centred on the classic memorable Text, perpetuates logo/phallocentrism. And at the centre stands the neutral He.

To inscribe femininity is a problem of power. As writing it must reverse logo- and phallocentrism, decentre both Logos and phallus. This is the work of what one can only call post-feminism (since feminism, as textuality and sexuality, is too close to the logo/phallo/centre). It will implicate the power in multiple textuality. So far one way-station has been to turn to texts designated as private and ephemeral – the letter, the tape-recording, the shopping list, the recipe. But really post-feminism writes itself as a new writing which we do not write yet. In a little multiply-authored volume entitled *Lessico politico delle donne (Women's Political Lexicon)* the compilers of the literature section say this:

> So it is body-word. Not the language of the Logos. The immediate incidental word. Not the discourse of order and of knowledge. The word that frees itself in a total unproductivity, that does not know the rules of the game. The word that flowers in the silence of the night, in the time of repose and stasis, absenting itself from the rhythm of daily work. The word of dispersion, of shopping, not of acquiring and consuming.
>   In short, the word of loving.[4]

Post-feminism is a language of the body – which is not a *simple* language of the body, because there is no simple language any more – but a way to reinscribing both the textual and the sexual, aligning them differently. It decentres logos and phallus (or will do so) by rejecting male memorability in favour of forgettability, by erasing the categories of classic textuality, Author, Text and Reader. It can do so because there is already a new power in writing: writing which is now multiple and multiform, in fields which interrelate the verbal and visual in variously differing ways. So in many respects we are already there; we live in a frame of forgettability, erasures are already occurring, we are decentred; we already write and read the new textuality. But not in any simple way.

On Tuesday 11 May 1982, *The Sun* carried another of its anti-Argentine, pro-Thatcher cartoons that had been appearing with regularity throughout the Falklands crisis. As a right-wing tabloid newspaper *The Sun*'s position *vis-à-vis* military action in the Falklands was never in doubt: it spoke a standard right-wing militarism, full of allusions to British courage during the blitz and harmonious understanding with the American ally. And at the same time stories were steadily run on the brave wives left behind, the agonising wait for the women whose husbands had been on board doomed ships, the grief-stricken mothers who talked of their dead sons in terms of pride that they had given their lives for freedom and their country. The *Spare Rib* editorial of June 1982 wasted no words concerning the implications: 'On its own, the sickening media coverage of the "boys going off to fight" while their girlfriends and mothers wait at home for their return would be reason enough for feminists to oppose the conflict. Lest *we* forget, war makes "men" of boys and "girls" of women'.

The Sun cartoon however highlights a confusion at the heart of all militaristic rhetoric. It shows Margaret Thatcher wearing a cross between a Churchillian siren suit and battledress, with a Montgomeryesque beret, rising out of the water and holding a huge shopkeeper's weight marked TASK FORCE over a tiny cowering rat, dressed only in a general's hat and clearly marked with the letters JUNTA across its back, squatting on what can be taken to signify the Falkland Islands. The caption below the cartoon reads: DROPPING IN ANYTIME NOW. On Thatcher's face is a kind of half-smile, with the tightness of the mouth and the grip of the hands on the weight denoting resoluteness.

Thatcher's own war rhetoric made much of her maternal role, and constantly utilized the emotive phrase 'our boys'. But at the same time, as the person responsible for taking military decisions she occupied a role very far from that of wife and mother. Within right-wing ideology the passive role of women is accentuated in time of war: woman as such is erased, her attributes being distributed elsewhere (in *The Sun* leader of 12 May for example, the following sentence is printed in dark type and underlined: 'It is not jingoism to love one's country and to insist that she is treated with justice and respect in the world.') But with a woman as Prime Minister, albeit a right-wing woman, the game of roles is altered. The cartoon shows up the ambiguities: Thatcher holds a weight in her hands, symbol of military might as designated by the caption across it, but also an iconic sign of domesticity. She is not depicted flying a Harrier jump-jet or engaging in direct combat of any kind. She stands, her femininity emphasized in the line of her breasts under the close-fitting jacket and her curly blonde hair fluffed out beneath the beret, with calm authority, holding the weight above the dehumanized Argentinian. The caption reiterates the blend of the domestic with the military; the phrase itself is conversational and connotes visiting a friend, but the explicit sign of the weight removes all doubt about what is implied.

The ambiguities become clearer if we attempt to modify the figure of Thatcher in the cartoon. If she had been depicted in full battledress and armed, for example, the connotations of domesticity and motherliness would have disappeared; if she had been portrayed wearing feminine clothing, one of her blue suits and blouses with large bows at the neck, the connotations of military power would have been lost. She had to be masculinized, but only up to a point. What the *Sun* cartoonist had to do is portray a woman in a role that the newspaper's own ideological position sought to suppress. This exposes the contradiction that lies at the heart of fascist dialectic. Maria Antonietta Macciocchi has summed up the traditional role of women in fascist ideology with her image of women wearing a long chain of saucepans on their backs 'like a noisy metallic tail', but when a right-wing woman assumes the power traditionally reserved for authoritarian males, right-wing image-makers are faced with a dilemma: this is our leader, but this is not Man; it is Woman/Man and therefore a polymorphous sexuality must be textually depicted.

'This exposes the contradiction', we say, as if it were self-evidently exposed. Yet that would be to ignore the role of the Reader. The ambiguities of *The Sun* text, inherent though they may be, only emerge to a certain kind of Ideal Attentive Reading. Meanwhile as text *The Sun* is part of a whole contextual framing that calls for a very different Ideal Reading, which is not supposed to acknowledge the plurality of possible readings and for which irony and ambiguity are not supposed to exist. We have a general problem concerning reading here. For the Ideal Reading which denies plurality is not restricted to reactionary male-determined texts. It is a problem of textuality generally.

The cover of the March 1982 issue of *Spare Rib* offers an image every bit as ambiguous as *The Sun* cartoon but entirely 'understood' so long as the reader takes up an Ideal Feminist stance. The bright yellow cover frames a still photograph of a group of women protesting about male violence. Four placards are visible, one foregrounded reading WOMEN SAY NO TO MALE VIOLENCE, one held above the group at the back reading WOMEN ARE ANGRY ABOUT MALE VIOLENCE, and two that are partially obscured by heads and shoulders: WOMEN GET ATTACKED [EVERY DAY]; MALE LAWS, [MALE STATE, MALE VIOLENCE]. One of the protesters, holding a pen and board, is standing in front of the group, obviously collecting signatures for a petition. She is very young, in dark punk gear, bondage trousers, T-shirt, rows of badges, and her hair stands up in long greased spikes. Her face is half-turned towards the other centralized figure in the photograph, an old lady, half a head shorter, in a pleated skirt, short coat and fur-lined hat. We can see the old lady's face in profile but cannot determine the expression. Her left arm is slightly raised towards the girl with the petition. The women in the group behind are looking out away from the camera and away from the two women who are looking at each other in the foreground. The caption underneath the photograph reads 'Women together against rape', and the assumptions to be read into the photograph are quite clear: old and young, punk and traditional are united in sisterhood against a common cause. This caption is more than just another writing however; it is itself a reading of the photo and one which denies alternatives. It translates the writing in the photograph which speaks of 'violence' into a writing which speaks specifically of 'rape'. And through the word 'together' it frames the visual action as being un-ambiguous. Yet this same photograph if found in *The Sunday Telegraph* could be read as the opposite of sisterhood. The old lady's upraised arm could in that context be a sign of rejection, of protest against the outrageously dressed androgynous creature who has blocked her path. And what could be made of the gazes which 'evade' the camera? Do they perhaps speak fragmentation or alienation rather than solidarity? Of course at one level we (i.e., Sophisticated Readers) will concede that there are as many readings as there are readers, but it remains the case that the *Spare Rib* cover starts from the assumption that there is an Ideal Reader who will identify with the ideology of the text. Thus even though it is a text which sees itself as self-consciously deviant it reinforces the *status quo* insofar as it uses the techniques of patriarchal discourse and denies a plurality of voices.

This is one example of how we stay close to the logo/phallo/centre. In a rather different way Judy Chicago, having produced the extra-ordinary artistic achievement of her work *The Dinner Party*, can still say: 'I feel that unless *The Dinner Party* is permanently housed I will not have achieved my goal of introducing women's heritage into the culture so that it can never be erased again – I would be content to see it in a simple, triangular room in a museum, cultural institution or university, or as part of a larger women's institution'.[5] Her art should be displayed and not only in book form, but still, memorability through institutionalized acknowledgement becomes the frame within which she considers her artistic text will speak fully. And who then speaks? She or the institution? Woman or phallus?

Xavière Gauthier back in 1974 succinctly defined the problem which textuality poses for women:

> Throughout the course of history they have been mute, and it is doubtless by virtue of this mutism that men have been able to speak and write. As long as women remain silent, they will be outside the historical process. But if they begin to speak and write *as men do,* they will enter history subdued and alienated; it is a history that, logically speaking, their speech should dis-rupt.[6]

The textual problem is twofold. On the one hand, there is the question of the production of texts which might find a language and voice to be more than a variation of established forms; but that production is also a problem of reading. Finding a voice involves reading; even Authors are also Readers (of their own texts and others'). Finding a voice cannot involve any return to neutrality, to the centre, to an Ideal Reading. For textuality to be more than a mirror image of the accept-able face/penis of male culture, an acceptance of pluralism, of frag-mentation, has to emerge in the reading process.

This fragmentation, we say, is already with us, since we live in a world of multiple textuality. The classic age of the Book is over – that age which produced the classic constructs of Author, Text and Reader and set them within a frame of memorability. George Steiner has defined that age as follows: it comes after print, when the Book can assume a definitive textual presence in multiple identical printed copies, and it 'favours particular formats . . . say the bound volume over the pamphlet, the in-octavo over the folio . . .'[7] This classic Text produces the classic Author as memorable, larger-than-life Identity. Before this age books might have a shadowy attribution or none at all. Shakespeare even, who can be accused of being Bacon, is not an Author in this sense. Sir Walter Scott, who is the first to be accorded the memorial of knighthood for literary production, clearly is: he stands at the zenith of this history of the Author. Alongside him we find the classic Reader, 'a man', as Steiner says, 'sitting alone in his personal library': such a construct embodies 'a number of implicit power relations' – the production of books plentiful and cheap enough to create private libraries, the architectural construction of a private library space within the house, social relations with servants and family which preserve the peace in and around that space, and a commitment to silent intense reading as the 'real cultured' form of reading. This is the 'classic act of reading – what is depicted as *la lecture* in so many eighteenth-century genre paintings and engravings'.

These classic forms have a very short history, they become fully articulated only in the eighteenth century, since they express power relations which only then become fully operative. They are fictions of those relations, both produced by and expressive of them, but they are fictions with a continuing potency to create Authors, Texts and Readers in their image which is not exhausted even yet – even in textual fields beyond the Book. We stress here what they *were* because of what they still are. Even when we live in a world of multiple textuality, where the proliferation of texts and textual fields means that it is a contradiction for texts to be memorable, we still strive for the memorable Text. Even though Barthes has told us that the Author is dead and Foucault says that 'the Author must efface himself',[8] there are more 'Authors' than at any time in history. The question arises: how should the 'Author' now be written? Either dead or effaced, perhaps the construct should in Derridean style be considered under erasure – *sous rature* in Derrida's technical phrase – and so be written thus – the ~~Author~~.

Let us look at a non-traditional textual field, yet one which is full of ~~Authors~~, rock recording, in order to see how the classic constructs, although compromised and under erasure, still survive. Within rock the question 'who speaks?' has always been insistently posed because of the nature of the recording (or 'trace', to continue the Derridean theme). Is the songwriter the rock Author (as would be the case in literary discourse)? Is it instead the producer? Or is it the singer? The last is the most obvious answer. Elvis Presley 'makes' 'Jailhouse Rock', not Leiber and Stoller who wrote it. Elvis 'makes' it both because he records it but also because 'Jailhouse Rock' becomes unthinkable apart from him. A definitive Performance Text emerges, which is the original 1958 recording. But the history of rock makes it clear that other answers are possible. Do the Teddy Bears, in the same era, make

'To Know Him is to Love Him'? Yes, but so does Phil Spector who writes and produces it while still in high school. And it 'makes' him the first great Producer/Author while the Teddy Bears fade into anonymity. In rock there is no simple solution to the Author problem. Today the claims of the Producer to be rock Author have gone so far as to become (as in film) a form of auteurism. No LP sleeve can go without its credits and the producer's name must be high on the list. But this does not prove the existence of any classic Author: on the contrary the Derridean argument applies. There is no one Author who speaks in rock but a range of different voices: writers, producers, singers, instrumentalists, engineers, etc., all of whom contribute to the Recorded Trace. The discourse of rock is produced through a continual play of difference – different voices working in different ways at different times to produce the trace, not in one pure moment of space-time but through deferrals and different takes, mixed in multiple overlay and then remixed. The Author and Presence are erased, in their place the Author and Derrida's *différance* – the play of differing and deferred time and place.

This is the textuality of rock: no Author, similarly no pure Text. The multiple nature of multiple recordings produces Texts whose sole principle of coherence is in some shared name (that name may be of a group, like the Rolling Stones, or of a song, like 'Yesterday', but in either case the name guarantees the sound that will be heard). In such a context there is no pure Reading, and indeed rock produces multiform readings. It is read as background – to talk or to working, to meals and to this writing here; it is equally read as foreground text in an analogue of classic Reading, alone in the record-lined room (an act of solitary silence intensified by wearing headphones); or one can foreground the text at a less intense level, in a kind of rote reading/multiple listening (this is how, through repetition, much pop-rock is read). Thus there are multiple kinds of reading and in addition different levels of reader engagement, between which one can switch constantly – in other words Reading, not Reading.

The classic constructs are therefore all under erasure; in addition the classic frame of memorability has been reversed. Rock's discourse – for commercial reasons but not commercial reasons only – is open-ended, a constant production of records, tapes, playlists, etc., different writings in which the only constants are erasure and supplementation (re-recording alongside and as part of new recording). For memorability as frame therefore, read forgettability.

What we say of rock can *a fortiori* be applied in all modern textual fields (film, TV, and the like, as well as the Book). In all the frame is forgettability and the classic constructs are under erasure. The production of texts and of textual fields has multiplied to the point where only a structural amnesia can deal with them. Each textual field produces new texts in an open-ended progression and increasingly these traces are designed to replace, not memorialize, older ones (the fiction is *progress*: the creative principle not the classical mimesis but the modernist 'there is nothing in principle that cannot be said'). Modern textuality is Borges's Library of Babel, wherein all reading demands and produces forgettability. There is skim reading, plundering reading, mindful and mindless reading, but little of the classic memorable reading – the kind which could read Virgil or Milton and understand the allusions without the aid of notes. (The student reading for exams must remember the content for each, but only until the exam has been written when it must be forgotten in favour of the next. Empirical studies show that people cannot remember more than two items from last night's TV news. Such forgetting is not specific to TV reading or schooled reading, it is a general condition; these are specific forms of a generally multiform reading.)

Multiply-multiple textuality cannot tolerate memorability: its texts ~~[Texts]~~ must become in sum unmemorable, their *auteurs* becoming a string of credits disappearing at speed up textuality's screen. Yet in all textuality phallocentric classicism fights paranoiacally on. It cannot maintain in any simple fashion its old fictions – where the Reader was self-evidently as Steiner says 'a man', and likewise the Author, a male fiction whose power was acknowledged in male names even where the writer was biologically female like George Eliot or George Sand; it cannot even maintain a masculine writing for, as Virginia Woolf realized, the linguistic basis of the Text, the Sentence, was male,[9] and now that too is under systematic attack, in the discourse of inscribing the feminine. All this implies the erasure of a historic masculinity. Phallocentrism itself comes under erasure. But it is erasure, not death. Residual phallocentrism remains, claiming to be neutral and desexed: it is the neutral Auteur, male or female, and that neutral Reader, the Critic. Nothing is more intimidating than this invisible (male) judge, the modern inquisitor, the examinatorial and disciplining Ideal Reader who haunts modern ~~Authors~~ throughout the lifelong process of producing ~~Texts~~ from earliest schooldays, and who frequently intimidates us into producing nothing.

Neutrality + Invisibility = Male

How does this modern textuality relate to the problem of inscribing femininity? Our answer has several stages. To begin with we would argue the following: residual phallocentrism cannot be ignored, but neither can the power of the new multiple writing. The attempt to inscribe femininity responds to both, which is why it can be no simple language: it embodies contradiction, erasure, the paranoia of auteurism, residual idealism and so on, but it begins already to write itself. Let us return once more to rock and to how women function within its textuality. Rock's history begins as unabashedly sexist. Women begin as absence or at best Other: they exist as song-titles (e.g., the objectifying 'Be-Bop-A-Lula'), occasionally as writers (Sharon Sheeley with Eddie Cochran) or as singers who generally mirror the masculine discourse (e.g., Connie Francis's 'Where The Boys Are, That's Where I Will Be' – and what of the girl singer in the Teddy Bears, who now is to most of us a faceless voice, Absence replaced in the mirror by Spector?). Women in the 1960s become more of a presence, but it is instructive to run down the categories in *The Rolling Stone History of Rock and Roll*.[10] There are some forty named male groups and individuals but only one named female category, 'The Girl Groups' (which proves to be Motown groups like the Marvelettes and Supremes) and two named individuals, Aretha Franklin and Janis Joplin. The conclusion appears clear: women were a secondary presence who had to be black or sound black – acceptability in exchange for ghettoization. But that proves a little too neat, for there is one (neutral) category where women figure alongside men, equal in numbers and stature: that category, it is no coincidence, is the singer/songwriter (*Rolling Stone* lists Leonard Cohen, James Taylor and Paul Simon alongside Carly Simon, Laura Nyro, Joni Mitchell and Carole King). Here writing adds a dimension of power within the general textual field. The woman as writer has a right to voice which goes beyond the writing. Songwriting plus singing doubles the texts and thus the textual power, giving the right to be other than Other. That does not in itself transcend phallocentrism: sometimes it appears only to produce a more sophisticated tokenism, i.e., as rock proliferates into a network of sub-discourses each gets its women's section: women's easy listening, Linda Ronstadt; women's punk, Siouxsie; women's heavy metal, Girls' School. But however ghettoized, women become a generalized presence.

The singer/songwriter exploits multiple textuality, and in multiple ways that textuality gives women a voice. Consider the construct, the 'rock voice'. While the rock singer has been archetypically male in gender, the register of the voice has not, but is instead curiously ambivalent: from Little Richard to Paul McCartney to Stevie Winwood to Sting it has been predominantly the male head register; it has always been available across gender lines as a shared voice, alongside the female chest register (which has been the predominant range for women rock singers). So if one poses again the question 'Who speaks in rock?' the answer is both male and female, for the voice is not based exclusively in one gender: and indeed the ambivalence goes further, for it is not only the Authors who speak; there is a supplementary speaking by Readers, since one widespread form of rock Reading is joining in and singing along – by both males and females along with both male and female recordings.

Now, in a recent development, that of the now-ubiquitous rock video, there is a fascinating twist in the play of rock voices; five years ago the video was a marginal supplementary text but now, despite all the overkill, there is no likelihood that it will relapse to that status. And we would suggest that within the field of video an easily-overlooked multitextual breakthrough has been engineered by a woman, Toni Basil. This is not to say that she is the first, only or most successful video *auteur,* for clearly the field has discovered a cultural prominence which goes beyond the work of any one video-maker. Nor is it simply to say that she has a certain recognition within the field for her work; while she can claim certain credentials – a training in dance, work on movie and video shorts from the early 1970s, as well as being a singer/songwriter – there is again nothing unique in such qualifications; other prominent names (e.g., Godley and Creme) can claim similar backgrounds. What we are concerned with is the creation of a video 'voice', the engineering of a multitextuality which embodies a new kind of textual discourse. The video began as a marginal supplement produced in two thematic forms, the one centred on the musicians, represented in concert performance or studio recording, the other superimposing a totally separate video text, an old cartoon or movie clips, as a kind of contrapuntal gloss; it has come, in its modern forms, to play variations on these early themes – playing with computer-generated special-effect counterpoints, using multiple shots of the musicians in and out of performance, producing original video texts which play off the music, sometimes underlining it, sometimes ignoring it (i.e., retelling the musical story, telling a different story, refusing a story completely). Most respond to the demands of rock economics and function as vehicles to promote instant memorability and profits. But all have come more or less successfully to terms with the multitextuality of the discourse.

Toni Basil, we would argue, is the *auteur* who first (and so far best) worked her way inside the discursive possibilities, pursuing, if you like, the logic of the supplement and moving the video to its present location as rock's supplementary centre. The process can be seen in her 1981 LP (produced in both audio and video versions) *Word of Mouth.* This dual publication by definition rules out the possibility of there being one Definitive Text: but as ~~Text~~ it also reveals the kind of complexity which Basil worked out. It is not the music *per se* which is a breakthrough (the phallocentric dream) – it remains rock – it is the combination of texts which can each be read in their own right but which together form one supervening ~~Text~~ which is new. The video LP takes a conventional rock text and sets it with a coherent yet independent video text. Within that Basil works with a group of 'street dancers' whom she assembled to produce, in conjunction with her own trained dancing, a dance text which is in its way a new writing of rock dance. Taken in sum, the overlay and combination of texts works as an acceptance and exploitation of the principle that rock is in essence ~~Text~~, with all that that means. The principle of coherence which holds *Word of Mouth* together is assuredly the author-function Toni Basi, but only through *différance*, since where there are such different subtexts, *and* no one Definitive Text, she can only be decentred presence. Similarly all reading or any one reading of the text is 'differentiated', since to make a 'full' reading is impossible without multiple reading of both audio and video versions, for each in its systematic differences is incommensurate with the other. Describe, if you like, the prior relationship between music and video as vertical, talk of the former relation as paratactic and the latter as syntactic (or contrapuntal versus harmonic); name the change even as one which produces a holographic intersection of previously perspectival texts – whatever metaphor of transformation one prefers the point is that the video before Toni Basil is a quite different animal (i.e., textual intervention) from what it then becomes. She, as author-function, has realized and made real a multi-textuality where before there was a dispersal of secondary texts around the music.

Is it coincidence that a woman should speak this new textuality? We think not. We would draw an analogy with 200 years ago when not only did a new non-classical literary discourse begin but also a new doctrine of creativity – genius not mimesis – which erased the old rhetorical culture. At that moment developed a new generalized power of writing. Male romanticism was one part of this, but while glorifying genius it focussed its efforts on the traditional high-status authorial voice, the poetic, looking phallocentrically backwards and treating prose as an afterthought. Into that 'afterthought' stepped women. Possibly the single most important romantic text – but written in prose, by a woman, and therefore marginalized on both counts – is Mary Shelley's *Frankenstein*. And then there is Austen who developed her own kind of reflexive, internalizing prose-writing, taking, as Walter Ong has pointed out, what had long been a feature of verse drama, the practice of close plotting and fine-grained characterizing, in order to produce the close-plotted novel.[11] Ironically (or perhaps predictably) the poetic voice became secondary to prose during the next few decades since prose forms better expressed the power of the new writing. Where women had first written anyone could copy and thus both men and women, following Shelley and Austen, appropriated the various forms. Similarly Basil first exploited rock's multiple textuality while residual phallocentrism was making the most 'creative' men concentrate on the traditional high-status areas of rock writing – music and lyrics – in the quest for memorability. Now – as 200 years ago, and as happened with Sappho, the first Author to write a personal poetry of the self – men step in to reappropriate the new discursive voice as being essentially theirs. In each case the Other writes the new supplementary writing first, and once the writing has been written so that 'anyone' – any neutral One – can appropriate it, then male *auteurs* swamp the field and male neutrality works once more to render the Other invisible.

At this point we can no longer evade the problem contained in our title, the relation of textuality to sexuality. The two constructs, it is becoming clear, are mutually related. The phrase 'inscribing the feminine' declares as much. This article was almost completed when we discovered Elizabeth Abel writing in almost identical words to ours: 'Sexuality and textuality both depend on difference'.[12] More than that, in the historic present they are both traces built of the same *différance*. Let us take Foucault's contention that sexuality is a construct of the nineteenth century, and we cannot avoid the coincidence with this historically new textuality, a coincidence whose points can begin to be specified.[13] A new (prose) writing of the text graphs on to a new writing of the sexual, for the new sexuality is decidedly written. It is discovered through the case-notes which doctors (even before Freud) begin to keep and it is expressed in the still-continuing waves of texts produced by doctors and other experts. All this writing is an expression of the new generalized power in writing, as Foucault's work from *Discipline and Punish* (1975) on has shown. Disciplinary power operates by turning each Person into an archive: more generally Persons become Texts to be produced and read, they also produce themselves as Texts, hence as Foucault says in his *History of Sexuality* (1976) this is the most confessional society in history. Writing hereby becomes multiply inscribed in the Person. The Person is in some originary sense the Author of the self as Text, but that Self-Text can then be read by the experts who turn it into writing. That division of labour proves that the Person is only ~~Author~~ alongside the expert who is also ~~Author~~ (both of writing and through therapy of better Persons). And similarly both Person and expert become ~~Readers~~ of the Self-Text; the Person reads internally, the expert from without, so that there is no one Ideal Reading, only a multiplicity (inevitably because the Self-Text is of course a ~~Text~~ changing through time and with the perspective of the Readers). Thus the Person (male or female) is the product of modern textuality.

Sexuality (male and female) follows its contours and contradictions. We live a textual sexuality which displays the same conjunction between erasure and intensification of the old classic idealizations: textuality/sexuality. Sexuality has become polymorphous, there are no interrelations, positions and multiplicities which are in principle inadmissible, no sexual text which cannot be written in some textual field or other. But there is intensified pressure towards the ideal: the memorable relationship within the frame of multiply forgettable ones: the sexist ideal – to become a Person and achieve identity through sexuality alone (certain Persons function as such sexual Texts – Brigitte Bardot, Robert Redford or, within video, Duran Duran) and the many texts which detail their star-crossing interrelationships make them Texts of a quasi-legendary status. Such an ideal even when expressed by women remains residually phallocentric: as textuality, containing within it still the classic ideals, it is still a male sentence passed on (to) women. Even the non-sexist ideal, the open relationship, comes into question: for as Beatrix Campbell says, the sexual revolution was 'primarily a revolt of young *men*. . . . The very affirmation of sexuality was a celebration of masculine sexuality'.[14] This is not because sexuality must always be ultimately male; but to date there is residual phallocentrism in even the most reflexively open sexuality – the trace of its textuality.

This is our textual/sexuality – a product and expression of power relations and of writing, still close to the logo/phallo/centre. What finally does this mean for the field which must explicitly combine textual and sexual discourse, feminism? We return to our earlier criticism concerning the Ideal Feminist Reader. Such an ideal suggests that within multiple textuality and within *différance* a point of absolute discontinuity can be found: women's language, women's texts, women's reading. Such genderism is still residually phallocentric. The notion of the authoritative reading, where only the Ideal Reader will cut through possible ironies and ambiguities belongs to a patriarchal pedagogic system; it perpetuates the power of the phallus by arresting the play of difference.

Is it significant that Cixous, writing from within feminism, does not single out feminist writing as the new inscription of femininity? She names but three French writers of this century through whom inscriptions of femininity have come out: 'Colette, Marguerite Duras . . . and Jean Genêt'.[15] Feminism, because of its position as non-male discourse, has long realized the inadequacy of the old classic Author/ Text/Reader categories. It began the first explicit erasures of them: women too became authors, the battle over the male sentence was begun and gradually it became untenable that the Ideal Reader was male. But these erasures led not to a general acceptance of erasure but the establishment of female antitheses: neo-classic female Authors and alongside them the Feminist Reader (who subjects texts to a feminist version of the classic intense silent reading). Antithesis has maintained genderism, for instance in the search for a women's language and, a related problem, for an adequate feminist theory of the Work. Neo-classic feminism has tried to solve this by creating the category of 'great books by women': but this perpetuates the classic construct of the Author while also reducing the criterion for great writing (and more generally for inscribing femininity) to what you have between your legs. (It is partly for this reason that Cixous includes Genêt as one through whom inscription has begun. There is no *gender*-based women's language.)

These are contradictions which accentuate the crisis of a feminism inscribed within patriarchal discourse. Yet we believe that a post-feminist writing is beginning to emerge. We chose to consider Toni Basil as one example of a woman creating a discourse that deconstructs linearity; and in other textual fields a similar process can be discerned. Texts are being produced which raise questions of the possibility of a discourse away from the logo/phallo/centre. Within traditional writing fields such women as Marthe Robert, Christa Wolf, Adrienne Rich and Dacia Maraini, to choose writers from four different social contexts, have challenged the linearity of literary forms. All four in various ways have questioned the rigid demarcation lines of traditional literary production – between the text designated as criticism and the text designated as fiction, between autobiography and the fictional process, between performers and audience, and all have widened their concept of the work to include such ephemeral texts as diaries, notes and jottings, tape-recordings and verbatim transcripts of conversations. This emphasis on the fragmented, on an idea of reading that is multivarious because of the interweaving of types of text, is indeed an alternative writing in which the public and the private are merged and become indistinguishable. It is to turn the power in multiple textuality directly against phallocentrism and decentre it. This is of crucial importance for the whole practice of feminism. For feminism as interpersonal relations is committed to the right to an equal voice: women have the right to be multiple, polymorphous ~~Authors~~ and ~~Readers~~ of themselves and others. But at the level of writing feminism has despite all efforts to the contrary continued to produce *auteurs* and Definitive Texts. And what is feminism if at its heart phallocentric power relations continue to be inscribed?

We were well aware when we began to write this of various complexities. We have been writing as two writing a common text 'together': that commonalty does not reside in our sex – we are one female, one male – but 'together' sums up how we have produced our ~~Text~~ through conversation, notes and drafts exchanged and even writing two versions of this conclusion simultaneously, versions which are now merged. 'Together' extends beyond the two of us as well: to find the same being written – differently – by Abel, for example, increased our awareness of writing in a shared discourse. But 'together' has its limits. The final ~~Text~~ cannot simply overcome the old interplay of power between Author and Reader – not and remain ~~Text~~. So we accept that among our ~~readers~~ lurking anonymously somewhere, is an Ideal Reader (whom we have not been able, in our writing, to ignore): we are aware that this Reader will perceive in what we have written defective scholarship, or a defective feminist standpoint, or both . . . but we are even more aware of our power as Authors to impose *our* Reading.

NOTES AND REFERENCES

1. Cixous, 'The Laugh of the Medusa' (1976), in *The 'Signs' Reader: Women*

Gender and Scholarship, eds. E. and E. K. Abel, University of Chicago Press, Chicago 1983, p. 282.

2. See Derrida, *Of Grammatology,* trans. G. C. Spivak, Johns Hopkins University Press, Baltimore, Md. 1976.

3. Cixous, p. 283.

4. See *Lessico politico delle donne 6: letteratura, cinema, arti visive,* edizioni Gulliver, Milan 1979.

5. See Judy Chicago, *The Dinner Party,* Anchor Books, New York 1979.

6. Xavière Gauthier, 'Existe-t-il une écriture de femme?', *Tel Quel,* No. 58 (1974), p. 96.

7. George Steiner, 'After the Book?' (1972), *On Difficulty and Other Essays,* Oxford University Press 1978, p. 189.

8. Foucalt, 'What is an Author?', *Screen,* XX, 1 (1979), 13–33.

9. See Virginia Woolf, 'Women and Fiction', in *Women and Writing,* The Women's Press 1979, pp. 43–52.

10. See *The Rolling Stone History of Rock and Roll,* ed. J. Miller, Picador 1981.

11. See Walter Ong, *Interfaces of the Word,* Cornell University Press, Ithaca, N.Y. 1977.

12. Elizabeth Abel, 'Editor's Introduction to *Writing and Sexual Difference* Issue', *Critical Inquiry,* VIII (1981), 173.

13. See Foucault, *A History of Sexuality,* trans. R. Hurley, Allen Lane 1980, Vol. I.

14. Beatrix Campbell, 'A Feminist Sexual Politics: Now you see it, now you don't', *Feminist Review,* No. 5 (1980).

15. Cixous, p. 283.

Chapter 13

THE UNCONSCIOUS AND CONTEMPORARY CULTURE

DAVID PUNTER

My starting-point for this essay is a concept of the 'social unconscious'; that is, a set of processes at work in society underneath the level at which conscious forces, motivations, volitions come into play. I assume that one task for the cultural critic is to explore these processes. But this exploration cannot be a simple one, because the project of bringing the darkness into the light contains, and can only work in terms of, a paradox. The best attempts to work in this area – I am thinking of Freud, Barthes, Jameson – have taken on this paradox in varying degrees[1]; Barthes in particular has suggested to us that what must be involved is a certain self-reflexivity, a radical questioning of the self which is doing the investigating, and in the more recent work in the field it is becoming increasingly obvious that this self-reflexivity is bound of necessity to generate different forms of writing. To put it at its simplest, we can say that the very forms of narrativity in which we might conventionally choose to express our perceptions of the world are themselves statements, of an implicit kind, about the amenability of the world to coherent interpretation; but behind the assumption of coherence there lies, not a neutral rationality, but precisely a *desire* for coherence; and this has to be reckoned into the account we give.[2]

The seven pieces which comprise this essay are attempts, of differing kinds, to render various experiences of cultural encounter, and to do so in a way which does not seek to eschew the moment of subjectivity. But I have also assumed that this 'moment of subjectivity' is not something which is given to us as a 'natural' responsiveness to experience, but rather something which is itself constructed by the shards and fragments of culture which continually address us, and which address us in a particular form in a culture where the 'fragmentary' has itself achieved a peculiar status[3]: in a world where we are continually exposed to bits and pieces of experience, conveyed to us at high speed through specific technological developments which largely appear to us as beyond our control, the most useful forms of writing will replicate that fragmentation at the same time as questioning it. Writing comes to approximate to the filmic image, the broken flow of television programming, a set of 'depth pictures' each with its own root in unconscious process.[4]

I would only want to add that the seventh of the pieces, 'M1 Gangsters', might be considered by readers as an 'optional extra': the other six deal with, or at least begin from, cultural phenomena – changes of style, prevalent attitudes, structures of power and control – which I take to be quite familiar, while the seventh attempts to take a structure of narrative itself as a starting-point. But it is possible that this cannot be done; in which case, it might be worth thinking about the 'limit of narrative' which we are forced up against when we come to investigate our own ambivalences, the difficulty of manifesting a 'pleasure of the text' when the text itself is a psychological construct and thus already at a specific remove from empirical evidence.

I have not supplied a conclusion, because I would prefer not to 'naturalize' these pieces by drawing them back into the web of universal interpretation; but there are some themes which I believe to emerge within and between them which you might want to bear in mind as bases for further work, and they can be listed quite readily. The specific intersections of commerce and culture; the complex relation between phallomorphism and the new technology; the connection between spatial arrangements and the structures of power and control; the fear of annihilation and the means we devise to allay it; the generations in relation to decades and other forms of temporal patterning; the condition of the lyrical: these are the points at which I would begin to see some kind of pattern or shape emerging among these pieces, but for the individual reader those shapes might be quite other.

FROM PUNK TO NEW ROMANTIC

The trajectory from punk to new romantic, in one sense a customary reversal of styles (chains to looseness, gaudy to pastel, rocker to hippie), and thus modelled on an already institutionalized process of change, can also be seen in terms of a sequence of adjustments to power. The removal of the mechanisms of social and industrial control from the hands of humans, the arrival of the new technology, is necessarily accompanied by a mystification, of discourse among other things: computers give birth to their own languages. But that removal cannot be 'shielded' (in the nuclear sense) at the actual point of impact: unemployment, redundancy, superfluity. The first response seems to have been an ironically self-cancelling aggressivity: the chains are not weapons but the signs of bondage, self-hobbling, reminiscent of Kurt Vonnegut's religion of God the Utterly Indifferent, with its apparatus of visible handicaps.[5] If that response is built on the ruins of individual power, and reflects imprisoning within a newly useless self, the next response is more frightening, because the new romantics demonstrate how the removal of power to inaccessible reaches is accompanied by the growth of a fantasy of power which is exempted from reality-testing. The styles of the new romantics are public-school, dancing while Rome or London burns[6]: whereas for the Clash, London really was burning and the flames at least provided spectacle, and could be reflected in the violent reds and greens of the coxcomb, the new romantics are looking fastidiously in a different direction, in towards the imaginary realm of the dance hall and towards the imaginary network of a circuit of clubs and known 'personalities'.

The punk movement had no personalities: there was no public arena to be striven towards, and thus each individual punk was as pure a manifestation of an ethos as any other. The new romantics resurrect the fiction of fame; that, even amid overpopulation and the rule of the commodity, the individual can construct a stage for the display of heroism. What is encoded is the struggle of the self, driven beyond endurance by experience of constriction, taking flight into a realm of lightness and swirling shapes, reincarnating, like the Great Gatsby, a background for the unspecified great action: 'I will do such things, What they are, yet I know not . . .' Punk enacted commodity, packaged, interchangeable, the challenge of the parcel within which the human shape becomes unrecognizable; the new romantics exaggerate the shapely, pretend that the stylish appearance of success can compensate, put into parodic practice the lessons of the school careers officer about self-presentation and turnout. Punk knows that where there are no jobs, and where claims about leisure training are acts of bad faith, this *matters*; for the new romantics, the living fiction is that the systems of support and achievement can be bypassed, that the façade of the good life is available.

Every aspect and manifestation of aberrant behaviour can be glibly characterized as a reaction to the bourgeoisie; what is significant for distinctions here is the bourgeoisie's arrogation to itself (in a way which did not interest successive aristocracies) of the reality principle. It is this which selects and distributes alternative roles: punks and new romantics live out despite themselves the risqué fantasies of a secure group of which they are not a part, pushed successively down and up the social scale. Bourgeois security lies – now – in knowing that the social scale has ceased to exist in the sense of a ladder to be climbed; the location of an alternative group subjectivity within the trappings of an outmoded upper class, as with the new romantics, plays as safely into the hands of a rigidified power structure as does the enactment of a bondage which is otherwise invisible, locked away in prison and factory. It is as if the middle class, having locked its rivals safely away in cul-de-sacs, can now afford to spend a little time watching false and staged representations of those rival groups enacting their own redundancy, their own inappropriateness in the world of computers and information deluge.

What is also available in the trajectory of styles is a range of images of Englishness, from the punks, locked claustrophobically into an England as gaol, as defeat of aspiration, to the new romantics, laying claim to a mythic Europeanism (Cabaret Voltaire, Spandau Ballet) which only really appropriates uncomprehended shards of foreign culture. Either way, the impulse is to pull out, from the Common Market, from a failing competitivity; and then to close in around the uncomfortable remnants of imperial power, squeezing the pips. But where the punks found no residual juice, were content with hearing the rasp and abrasion of a system which had no goods to deliver, no offerings for the fulfilment of desire, the new romantics imagine an irrigating flow, as though the dry bones of England can be made to live again by creating more channels of communication, by claiming that a new aristocracy can form a vital grid across the country, albeit a grid mapped on to metropolitan domination.

It would be easy to see the style of the new romantics as feminine, flowing garments and flowing locks, but this is caught up in an assimilation to the perennial style of the privileged, those whose clothing will never need to be adapted to prevent mauling by the machine. For the heavy machinery mimicked in the clumsiness and rattling rhythms of punk is, after all, defunct: the new sources of power are noiseless rooms, flickering banks of lights, the soft whir of computer tape. There is a correlation here with the commercial rise of video, which also transforms linear time into an available and manipulable series of playbacks, but in the world of commodities cause and effect are mystified: perhaps it was the imperative of the new technology which came first, and the dreaming and flouncing of the new romantics emerges just on cue to fill the otherwise empty cassettes of the manufacturers. Certainly the impact of Japanese technology preceded the obsession with oriental aesthetics, which it is now in a market position neatly to encapsulate.

What happens also at this point of transition is a move away from the tradition according to which teenage style clustered around music, towards a more polyphonic ensemble of media: punk and new romantic music is an accompaniment, not a prime mover, a throwaway adjunct to a style held more truly and more steadily in a set of social behaviours. But the availability of these behaviours for public consumption is different: punks laid claim to the streets, asserted that what went on there was of a larger order than the domestic, whereas the new romantics merely pass through the streets accidentally, faces averted, dresses held high, on their way from one outpost to another of a mythic café society. In punk, then, the dispossessed self conceded that it has nowhere to go: the new romantics refuse the fact, find their summation in the airport lounge where everybody is of interest on the grounds of where they might be going to, or coming from. Thus the stasis of the social and career ladders is bypassed, and an alternative mild gradient set up within the hidden and closed society; as higher education closes down, or closes in on the few products of real educational privilege, the concept of 'opportunity' becomes all-pervasive but fatally vague, as though now there is always something exciting just around the corner, even if we cannot formulate what it might be.

In this transition, then, we can find the self colluding in its own superfluity, constructing a flimsy world. Teenage culture in the West has been preparing for this for generations, drawing boundary lines around an age group, but whereas previously there was an element of preparation contained within the withdrawal into the Long Hut, now teenage culture can conceive of itself as terminal, can draw into itself adult styles – must, indeed, do so because the bridges to be crossed on the regular route of maturation are down.

STEREO

The silver and the lights, symmetrical gleaming boxes encased in black, stacked: a neat segment from the cockpit of an aeroplane, or the boxed controls of the anaesthetic machine, precise speed and precise control, the flicker of a green dial between life and death. The controls have their own life, insulated from sound, yet being in charge of this magic array is not exactly a matter of taste, but a participation in a knowledge, which has its own material forms of proof: trade magazines, arrangements of statistics, hierarchies of abbreviations, an invisible and soundless network, modelled curiously on an older circuit, the radio hams, but freed now from the element of danger. The choices to be made are not on a spectrum between sense and a splitting screech, but a question of minute shading, balance: as though the successful conclusion is to be a complete poise, sonic angels balancing on a pinhead. Into the cluttered living space, this bank of equipment brings a different order, partly material, partly the imposition of a hidden geometry, bisecting angles, valorizing some listening positions at the expense of others, sorting out those visitors who share the knowledge from the clumsy ones who do not and whose world remains bounded by the armchairs and soft forms of cloth and carpet.

The styles change: the radiogram, hopelessly obsolete, has passed under the vague heading of Victoriana, because it foregrounds conformity to the aesthetic of the polished surface and the rounded wooden edge, the metal and clockwork brought within the purview of duster and polishing rag. The portable record player, in its day proud of compactness and storability, is now a child's toy, archaic as bakelite, its snazzy coloured plastics yellowing with age. The newer scattered systems, separate decks and amplifiers, still survive but are having to fight: foregrounding (correctly, according to the new aesthetic) the architectonic, they nonetheless do not permit the absolute compacting of control of the new, stacked systems, and bespeak a less than adequate dedication. Split among the neat ferns and modernist ornaments, they represent decoration and amateurism, now superseded by the consolidation of technical mastery. Scattered, those systems relied on movement, on a ranging of equipment, an age of expansiveness where all pleasures could fit into a wider concept of entertainment: with this new style, entertainment is as old-fashioned as *Sunday Night at the London Palladium,* technical excellence has moved easily to the top of the list of priorities, and specific records, tapes, programmes have become examples, the illustrations which provide evidence alongside, but subservient to, the already complete text of the equipment itself.

What is also present here – and what constitutes the imagistic integrity of the text – is an interlocking series of devices: a sequence of turns of the various dials can produce a sound (meaning) so nearly identical to another sequence that only the skilled reader can effect the distinction, yet the route we must follow to produce these near equations already involves the all-important mastery of technique. Women could manage a radiogram, children a portable: here we are in an exclusive world of the male, a minutely articulated system which serves to effect differentiation and to manifest control. From this panel, the room itself can be manipulated, its dimensions pulled inside out, with minimal effort: the machine becomes an extension of the body, and the bodies which need extension, which continually cry out for perfect reproduction and yearn after what is denied, are male. This is a tiny approximation to the grander prostheses of radar, computer-controlled microsurgery, electronic surveillance systems: a foretaste of the rôle of the male in the future, at the controls of starship or home computer, untrammelled by soft edges, the silver boxes surrounded by the dark, eyes and ears drawn inward, the apparently shrunken senses really cultivating a power through intensity and penetration, turned phallomorphic and probing into the silence and the dark, producing sound at the turn of a dial or the flick of a switch, endlessly manipulating, 'experimenting, experimenting,/with long damp fingers twisting'.[7] From the machine we can extrapolate the shape of the male body of the future, grown intense and sensitive at the edges and tips with the desire for control, conjuring images from the dark, the male as heroic wrestler with imprecision or as artist/hunter, accustoming itself to the atrophy of the useless, hearing about the wars through which that atrophy is continually performed in perfect stereo.

Like a phantom phallus, this system projects itself into the world along lines of excess, appropriating and cordoning space: the stereo becomes a *symbol* of force, with always too much power, always a wattage whose potential goes wildly beyond use, like the cars which could reach a hundred in a few seconds if there were a place to do it; but then, as with the stereo, the projected place can only be an airstrip, with the expected consummation a takeoff, a machine to negate the world and achieve an untrammelled overview. Such machines are thus insistently male: washing-machines do not possess excess power, do not, as do the stereo or the car, offer an overdrive which will blank out consciousness through sound or speed. But then, washing-machines are not weapons, as the male technologies are, weapons for attack and to safeguard self-differentiation; and, paradoxically, the stereo is also a weapon for silencing, a gigantic megaphone for the (male) voice of the operator which will drown out competing voices, as the adolescent uses his sound system to drown mother as she calls up the stairs. And with headphones, the silencing becomes a mechanism for total withdrawal, for an apparent retreat but into the strong fortress of the (male) self, where plans can be laid and hatched and the domestic excluded.

The illusion is that the bank of equipment is endlessly extensible: that there will be ever more closely matching machines (matching to prevent too many initiates) to figure power in the world. But the construction of the chimera is more complete than that: fully wired for sound, the operator turns himself into technology, separates sensuous accuracy from material being, locates himself according to the intersections of the airwaves as a counterbalance to the constricting immediate geometry. The turntable has a stroboscope, rounded form controlled and pinned down by an approximation to the dangerous accuracy of the laser, of the guided missile. Like Macavity, the male at his controls is never on the scene of the crime, his ego defences lying in increasing remoteness, endlessly seeking to circle above the gross matter of the planet, but now also compensating for the collapse of the dream of space travel. Thus life and death, the bursting bomb and the burst eardrum, become a question of fine tuning, of 'homing in', as though the true way for the male to come 'home' is in a cloud of stars signifying glory and death.

DIY AND THE MIDDLE CLASSES

Among the many threads drawn together, and exploited, in DIY is an imagining of the future. Fears about what is to come used to be global as in Jules Verne, and the narrative hero was able to react (as atomic scientist, politician, traveller) on a global scale; John Wyndham and

Nigel Kneale typify a change of subject location, whereby the cosmic (or national) disaster is given to us and experienced through the specific disruption of local structures of power (the hospital, the plant research institute, the town hall).[8] DIY is a preparation for this experience, where the intricate web of specialism will be proved flimsy and we will have to reabsorb into ourselves the skills of survival and demonstrate that the spirit of Crusoe still lives within the bourgeoisie; it is thus simultaneously a statement about power and control, such that the middle classes assert in advance that whatever the next world order will be, they will be able to dominate that too through flexibility and adjustment. Thus also, there is something contained about atrophy: as when a limb is amputated the subject still experiences a presence, so the middle classes, self-shorn of manual skills, still flex the missing limb, hoping to conjure it back into existence.

But of course, ideology is a realm in which material constraints are manipulable, and thus it is possible that these flexings and petty insurrections will indeed induce new growth; and thus the middle classes, central power source of the social body, will be able to dispense with the Other and take on the shape of a whole society, a society which will have the further advantage of being radically slimmed', and in fit shape to inhabit the changed world. The rejection of the unemployed millions would thus become a real casting into the outer darkness: excluded from the fallout shelters as they have been excluded from labour, the working classes would be shifted into the category of total commodity, visible only on the radar screens and computer printouts from which the new controllers will, safe inside, be reading' the shape of things to come.

The difficulty of imagining that new world, and the hesitancy about preparation, are symbolized in the burgeoning of DIY, from handsaw to complex power tool. The middle classes, it seems, cannot resist the phallic, even when it is accompanied by a reliance on what might become unavailable power sources; but then, the dim myth of the post-nuclear future has probably to do with individual generators of electricity, indeed with individual stockades, complete with various power supplies, within which bourgeois families may wait out a time of change, untouched and untarnished. Within that too, there are visions of improvement: that the manifestation of those stockades, those pioneer dwellings in an otherwise empty land (or populated only by gangs of working-class youth who, exempt now from police control, are fit game for shooting), will allow the middle classes to regain the family ramifications which they have lost, to reaccept the sense of cousinhood which has been wrecked by mobility and competitivity. Within the wooden walls (for, the myth goes, we will have crept by then from the underground shelter, perhaps sending the dog up first to sniff the new air), we will refind the exhilaration of self-sufficiency, and, in time, also the joy of fresh communication: untrammelled by the 'usual channels' (which we have constructed and by which we now find ourselves bounded), we will be able to devise new discourses, new methods for sending out messages to the next compound and discovering whether life still exists after slimming/beyond the family.

DIY is thus about changes in space and about the future towards which those changes might point, and here it shades into a conflict between two different wider models of spatial modification, on the one hand 'extensionism', and on the other the camping holiday and the weekend cottage, from Godard to Posy Simmons. Essentially, this is again an issue of class: the perpetual extension of the house, the working-class habit, bases itself firmly on the original space and claws back marginal territory, adding a room here, an extra alcove there, redesigning and pushing back the loadbearing walls, filling out frontage. Meanwhile the middle classes, at camps in the Dordogne or rebuilding rural slums near the Norfolk coast, are reclaiming different types of space: bolt-holes, advance guardposts for a different kind of living. On the one hand, the single stout and capacious structure (equivalent of the heavily armoured – wallpapered – naval cruiser, or the solidly equipped and old-fashioned military regiment), on the other a network of lines traced across the country, outposts, choices (the equivalent of submarine warfare, or of strategic options, including the possibility of going to ground). Of course, it is possible that this supposed battle of the future against an alien power is itself a cover story for a class battle perceived much nearer at hand than that, in Toxteth or in Brixton; indeed, that the epidemics of our future imagining are already with us as 'violence' (in its middle-class definition) spreads into the hitherto inviolate suburbs and as the informational network of the bourgeoisie (the country retreats, the *Guardian*) is developed and opposed by other images of network (the 'black' economy, with all the dualities of meaning produced by that phrase).

Thus the armchair strategists and the specialists in guerilla warfare take up their stations within the institutional apparatus of the state, demonstrating by so doing the point which they will continually try to impress on the public: that those institutions are hollowed out, riddled with woodworm, façades behind which dwell and fester the agents of subversion. Skilled in DIY, we are already coming to know how to recognize the various kinds of rot which might afflict the 'house' of Britain (the house of Windsor, the House of Commons) and to be able to deal with them. Of course, the ideological projection also offers its pleasures, even to the radical consciousness: after all, this reclaiming of skill and material contact can be seen as a previously suppressed part of an essential materialism, regaining touch, moving back into a genuine inhabiting of an otherwise alienated world, attempting a differentiation of labour which will move beyond the locked divisions of class warfare. Thus, of course, socialist intellectuals, contaminating agents of damage to the societal and domestic fabric, are given an apparent choice, between public and private arenas for development; and this is a holding device to prevent spread but also a pre-testing of choices to come (about the stability of the economy, about expansion, about cottage industry).

There is another sense too in which DIY represents a 'waiting for the end': a sense that, when there is a calling to account, we may not be able just to say, 'I have been a computer operator, or part of a technical team', but may want to be able to pronounce a discourse with greater historical validity: archetypally, for so many reasons, 'I was a carpenter'. To have tied a life in so closely to a bundle of temporary specialisms may, in the end, make us feel queasy: how shall our biographies be written when the advance of technology and control has rendered the very names of our labour meaningless? Yet there is a question behind this, about the account and to whom it is to be rendered, to God or perhaps to the Goddess, to women, of whom perhaps we fear that they may be ironically recognizing the inexplicability of these male lives spent in the service of unintelligible goals, and even worse, recognizing the regressive and infantile pleasures which are grafted into them. On this account, it may also be necessary to list an assertion of virility, through power drill and bradawl; and again, a skill at 'making' which will revalidate masculine work against the threatening combination of production and reproduction which is possible only for women (although the State is rapidly generating devices to render that threat redundant).

Just so, there is a hovering question about the addresser of the imperative in 'Do-it-yourself': the State, restless in its operation of an over-complex commercial traffic; the sublimely rude tradesman of bourgeois nightmares, who offers to come only in three years' time; the wifely stereotype, both challenging virility and refusing assistance; or that part of the self which ironically and painfully thinks it recognizes a basic social Hobbesianism, which thinks it 'knows' the selfish secret of life. Against all these addressers, the home workshop is a spatial defence, and also a temporal one: an area where a little can be 'carved' out of the surrounding structures, where a stamp can be pressed into the given shapes of life and housing.

THE BOOK DEPARTMENT

Neither a bookshop, with its implicit apparatus of technical and specialist assistance, nor a station bookstore, home of an unashamed and time-bounded consumerism, the book department in a large store offers its own grid of power and popularities, its own version of the science of knowledge, all the more potent for its obvious immersion in a wider science of uses and functions (hardware, crockery, gifts). Its entrance lies through the Children's Books, because their sales depend on colour, foregrounding, accessibility: the cost of books mauled is well justified by the unexpected purchases to silence a demanding infant. The sections which are set aside for men-as-husbands (do-it-yourself, hobbies) are more initially puzzling, technical manuals alongside coffee-table and workbench extravaganzas, but this is because they cater for an 'uninformed' public: the assumption is that most of these books will be gifts, welcome or unwelcome, from women, who know nothing, to men, who will value the thought more than the efficacy.

The lines which run through the fiction sections are more complicated again, in one sense more archaic: Penguin classics in black covers can still be unself-consciously referred to as Black Classics, though not in London or Liverpool. It appears initially as though a primitive classification is carried through: Romance, Horror, Crime, Westerns. But this is not a classification imposed, rather the recognition of a writing and publishing practice, although the end term of the series (Pornography) is still suppressed. What the genres do, among other things, is serve as parentheses, within which another, different category, sub-labelled Fiction, has its home, stripped of the recognizable marks of difference; classics which have recently been televised are neatly removed and placed into a separate category of their own.

The 'genres' flourish on repeated consumption: 'I'd like one of those which I haven't read yet'. They are finite, collectible; they embody the possibility that, with sufficient voraciousness, all the Science Fiction in the world might be amassed or consumed, like the endless parts of the Reader's Encyclopaedia of Human Knowledge (in weekly instalments). Each individual artifact is readily decipherable as a fit member of a class, the hand-drawn covers and cheap paper of Romance immediately distinguishable from the glossy raised covers and lurid blacks, mauves and turquoises of Horror. The slightly older genres can afford a little more discretion, but only because their overarching sign has a little more history, a little more evolution, and has turned further into a hieroglyph, an arbitrary language: the green covers of Crime do not carry a direct signification of content, only a reference back to a preceding chain of signifiers. The Fiction category is turning itself into this kind of sign as well (English Classics), grey covers representing the grey area between the poles of the rainbow.

The Biography section bulks large, hardback rather than paper, royal and aristocratic insignia replacing the commercial logo, as, inside, the leisured manners of an older writing practice survive against the quickfire of the genres. Biographies are respectably clothed in dust-jackets, lives without real revelation; what is also encoded is longevity, the length of the life assimilated to the assumed length of possession. A neighbour might not return Crime or Romance, but

Biography becomes property, even if the actual practice of rereading has died, to be replaced by an empty space for the reader and a filled space only on the bookshelf.

Across this grid lies a different one, which takes up the lesson that the same reader may, from time to time, buy from different genres, and which thus seeks to juxtapose them and achieve sale by contagion according to a wider conception of taste and desire for information: Paladin, Picador, Abacus, distinct revolving stands to represent a more sophisticated version of time and space than the steady ranks of the other classifications. Here there is a discreet obeisance to the assumed myriad-mindedness of the middle-class reader: a little magic, a little new fiction, a little nostalgia, perhaps even a little sex. Penguin's children, now that the sole parent has grown flabby, are coming into their own, sprightly and lean, counterposing modernist spaciousness to the neo-Victorian clutter of the older covers.

The basic grid is crossed again, and differently, by the Fine Books section, where the 'fineness' of Dickens or Hardy is floated on the same exchange as the 'fineness' of imitation-leather book-jackets and as the further 'fineness' of art reproduction. Taken altogether, these constitute an impregnable stockade of taste, sealed in glass, multi-volumed, parodically similar to an eighteenth-century library. The discourse of 'quality' and 'sensitivity', the whole paraphernalia of a devalued aestheticism, is here translated into an undifferentiated commodity, quality transformed into quantity, the regressive pleasure in the 'matching sets' of the stamp album replacing sequentiality and even history itself. This is the point at which surplus profit can be turned back into investment, the Wall (Street) of Art.

The Hobbies shade imperceptibly into the Household Hints, female work equated with male leisure, cooking with pigeon-fancying, economies of time with expenditure of time: most of the books here cannot be read, but are the figures for lost authorities and unavailable assistance, codified advice to the consumer at sea in this store itself and in thousands like it. Here are the dreams of ideal homes, and the wish for a self-enclosing knowledge which will no longer be dependent on untrustworthy tradespeople, alongside the replacements for the knowledges unacquired during maturation. And next to them, the further instructional props for life in the twentieth century: home health, physical perfection, aids to the relaxation of mind and body, the fragments of the New Science of the suburbs.

The counterpointing of grids reflects uncertainty about the time and space of the reader: how to lodge these books in domestic interiors divided between television space, workshop, kitchen, in stretches of time rigidly planned from workplace to TV schedule. What, perhaps, differentiates Fiction is that it presupposes a reader with time and space to return, to receive instruction of the imagination from a non-instructional text and to derive satisfaction from a product lacking the skeletal formula which, in the 'genres', engages prediction. The sub-fictional genres have absorbed, and now refract, the dreadful literary/critical lesson, that plots can be typed and numbered, that there is a limited range of narrating positions and of reading arcs: within them, we can abandon the effort at wider judgement, and settle instead for quantitative estimates of deviance from the norm; we can become ourselves the credit-rating computer which passes a strict judgement on structural conventionality. The pleasure of the genres does not derive purely from sameness, whatever the critics may see, any more than does the pleasure of Bach, but from a certain kind of fineness – not, certainly, fineness of style or of imaginative perception, but fineness of tuning, so that the most minute of variations can evoke a series of rememorations of previous instances. In this sense, each genre constitutes a single text, and that structure is being reabsorbed into the higher and more 'literary' forms, Robert Coover, Italo Calvino and Borges providing us with texts where the variations are played and tuned within a single cover.[9]

But the price of all this is that the 'classic' text thus becomes the incommensurable: the genres become a series of defences between the literary and the reader, but not in the sense of walls to be scaled, rather of pleasures to be experienced without the effort of changing worlds. At this point the arrangement of the book department becomes inseparable from the fate of the literary itself, mediated as it is, through television and the dominant media of habitual learning, in the shapes of psychobiography, sensationalism, sexual perversity; bracketed, as in the book department, as the indistinct. In the genres, success and failure for the reading self are clearly marked: either we triumph over the aliens/foreign spies/resistance of our mistress or lover, or we are understandably overwhelmed by prodigiously superior forces of monsters/undercover agents/objectionable family members. What is excluded from the genres is the possibility of *not* attaining to a global knowledge of this kind, of remaining in doubts and confusions; perhaps the fear, for us, of being no longer a world power, but worse than that, of not knowing whether we are or not. And so the genres and the instructional texts close in around the English 'literary', protecting but also strangling the arena of doubt and interchange, squeezing readerly space into a spot beside the dinner plate and readerly time into ten minutes before sleep.

THE BOOK CLUBS

Several versions are available of the book as commodity: fetishism is present in the chains of genre titles, in the glass-doored alcoves for fine art books, in the privileging of publishing house and imprint. The commodity peddled by the mail-order book clubs falls at a particular intersection of history and value, an intersection secretized and effectively silenced by its removal from the processes of direct purchase and choice. Responsibility can be removed from the purchaser: here we have a selection made by an anonymous – although occasionally very public – panel; the books carry a guarantee, both of their lasting value and, by virtue of uniform binding, of their approximate equivalence. A market which would otherwise be puzzling, even embarrassing, is sanitized: it appears, of course, appropriate that in the fantasy of gentlemen's clubs and smoking-rooms which is woven by the advertisements we should not have to tangle directly with the arcane whims of booksellers, should not have to expose ourselves in person to the possibility of exploitation by the bearers of superior knowledge.

At one level, the value is floated on the common seas of exchange. The talismanic words flow like honey: gold, calf, leather, illumination. All is texture: these are books to feel, and also books which will glint at us, whether they are touched or not. Their physical surfaces are both glossy and pitted, demonstrating a sere resistance to the weathering of time. Their cornerings and clasps move us back to a variety of valorized traditions: through the caricature treasure-chest into the world of piracy and hoarding, through their seals into the stamped significance of legal documents, wills, property transactions, through their esoteric garb, loaded with half-understood signification, into the realm of magic and alchemy. Between these covers lurks the elixir of life, the perennial philosophy which we may be privileged to invoke over against the accumulating weight of trash. The book itself suggests other trappings, while at the same time obliterating their necessity: bell and candle, leather inkstand, leathered desk. Set in the veneered bookcase, they represent an entire world, a world of privilege, reminding us ambiguously of the rarity of literacy.

But the element of history is also more personal, more familial than that. There were bookcases in our youth, yellowing volumes of Scott and Mrs Hemans holding out promise – but it was a promise we never claimed; when we opened those treasure stores, we could still not find the key. Something was still withheld, the trick of the psyche which would somehow render those secrets available. They could not be read: they pertained to a past age. But perhaps, the myth goes, ownership was the important factor: perhaps now we have ourselves taken part in the procedure of embalming, we will prove able to probe the body, the body of discourse, the corpus of the past. But even if not, there is a further possibility; that these volumes will, for our own children, serve a similar function, will persuade them, if they should by chance call attention to a tawdriness in their surroundings, that culture was, after all, available to them too, that we had done our best that 'books should be part of their childhood'.

Introduction to contemporary cultural studies

For we – or our fathers and mothers – sold off the real thing, discarded it to make room for the neater electronic media. In doing so, we thought we had merely exchanged one model of familial incorporation – stories at bedtime, father reading the evening Bible – for another, centred comfortably around TV and radiogram. Perhaps we are now suspecting that this is not so: an easy way to displace the fear is by a gesture of return, by seeking again to reopen those channels of communication which the 'generation gap' appears to have severed. And so, from the book clubs, we buy back our history, alongside the genealogical investigations and the new, miniature piano. These are the books, we are asked to suppose, over which grandmother and grandfather pored in the cold evenings; therefore they might also be the tools with which we can rebuild the familial and societal security and stability for which they stood. We can weld together the generations by bringing about our children's adherence to these coded values; who knows, perhaps there is even a possibility that in time to come they, the children, may be able to provide *us* with the key, that they, with the benefit of further education, may be able to direct us through these over-lengthy narratives and interminable verses in the selective ways which we could not ourselves find.

The exercise in social reclassing which is here offered to the lower bourgeoisie is complex. On the one hand, there is the possibility of overcoming the thwarting of aspiration: that rise into the upper-middle class which at one time seemed a reasonable hope requires, obviously, at least the beginnings of a library, in itself but also as an antidote to dad's do-it-yourself manuals, mum's occasional thriller. But on the other hand, there is the chance to recapture a common culture, to revive a legendary time when these texts were the common currency of the land, when ploughman readers read ploughman poets, when damsels, however uneducated, shivered to the strains of chivalry and the sonorities of Tennyson. For those stuck in aspic, transfixed by the television, either kind of movement will do: from the crowded and repetitive suburbs out to the country, whether it be to the big house or to the comfortable cottage just down the road.

And, of course, there is a question of time. What is disastrously puzzling about literary culture is again this question of choice: with fashion, with pop music, even with film, there is a track laid down – styles alter and we can position ourselves, in various ways, in relation to them. But the literary never offers us a fair chance: most of it has already happened, that which is happening now is, presumably, inaccessible without some recapitulation, but how long would that take? Books do not even prescribe, of themselves, a reading time; how long are we *supposed* to take over *Great Expectations,* over Byron's tales? The book clubs solve this problem at a stroke: once a month the deliciously bound volume lands on our doormat amid the advertisements for central heating, the mounting heap of appeals for work from unemployed small tradesmen. Here there is not only uniformity in space but regularity in time: the pleasures of a series, the reduction of difference to an assimilable rhythm, even the further advantage of the possibility of reneging, of being naughty and not eating up our food.

And there is the expense. Here questions of pricing are reversed: it is not a question of a bargain, but of the investment of as large a sum as seems reasonable in the future. For these books promise both past and future, they conquer death: perhaps no cost could be unreasonable. Besides, it is hard to see how we could regret the payment: if the gilt chips and wears, if the leather cracks, we still have George Eliot or the *Encyclopaedia Britannica* on our shelves, and their dilapidation only contributes to the fictions of use-value. Here, too, is a property which we shall never throw away, which will not run out of batteries or lose its wheels, and which will reverse the process of time, gaining value as we, ourselves, wish to do; attaining to the reverence for wisdom which, as we remember, our grandparents were privileged to experience, but which we suspect does not lie in store for us. These objects will be spared the indignity of age: on our behalf, they will hold to the quiet authority lost to us in the shouting-matches, the petty arguments and jealousies, which sully our maturity.

EXAMINATIONS

The interrogation, the night boot at the door, the moustached colonel flanked by executioners, have been outlawed in the British ideology: in the school history books the last image of arbitrary power is the Court of Star Chamber, in the literature the looming castles and flickering candles were exiled at the end of the eighteenth century to Southern Europe, to the proto-banana republics of city-state Italy and the fortress-dominated deserts of a mythical Spain. Now the imagery is safely sanitized through Ruritanian comedy, exiled even as post-imperial responsibility to the secretive fumblings of the US in Central America, where we can pleasurably watch paper generals get what they deserve. Twelve good men and true are empowered to look into conditions of questioning; Judges' Rules cover the immediate and unsurveyed power of the police, exercised in police-station back rooms and in city-centre multi-storey carparks, with the patina of 'due process', as though those paternal and bewigged figures are capable of umpiring a safe adversary conflict between policeman and villain.

Instead of interrogation, we have examinations: in place of the model of the city state and the power of the Medicis, we have a refined version of Teutonic classification systems, with all the apparatus which has historically accompanied them. At root, there was a strong connection between the educational and the administrative state apparatuses: those examinations were the testing ground for a post in a proliferating civil service, the professors of philosophy in the Kantian tradition were also the intellectual guarantors of the legitimacy of the state. From that nexus sprang an apparently metaphysical debate which was at root political, which acted as an ideological justification for a separation of ideality and actuality, so that an existing political system, however corrupt, could be seen as a manifestation of a supra-phenomenal eternal order, a bourgeois extension of the divine right of kings. Doing well in those examinations was thus not merely a matter of personalized achievement; it carried also with it an initiation into responsibilities, demonstrating not simply absorption of an ideology but an operational fitness in the procedures necessary for handling the further dissemination of that ideology. Hegel, Chekhov, Kafka are the fantasists of that condition, where the transmission process between a humanist education and a bureaucratic version of political power was direct, and the examination served as guarantee of the required stability.

The essential features of this process are uniformity and distinction: a laboratory equalization of background against which minute discrimination can, we are told, stand out clearly. Thus the process of differentiation is itself dual: on the one hand, there is the differentiation among candidates, on the other the continuous practice of minute discrimination as a validation of the unfailing skills of the examiners. What the candidate cannot see is the process which takes place behind the mirror: the way in which the artificially calmed battlefield of the examination room has superimposed on to it the image of the war-room itself, where, under the guise of a more or less caring and accurate version of assessment of achievement, minutely various intellectual and political positions are staked out and evidenced, and the examiners come to direct grips with the control panels of society, dealing in percentages, classifications, specific balances of excellence; and all this uniquely safely, for in the examination process there is typically no one-to-one encounter across the all-important boundary, and no recourse of appeal from judgement.

Thus the examiners demonstrate to each other that their powers are not failing with age, that the curves of normalcy and aberration they carry in their heads and in their briefcases are not isolated fantasies but the material of a shared interpretation of value. As if, it may seem, by a miracle, the examiners agree: we should hardly be surprised, for they are there primarily to agree and thus to vindicate the integrity of the order to which they have given their allegiance. Secondarily, they are there accurately to measure the margins of dissent: not in the scripts which they mark, for these are merely the raw material of a formation process, but in the valorizing responses made by their colleagues. Minutely, the levels of permissibility vary year by year: the older and wiser heads are in a position of assessing the very flux of social acceptance, of viewing the tiny yawings of the craft of state as its centre of gravity shifts slightly with the generations.

By implication they are, of course, also in a position to make corrections to the vessel's course, although the means need not be crude. Boards of examiners are often created *ad hoc*, so there is little need for deliberate exclusion: what is easier is to establish the firmness of the centre, and to wait for the evidence of this conservatism to effect its own stabilizing power. For those new examiners who may be disposed to question the nature of this centring, there is always a space: on the one hand, they may be allowed to represent the State's benevolent concession to eccentricity, while on the other they may be conveniently exposed to the petty exercise of liberalism by means of which the bourgeois order maintains its grip.

Meanwhile, out in the examination room, the other necessary miracle occurs, and the organizing authority thus repeatedly demonstrates the power of its hegemony: there is, again, no revolt. The hundreds of candidates do not – again – experience their collectivity; they are, again, and at the drop of a piece of chalk, separated, atomized, reduced down to separate particles, and bow their heads before the puniest representative of that authority, albeit begowned or swordsticked. Again the frisson occurs whenever the lone candidate dares to raise a hand: will this be the signal, or the initiation of a transgression? But no, whatever the request was, it initiates only the conduct of an almost silent discourse: the invigilator bends caringly over his individual charge, having taken his own time to attend, and thus made and proved his own judgement of urgency. Thereafter the culprit is broken: no possibility there of change, and with each carefully handled 'incident', however trivial, the subjugation of the masses is more strongly reinforced. In the end, the dried-up residue of rebellion is pointlessly enacted, in the early leavers: but this only confirms the overall message, that only in some entirely other place, beyond the enclosing walls of this room, is there an available image of freedom, but at far too high a price for the majority.

The substance reflects the form: this is not the arena for risk. Thus the examination produces the familiar double-bind: lurking in the shadows is the image of the brilliant script, which is offered in terms not of a formal perfection but of a master-stroke, the single god-given answer which will convince that here is the potential hero of a generation. But this is, of course, not really possible, however much candidates may brag afterwards: and thus the image of the perfect answer to the all-consuming questions of the State is continually withheld, proffered but out of reach, confirming in advance the authority of the Board, convincing the candidates that it is better to be safe than to take the risk the effects of which, after all, nobody will ever see.

Because scripts are, effectively, not read. Indeed, they are pored over, but in conditions of the utmost secrecy, prior to the inevitable shredding, and thus confidentiality is assimilated to a bureaucratic secrecy. Thus also, the value of subjectivity is undermined: what is implanted in these future civil servants, administrators, men and women of paper, in a conviction that, in the afterlife, all judgements are provisional insofar as they cannot approximate to these defining conditions of objectivity. It is thus on the image of the unattainably accurate examination that the later operations of society are super-imposed: the check on the social security applicant's living conditions, the tax enquiry. Somehow, through the multiplication of these uni-lateral discourses of power, the longed-for conditions of certainty might be achieved; meanwhile, the evidence of the individual is to be treated as unreliable, merely as a partial text for interpretation.

Thus also a myth of finality is inculcated and fostered: that, some-where at the end of the learning process (for the assumption is that there must be such an end), there will be an accurate and reliable reckoning. In the meantime, raw experience is devalued: it is to be treated as preparation and revision, the early stages of a process which stands under the sign of teleology. Death itself is at stake in the examination room: on the pass lists, there will always be at least one name which does not appear at all, which has vanished off the end of the spectrum of the acceptable, to stand as the sign for a still present fate, as the evidence of the power of life and death. The examiners do not need to don the black cap; we don it ourselves as we participate in the process, as we submit to the procedures which will include in their end result the silent exclusion of one of our number, and which will thus validate our claim to further life.

M1 GANGSTERS

You know the scenario so well. It is the barely submerged substance of so many newspaper stories, the continuous site of fraud and intimida-tion, petty blackmail and urban fear. It is the scenario, the ambience which *Z Cars* portrayed as 'realistic'. The myth, then, that we are concerned with is not simply a place, certainly not an attitude of mind: rather, it is the occupant of a specific ideological fold, a *mise-en-scène* compounded of pleasures, taboos, transgressions, it is a composite image within which, like a cog in a gearbox, is enmeshed a specific image of the self, like the images bound up with royalty, stardom, the soap opera. As we imagine this scene, we find that parts of us which we cannot habitually mobilize have been living there, inhabiting this imagined discourse, seemingly without knowledge: like the way, en-meshed with Philip Marlow, we find mobilized within our selves a particular set of attributes, the laconic smile, the sauntering walk, the power in reserve, the bad luck. For it is the strength with which we engage with these alternate selves which demonstrates the dispersal of our subjectivity; it is the difficulty of mobilization and the taboo under which that process operates that is the gauge of our alienation, of the distance to which parts of our scattered selves have been flung in the always-already-past collision with the demands of authority. Thus the thrill of fictions: the surprise of being introduced to a landscape, and finding, there already, at home, a self – and one more organized than our pseudo-unitary subjectivity, because it is there in fantasy only, and can afford, psychically, the homogeneity, the collection together in one place, which for us, living with the risk of being permanently bound within our own shape, would be death.

This particular scenario has added resonance because it is mediated through both fact and fiction, film and news: the refractions of the image are multiple and, for all that, there is something held in reserve, a part of the plot which we will never know, for conspiracy is of the essence. The first element is a place, a recognized geography which can have many existences: a multi-storey carpark; a motorway café; a brief and unexplained encounter between the drivers of two cars. The place is constructed of these ingredients: anonymity – it belongs to nobody, or to a faceless department of State or council; neutrality – it is subject to regulations only in ways which have no bearing on the business to be conducted; danger – the drop from the uppermost floor, or the sudden flare of an engine straining, or the flick of a lighter which reveals the expected contours.

The second element is a discourse, because this place signifies as the site, the only possible site, for a discourse. It will comprise half-grasped threat and nuance; it will be anchored deep in ageing resentments; but still it will gain its sharpness and focus from the fact that here something important is at stake – money probably, but also a sphere of influence, domination of a territory, a monopoly on a particular black-market exchange. In the wings of this discourse hover the paraphernalia of sharp dealing: secondhand cars, bonded warehouses, tax evasion, payoffs, protection money.

The third element is imbalance, because this geographical/discursive site gains its purchase in our imaginations from the enactment of an unfair fight. It is here that the faceless thugs come for their instructions; here that large men in suits put the frighteners on mavericks and upstarts; here that the hideous birthday party is held which ends in victimization and scarring.[10] Whatever transaction takes place, a mark will be made; probably on the flesh, though where nobody can see, also on the mind and thus on future behaviour.

The characters, the selves and anti-selves, neatly engage us but within limits, for the assumption is that everyone who gathers here, transiently, is a gangster: in the encounter we are depicting, there is no carrier of a value we care about, only the various hierarchs of an order which itself, to us in our safe houses, is threatening. We can therefore view the battle of nerves with equanimity, as long ago we watched the rough boys sorting out their differences, and learned that it was better not to get in the way (and before that learned the same lesson about our parents' bedroom). For this encounter, which is even now being prepared, will be an enactment of patriarchy, a version of rape, a visiting of strength on relative weakness, and there will be, among other things, a process of feminization available for our complicated delectation.

So in this scene that we are filling in, a trade-off will be offered, or perhaps a warning issued; the hands will be gloved, and the suits unostentatiously expensive. What is at stake will probably be a contract; we shall watch the ripples from this controlled firestorm moving through the local radio and television programmes, surfacing as the success of such-and-such a tender for a housing project, or as a change in the habitual supplier of council dustcarts. Small commercial fortunes are on the line; there may be whispered threats about the safety of children, wives. The shadow of Poulson and T. Dan Smith will be in the air, and of Hitchcock's image of the body rolling helplessly out of a sack of potatoes, the unfathomable clue.[11] There will, perhaps, not be violence, although there may be jostling, and there will certainly be physical stances, shoulders squared, eyes flicking, tension.

It will be dark, although not so late as to arouse suspicion; it may be that neither party is clear about who has paid the police to stay away, but stay away they will. There will be calculating of odds, for the kind of power which exists in this fold of space is perpetually hovering, a balance of wreckage which hangs suspended, a fist drawn back for an undelivered blow. There will be the possibility that much can be deflected: that behind the aggro, there is the chance of an alliance against a further shadowy enemy, but on terms. The common currency will be Christian names, drawled or squeezed from between tight lips; or it may be that there will be other unuttered names present, the names of principals. It may be that everybody concerned will declare himself an agent; and it may even be true.

Not, of course, an undercover agent, or anything so melodramatic: merely a respectable agent for certain business interests, transacting a little business in the customary way. Certainly the theory will be that all this is sanctioned at a higher level, that this is the way things are done everywhere, that other pretensions are sanctimonious. It will not do to be fat, or drunk, or to care very much for one's relations: all this would be evidence that a certain fitness is sliding away, and that the balance is about to be decisively tipped, and if that were to happen the scenario would be different, would be less intricate, for then some of the cards would be visible on the table, whereas here nobody is yet sure what has been dealt.

If the interests at stake are sufficiently important, or diversified, regional distinctions may be mobilized: the hard men of the North come down to clean up on an untilled acre. But whether in this form or another, person and image will already have interacted: Humphrey Bogart and Jimmy Cagney will be somewhere in the air, investing this transaction with the faintest glint of glamour, light reflecting off a penknife, or perhaps it is coins between the knuckles. This is the pulse of commerce, the personal contact which has been outlawed from the world of office-blocks and wide desks; although it is nevertheless to those desks that reports will be offered, in the tersest of monosyllables and from call-boxes, in the morning.

We do not need to flesh out the sign still further; we all know this is the way things get done. There is the shoulder in the back when it seems as though business has finished, the smart Granadas racing away along the motorway, the belated cigarette, the new counting of odds. For us too, things would be simpler and more exciting if they were done this way: simpler because we are imagining each encounter as self-sufficient, more exciting because here is a precise use for words, words as act and gesture, threat and bargain, instead of as a vortex or whirling in the dark. Here each word is placed carefully; these men are the masters of tact, because in this version of Diplomacy everyone has agreed to the rules, and the least slackening of a poker-player's jaw will be noted. Here every hesitation, every moment of silence, is loaded, a mine of information; every gap left in the account given is a silence into which death may pour.

NOTES AND REFERENCES

1. The classic texts are Freud, *The Psychopathology of Everyday Life;* Barthes, *Mythologies;* Jameson, *The Political Unconscious: Narrative as a Socially Symbolic Act,* Cornell University Press, Ithaca, N.Y. 1981.
2. I am referring here also to Derrida's arguments in, e.g. *Of Grammatology,* pp. 87–93.
3. See also my 'Theory, Writing, Experience', *New Literary History,* XV (1984), 413–24, which refers back to 'Literary Theory in the University: A Survey', *New Literary History,* XIV (1983), 411–51.
4. Cf. my *The Hidden Script: Writing and the Unconscious,* Routledge and Kegan Paul 1985, ch. 9.
5. The reference is to Kurt Vonnegut, *The Sirens of Titan,* Dell, New York 1959.
6. I know that the new romantics are referred to here and throughout in the present tense, and that this, of course, is part of a process of built-in obsolescence.
7. Roy Fisher, 'Experimenting', in *Collected Poems 1968,* Fulcrum 1969, p. 43.
8. See, e.g., John Wyndham, *Trouble with Lichen,* SF Book Club 1962; Nigel

Kneale, *The Quatermass Experiment*, Penguin 1959; from the 1953 television serial.
9. See, e.g., Robert Coover, *Pricksongs and Descants*, Cape 1971; Italo Calvino, *Invisible Cities*, trans. W. Weaver, Secker and Warburg 1974; Jorge Luis Borges, *Fictions*, ed. A. Kerrigan, Calder 1965.
10. The reference is to Pinter, *The Birthday Party*.
11. The reference is to Hitchcock, *Frenzy* (1972).

Section D
NEW DIRECTIONS

Chapter 14

THE STORY SO FAR: AND FURTHER TRANSFORMATIONS?

RICHARD JOHNSON

POLITICS AND KNOWLEDGE: THE MAIN TENSION[1]

Cultural studies has developed in an intimate if critical relationship to academic knowledges. The debts to literary studies, social theory and social and historical research are especially deep. But the work has been propelled by other motives. Sometimes it has arisen from the needs, demands or 'spearhead knowledges' of the new social move-ments. Sometimes it has been fuelled by anger with the rigidities of 'old left' mentalities. Sometimes political frustration has been expressed as an attempt to understand a particular conjuncture. Agenda of research have been found in the everyday life of subordinated social groups, or in sides of daily life which 'serious' analysis has ignored. Very often researchers have sought to understand personal pilgrimages or blocks. Cultural studies, in other words, has been formed in a two-sided and highly contradictory relationship between academic knowledges and political aspirations.

Certainly this way of seeing things has some power in explaining our tradition. In the first, class-based phases, a critique of literary criticism provided a way of expressing an affirmative relationship with working-class culture.[2] A critique of conservative historiography and the con-struction of an alternative, democratic view of the national past pro-vided a way of renovating Marxism.[3] The leading modern instance of this dynamic is the feminist questioning of past knowledges, academic and 'radical', for their masculine partisanship, gender-blindness and neglect of women. Again, a whole new wave of work in cultural studies has been associated with very palpable political commitments. Cul-tural studies has been at the centre of several such reappraisals: it is a critical tradition, twice or thrice critiqued.[4]

This tension throws light too on everyday dilemmas. Each new group of researchers must battle their way through these contradic-tions or learn, at least, to 'ride' them. Do we start from 'the debates', half-removed from academic knowledges, but clearly bearing their impress? Do we have more than half an eye on considerations of academic prestige or self-justification? Or do we seek some directly 'political' entry to the topic, starting from a definition of popular needs? The depth of the contradictions depends on the extent to which academic knowledge-forms have *already* been transformed, but there remains a world of difference between even the critical knowledges and the forms which will build a new politics.[5]

This distance is reproduced by the social divisions which underlie the production of academic knowledge. While these divisions remain, I think we have to work both sides of the relationship. Of course, the relationship with academic knowledge has to be somewhat detached. Most of the real gains have been made through critiques. But I mean critique in the strongest sense: not rejection or criticism merely, but also a taking over and transforming of positive elements. It is in deciding what *is* positive that the other relationship has been so important. We have picked elements for their usefulness for cultural analysis but also for their potential as politically-active insights. In existing circumstances, anyway, we cannot leap into some wholly different way of knowing, divorced from knowledges which occupy the space of systematic thinking in our society.

If this analysis is right, however, neglect of the political connections is more likely. As academic knowledge, as a 'new discipline' even, cultural studies would lose its dynamic. There is a more than usual danger of this happening. This follows from some successes on the academic side, including the installation of cultural studies as a first-degree subject in several polytechnics, the development of journals, meetings and overseas links.[6] This sets up a marked tendency to academic codification and, where teacher attitudes are pragmatic, encounters for students with just another orthodoxy. Even where the subject remains, as it usually does, open and experimental, the impulses that made us critics may no longer be immediate to our students. How can *they* occupy a critical tradition critically, that is, productively?

In addition cultural studies and allied subjects (e.g., 'media' or 'film' studies) have a larger influence on academic disciplines, especially English, sociology, and that uncomfortable hybrid called 'communication studies'. More recently there have been productive engagements with linguistics, historiography and the whole area of visual art and design. This means fresh infusions of enthusiasm, but also the reproduction of disciplinary tendencies on the new ground. More deflating, perhaps, is the takeup of selected elements from cultural studies back into traditional disciplines, but disconnected from the political preoccupations that first gave them life.

Something like this tension has been present throughout the post-war history of the New Left. Indeed, a pessimistic reading would stress a secular tendency to academicization and therefore to separation from popular forms. But I also think we are more conscious of this divorce today. A sense of the connection between knowledge and power among the knowledge producers themselves may well turn out one of the significant developments of the 1970s. It has many manifestations: in the theories of Bourdieu and Foucault, in the critiques of science or scientism by radical scientists and radical philosophers, in the extensive concern with knowledge, control and social reproduction within the sociology and social history of education, and in the feminist critiques of academic knowledges, agenda and social relationships.[7] More practically the commitment to collective or community-based forms of knowledge production has often expressed dissatisfaction with the academic norms: 'normal' competitiveness and hierarchical authority especially. Even within the radicalized strata, there have been swings of emphasis here. We might compare the singular affirmation of 'science' characteristic of the early and mid-1970s and associated with the philosophy of Althusser with the less epic, more sceptical mood associated with Foucault's analysis of the many forms of 'knowledge/power' and the decline of the 'universal' intellectual. Academic and professional knowledge-forms now look much more like parts of the problem than parts of the solution. So the issue is now posed still more sharply, just as academic professions themselves become much more difficult to enter: what can be won, if anything, from academic concerns and skills for knowledges useful for popular emancipations?

One condition for winning anything from these forms is a sense of a collective project different from the usual academic purposes, themselves almost always individualistic in form. Maybe this has been the one most important resource in 'the story so far'. Only from such a standpoint can collective priorities be properly discussed. If we do not debate central directions of our own, we will be pulled hither and thither by the demands of academic self-reproduction or defence and by the differing disciplinary versions. Even now, distinctively 'literary' and distinctively 'sociological' approaches are developing, closely related to theoretical fragmentations. This would not matter if one discipline or one problematic could grasp the study of culture as a whole, but this is not, in my opinion, the case. Cultural processes do not correspond to the contours of academic knowledges as they stand. Cultural studies must be interdisciplinary or a-disciplinary in its tendency. Each approach tells us about one small aspect of a larger process. Each approach is theoretically partisan, but also very partial in its objects.

If this is right, we need a special kind of defining activity which reviews existing approaches, identifies their objects, their good sense, but also their limits. Actually, it is not definition in the sense of an academic codification of cultural studies that we need, but *some pointers to further transformations*. This is not even a question of aggregating approaches – a bit of sociology here, a spot of linguistics there – but of reforming different approaches in relation to each other. I hope to make this very general statement more concrete in what follows.

GENERAL DEFINITIONS

One possible area of debate is over general definitions of the field. There is not very much that can be said at so high a level of abstraction. Yet it is important to say something to dislodge, at the outset, the more grossly inadequate views of culture.

One starting-point is the term 'culture' itself. There are problems with this term if we wish to state our preoccupations quite tightly. 'Culture' is important, rather, as a kind of reminder: first, of a history of struggles over meaning; second, of some theoretical and political rules-of-thumb characteristic of the 'culture' tradition. There is no solution to this polysemy: it is a rationalist illusion to declare 'henceforth this term will mean . . .' and expect a history of connotations to fall smartly into line.[8] The situation with 'ideology' is now rather similar, if not more confused.[9] So though I fly 'culture' as a flag and use the word continually where imprecision matters, I seek other, fresher terms. 'Cultures' or 'lived culture' may also have particular uses which it may be important to retain.

My own keywords are 'consciousness' and 'subjectivity'. For me cultural studies is about *the historical forms of consciousness or subjectivity,* or *the subjective forms by which we live* or *the subjective side of social relations.* Each part of these definitions is important.

I think of consciousness, first, in its use in *The German Ideology.* As a (fifth) premise for understanding human history, Marx and Engels add that human beings 'also possess consciousness'.[10] This is elaborated in the 1844 *Manuscripts,* but is a premise of all the later works too. It is implied when, in *Capital,* Marx distinguishes the worst architect from the best bee by the fact that the architect's product has 'already existed ideally' before it is produced.[11] It has existed in the architect's consciousness, in his imagination, as an idea and also in its first materializations, as drawings, as designs. Human beings, as a species or as a general-historical feature,[12] are characterized by this imaginary life, this subjective side. But 'consciousness' has always to be viewed in its relation to practical activity, to human productiveness, and therefore to all the forms of social division and co-operation. This anti-idealist conception of consciousness, in which, however, the subjective side is very important, is one fundamental starting-point for cultural studies.

In later Marxist discourse 'consciousness' has often been narrowed, qualified as in 'class consciousness'. It has also been inflected to mainly cognitive questions – more or less adequate *knowledge*. I think that Marx's 'consciousness' was wider than this (though with lots of blind-spots too!). It included a consciousness of self and an active, moral self-production. Human beings produce *themselves* in conscious, 'sensuous' activity, under conditions they do not choose but which, within limits, they may transform. These are essential stresses too, of course, in the 'culture' tradition.[13]

In practice, however, Marx was especially interested in the critique of conceptually-organized knowledges – Hegelian idealism, French socialism, English and Scottish political economy. Despite the importance of his early critiques of religion, the contest with particular ideologies tends to replace the concern with everyday practical consciousness.[14] In his most interesting text on the character of thinking he tends to bracket out the other modes of subjectivity – the practical, the aesthetic, etc.[15] This is why it is so important to stress the meanings which in later debates have gathered around the term 'subjectivity'.

This includes all the features of 'inner' states traditionally ascribed to aesthetic or emotional life and, conventionally, to femininity. Actually such features enter into all subjective states: even *men* take *pleasure* in *knowing*! It includes centrally the 'who I am' or 'who we are' of culture, the formation of individual and collective identities. Also expressed in the modern debates around subjectivity is the very Marxist insight that subjectivities are produced not given, are objects for inquiry not premises or starting-points. The question is how we got to be who we are. 'Subjectivity' similarly includes the possibility that some impulses are subjectively active – they *move* us – without being consciously identified.

When discussing the circulation of capital, Marx continuously uses terms like 'forms', 'social forms', 'historical forms', etc. This language of 'forms', which I see as crucial for our own definitions, sometimes occurs in his discussions of consciousness or ideology: 'a distinction should always be made between the material transformation of the economic conditions of production, which can be determined with the precision of natural science, and the legal, political, religious, aesthetic or philosophic – in short, *ideological forms* in which men become *conscious* of this conflict and fight it out.'[16] This famous passage sketches a parallel project to Marx's main concern, a project equally concerned with forms. Marx was mainly concerned with the socio-economic conditions and their characteristic capitalist forms. He looked at social totalities from a particular point of view or set of abstractions: the forms through which human beings produce and reproduce their material life. Cultural studies also looks at social totalities, but from the different complementary point of view implied in the 1859 'Preface': the regular but transient forms through which human beings 'live', become conscious, and sustain themselves subjectively. This is a kind of *means*, a kind of *subsistence*, equally essential to human existence, *but in a different way*, to tools, food, shelter or a means of procreation. It includes Marx's 'ideological forms' but also such everyday phenomena as the stories about the day which we tell ourselves as we wake up of a morning, which help us get up, or send us snuggling back under the bed-clothes!

In its stress on 'forms', a Marx-influenced cultural studies converges with the various structuralisms, a second major influence on our definitions.[17] The indispensable structuralist contribution has been to draw out *the peculiar objectivity of the forms we inhabit subjectively,* the *objective* side of *subjectivity*. Subjective forms do not only exist as ideas, meanings, feelings in the heads and bodies of persons. Indeed in these states, they have a certain inscrutability. Fortunately for the possibility of systematic understanding, they exist also in objective embodiments: as language, rituals, discourses, ideologies, myths and all kinds of systems of signification. All these systems have their own rules, conventions or principles which underlie the possibility of producing meaning at all. Since these rules are daily learnt and activated by members of a community, they have a special kind of materiality of a profoundly social and conventional kind. In this way structuralisms (a composite here a very wide set of influences) have shown us how cultural forms have a shape, a hardness and a determinacy of their own, not to be reduced to a mere reflection, or to an individual existential flux of impressions and feelings. It is in the encounter with traditions *without* these insights – reductive Marxisms, for example, or some traditions in phenomenological sociology, or old-fashioned kinds of literary appreciation – that the debt to structuralism becomes so evident. Culture can be studied, systematically, precisely because it is understood as a social product with its own forms of objective existence and its own real shapes.

I hope I have said enough to distance us from all the partial and trivial views of culture which still regularly reappear on the scene. I am thinking of the definition of 'culture' as light relief which one sometimes finds in hardnosed positivistic sociology – you know, a matter of leisure or popular pursuits or, at best, of imponderables we cannot quantify. Cultural studies from such a viewpoint seems a matter of 'opinions'. On the other side, the high-cultural definitions continually recur: culture is limited to particular genres or high-art practices, or to the popular *equivalents* of such texts. It is after all possible to retain most of the old definitions and methods of analysis and apply them to new objects: from 'the novel' to 'the thriller', from art cinema to 'Hollywood' or television. The tug of amateur or professional enthusiasms also exercises an influence: in some quarters cultural studies equals sub-cultures. Of course these are all important objects, but we must not *limit* ourselves to particular kinds of text, or specialize practice, or institutional site. *All* social practices can be looked at from a cultural point of view. The more important may be the least 'culturally' (old sense) obvious. This goes for factory work, trade-union meetings and for life around the supermarket, as well as the more manifestly 'cultural' spaces like schools, art galleries or (misleading unity!) 'the media'. Subjectivities are powerfully formed in all these places through the conscious social practices of the agents.

CIRCUITS OF CULTURE: AN HYPOTHESIS

I find it helpful to propose a kind of realist hypothesis about the state of knowledge in our field. What if the existing theories, their methods and their results actually correspond to different sides of the same process? What if the process is more complex, in sum, than any one version suggests? What if the theories are true as far as they go? What if they are false if stretched beyond their competences?

Assent cannot be expected to the premises of such an argument, just like that. Premises have to be judged by results. But this starting-point has an immediate appeal if it helps to explain the theoretical and disciplinary fragmentations of cultural studies as a whole. Of course, the fragmentations could be explained in simpler 'rationalist' ways as products of the diversity of theories, each with its own discrete 'object'. Perhaps we are surrounded by a litter of problematics – superseded but slow to go away. Alternatively we might focus on the detailed divisions of intellectual labour, the interests and forms of cultural capital that accumulate around them. This would take us a long way, I am sure, but we might also seek to relate different approaches to the processes they seek to grasp. Theoretical divisions may arise from different standpoints or viewpoints *in relation to cultural processes themselves*. The regularities of cultural processes themselves create or sustain different points of view, different preoccupations. These are *related* to divisions of labour and are given a certain fixity by specific theories. This would explain not only the fact of 'difference' (which any old rationalist or relativistic theory can cope with!), but the *forms* of differentiation and their *persistence*.

To take this further we have to hazard some description of the different aspects of cultural process. Such a description could not be a finished theory or abstraction – if such exists. It would have to start by taking different approaches at their word, identifying their different objects and linking them. The value of this would be pedagogic, illustrative. It could explain why theories differed, not sketch an ideal approach. At most it might signpost some future transformations.

I find it easiest (in a long tradition of the Birmingham CCCS, where I work) to represent such a description by a diagram. The diagram

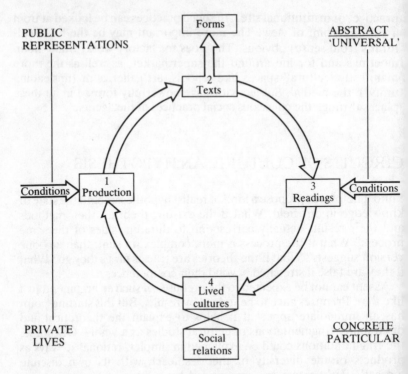

PUBLIC
REPRESENTATIONS

ABSTRACT
'UNIVERSAL'

PRIVATE
LIVES

CONCRETE
PARTICULAR

represents a circuit of the production, circulation and consumption of cultural objects. Each box represents a 'moment' in this circuit.[18] Each moment depends upon the others and is indispensable to the whole. Each involves distinctive changes of form, real transformations. If we are practically preoccupied with one moment and familiar with its forms, the other moments may not exist for us. We only see the results of processes; the acts of production disappear in the product. Cultural objects require to be produced: putting together a book, a television series, or a public ritual takes a lot of work. The form of the production process, however, is not evident when we read the product as a 'text'. Similarly all cultural objects are read by persons other than analysts. It is difficult to predict the forms of this reading from the text. The experience of authorship rather confirms this. Our communications are always returning to us in unrecognizable forms. We often call this *mis*-understanding. Academics call it '*mis*-reading'. But so common are these 'misses' that we would be wise to regard them as normal. To understand them properly – as transformations of meaning – we would have to grasp the specific conditions and practices through which the product was 'consumed' or 'read'. These conditions include all the asymmetries of power, cultural resources and knowledge that relate readers to both producers and analysts, as well as the more fundamental social relations of class, gender, race and age (to list only primary ones). We would also need to know about the cultural elements already present in the reader's own milieu: readings are intimately connected with the next moment in the circuit – 'lived cultures'. These reservoirs of discourses and meanings are in turn a raw material for fresh cultural production within the group or milieu itself, or through more specialized, public means.

At each point around the circuit, then, there are changes in form: conditions or means of production; the products or texts; the different socially-located readings or uses of the product; the intersections of these with the lived ensembles already in place; the moment of production again. But different social practices, of a more or less specialized kind, also inhabit the different moments: cultural production; cultural analysis; cultural consumption; and conscious practical activity in a broader sense. Finally each moment is also a place in a system of social divisions, especially those associated with professionalized forms of cultural work: producers (e.g., media professionals), analysts (e.g., literary critics) and 'ordinary readers'. These specialized roles intersect in important ways with the broader social divisions (e.g., most media professionals are men and all are middle-class).

An example may clarify some points. We can whizz a Mini-Metro car around the circuit. This is a pretty standard later twentieth-century product of capitalist business. Like most products in our society it takes the form of a material commodity. It was also endowed with an especially rich set of meanings: it was the car to save the British car industry by beating rivals from the market and by providing pretexts to discipline the Leyland workers. So it was material and politico-cultural production combined. In one television advertisement, a band of Metros pursued a gang of foreign imports up to (and apparently over) the white cliffs of Dover, whence they fled by landing-craft. The Metro was a nationalist hero in an epic of the Dunkirk evacuation, played backwards! While our analyst abstracted forms for study – epic narrative, popular memories of the Second World War – 'ordinary readers' made their own sense of the thing. (But, of course, there were no 'ordinary readers', only groups of *extra-ordinary* ones transforming the Metro-text in *different* ways.) Beyond these readings, the car found places in the practical activity and common sense of some consumers: a way of getting to work or taking the kids to school or expressing a kind of zippy independence. The Metro-text also contributed some new versions to the public themes of industrial 'peace' and national renaissance. Much of this had then to be sifted by market researchers, capital's own cultural accountants. The use of similar strategies for selling cars and weakening workers' collective power suggests considerable accumulations (of capital, power and meanings) from the episode. The Metro became a little paradigm, though not the first, for a much more diffused ideological form – 'the nationalist sell'.

SOME CHANGES OF FORM

I have talked rather vaguely so far about changes in form. In so brief a discussion it is only possible to specify a few key transformations. These are represented on the left and right of the diagram, in poles from top to bottom. The circuit involves a movement from private to public forms and back again.[19] Cultural production is often, but not always, a process of rendering public, a public-ation. Cultural consumption is always a process of rendering private again. Publicity and privacy are accompanied by more general changes of form: from the relative concreteness of private forms to the relative abstraction of public ones, and from a more particular to a more general scope of reference. Let us see what the Metro can convey to us here.[20]

As a designer's brainwave, even as a manager's 'concept', the car remained private. Nor had it acquired a distinct or abstracted existence. The idea emerged in the course of practical activities: at boardroom briefings or at Saturday's game of golf. In the course of being 'put on paper', 'kicked around' and 'launched', it acquired a material shape and a cultural form – a name. In 'the full glare of publicity', it became 'a great public issue'. Obviously, it became concrete: you could see it, buy it, even drive it. In another sense, it became abstract, separated or abstracted from the forces which produced it. There it is, a super red shiny thing, in the showroom, surrounded by its texts of Britishness. Who would know from this display who conceived it, promoted it and suffered to build it? Who could predict exactly what uses or meanings it might have for anyone? What use is it going to have for the harassed looking woman with two children in tow who has just walked into the showroom?

So the car became public in the obvious sense of 'wellknown'. But it also became *worthy* of public attention in some sense; publication involved *evaluation*. Moreover these evaluations were held to apply very widely, even, within political limits, 'universally'. The Metro was a lesson to the nation. It spoke for us all. Yet note how the harassed looking woman and her children (all of whom have decided views about cars) pull us back from these abstract universals, these claims for others, to particular conditions and stories. You won't be surprised to hear, when you get into conversation, that she has just finished the weekly shopping and is expecting another baby.

Just as publication involves abstraction, so 'reading' involves what we could call clumsily 'concretion'. Even as readers decode public messages, evaluating Metro cars for instance, many more determinations than 'the text' come immediately into play. This moment is *manifestly* concrete. All this implies a different theory and method of research from our analyst's abstraction of forms from texts.

PUBLIC AND PRIVATE FORMS: EPISTEMOLOGY AND POWER

These differences of form affect the possibilities and conditions of social knowledge, including those of 'research'. Public forms range across the whole social surface, though they are differently attended to, understood and used by different social groups. The forms themselves are easy enough to study: researchers are more likely to have problems of selection than availability. Some discourses are fertilized through all the main public channels – the media, academic and professional knowledges, discourses on high culture or high politics. They flourish in exotic, luxuriant forms like the discourses on monarchy in Britain.

Other cultural moments, dubbed 'private', are more hidden, both from the public gaze and from the social worlds of others. They form a tough and shrubby undergrowth well away from the limelight. These forms are not actually 'private' in the sense in which they are defined in dominant versions of the public. They are not of personal relevance to individuals only: they also express social or communal concerns in ways the public forms do not. They constitute little 'publics' of their own which may have the capacity to challenge and even to transform the dominant public definitions. Yet I retain the term 'private' because it indicates real subordinations, real resources and real limits. The strength and limit of 'private' forms is their particularity and concreteness. They are adapted to the life conditions and historically-produced needs of particular groups. Often, they do not pretend to define the world for others. They are embedded in everyday social intercourse in very specific sites and occasions. In the course of their daily lives, women go shopping and meet and discuss the various doings of themselves, families and neighbours. Gossip is a private or more correctly privat-ized form which is rather stigmatized in public evaluations and often 'put down' in the lived cultures of male groupings. Yet it is a vehicle, not only for the central concerns of a social group, but for matters which are essential to human life and to all social arrangements (procreation, child care, health, food, and intimacies of all kinds). Like all such forms it is deeply and manifestly contradictory, mounting collective resistances, but also divisive.

A full knowledge of forms of this kind requires membership of the group concerned or some mode of entry appropriate to an outsider. The conditions of inclusion and exclusion differ widely according to the case and, perhaps, according to the degrees of power at stake. But knowledge of these forms is not reliably available through the public representations. There are several reasons for this.

Sometimes matters with a salience for subordinated groups do not appear publicly at all. It is not that they are naturally or necessarily private: it is a work of power to privatize them: the condescensions of the powerful, the secrecies of the oppressed. The criteria of public significance are not as neutral or universal as they appear. They have a long-term tendency to correspond to the overall relations of force in the society and, more complexly, to the state of struggles in particular domains. As we have seen, public forms universalize, but they cannot abolish real difference or resolve real antagonisms. They therefore express some interests more adequately than others, but always as though these interests (e.g., selling cars) were universal. Public representations like State institutions have none of the modesty of everyday life: they speak loudly and continuously for 'us all'. But this community is partly illusory: it is community structured in *dominance*, its universality *qualified*, its criteria of significance *weighted*. Even the public/private split itself, as an ideological construct, is relative, historical, subject to struggles. There are no matters which belong intrinsically to either sphere. Even a notion of 'spheres' may be too static to grasp just how the distinction *works*. We might think instead of a continually shifting and contested boundary or relationship, policed and challenged in very particular ways.[21]

More commonly, for instance, 'private' matters do appear in public. They may even be given meanings similar to those through which they are lived by subordinated groups – private forms, publicly represented. This is why, once we understand cultural differences, subtle *differentiated* readings of public forms *can* be made. But public forms tend to frame and evaluate such representations in ways that bend them back to middle-class and male definitions of significance, or at least contain their potential for disturbance. So shop-floor humour or the forms of gossip *do* find public representation, but they tend to appear as 'entertainment' (e.g., comedy turns or soap opera) or are dignified in some connection with public figures (the unending *royal* gossip/soap opera). Such framings, fictionalizations and other transformations do not necessarily altogether vitiate the elements of good sense present in the lived moment. Again we have to take account of the particularity of *readings*. In general, we should not assume that public-ation only acts in ways that seem demeaning to the relevant actors, or act, in practice, to repress. There is no substitute here for the close analysis of instances: there are few *general* conclusions to be drawn short of empirical researches, save the warnings against simplifications.

Very often, however, public representations manifestly act in openly punitive or stigmatizing ways. The elements of private cultures are robbed of any authenticity or rationality. They are reconstructed as dangerous, deviant or dotty.[22] Similarly the experiences of large social categories are presented as pathological. They are problems not of society or of power, but of the mal-adjustments of the social group itself. This much-documented and unendingly repeated process is 'representation' with a vengeance: not as subjects demanding redress, but as threats, patients, clients or, at best, as victims. But this is only the most extreme case of the more general condition; a knowledge of cultural processes must remain incomplete (or worse) if based on public knowledges alone.

More generally, our discussion suggests three warnings against simplifications. First, the conditions of knowledge differ depending on which moment of the circulation of forms we have in view. The broad distinction public forms/private forms is especially important here. Second, a fuller knowledge of cultural processes depends upon grasping, theoretically if not in detailed researches, the whole circuit of transformations. Public and private forms are not hermetically sealed one against the other. There is a real *circulation* of forms. Third, to study culture is to be necessarily and deeply implicated in relations of power of the most subtle and intricate kind. Cultural studies is *part* of the circuit it seeks to describe. It may, like most academic and professional knowledges, *police* the public/private relation and confirm its present forms. It may transgress and critique it. It may become part of the routine surveillance of subordinated populations, supplying useful knowledge to controllers. It may attempt to represent such groups more adequately. It may monopolize social knowledges and skills or seek to diffuse them. In an important sense the 'political' side of the cultural studies relation is not a matter of choice at all: it is an ever-present condition of the work.

FORMS OF CULTURE; FORMS OF STUDY; 'CULTURALISM' AND 'STRUCTURALISM' REVISITED

The first use of the model is to help to account for the persistence of two clusters of approaches, the characterization of which is familiar from previous debates.[23] On the one side there are those who define the object of study as whole ways of life or cultures, viewed in their full material contexts. This is often accompanied by a suspicion of methods that abstract, especially of rationalist or *a prioristic* modes of theorizing. The central stress is upon the recovery of lost or hidden cultural elements, the self-productions of particular groups or movements. In oppositional forms of this practice, it is the cultural productions of subordinated groups which are rescued from the public condescensions, past or present. There is a strong stress, therefore, upon the activity of empirical research as a way of compensating for the selective traditions. The preferred forms of representation are the culturally rich social histories, or 'ethnographic' cultural description, or reminiscence, autobiography, or oral history, or those kinds of realist fiction which recreate socially located 'experience'. It is the term 'experience' itself which best expresses the key features of the approach.[24]

On the other side there are those who are concerned with analysing the production of meaning as a relatively independent or effectively autonomous process. This is accomplished by abstracting the means of signification or by privileging the discursive construction of situations and objects. Although the avowed theory is 'structuralist' or 'post-structuralist', there has been, in this tradition, a steady retreat from the 'sociological' or Marxist structuralism of Althusser which attempted to grasp the complexity of social formations as a whole. The preferred object is the public text or broader public discourse, most commonly in literary form. The preferred mode of working is 'the reading' by which texts yield up their rules and artifices, including their unspoken assumptions. It is 'analysis' which is in control here, rather than 'research'. If the first 'culturalist' set of methods owes much to the academic disciplines of history, anthropology, some kinds of sociology and older traditions in literary criticism, 'structuralist' approaches are aligned with the traditions of linguistic formalism and literary modernism.[25]

In the long run, this division is a sure impediment to the development of cultural studies. Much of the most interesting work transgresses it. But we can see why such a division might persist if we relate it to the different cultural moments. Culturalism finds its rationale in the structural features of lived cultures as forms of practical consciousness. The main methodological preferences correspond to the private forms and the problems of recovering and representing them. The typical procedures of structuralist approaches, by contrast, have an affinity with the public knowledge forms. Compared with the thick, conjoined tissue of face-to-face encounters, public forms are very much more plainly re-presentations which depend upon specific cultural means. They even come at us from a specialized apparatus – television set, film screen or radio. Of course, it is possible to describe the forms of gossip or of other live interactions formally, especially if we first 'fix' them for study in some way through tape-recordings, transcripts, video, photography or 'field notes'. Yet if we treat the products of this transformation as 'texts' only, we do seem to make a particularly violent abstraction from the original contexts of talk. This risks missing the original point of the form. As Paul Willis has shown, there is, for instance, an especially close relation between the practical activities of manual labour and the forms of shopfloor culture. Practical jokes, for example, often play upon labour skills.[26] The whole mode of the culture is to refuse the separation of manual practice from mental theory which is a feature of public (but especially academic) knowledge forms. Although there *are* limits to the more formal analysis of television programmes or films, they are not so obvious. The television programme is not so context-bound apparently. It is capable of meaningful appearances in a wide range of situations. Public media permit, indeed, quite extraordinary manipulations of space and time – witness the television revival of old movies.

I am arguing, then, that the evident concreteness of private forms underlies culturalist methods which attempt to conform study to these features. Structuralist method, with its stress on formal analysis, presupposes the real abstractions of the forms of public communication, from the printed book onwards.[27] I find confirmation of this in the difficulty with which either tradition approaches the objects of the other. Structuralist analysis has developed on the basis of the empirical study of literary texts (classic and avant-garde), film and, latterly, the varied genre of television. Even Foucault's histories of discursive formations, perhaps the most resourceful of 'post-structuralist' methods, focus on the regulative 'disciplines', usually upon the highly worked-up professional forms of knowledge/power, from the priestly confessional to modern medicine or the 'psychological' disciplines. They have had little to say, so far, about more everyday or common-sense forms of knowledge.[28] Social historians and ethnographers on the other hand often adopt a crudely 'external' view of public or dominant knowledges and are inclined to neglect the linguistic and discursive forms which are actually present in lived cultures themselves – and, in part, organize them.

Our model has a use, then, in helping to explain the larger theoretical divisions. But we can also make more refined distinctions on this basis. Each moment, or the positions and points of view associated with it, has tended to reproduce specific approaches to the understanding of cultural processes, each with their own tendencies to intellectual imperialism.

PRODUCTION-BASED APPROACHES: INSIGHTS, LIMITS

Many accounts of culture focus upon the production or the social organization of cultural forms. They take the standpoint, theoretically or practically, of more or less specialized cultural producers. I include here the knowledges of writers, artists, dramatists, media professionals and managers, advertisers, designers, experts in public relations, and, in their ideological tasks, professional politicians and administrators. But I include those theoretical and academic knowledges that look at cultural processes from a point of view which is bounded by the characteristic limits of vision of these groups. Liberal-pluralist theorists of mass communication, market researchers and public opinion pollsters and analysts take points of view closely related to the practical concerns of these professions. Much high-cultural or 'aesthetic' debate takes place within assumptions concerning the peculiar creativity of 'the artist'. As between academic disciplines, it is, perhaps, social scientists who have most elaborately developed this perspective.[29]

Marxist paradigms clearly conform to production-based studies in important ways, though usually, in some respects, as 'critical' or 'alternative' versions. Marxists have been interested in cultural production from two related points of view. They have been concerned to understand the specifically cultural resources of authority and the part which the organization of cultural life plays in the reproduction of capitalist social relations. But they have also been concerned to understand the relationship between revolutionary groups and parties and the lived culture of the subordinated social classes. They have taken the viewpoint of *oppositional* cultural producers, critics of the State's 'ethical' role, organizers of 'counter-hegemonic' movements. They have often seen themselves as 'specialists' in the sense of having a specific historical task or rôle.

Early Marxist accounts asserted the primacy of production conditions, often reducing them to some fairly simple version of 'the forces and relations of production'. Later, Marxist critics joined others in examining the influence of capitalist conditions of production and exchange on the 'authenticity' of cultural forms, including the popular arts.[30] In later Marxist accounts the forms through which culture or consciousness has been organized – often theorized as 'the superstructures' – has begun to be elaborated. In the work of Gramsci, for example, a production-based approach was greatly widened and Marxism hugely enriched in both of its major preoccupations. The baleful influence *inside* Marxism of high-cultural definitions of culture was also challenged in ways similar to the later British New Left. Gramsci's insistence that everyone is a 'philosopher' expressed the same point as the later democratization of 'culture', and had a similar source in Marx's emphasis on 'consciousness'.[31] But Gramsci was the first major Marxist theorist to take the culture of the popular classes seriously as an object of study and as a ground of Communist politics. On the other side of Marxist concerns, he was the first fully to theorize the ideological or cultural rôle of the bourgcois State and of the institutions of civil society. His writings about intellectuals, both as cultural producers and as a directing or organizing force, look back to Machiavelli, the French and Russian revolutionaries, and forward to the modern elaboration of intellectual functions into whole social strata with their own interests and internal organization. Reading the *Prison Notebooks* from a New Left perspective as late as the early 1970s was a real revelation, providing definition and confirmation of existing aspirations.

Two limits recur in production-based approaches. The first, more familiar limit is that set by a kind of economism. There is a failure to theorize what is specific to the production of cultural forms, or the cultural dimensions and conditions of production generally. Cultural production is assimilated to capitalist commodity production in general. There is insufficient attention to the *duality* of the circuit of cultural commodities: in part the accumulation of capital, in part the transformation of meanings. In cultural production, especially, tools and raw materials take an immaterial form. They include the stocks of knowledge and subjective forms that already exist, publicly and privately, and the codes and conventions through which meaning is organized. Of course, these too bear the imprint of being produced and reproduced under capitalist conditions. I would argue that the rules of language and discourse as well as the meanings of particular signs and words have already been deeply structured by social contradictions and struggles of social groups, especially by class- and gender-based conflicts. These repertoires then influence the future forms of production. As against this, Marxist approaches to production – studies in the political economy of the media or the leisure industries, for example – usually go for the most brutally obvious determinations: processes of competition, commodification, monopolistic control, imperialist expansion.[32] This is why the claim of some semiologists to provide an alternative 'materialist' analysis of cultural production has some force.[33] At least semiology understands that some of the conditions for cultural production are the means of signification.

The second limit is less easy to define: perhaps we should call it 'productionism'. The temptation here is to infer the whole tendency and history of the cultural product from its conditions of production. The 'vulgar' forms of this inference are familiar: we need only to trace a form to its social origin to know it in its essence – hence 'bourgeois ideology', 'bourgeois science', 'the bourgeois novel' and, of course, the search for all the 'proletarian' challengers. Notions of 'proletarian culture' as that 'genuinely' produced by proletarians show the same profoundly un-relational strand of thinking. More sophisticated versions can be found in left critics of 'mass culture'. Adorno's magisterial polemics, for example, proceed by some giant theoretical strides: they identify capitalist production conditions, trace their effects in the 'fetishization' of cultural commodities and find their perfect complement in 'the regressive listening' of fans.[34] These inferences or deductions render close attention to cultural forms or readers' uses quite redundant: capitalist production begets capitalist consumption.

It is now usual to criticize such reductions by denying that there is any necessary connection between ideological forms and class position.[35] I do not myself wish to deny such a relationship: in fact, I am quite sure that the social position of the producer deeply shapes the nature of the product. The problem lies rather with the wholesale and *a priori* nature of such identifications. They are not so much wrong as premature. They neglect the range of possibilities in all cultural forms (mass or élite). These are only grasped by close contextualized readings of products, analysts' readings which, however, are sensitive to the contradictions of textual forms and the *different* positions offered to readers. These need to be followed by an equally scrupulous attention to the actual modes of appropriation of the product by readers of all kinds. I do not see how many cultural product can be dubbed 'bourgeois' or 'ideological' until this whole circuit has been explored. If we retain the critical, negative sense of 'ideological', surely it is the *last* term to use in cultural analysis, not the first.

Even where accounts do not claim to be definitive, the absence of analysis of forms or of readers or of both is a real limit. I think this is a limit, for instance, in Gramscian approaches generally. Gramsci himself was much more the 'Leninist' than has sometimes been appreciated in discussions of him in Britain: he was concerned, above all, with the political *organization* of culture.[36] He was much less perceptive about the nature and conditions for the popularity of cultural forms, especially as these concerned questions of subjectivity.[37] This is also true, in my opinion, of Gramscian studies within the Birmingham Centre's own tradition, which combine a concern with the organization of public discourse and a critical analysis of their forms. *Policing the Crisis* and *Unpopular Education* for example are weakened as political diagnosis by their failure to reconstruct fully the popular meaning of 'authoritarian populism' or the crisis of Labour's 1945-ism.[38]

Our first case, however, is an interesting instance of a more general argument. Of course, we must look at cultural processes from the point of view of their production or organization. This must include *cultural* conditions but also *labour*: we cannot be for ever discussing 'conditions' and never get to 'acts'. At the same time we must resist the temptation to subsume all other cultural moments under the categories of production studies. This holds theoretically, and also politically in the light of the divisions of labour. For productionism is perhaps the deepest prejudice of all. Perhaps it is an ideology of all specialized producers: writers, artists, teachers, educators, communicators, agitators and *animateurs* of *all* kinds. All intellectuals tend to assume that it is *their* production which animates or sedates. They hold the productivity of extraordinary readers at bay, and think they can fix the meanings of their own products definitively. I think that even very perceptive 'producers' or producer-orientated critics – like Brecht or Benjamin for instance – have tended to think within the same limits.[39] It is by 'Man (usually) the Creator' that the really revolutionary moves are to be made.

This suggests two stages in rethinking these partial approaches. We have to grant independence first to each moment, rescuing it from the imperialism of others. But the line once held against all reductionisms, we have to recognize that the moments are not all that distinct. Production is an especially good instance here. In a better analysis, it must be treated as a feature of *each* moment. We can properly speak of texts or cultural conventions as 'productive', or as having the capacity to produce. We should certainly view readings as a process of production in which the product becomes a raw material for new meanings. Social groups certainly develop their own forms of cultural production which do not necessarily depend on elaborate divisions of labour. Yet productionism certainly exists as a tendency: there is no better instance, perhaps, of the relation between social divisions and theories.

TEXT-BASED STUDIES

'Writers have only produced texts, in different ways; the point is to "read" them.' Two developments underlie the emergence of this, the *critic*'s standpoint. It presupposes a separation between specialist and 'ordinary' readers, and between specialist producers and commentators on their works. Both developments are closely related to the growth of educational institutions. Academic institutions are the most common locations of the critics today, but it is important to note how many critical insights began life as producers' theories. I am thinking particularly of the practical-theoretical sources of modernism in theories associated with cubism, constructivism, Russian film-making and Brecht's 'epic theatre'.[40]

Skills in the formal description of cultural forms are mainly carried in the academic disciplines grouped together as 'the humanities' or 'arts'. These skills are indispensable for cultural analysis and the origins of cultural studies in the study of literature is no accident at all. Nor should it surprise that there has been continual methodological refreshment from these quarters. I have in mind the analysis of narrative, the identification of genre, the study of linguistic forms, and the common borrowings by cultural studies and the humanities from semiology and other literary structuralisms.

This sets up a situation which I find paradoxical. Modern formal analysis promises a systematic description of subjective forms. In this part of our study we are at a stage equivalent to that noted by Marx for political economy in the middle of the nineteenth century: a primitive but necessary stage 'when the forms had still to be laboriously peeled out from the material'. Yet there are real inhibitions to this development both within a Marx-influenced cultural studies and on the more literary side. Cultural studies retains a healthy suspicion of formalism and especially of the abstraction of texts from their conditions of reproduction, circulation and use. This suspicion of formalism sometimes becomes, however, an impatience with formal analysis as such. I think this is a quite misplaced prejudice. Formal analysis is a way of demonstrating the force of our 'cultural' intuitions. We need to abstract the forms from texts in order to describe them carefully or show how a 'preferred reading' or utopian moment is constructed. We need to be able to represent, with clarity, the variations, combinations, contradictions and subjective pressures of textually embodied forms. Was not Barthes right when he argued against a quixotic rejection of 'the artifice of analysis'?

> Less terrorised by the spectre of 'formalism', historical criticism might have been less sterile; it would have understood that the specific study of forms does not in any way contradict the necessary principles of totality and History. On the contrary: the more a system is specifically defined in its forms, the more amenable it is to historical criticism. To parody the well-

known saying, I shall say that a little formalism turns one away from History, but a lot brings one back to it.[41]

Despite Barthes' own subsequent flight from both history and 'totality', I find continual refreshment in this early formulation.

On the other, more literary side, however, indispensable tools of analysis are locked up in a technical mystique and academic professionalism and applied to a very narrow range of products. Possibilities are cooped up by the need to comment freshly on some well-thumbed text or much-disputed author. Linguistics is the paradigm case here: it offers an invaluable tool kit for cultural analysis, but is burdened by assumptions of scientificity which cultural criticism, in its current mood, finds bogus and self-aggrandizing.[42] Encounters with linguistics often therefore reproduce the paradox rather than enriching both sides.

An example of what may happen once barriers are down can be found in the case of the study of narrative and genre. This is one of the most exciting areas of intersection between cultural studies and formal analysis. It is becoming clear that narrativity or story-form is far from being a merely literary device and is a constituent moment of subjectivity more generally. Feminists working on romantic love, for instance, have traced the correspondence between the narrative forms of popular romantic fiction, the public rituals of marriage, and the subjective tug of 'romance'.[43] A similar argument is now being pursued around the forms of epic narrative or adventure story, the fighting fantasies of boy culture and the subjective forms of conventional masculinity.[44] As if on prompter's cue, the Malvinas/Falklands conflict crystallized both forms and conjoined them in a single history: weeping women at the quayside; gleeful men on the ships. Clearly epic and romance are not merely literary categories: they are among the most powerful and, in our society, ubiquitous of subjective forms. Men and women live, love, grieve, fight and die by them.

WHAT IS A TEXT?

If text analysis is indispensable, what is a text? In the case of the Metro, for instance, could we stop with the car itself, as Barthes once analysed the lines of a Citroen?[45] Led on to texts through advertising, we could hardly stop until we had studied the whole 'Metro-text', including the proliferation of public discourses on the future of the nation. This tendency of public texts to a polymorphous growth poses inescapable practical problems. Where does our text end? Too often, I think, we reach for a traditional solution: we bound our object by plumping for an author (where this is possible), an *oeuvre* or a genre. We bound the object by recognizably literary criteria.

Yet there are limits to this. If we want to know how different genres or media structure representations we need to work across them, comparatively. We need to trace the differences, say, between literary romance, romantic public spectacle, and romantic love as an inner narrative. Only in this way can the important conundrums be resolved: how far do ideologies of love seal women back into oppressive social relations and how far do they carry critical or utopian conceptions of relations between the sexes? We do not *have* to bound our study by literary criteria. Other options are available. We can organize around the choice of an issue or a theme, or trace a set of discourses across media and genre, or set out to study a particular historical conjuncture.[46]

Beyond this, it is arguable that there is a fundamental difference of object between cultural and literary studies. Certainly students of culture may take a single text as exemplary of a widely present form. Ultimately, however, the individual text is only a *means* to cultural study, a kind of raw material for a part of the practice. Cultural studies does not prize the text in itself but rather seeks to shift it from centre stage. In the end our objects are not 'texts' but the forms that people live by, in each moment of their circulation, including their textual embodiments.

FORMALISM: THE STRUCTURALIST FORESHORTENINGS

The abstraction of forms from texts is a necessary analytical procedure; the abstraction of texts from the other moments risks a formalism in the negative sense. Formalistic readings fix the real appearance of abstraction by privileging the moment of textual embodiment. An understanding of production and of reading is subordinated to the logics of critical analysis. This approach to culture, very characteristic of the literary and semiological structuralisms, is a true theoretical imperialism, and has often been pursued with missionary vehemence.[47]

There *is* an account of production within this paradigm, but it is a severely reduced one. If we think of production as involving raw materials, means of production, and socially-organized labour, semiological analysis looks at some of the cultural means but ignores the rest. It brackets out the usual concerns of a political economy. It is uninterested in social conditions of production. It neglects the human activity of producing. It substitutes for all this the 'productivity' of signifying systems. Though a conception of practice is much invoked ('signifying practice') it is practice without practitioners. As the elegant, one-sided exaggerations put it: myths speak the myth-maker, language speaks the speaker, texts read the reader, theoretical problematics produce the 'science' and ideology constructs the subject.[48]

These shifts, as illustrated, for example, by the development of the dominant 1970s kinds of film theory in the magazine *Screen,* formed part of a larger tendency to stress the means of representation or to criticize 'representation' as such for its tendency to 'realism'. It was argued that we had to choose between the virtual autonomy of signifying systems (and the arbitary, non-referential nature of the sign) or fall back on a consistent Marxist determinism.[49] In film criticism, for example, the cinema was treated as an autonomous signifying machine: the focus was upon the particularity of representation in the cinema or on television, not on the way discursive elements, first produced elsewhere, were pulled in and transformed. In this way cinematic texts and 'means' were abstracted from their discursive context (and 'contents'), the surrounding social relations, and the particular historical moment.[50]

Such accounts foreshorten in that they only grasp a quarter of our circuit. The focus is on the second, 'textual' moment; the discussion of production and readership must conform to its logic. The means of signification are not conceived of historically, as having their own moment of production. They are an assumed (or 'deep') structure. The *conventionality* and *arbitrariness* of organizing conventions is stressed but not their *historicity*. This is a general or theoretical absence which haunts Saussurean linguistics from the start. The rules of language determine the daily speech acts, but the everyday deployments of linguistic forms appear not to touch the language system itself. There is no true circuit of effects. The struggle over language is foreclosed. To recover a fully social language theory, it is therefore necessary to go outside the French semiological traditions, back to the critiques of Saussure marshalled by the Marxist philosopher of language V. N. Volosinov or across to the practically-applied linguistics of M. A. K. Halliday, William Labov or Basil Bernstein.[51]

READERS IN TEXTS; READERS IN SOCIETY

Structuralist approaches to 'the reader' are closely connected to the broader project of a theory of 'the subject'.[52] This characteristically post-structuralist enterprise sets out from a critique of humanist conceptions which are seen as typical of pre-modern philosophy. Here a simple, given, unified 'I' stands unproblematically and full of intention, at the centre of thought, action and aesthetic or moral judgement. Against this, structuralism insists on the radical constructedness of this 'I', its contradictory, fragmented and partly illusory character, and therefore the falsity of humanist theories in general. In attempting to explain how subjects are produced, structuralist approaches stress the discursive or textual means. The key insight is that narratives, images, or ideologies in general always imply or construct a position from which they are to be read. Although 'position' remains problematic (is it a set of competences or a real subjection?) the insight is dazzling, with many applications. We can now look at the work which photos do, for example, not merely in presenting a scene but in putting us in a place before it. Add to this a second typical insight – that these effects are disguised in certain ('realist') forms – and we have a heady brew indeed. Here formalist critic meets avant-garde practitioner and the hunt is on for radical or transformative texts which really show readers how they work.

These insights promise a way of connecting the analysis of texts with the study of readers. Of course, the concern with 'positionings' or 'interpellations' should not replace other text-based methods. We still need to know about the manifest and latent themes of texts or discourses, their literary or linguistic strategies, their ideological aspects and utopian moments. The legitimate object of all such readings is to identify the *pressures* or *tendencies* of textually-embodied subjective forms, the directions in which they may move readers, holding in abeyance, for the moment, a fuller investigation of all the other conditions. The difficulties arise – and they are very numerous indeed – if these tendencies are held to be realized in the subjectivities of the readers as a simple inference from the textual forms and the critic's own reading.

My view of the enormity of such a leap must be clear from the previous discussion. At the simplest level it is a matter of the absence of relevant material: we simply do not know, without further research, about readers very different from ourselves. But there are broader methodological inadequacies too. Textual analysis is not competent to handle the complexity of determinations that adhere around the act of reading. The whole pressure of formalistic work is to isolate the text for closer scrutiny. But the real tendency of the reading moment under everyday conditions is the opposite of this. Texts are encountered promiscuously: they overlap, coexist, pour in from diverse media, in differently-paced flows, mixing public and private forms. The reality of reading is intertextual, or, better, inter-discursive. No subjective form acts on its own; it must compete or combine for attention. Nor can we predict, in advance, from public texts in what combination of other elements it may appear to particular groups of readers. The logic of these combinations is not predictable from the public forms. It depends upon the cultural elements already in place in relation to the practical activities of particular social groups, and the long-term conformities between culture and situation. This includes the narratives of self which are already active, and the sense of individual and group identities.

PSYCHOANALYTIC SIMPLIFICATIONS

Even if we can specify the conditions and raw materials of a reading, there remains everything to say about the act itself and its products. We have scarcely begun to discuss this, partly because of vulgar productionist prejudice, partly because the absence of action on behalf of ordinary readers is a feature of all formalist accounts. Even those theorists (e.g., Brecht, *Tel Quel,* Barthes in *S/Z*) who are concerned with productive, critical or deconstructive readings ascribe this capacity to types of *text* (e.g., 'writable' rather than 'readable' in Barthes' terminology) and not at all to a history of real readers. The absence of production in reading parallels the ascription of 'productivity' to the signifying systems. At best, the act of reading is conceptualized as a replaying of unconscious experience.

I believe that there is still a huge potential in the critical use of Freudian categories and insights, as critical, that is, as the appropriations of Marx have become. Accounts of reading as a reliving of psychoanalytically defined narratives do have the virtue of bridging textual positions and real readers. I am sure that such analysis has identified, for example, some of the ways men use screen images of women and relate to filmic heroes.[53] Yet the gap between text and reader is bridged at a cost: a radical simplification of the social subject, a reduction to infant needs. Reading Freud himself, it is surprising to find how much psychoanalytic traditions are themselves simplified (despite the clever-clever obscurities) in the fashionable Lacanian versions. How can one specify, on this basis, all the differences that actually distinguish extraordinary readers? Surprisingly, even gender differences prove hard to grasp. There are distinct limits to procedures which discover in otherwise very varied texts and situations the same mechanisms producing the same effects.

One lack in these accounts is any attempt to describe the surface forms – the forms of inner speech and narrative – which are the empirically obvious features of 'subjectivity'. Perhaps it is thought 'humanist' to pay attention to 'consciousness' in this way. Without such an account, however, there is something spurious about claims to be working on 'a theory of the subject'. This is because the *explanandum,* the *object,* of such a theory has never been specified. What is it, precisely, that we are trying to explain? I would start from the fact of inner narrative.[54] Are not we all continuous, resourceful and sometimes frenetic story-tellers? Narrative form is not only universal in culture's objective manifestations, in texts that impinge upon us from 'outside'. We tell stories 'inside' our heads, in the imaginative world, that is, which accompanies our every action. We are not merely positioned by narratives we read; we position *ourselves* by our constant internal narrations. We use 'realist' forms of narrative to plan the future (it matters here that they are as 'true' as we can make them!). We use 'fictional' or fantastical forms to escape, divert, or take a pleasurable break. We construct stories about our individual and collective pasts. As well as repressing embarrassing or traumatic moments, we relive them imaginarily. Such memories and histories are important in constructing a sense of who we presently are. This is one way in which we secure some subjective continuity in the flux of events and meanings. This is how we struggle – individually or collectively – for some integrity or unity, for some *control* over our produced, fragmentary and contradictory selves. In relation to collectivities, this is one way in which to recover some older Marxist questions concerning 'will', struggle, solidarity and historical agency.

SOCIAL INQUIRIES

Studying the private forms imposes special requirements and disciplines. Of course, students of culture have access to private forms through their everyday social worlds. If we understand personal experience not as a unique existential flux but as encounters with representative situations and socially-available cultural forms, our own experience is an indispensable resource.[55] The first and still most important form of cultural studies is to make explicit what we know already implicitly as participants in a culture. The first condition here, however, is the recognition of major cultural differences and therefore of the limits of the representativeness of our own social world. Sensitivity to the cultural effects of the major social relations involving power (class, gender, race and age) is especially important to avoid the most grossly ideological conclusions.

If our everyday knowledge sometimes misleads, 'ethnography' or the practice of representing the cultures of others is a justifiable activity. We have to keep a discomfited eye, however, on the historical pedigrees and dominant tendencies of sociological and anthropological inspections, their origins, especially, in the State or philanthropic surveillance of subordinated peoples in capital's old metropolitan centres and on its imperialized peripheries. Merely to study cultural forms distances us from the main commonsense mode in all social groups – and I mean all. Intellectuals may excel in describing other people's implicit assumptions, but are as implicit as anyone else when it comes to their own. To render such accounts public is immediately to activate all the relations of power we traced around the circuit, especially where the practice crosses the major cultural differences.

I believe, however, that there are political discriminations to be made in the history of social inquiry. One tradition identifies itself as linked to 'political arithmetic', to nineteenth-century 'moral statistics', to Booth and Rowntree and to the eugenically-informed social researches of the early twentieth century. Perhaps this is an accurate pedigree for much post-war social science. It is a different tradition, in my opinion, from the strands that have combined in New Left research: traditions of popular history, autobiography and the kind of reportage represented in the nineteenth century by Henry Mayhew. The difference is a concern with the rationality or realism of popular knowledges and the espousal of 'the people', not as an object of scrutiny, but as an active political force. Even so, it seems wise to be suspicious, not of all 'ethnography', but of all accounts of the practice which minimize the distance between researcher and researched, or pass over the political risks and responsibilities. The ultimate object must be to try to break for ever the social divisions of research, and the distinctions between subjects and objects. In the meantime, the situation is very complex and full of unexpected traps. Social inquiry tends constantly to return to a bourgeois model: pathologizing subordinated cultures, normalizing dominant culture, helping at best to build academic reputations without proportionate returns to those who are represented. On the other hand, guilty attempts to correct these tendencies may have equally unproductive effects. Some of these are apparent in radical ethnography and its equivalent forms in social history.[56]

LIMITS OF RADICAL REPRESENTATION

One typical difficulty in such accounts is the attraction of empiricist or 'expressive' theories of culture. The condescensions of middle-class views of working-class culture (typically) have been met by assertions of its peculiar richness or authenticity. I think that Hoggart and others have been right to stress the temptations to romanticization which this produces. This has often been strengthened by 'old Marxist' assumptions about the proper state of consciousness of the working class and its epic destinies. Working-class cultural forms are seen as having a particularly intimate bond with proletarian conditions, their authentic expression, perhaps the only expression possible.

Such tendencies produce major difficulties, not least for researchers themselves. The researcher's own thinking must always be suspect if the spontaneous forms are seen as a completed knowledge. The only legitimate practice is to present an unmediated chunk of life experience itself, letting it 'speak for itself'. Perhaps the only legitimate stance for the researcher is invisibility.

For similar reasons there is a pressure to present lived cultures with which one sympathizes deeply as peculiarly homogeneous and distinct. Indeed, sometimes the 'cultures' replace the people and the social relationships. Cultures as whole ways of life are humped about by the same sort of people and bump up against other great slabs of meaning humped about by others. There is a definite tendency to what I call the 'continental plates' theory of culture in some CCCS and CCCS-influenced work.[57] The best corrective here is to remember that cultural forms express *social relations* and therefore subordinations as well as assertions of identity. A further corrective is to be sensitive to the forms of internal division *within* class cultures, especially those along the fractures of race and gender. The emergence of 'way of life' as a key figure of white racism and Conservative nationalism in Britain suggests some deep conservative convergences here.

The main lack, however, is any attention to the *means* of articulation of group identities. This is a common element in the empiricist devaluation of theoretical frameworks, the refusal to distinguish objective and subjective sides in experience, and the mysterious disappearances of researchers, organizers or militants. There is no better instance of this than the neglect of linguistic or discursive analysis in ethnographic or, until recently, in social-historical work. In the terms of our model, the circuit is again foreshortened. The creativity or productiveness in private forms is well understood, but not their relationship to the whole arc of public representations. Once again, however, it is important not to present these difficulties as though they were gratuitous theoretical mistakes. They are themselves the products of power and of attempts to mitigate or evade it.

CIRCUITS SUMMARIZED

My argument has been that there are three main forms of cultural studies research. These correspond to the forms of appearance of cultural circuits and the preoccupations that cluster around them. Production-related studies imply a struggle to control, transform or counter the more separated kinds of cultural production in our society. Such studies, implicitly or explicitly, address intellectuals of different kinds, including political forces with some emancipatory potential. Sometimes they seem to address or attempt to constitute political forces which do not yet exist.

Text-based approaches focus on the nature of the cultural products themselves. They too imply a particular political project, most commonly a truly transformative text, film, play, song, etc. There is a close historical affinity between text-based strategies and the preoccupations of the artistic avant-garde. Latterly these preoccupations have often migrated to the academy or, often more positively, have informed educational practices which have sought to produce really critical readers.[58]

Research into lived cultures has been closely associated with a politics of representation. If we think of this within a Gramscian framework, it involves two sides. On the one side 'organic intellectuals' (who may arise from the popular classes) learn from and work on the 'good sense' in common sense, the realistic insights in practical consciousness. They attempt to develop common sense into more historically-aware, critical and self-conscious forms, partly by supplying its 'inventories'. Lived cultures are thus given a 'public' or counter-hegemonic turn, able to complete at the level of universal significances characteristic of the public sphere. They may also be a means by which the public-private relation is transformed. On the other side, intellectuals of the popular classes are directly involved in the critique of the dominant philosophies. These cultural tasks are also, for Gramsci, organizational tasks, involving direction, education and leadership.[59]

In our society, however, these aspects of a general politics are themselves fragmented. They are often de-politicized and ascribed to specialists of different kinds: professional politicians, professional researchers, journalists and community workers for example. Because of the weaknesses in both our theories and our inherited forms of politics, elements of organicity have, for the present, to develop where they may: a research project here, a party branch there, a community project somewhere else. The partially-accomplished shifts in academic research models – broadly towards 'action research' – may be profoundly significant here.

So we have the kinds of fragmentation which the circuit model describes. Each fragment has a kind of realism in relation to its own moment. But the limits are plain to see politically, especially, perhaps, in internecine struggles on the left: 'hardened politicos' face 'bloody academics', while community workers struggle on regardless! Differences, with origins in a division of labour, are hardened up by the theoretical or disciplinary frameworks. The tendency to an over-ideological, 'over-textual' conception of political struggle (especially on the academic wing) owes much, for instance, to structuralist and post-structuralist paradigms.[60]

FUTURE SHAPES, FURTHER TRANSFORMATIONS

So, far from presenting an adequate account of cultural studies, the model allows us to identify some major limits. The practical implication is that the divisions themselves must be systematically transgressed, the skills generalized. But it is important to transform the skills too. This means breaking up the intellectual-practical 'sets' I have tried to describe. There are, in fact, inner connections and some real identities *between* the moments. The general model for an intellectual transformation is the transportation of questions and approaches from the study of each moment to the study of all. I have only room for two illustrations of what this might mean.

How might one transform formalist approaches to texts and forms without losing the real virutes of formal analysis? I chose this case because of the power, pervasiveness but also the limits of literary models of cultural study. I have already discussed the initial choice of object or 'text' and the need to escape from residually literary definitions. We also need to develop further form of analysis which hook up to and enable the studies of production and of reading. This may involve reasserting some unfashionable options.

It is possible to look for the results of production processes in texts, once the production process is partly known. There is more to this than 'codes' or the means of signification. A properly elaborate concern with the determinations which stem from production might replace the overwhelming concern with 'bias', at the moment the main form in which this connection is made. Like all the other insights around the circuit, this preoccupation needs thoroughly historicizing: we need histories of, say, televisual forms, in relation to histories of production. Nor can the re-emergence of 'history' (more concretely than in Barthes's advocacy!) be limited to media organization. In a real sense it is not the signifying machine that produces meaning, or even the industry, but the whole conjuncture.

Similarly, it is possible and productive to read texts or forms as representations. One way out of the anti-realist cul-de-sac here is to recognize that we are always analysing a representation of a representation. The object re-presented in the text is not a naked event or fact. It has already been given (usually competing) meanings in some other social practice. We need, therefore, to research the different versions in order to chart the transformations which occur across the representational practices. We could put together, for instance, accounts of the rituals, banners and lived meanings of peace movement demonstrators, their representation by the Ministry of Defence or the police, and the negotiation of these meanings on the television news at nine or ten o'clock.

What forms of text analysis would best serve the needs of the study of readership? There seem to be two main requirements here. First, our reading of texts must be as multi-layered as possible. If we identify the 'preferred readings' or 'dominant frameworks', we must also attend to subordinated versions, even when they appear in fragments.

We have to attend too to the contradictoriness and ambiguities of texts. We should constantly ask – could this be read differently? One of my favourite examples here is taken from a *Sunday Mirror* report of the major CND demonstration in October 1981: 'Police adopted a low-key, softly-softly approach and the protest passed off peacefully.' There is not space to give details, but I think at least five readings of this passage can be identified, each of which seems plausible within a given theoretical framework or set of prior expectations. These readings can be specified linguistically – as can the range of ambiguity. It is also possible to suggest that *one* of the readings corresponds most closely to the general tenor of the *Mirror*'s report (and indeed to the dominant framework for comprehending CND demonstrations in the popular press). This leaves the matter to be settled, elsewhere, where it belongs: in concrete studies of readerships and the larger historical contexts. In the meantime, the five (or more) answers to me please – on a postcard!

A further main requirement is that analysts abandon, once and for all, the two main models of the 'critical' reader: the primarily evaluative reading ('Is this a good/bad text?') and the aspiration to text analysis as an objective science. Both prevent us really relativizing our own reading and therefore learning from it more fully. 'Scientific' readings remove from our conscious consideration the common-sense knowledge we all possess of the larger cultural contexts within which meanings are produced. They hide away our very real social involvement in the meanings, involvement which is active nonetheless. The skill of multiple readings, hypothetically stressed or weighted, is not a fixing of one version, but a capacity to inhabit several. In developing this skill we draw on wide 'amateur' knowledges greatly superior in range though not in explicitness to any technical equipment we may acquire. I have already stressed the real limits of 'representativeness'. These remain, but it may help if 'the analyst' is, in fact, a group. None of this is to deny the real disciplines of reading. Reading *must* be 'close' in the sense of careful, explicit, and attentive to 'words on the page', but not 'close' in the sense of confined.

My second, partially-realized example is what I call 'best ethnography'. This includes some ethnographic work from Birmingham ('best', mind you; not 'perfect'!).[61] These studies succeed because they have broken from many of the limits of expressive theories and the limitation to private forms. There is a discursive or formal element in the analysis. Abstraction and formal description – for example of 'style' – is used to identify elements in a whole lived ensemble. Connections are sought between lived cultures and public forms. The moment of 'reading' is attended to, typically as group appropriations of mass cultural forms. There is an injection of 'textual' reading in ethnographic study, the result of a broader structuralist influence. Cultural forms are also related to an analysis of social relations. This is one reason why feminist work on girl culture, for instance, has been as preoccupied with theorizing women's position as with talking to girls. So a form of cultural analysis, influenced by structuralist insights, is combined with a sociology of social relations and a strong sense of everyday cultural productiveness.

It is only with combined skills of this kind, not through theoretical purism, that cultural studies can come to terms with the really important questions. For me these are twofold. First, there is the problem of the popularity, the pleasure or the use-value of subjective forms. Why do some forms acquire a popular force, constituting subjectivities, providing principles of living, becoming 'life'? In what different ways are subjective forms inhabited or used? Under what conditions are they inhabited playfully, ironically, satirically, in parody, or in 'deadly earnest'? What needs or wants do they supply? But, second, it is important to retain or reformulate an older set of questions, without which there is a certain epicurean relaxation of tensions, a certain populist collapse. I do not want to sound too puritan here (who does today!), but we really must not drop, in the hot pursuit of 'pleasure', a concern with political tendencies or results. Do *these* forms, in *this* conjuncture, lived like *this*, by *this* social group, tend to reproduce existing forms of subordination or oppression? Do they hold down, shackle or contain social ambitions or the possibilities of social individuals? Do they define wants modestly, partially, unequally, in ways far from disinterested? Do they promise a lot and give little? Are they *really* dreams that can come true? Do they stay within the existing horizons, not recognizing that relations will change as they always have done? More concretely, what admixtures do we find, in particular forms, of ideological closures and utopian possibilities, of 'traps' and 'openings'? Under what circumstances might the closures be opened and the utopias realized?

NOTES AND REFERENCES

1. This paper is a much-shortened and extensively revised version of a talk given at the Department of English at the Istituto Universitario Orientale in Naples and published in full in the journal *Annali Anglistica* and as a CCCS Stencilled Occasional Paper ('What is Cultural Studies Anyway?', CCCS Stencilled Paper No. 74). I've learnt a lot from giving this paper, in many different versions, to people interested in cultural studies in West Germany, Holland, Italy and Britain. But a special thank-you to my MA Reading Group at the Birmingham Centre in 1983–4 for engaging so constructively with its obscurities.
2. The key texts are Hoggart, *Uses of Literacy;* Williams, *Culture and Society;* Williams, *Long Revolution.*

Introduction to contemporary cultural studies

3. I am thinking of the Communist party Historians' Group. See Bill 5. For a (too brief) attempt to extend this argument, see Richard Johnson, 'Educational Politics', in *Is There Anyone Here from Education?* eds J. Donald and A. Volpen, Pluto 1983.

4. Is it necessary to add that no critiques are ever 'permanent', no victories ever securely won? In some ways, the two major modern reappraisals – from feminist and antiracist viewpoints – have only just begun, especially, perhaps, the latter.

5. For a (too brief) attempt to extend this argument, see Richard Johnson, 'Educational Politics', in *Is There Anyone Here from Education?* eds J. Donald and A. Volpen, Pluto 1983

6. There are degrees called 'cultural studies' at the Polytechnics of North East London, Portsmouth, Middlesex; and communication studies (or allied) degrees with cultural studies elements at Sheffield, Sunderland, Bristol, Central London, Wales and Trent. The Open University Popular Culture course is another important educational focus. Journals include *Media; Culture and Society; Screen* (now incorporating *Screen Education*), *Ideology and Consciousness; Block; Schooling and Culture; Theory, Culture and Society; LTP: Journal of Literature, Teaching, Politics; Formations.* More general journals (e.g., *Feminist Review, History Workshop Journal, Marxism Today, New Socialist, New Left Review, Race and Class*) often have overlapping interests. A Cultural Studies Network became a Cultural Studies Association in February 1984.

7. See, for example, Bourdieu, 'Cultural Reproduction and Social Reproduction', in *Knowledge, Education and Social Change,* ed. R. Brown, Tavistock 1973; Foucault, *The Archaeology of Knowledge,* trans. A. Sheridan Smith, Tavistock 1972; Brian Easlea, *Science and Sexual Oppression,* Weidenfeld 1981; Geoff Whitty and Michael Young, *Explorations in the Politics of School Knowledge,* Nafferton 1976. Thanks also to Maureen McNeil for very interesting discussions on these themes, especially her papers for the MA course at CCCS and for the Osnabruck Conference in 1983. The revised version of this paper is influenced especially by arguments about the effects, on knowledge, of the divisions of labour.

8. The classic treatment of 'culture' from this accumulative perspective is the entry in Williams, *Keywords.* See also, with respect to my later discussion, the entries on 'Unconscious' and, in the new edition, 'Subjective'.

9. I find myself at odds with many strands in cultural studies which now prefer the term 'ideology' as the appropriate general category. They opt for a usage in line with the more expanded and potentially 'positive' sense in which ideology is used by Lenin and, later, Althusser. Ideology is applied in the OU Popular Culture course, for instance, to the formation of subjectivities in general. If stretched thus, I would argue, the term uses its usefulness – why would not 'discourse', 'cultural form' or even 'culture' do just as well, since subjective effect is part of the general cultural process? On the whole, I wish to retain the 'negative' or 'critical' connotation of 'ideology' in Marx's usage, though not, as it happens, the usual accompaniment, a 'hard' notion of 'Marxism-as-science'. It may well be that all our knowledge of the world is 'ideological' more or less, rendered partial by the operation of interest and power. But I still want to be able to make discriminations between knowledges or forms of subjectivity, and see

them as more or less 'ideological'. Moreover the 'expanded' or 'neutral' use of ideology cannot lay to rest the older negative connotations: these resound whenever we use the word, whether we like it or not. The dual history of usage is recapitulated in the work of Jorge Larrain: see *Marxism and Ideology*, Macmillan 1983, and *The Concept of Ideology*, Hutchinson 1979. The outcome is that I now prefer to use 'ideology' or better 'ideological' sparingly, always adjectivally and at the *end* of an argument, not at the beginning!

10. Marx and Engels, *Collected Works*, Vol. V, p. 43.

11. Marx, *Capital* (3 vols.), trans. B. Fowkes, Penguin 1976 Vol. I, p. 283.

12. 'Species being' is the general Feuerbachian term used in the 1844 *Manuscripts*; later Marx refers to such universals as 'general-historical' categories, true, that is, of all history. I think this is a significant shift, preferring more or less long-term *historical* determinations to some conception of a biologically or philosophically absolute human nature.

13. Indeed 'culture' in many early New Left uses is simply an English 'translation' for 'praxis'!

14. For this imbalance in Marx's thinking and much else of value see Victor Molina, *Marx's Arguments on Ideology*, unpublished PhD thesis, University of Birmingham 1983.

15. Marx, *Grundrisse*, trans. M. Nicolaus, Penguin 1973, p. 101.

16. 'Preface', *A Contribution to the Critique of Political Economy*, Lawrence and Wishart 1971, p. 21.

17 'Structuralism' in its general influence on cultural studies has been extensively discussed elsewhere. See, for example, Stuart Hall, 'Some Paradigms in Cultural Studies', *Annali Anglistica*, XXI (1978); Hall, 'Cultural Studies: Two Paradigms', *Media, Culture and Society*, II (1980), 57–72 (reprinted in part in *Culture, Ideology and Social Process*, eds Tony Bennett *et al.*, Open University Press and Batsford 1981). See also the introductory essays in *Culture, Media, Language,* eds Hall *et al*. For a more general literary introduction see Terence Hawkes, *Structuralism and Semiotics*, Methuen 1977.

18. The diagram is based, in its general forms, on a reading of Marx's account of the circuit of capital and its metamorphoses. For an important, original and, for me, very formative account, see Molina, *Marx's Arguments*. I hope this important discussion will be published in whole or part. Also important is Hall, 'Encoding/Decoding', in *Culture, Media, Language*, eds Hall *et al*. My approach is also influenced by what I learned about Marx's method when writing 'Reading for the Best Marx', in CCCS, *Making Histories*.

19. My thinking on 'the public and the private' is influenced by various strands, often, perhaps, to my confusion. I am influenced, in general, by the feminist questioning of existing (perhaps any?) forms of the public/private distinction. This questioning will be profoundly transforming in the long run. Another important strand of discussion is to be found in many North American libertarian or New Left discussions (see, for example, Richard Sennett, *The Fall of Public Man*, Cambridge University Press 1974). Finally I have been much interested in what I have been able to learn of discussions in Germany. See Habermas, *Strukturwandel der Öffentlichkeit*, Neuweid, Berlin 1962; Oskar Negt and Alexander Kluge, *Öffentlich-*

keit und Erfahrung: Zur Organisationsanalyse von bürgerlicher und pro-letarischer Öffentlichkeit, Suhrkamp, Frankfurt am Main 1972. For an extract from Negt and Kluge's work see *Communication and Class Struggle,* eds A. Matterlart and S. Seigelaub, International General, New York 1983, Vol. II. For a summary of Habermas's argument on the public sphere see eds Matterlart and Seigelaub, Vol. I. More work is becoming available in English, mainly through North American interest. For a summary of the arguments see Michael Bommes and Patrick Wright, ' "Charms of Residence": The Public and the Past', in CCCS, *Making Histories.*

20. I am sorry to say this illustrative case is completely hypothetical since I have no contacts in the British Leyland management. Any resemblance to persons living or dead is the purest instance of the power of theory!

21. I am grateful to Mariette Clare and to the CCCS Popular Memory Group for discussions about the public and the private. I draw heavily on these discussions here.

22. There is a very large sociological literature on these forms of stigmatiza-tion, especially of the deviant young. *The Manufacture of News,* eds. Stanley Cohen and Jock Young, Constable 1973, was a pioneering collec-tion.

23. For my own attempts at defining this division at more length see 'Histories of Culture/Theories of Ideology: Notes on an Impasse', in Michèle Barrett, Philip Corrigan *et al., Ideology and Cultural Production,* Croom Helm 1979; and the essays in *Working Class Culture,* eds John Clarke, Chas Critcher and Johnson, Hutchinson 1979.

24. And its limits: see the discussion in *People's History and Socialist Theory,* ed. Samuel; and in Perry Anderson, *Arguments within English Marxism,* Verso 1980.

25. For this connection see Jonathan Culler, *Saussure,* Fontana 1976. For Russian formalism see Bennett, *Formalism and Marxism,* Methuen 1979.

26. Willis, 'Shop-floor Culture, Masculinity and the Wage Form', in *Working Class Culture.* eds Clarke *et al.*

27. Real abstraction in the case of the book form is interestingly discussed in Benedict Anderson, *Imagined Communities,* Verso 1983.

28. Exceptions are Foucault's passing interest in 'popular memory' and the discussion of alternative conceptions of crime in *Discipline and Punish.* But 'discourse' seems overwhelmingly to reference the most worked-up knowledge forms, 'philosophy' in Gramsci's usage.

29. There is a great deal of practical knowledge about 'communication' in the writings of professionals in these areas. Liberal pluralist traditions of media research in North America are recently reviewed – in ways pro-foundly ignorant of European traditions – in Shearon Lowery and Melvin L. De Fleur, *Milestones in Mass Communications Research,* Longmans 1983. The work on media in cultural studies has been based in critiques of these traditions. See, for example, the different approaches illustrated in *Culture, Society and the Media,* eds M. Gurevitch *et al.,* Methuen and Open University Press 1982.

30. These approaches are interestingly reviewed in Alan Swingewood, *The Myth of Mass Culture,* Macmillan 1977. For the Marxist critics see David Held, *Introduction to Critical Theory,* Hutchinson 1981. There are also

several really close empirical studies of media production which are essential correctives to the philosophical sweeps of these classics. See, for example, Philip Elliott, *The Making of a Television Series*, Constable and Sage 1972; Philip Schlesinger, *Putting Reality Together: BBC News*, Constable and Sage 1978; Hobson, *Crossroads*.

31. Gramsci, *Prison Notebooks*, esp. the section on 'philosophy'.

32. See, for instance, Murdock and Golding, 'Capitalism, Communication and Class Relations', in Curran et al., *Mass Communication and Society*; Murdock, 'Large Corporations and the Control of the Communications Industries', in eds Gurevitch *et al.*

33. These claims have an origin in Althusser's statement that ideologies have a material existence. For an extension see Coward and Ellis, *Language and Materialism*. This is a rather different perspective from Marx's argument that under particular conditions ideologies acquire a 'material force' or Gramsci's elaboration of this in terms of popularity.

34. See especially Adorno, 'On the Fetish Character of Music and the Regression of Listening', in *The Essential Frankfurt School Reader*, eds A. Arato and E. Gebhardt, Blackwell 1978.

35. This applies to a wide range of structuralist and post-structuralist theories from Nicos Poulantzas' arguments against class-reductionist views of ideology to the more revisionist positions of Barry Hindess and Paul Hirst and other theorists of 'discourse'.

36. I think that the predominant receptions of Gramsci in Britain have been anti-Leninist, especially among those interested in discourse theory. But it may be that CCCS appropriations also underestimate Gramsci's Leninism, I am grateful to Victor Molina for discussions on this theme.

37. I have in mind Gramsci's tendency to envisage the forms of mass attachment to Marxism as a form of 'faith', and his rather mechanical ideas about pedagogy. But I recognize that all this is based on a rather narrow reading, limited by available translations.

38. Hall et al., *Policing the Crisis: 'Mugging', the State and Law and Order*, Macmillan 1978; CCCS Education Group, *Unpopular Education: Schooling and Social Democracy in England since 1944*, Hutchinson 1981.

39. See Benjamin, 'The Work of Art in an Age of Mechanical Reproduction', in *Illuminations*. Again, the key lies at the production end, here in the transformations of conditions of production.

40. Particularly useful introductions to these combined impacts are: Sylvia Harvey, *May 1968 and Film Culture*, BFI 1980; Bennet, *Formalism and Marxism*.

41. Barthes, *Mythologies*, p. 112.

42. There are, however, some valuable 'breakouts' from a technical linguistics in the direction of cultural studies. See, for instance, the work of a group of critical linguists, initially brought together at the University of East Anglia: Roger Fowler et al., *Language and Control*; Gunther Kress and Robert Hodge, *Language as Ideology*, Routledge and Kegan Paul 1979. Also a group of linguists who work with Professor Utz Mass at the University of Osnabruck, West Germany. I am especially grateful for discussions on these themes with Gunther Kress and Utz Mass.

43. Much of this work remains unpublished. I very much hope that one of the next CCCS books will be on this subject. In the meantime see CCCS

English Studies Group, 'Recent Developments', in *Culture, Media, Language*, eds Hall *et al.*; Rachel Harrison, 'Shirley: Romance and Relations of Dependence', in CCCS Women's Studies Group, *Women Take Issue*; McRobbie, 'Working-Class Girls and Femininity', in *Women Take Issue*; Myra Connell, 'Reading Romance'; Christine Griffin, 'Cultures of Femininity: Romance Revisited', CCCS Stencilled Occasional Paper No. 69; Laura di Michele, 'The Royal Wedding', CCCS Stencilled Occasional Paper, forthcoming.

44. Much of this work is in connection with the Popular Memory Group in CCCS and will be published in a book on the popularity of conservative nationalism. I am grateful to Laura di Michele for opening up this area in relation to 'epic', and to Graham Dawson for discussions on masculinity, war and boy culture.

45. Bennett's example of the James Bond phenomenon is an even better illustration of the problem. See 'James Bond as Popular Hero', *Open University Popular Culture Course*, Unit 21, Block 5; and 'Text and Social Process: The Case of James Bond', *Screen Education*, No. 41 (1982), pp. 3–14.

46. Examples of organizing through a theme include Hall et al., *Policing the Crisis* and CCCS Education Group, *Unpopular Education*. For a more recent example, see CCCS Media Group, 'Fighting over Peace: Representations of CND in the Media', CCCS Stencilled Occasional Paper No. 72. An example of a project organized around a conjuncture is 'Jingo Bells: The Public and the Private in a post-Falklands Christmas', a set of studies which will, I hope, appear in a collection of recent CCCS media work.

47. One key example is (or was) the project of *Screen* in film criticism in Britain. Initially *Screen*, like its French model *Cahiers du Cinéma*, combined both formal and historical analysis (see for example many of the items collected in *Screen Reader: Cinema/Ideology/Politics*, ed. Ellis, SEFT 1977). In its campaigning 'middle' period, *Screen* adopted a much more formalist approach, from which it has somewhat retreated. In much of what follows I have *Screen* in mind, and draw on a long, largely unpublished critique written by the CCCS Media Group of 1977–78. Parts of this paper were published in *Culture, Media, Language*, eds. Hall et al.

48. The original version appears to have been Lévi-Strauss's on the subject of myth.

49. See, for example, the culmination of a long exploration of Marxist heterodoxy in Anthony Cutler *et al.*, *Marx's Capital and Capitalism Today* (2 vols), Routledge and Kegan Paul 1978.

50. For elaborations of these arguments see CCCS Media Group, 'Screen Critique', and Johnson, 'What is Cultural Studies Anyway?'

51. See especially, as a direct critique of Saussure, V. N. Volosinov, *Marxism and the Philosophy of Language*, trans. L. Matejka and I. R. Titunik, Seminar Press, New York 1973, esp. pp. 58–63.

52. For a summary of approaches see Coward and Ellis, *Language and Materialism*. Again I have film criticism in mind here as the particular example, considered more fully in 'What is Cultural Studies Anyway?'

53. See the by now famous analysis in terms of 'scopophilia' in Laura Mulvey, 'Visual Pleasure and Narrative Cinema', *Screen*, XVI, 3 (1975), 6–18. See also Colin Mercer, 'Pleasure', *Open University Popular Culture Course*,

Unit 17, Block 4.

54. Is it significant that in his classic text on narrative Barthes does not mention internal story-telling despite his stress on the omnipresence of the form? See Barthes, *Image-Music-Text,* trans. Stephen Heath, Fontana 1977, p. 79.

55. And some of the best, most influential work has been produced, explicitly, on this basis. The obvious example is Hoggart, *Uses of Literacy.* Feminist work too has actively promoted the importance of these insights.

56. For episodes in the history of orthodox social inquiry see Philip Abrams, *The Origins of British Sociology 1834–1914,* Chicago University Press, Chicago 1968; M. J. Cullen, *The Statistical Movement in Early Victorian Britain,* Harvester 1975; Gareth Stedman Jones, *Outcast London,* Clarendon Press 1971. The continuity between nineteenth-century inquiry and post-war sociologies is argued in CCCS Education Group, *Unpopular Education,* where the difference from New Left traditions is also argued. For the problems of research and social divisions see CCCS Popular Memory Group, 'Popular Memory: Theory, Politics and Method', in CCCS, *Making Histories.*

57. There is, for example, more than a trace of 'continental plates' in *Resistance Through Rituals,* eds Hall and Jefferson, especially in parts of the first chapter.

58. *Screen Education* was an important focus of these 'translations', but I am thinking of the growth of a critical media studies in secondary education and in higher and further education generally.

59. The main source here is the *Prison Notebooks.*

60. Most poignantly, perhaps, in some appropriations of Gramsci.

61. What follows is based, in rather too composite a way, on the work of Willis, McRobbie, Hebdige, Griffin and Hobson, and on discussions with other ethnographic researchers at CCCS. See, especially, Willis, *Learning to Labour* and *Profane Culture;* McRobbie, 'Working-Class Girls and Femininity'; Hobson, 'Housewives: Isolation as Oppression', in CCCS Women's Group, *Women Take Issue;* Hebdige, *Subculture,* Methuen 1979; Griffin, CCCS Stencilled Occasional Paper No. 69. There is a great need to identify systematically what has been particular to this tradition of ethnography.

Chapter 15

SITE VISIT: LOCAL CULTURAL INTERPRETATION

JOHN BROADBENT

INTRODUCTION

The material below is excerpted and slightly adapted from the printed programmes of three workshops held in 1981–82–83. These workshops, called DUET 2, 3 and 4, were mounted by the Development of University English Teaching project at the University of East Anglia, Norwich. Each of them had about thirty members, mostly academic staff working in English literature/higher education departments in the UK, but also including some overseas members, some research students, writers and undergraduates. The advertised aim was to develop the theory, practice, teaching and personal resources of men and women engaged with English and related subjects at the level of higher education. In structure and conduct the workshops derived from several different traditions, including the group relations work of the Tavistock Institute; various kinds of facilitation derived from the 'growth' or humanistic psychology movement; drama teaching, and other experimental teaching methods of a familiar kind. The convening staff usually consisted of about four academics and two lay people who would between them have a certain amount of experience in consultancy and leadership with groups or institutions, in therapy, and in creative writing, as well as in teaching and scholarship; there would also be two students as administrators.

Each programme was a document of about forty pages, briefing members some weeks in advance of the workshop. It opened with a section on context, and on the situation in literary studies, before going into details about the workshop itself. Most of these excerpts are from the context sections. The point of presenting them here is to show examples of contemporary cultural study which were produced for a specific purpose, for a specific community (the workshop), and by an actual group of people: although I wrote them, as director of these workshops, they were based on facilitated discussion and writing at preliminary staff meetings, as well as on informal discussion and revision provided by individual colleagues.

DUET 2: 1981

CONTEXT

DUET 2 is being held in the context of a sharpening political situation, and cultural flux. These events may be seen in the bad sense of crisis, as class antagonism, insoluble economic problems, illiteracy, truancy from cultural norms; or they may be seen in the better sense of crisis – decision or turning-point – as renewed political evaluation, fresh realism about wealth, the possibility of an élitist culture shifting into something shared.

It is within those crises that universities themselves face a new experience: some of us may be 'redundant'; some of the children who would have been our students will not reach higher education. Gain or loss? Since Robbins founded the new universities they have been largely recuperated into the existing system; and the UGC's cuts seem to have instinctively favoured conservative academies. But if intellect, imagination, growth are suppressed in one area, they will shoot up in another; so it is possible that the cuts will produce new development: the hard-hit universities will have to alter their actual structures radically; the advantaged may no longer be able to rely on other people to do their innovating for them.

Within the higher education system, English as a subject is going through a period of both creativity and inertia. The recent publicity given to debates at Cambridge about structuralism, film studies, and individual appointments, showed that the public recognize that such disputes are about political power; and also that the dialectic between structure and subjectivity is central for individual experience. Yet the dispute itself showed that although we are rich in theoretical sophistication, and in media, languages, skills, at the same time we are poor in our failure to accommodate and apply them, in our fear of the strange, lack of joy in our own resources. That is in itself, again, a model of the larger economy of the country.

The public context

It is easy to construct an analysis of context in the terms used by the politico-economic system itself. The country has decided on a series of reductions in public investment in the hope of private material gain, at least in the long run. There is an assumption that if we retrench now, there will be a long run and something like the past will be restored in it. The nation's current policy is a radical one, but it is aimed at the economic surface of things. Little energy is being directed at understanding the historical alterations which have overtaken the past and altered that hoped-for future already: endemic 'unemployment', rela-

315

tive poverty, shortage of fuel, the burgeoning of new cultures and political systems, diversification of our genes. Yet that sentence itself is characteristic in its dependent assumption that somebody else should be directing the energy. We seem as a populace to lack the will to meet the realities of our condition, good or bad. Or is it rather that we are in advance of our leaders and their media, hence ignore their admonitions while we wait for them to catch us up, or wait for the apposite moment – the moment when the paths of Zhivago and Lara crossed in a casualty clearing station, in a public library? Either way, there is a sense of waste and loss, of capability being put on the dole or parcelled out in safe routine, of the potential for this or that peculiar excellence, or peculiar inability, being suffocated by an uncaring airless uniformity.

> As a tentative definition of 'sick society' we can say that a society is sick when its basic institutions and relations, its structure, are such that they do not permit the use of the available material and intellectual resources for the optimal development and satisfaction of individual needs. The larger the discrepancy between the potential and the actual human conditions, the greater the social need for what I term 'surplus-repression', that is, repression necessitated not by the growth and preservation of civilization but by the vested interest in maintaining an established society.
>
> (Marcuse, *Negations: Essays in Critical Theory*, Penguin 1968)

Cultural context

The challenge for us, though, is to confront the context in the terms that literary people use (which may make Norman O. Brown more relevant than Marcuse). The sense of loss, and passivity in the face of it, seem to be partly historical. It is as if we were grieving not merely for present ills but for our lost empire and loss of creativity – lost parents or gods, perhaps. Numerous recent books are about the empire, or exist as quotations of books that were written within it: J. G. Farrell's *Singapore Grip*, Paul Scott's *Raj Quartet*, etc., Susan Hill's *Strange Meeting* (Wilfred Owen) and Paul Fussell's *The Great War and Modern Memory*, John Fowles's *The French Lieutenant's Woman* (*Persuasion*, Hardy, etc.), Frederick Bush's *The Mutual Friend*, *Apocalypse Now* . . . This is not surprising: Peter Marris in *Loss and Change* draws continuous parallels between individual bereavement, and the effort societies must make to rediscover meaningfulness as they change, now, at a rate faster than the change of generations.

Two recent novels about the future start with the acceptance of generational loss: in Doris Lessing's *Memoirs of a Survivor* the woman does not hold on to her own visions of a safer past or future. In Russell Hoban's *Riddley Walker* the hero sees his father die and takes his visionary powers over from him. In each novel, the child relates to the past and to safety through a transitional animal later abandoned: a cat-dog in Lessing, a wild dog in Hoban. Lessing, a South African, ha

316

been primarily a political writer and is now writing science fiction; Hoban, an American, has been primarily a writer for children. In them we see the canon of 'English literature' changing. Another symptom is that Marris's distinguished study of loss and change has never been taken up by the media; and like other delineations of the human condition recently, it is written with rich literary gifts yet not in a literary form. A precursor of Lessing's work, called *Memoirs of the Future,* was written by the psychiatrist Wilfred Bion. Bion was the doyen of group relations training in Britain, and at one time Beckett's analyst. His novel was published in South America and barely heard of in this country. It seems that the syllabus is dispensable: the literary imagination lives on the outer margins of the academic subject.

Universities

Suppose we ask what unconscious purpose for society – what purpose as a great writer would apprehend it – is being served by the contraction of education now? The contractions, instead of giving birth to new life, are punishing it; and this punishment recurs at other levels, in centres for retaliatory detention, in the unemployment of school-leavers. It is as though there were a general attack on young people, underneath the permissiveness, the declared concern, the commercial blandishments. The implied myth is of sacrifice: the young (and their mentors) are to be sacrificed to redeem the excesses of the 1960s? or perhaps as a way of rejecting the future, ensuring it does not arrive? Yet sacrifice does not involve killing merely: it is sanctification. Perhaps we are seeing the sacralization of certain groups in society – the unemployed, the young, the black – so as to permit other groups to be unholy.

> Shall not the councillor throw his curb
> Of poverty on the laborious?
> To fix the price of labour;
> To invent allegoric riches.
>
> And the privy admonishers of men
> Call for fires in the city,
> For heaps of smoking ruins
> In the night of prosperity and wantonness.
>
> To turn man from his path,
> To restrain the child from the womb,
> To cut off bread from the city,
> That the remnant may learn to obey.
>
> That the pride of the heart may fail;
> That the lust of the eyes may be quenched;
> That the delicate ear in its infancy
> May be dulled; and the nostrils close up . . .

(Blake, *Song of Los* (1795), plates 6–7)

317

An alternative reading (or writing) of the situation, a student suggests, would be in terms of propitiation: making sure, by virtuous thrift and stern measures, that the future does arrive, albeit in a slimmed-down form. Propitiation of the gods would go along with 'deterrence' at many levels: instead of an achieved sacrifice, a static threat – to withhold education or employment, or love, unless the generations behave themselves; ultimately, a threat to blow the world up, unless.

Again, how would a serious work of literature treat a university now, from the inside? It seems from recent novels that one fantasy held by the media and by universities themselves is that all forms of experimental or marginal activity form one suspect lump: so that left-wing political machinations, irresponsible sexuality, structuralism, developmental teaching, sociology, encounter groups, constitute a syndrome. This is a warning that when we come to defend ourselves against cuts, we are likely to adopt a mollusc-like posture in which every kind of experiment or marginality, good or evil, would have life withdrawn from it. One of the most radical changes of the 1970s, the unionization of academe, may turn out to be a conservative force; loyalty may lead us to defend practices which truly are redundant.

Literary studies

In English studies we may complain of cultural poverty; yet from another point of view our problem is how to manage infinite resources. As waves of development reach us – in literary theory, linguistics, the forms of fiction, film and drama, maturer cohorts of students – it is difficult to know how to adjust our syllabuses; or adjust our expectations about critical methodology when we mark scripts. We may realize that the forms we teach in continue to mirror an earlier world: the lecture, being an image of the renaissance schoolroom, or the Victorian factory, prolongs that model into our students' future behaviour as managers, teachers, broadcasters. We continue to write, and require students to write, in modes which have been superseded by changes in communication: the article, the essay, barely exist outside academe. Yet some of these challenges have been seized as opportunities: the Open University, for example, designs courses in literature which harness the multi-media resources of technology to the interdisciplinary resources of the subject; and produces textbooks written for the student rather than for any individual scholar's fame.

(Between DUETS 2 and 3 the cuts for universities were specified and began to be implemented; the Falklands campaign was fought.)

318

DUET 3: 1982

CONTEXT

> New York makes one think about the collapse of civilization, about Sodom and Gomorrah, the end of the world . . . I am not sure that this is the worst of all times. But it is in the air now that things are falling apart, and I am affected by it . . . But suppose it to be true – true, and not a mood, not ignorance or destructive pleasure or the doom desired by people who have botched everything. Suppose it to be so . . . There are still human qualities . . . We are an animal of genius.
>
> (Saul Bellow, *Mr Sammler's Planet*, Weidenfeld 1970)

> 'It's [London] threatened, you must see that.'
>   'By pollution and the collapse of its internal workings and services?'
>   'Yes, but much more by lack of faith. We are out of love with it because we're out of love with ourselves. What might really destroy us is human self-disgust.'
>
> (Maureen Duffy, *Capital*, Cape 1976)

Perhaps the context, of doom and genius, thanatos and eros, is what we have always lived in. But we are more aware of it. Part of the evidence for both is that serious writers are exploring the future. The 1981 Booker Prize went to one of the Raj-nostalgic texts we commented on in DUET 2; but the runner-up, *The White Hotel*, is precisely about eros and thanatos, the unconscious, acting out more and more directly in history.

Even so, it lags behind other works which have flown freer of documentary – many written by women (Lessing's *Shikasta* in the Canopus series and others we referred to last year) or by non-literary authors: *The Archaeology of Knowledge* ends with a dialogue between Foucault and his autocritic, just as Bernard Sharratt's *Reading Relations* contains several kinds of reflexivity. Gregory Bateson began *Steps to an Ecology of Mind*, and ended *Mind and Nature* (his last book, 1979) with dialogues between himself and his daughter.

Academic departments: interpretative communities?
One theme of DUET staff discussions so far has been the difficulty of talking about serious matters in professional terms. Even though we work in interpretative communities, we may find ourselves being 'swamped by the machine' as one person put it: the professional group turning into a deadly threat, excess of structure producing apathy or anarchy. We meet externalities, or individualistic trivia, when we want *communitas*, the tender metaphysics of Bateson's dialogues. This is presumably a defence against the chaos, and the femininity, of our subject; an assertion that it is hardware. In the same way, in our departments we don't usually invent modes of working that reflect the

fearful symmetry of our subject.

'Guided fantasy' is used in some kinds of developmental work, and can be adapted to creative writing classes. In one example the guide, having asked the class to imagine a place, and imagine meeting a figure there, says, 'Now ask the figure its name'. Pause. 'Now ask the figure its real name.' The context of DUET 3 is the end of the world, the Falklands, the cuts, unemployment . . . But when we ask the second question, what those names signify, what answer do we hear? In 1972 Angela Carter produced *The Infernal Desire Machines of Doctor Hoffman:*

> I lived in the city when our adversary, the diabolical Dr Hoffman, filled it with mirages in order to drive us mad . . . Hardly anything remained the same for more than one second and the city was no longer the conscious production of humanity; it had become the arbitrary realm of dream . . .sometimes the proportions of buildings and townscapes swelled to enormous, ominous sizes or repeated themselves over and over again in a fretting infinity . . . Frequently, imaginary massacres filled the gutters with blood and . . . created a deep-seated anxiety and a sense of profound melancholy. It seemed that each of us was trapped in some downward-drooping convoluted spiral of unreality from which we could never escape. . . Statistics for burglary, arson, robbery with violence and rape rose to astronomical heights . . . I was terrified to realize how much the autonomous power of the police had grown.

But it was not until ten years later, when most of that had come true or come to the foreground, that the book was paperbacked.

Through Angela Carter's excerpt we can hear an answer to what the Falklands' real name may be – the false islands, the antipodes upon which national chagrin can be projected, in fantasy, television, shelling; part of the mirage of Dr Hoffman. But can we go on with this discourse at the departmental level? As individuals we may have been reflecting on the mythology of the 'cuts': the castration of Abelard; Hedda burning the book; the rape of Philomel and the cutting out of her tongue to silence her; the closing of drama departments as if for civil war, lest they mock Angelo, Malvolio, Prince John of Lancaster. Philomel wove her story into a text but we seem to lack the institutional forms which would produce such a thing.

Do we have to be bound by despair? Another interpretation of the cuts might be cutting loose, for the individual now offered the chance to drop the apron-strings and remake a life; or the sub-group that might cut out a new space for itself inside a department. Are we in any case, by seeing the context as doomladen, trying to privilege ourselves into an arcadia which relies on other people to fashion the sheep-hooks?

The return of repressed change?

The mechanical printing of the nineteenth century, its back-to-back housing, rote learning, factories, exams and lectures and set books, were components of a single structure – McLuhan called it the Gutenberg galaxy. It began to collapse with the work of Freud, Joyce, Faraday, late Ibsen, Einstein, Chekhov. For Britain, the shift in technology to the electronic, and in thought to the organic and relativistic, coincided with the loss of empire. Naturally enough, institutions and habits belonging to the gone epoch lingered through a nostalgic obsolescence, for we had two losses to mourn.

The 1960s may have marked a peak of adaptation to the realities of change in the twentieth century. Has that decade been suppressed, or are we reimporting its skills into the 1980s? Certainly many of the knowledges planted then are only now flowering in the open – tectonics, linguistics, electronics, 'groups', divorce, television. . . .

For English as a subject, in England, much of that adaptive energy was recuperated into the existing system; or it was absorbed by the effort of setting up new academic *structures*. To that extent, the 'crisis in English studies' is the same as the crisis in Britain, or British Leyland: we did not dare to invest, or to reinvent. Yet this is contradicted by the existence of our playful fiction, the Colin MacCabe controversy, the *LTP* journal, British astrophysics and molecular biology . . . and by DUET? There is a puzzle about suppression and renewal, of which DUET and even this document itself (commodity fetishism, or greeting?) are examples. The time scales seem to slide over each other. It was only a hundred years ago that literacy was offered to everybody in England. And at that moment curved space, electricity, psychoanalysis were beginning. In 1897, when children were suppsed by Dr Boyson to be reciting in rows, some of them were being taught by Lawrence and Ursula Brangwen; and in the States John Dewey was writing:

> Education, therefore, is a process of living and not a preparation for future living . . . That education which does not occur through forms of life, forms that are worth living for their own sake, is always a poor substitute for the genuine reality, and tends to cramp and deaden.
>
> (*My Pedagogic Creed*, 1897)

THE WORKSHOP: IDEAS

The design aims of DUET are summed up in Dewey's 'Forms that are worth living for their own sake'. His statement implies a structure, and a creature. Over the last twenty years, similar metaphors have run through advanced educational thought:

> Instead of focussing on one thing at a time . . . teaching becomes a process of focussing on points of contact and connection between things and

321

ideas . . . Natural phenomena as now conceived by the sciences must be understood as a dynamic, a drama.

> (J. J. Schwab, 'The concept of the structure of a discipline' (1962),
> in *Guiding Learning*, ed. M.D. Glock, Wiley, New York 1971)

a theory of instruction . . . is principally concerned with how to arrange environments to optimise learning . . . The task of the . . . teacher is to provide exercises and occasions.

> (J.S. Bruner, *Towards a Theory of Instruction*,
> Oxford University Press 1960)

. . . ability to structure complex subject matter and to sustain extensive networks of reference points and concepts . . .

> (Gabriel Chanan and Linda Gilchrist, *What School is For*,
> Penguin 1974)

Connection . . . drama . . . networks; the subject as a symbolic arena like a novel; the teacher as a writer of occasions, environments; creating structures . . . living forms . . . These metaphors show how closely educational theory has matched literary theory. In section xii of *S/Z*, on 'The weaving of voices', Barthes writes:

> The five codes create a kind of network . . . through which the entire text passes (or rather, in passing becomes text) . . . We are, in fact, concerned not to manifest a structure but to produce a structuration . . .

DUET is offered in this spirit. It is potentially a matrix in the sense of womb, and in the sense of network; but it is not fully a matrix of either sort except as we, in Barthes' sense, 'produce' it.

Why teaching?

DUET's trajectory towards teaching can embarrass because it is less respectable than research. Yet it may be the beginning of research about what we don't know, and DUET's trajectory may be towards the future, and its literature and criticism, which lie in the hands of our students. A creative writing exercise at the University of East Anglia recently was dominated by two grandfather clocks; two portraits; and characters who changed from Methuselah to a young girl, from eleven years old to twelve, from a little boy to an ageing man. These fragments seem to be about Tiresias, or Tithonus; reluctant transition into adulthood. But also about the future's absence. There used to be a time – grandfather's time; people used to grow up – there they are on the wall – and live to immense old age; but now we shan't get much beyond puberty. Those, perhaps, are some of the concerns that lie behind the 'essays' students write. One writes of Wordsworth's poem 'Yew-Trees':

> The shadows of our experience seem to gather, even at mid-day, and are mirrored by this strange interplay of nature.

Study casts the shadow of old age, or the tutor's shadow, on to the student's prime and brings with it the shadow of the nuke: how can fathers not be death? But in this strange interplay there are perhaps the seeds of a new kind of criticism, and of new knowledge.

(Between DUETs 3 and 4 a Conservative government was re-elected with an overwhelming majority; nuclear protest grew, centring on Greenham Common; the universities survived the cuts without, it seems, redundancy, but were asked to consider more cuts; unemployment continued to increase.)

DUET 4: 1983

CONTEXT

Destruction or transformation?

This January I was visiting the library of the Tavistock Institute. It has always pleased me with its inversion of the canon of university libraries: here science and art – Sophocles, Darwin, Husserl – fit into the interstices of juvenile delinquency, marriage guidance, guilt and reparation, as in real life. But that day Freud, Klein, Bion, all disgusted me. Then, in a limbo of the gender section, I found Frédérick Leboyer's *Birth without Violence* (1974). The text runs like a poem in and out of closeups in which the Oedipal triangle, and the art/nature dyad, hold in harmony for a moment. A newborn baby crumples at the centre of a star formed by its own thigh, its mother's thigh, and the tender hairy forearm of the writer-photographer-gynaecologist. Leboyer explains that he does not slap the baby and at once cut the umbilicus, as in western orthodoxy, but lets the baby change from its mother's oxygen to that of its own lungs, so that

> for an average of four or five minutes, the newborn infant straddles two worlds. Drawing oxygen from two sources it switches from the one to the other, without a brutal transition, with scarcely a cry . . . Grant this moment its slowness, and its gravity.

A brutal enough transition is in orbit for us; and submission or silence are the easiest response to whatever the preliminary, pre-nuclear 'cuts' impose upon us. It is a menacing context in which to mount a workshop on the teaching of literature. At a staff meeting in March one of us said, 'The hidden statement of everything being written now is "I am frightened" '. During a discussion with students last year one said, 'It is death which shadows most of our thoughts'. Another spoke of 'a sudden flash, and *it is here*!'. She meant not only the flash of a nuclear blast, but the abrupt arrival of the post-industrial world, and living on the dole, through machines, in a violent culture. This fatedness ghosts or wastes institutions, rituals, education in advance, by pre-fusion.

The complexity of meaning in that flash indicates that the fear we attribute to the threat of holocaust may obscure the fear of a different cataclysm: the transformation of consciousness. Alix Pirani has written:

> the stress of unchannelled, festering and fidgetty energy is becoming intolerable. We're carrying the tensions, the too-much-holding, in our bodies and in our minds. And we're picking them up, of course, from the whole climate of our present civilisation, which I think is on the verge of breakthrough to transformation, poised in that place where the stress of holding, the crisis of power, the longing for release, are acute.
>
> ('The creative process', *Self and Society*, X (1982))

Some kind of transformation is in the air. Evidence is thin because in a time like this, literature and the arts may do no more than reflect the decay of the old order. Documentary has energy – the ranting poets, *The Boys from the Blackstuff*, the improvisatory drama initiated by Tony Garnett in *Cathy Come Home*, Tony Parker's oral reportage in *The People of Providence: a housing estate and some of its inhabitants* (1983):

> Sit on my arse and take the sick that's all I'm good for. Forty-fucking-two and that's my lot. Gets you down, you know, it really fucking does . . . Oh Christ, I get so fucking fed up I can't tell you, I can't put it into words.

He can't put it into words because it belongs already to a gone world. Other kinds of writing, almost always with an element of fantasy or futurism, do take us to the edge of transformation: the concatenation of youth and age, mysticism and camp, in Anthony Burgess's *Earthly Powers* (runner-up to Golding's Booker-winning *Rites of Passage*, also homosexual, and carefully portentous); and in Iris Murdoch's *The Sea, the Sea*, of which the hero is, once more, old and homosexual; Antonia Byatt's effort to relate past and present, genius and mental handicap, in *The Virgin in the Garden* . . . well, we all have our lists. But from most of these the life of the mass of people is excluded; and few of them use, except in broken sentences by weakened characters, the transfigured language you do sometimes hear strongly in Rilke, or in some feminist writing, at least from France. In Britain there seems to be no language which,

> as it develops, will not degenerate and dry up, will not go back to the fleshless academicism, the stereotypical and senile discourses that we reject. If a music of femininity is arising out of its own oppression, it materialises through the rediscovered body.
>
> (Chantal Chawaf, 'La chair linguistique' (1976), in *New French Feminisms*, eds Marks and de Courtivron)

Indeed, in Britain the media of all sorts are now barely able to express simple concern. They report on other articulate utterances – Greenham women, Brixton blacks, punk braves – to admire or regret, or more often to sneer. Disturbance is contained by locating it in places with bad labels: in Toxteth, in Belfast and Derry, in the Falklands, the mines. The common is enclosed, and concreted over, so that we shall not experience it inside ourselves.

It is by denying experience that the managed media also inhibit transformation. The life of the individual can illuminate institutions and cultures. Of the individual, Daniel J. Levinson says:

> To gain a genuine sense of integrity, a man must confront the lack of integrity in his life. During the Late Adult Transition [post-capitalism?], everyone at times has a sense of utter despair. This always has some basis in actuality as well as in irrational self-accusation . . . Whatever our values, we cannot live up to them fully.
>
> (*The Seasons of a Man's Life*, Knopf, New York 1979)

Students confront both the sterile and the generative encounters with their subject. Here are two, writing about their own development, dynamically and tenderly:

X. [After narrating a dream in which she had wept in the context of an abbey, beautiful singing, and rowdy students of nuclear physics] I cannot avoid making a connection with Wordsworth's poem here: my dreams play quite a large part in my life; I seem to remember them more than most people, and in general they seem to be more vivid and of longer duration than others do . . . As I was reading 'Tintern Abbey' for the fiftieth time, I came across this section, which I had never registered before:

> thy mind
> Shall be a mansion for all lovely forms,
> Thy memory be as a dwelling-place
> For all sweet sounds and harmonies.

Y. This connects my personal understanding of memory, time, dreams, unconscious peace and quiet [guilt?], and what Wordsworth was all about . . .

[After narrating the loss of a seaside windowseat which gave her a Wordsworthian view in earlier years] I do long to return to my non-committal repose sometimes, but like the poems in Blake's *Songs of Experience* I cannot return to the innocent state . . . Like Wordsworth I now have a vision, a thirst for reason or satisfaction in what I do, and doing it is not enough. I do not regret this state, but I cherish my memories of the past and accept that I have moved on . . . I must add at the end of this work . . . that I really think this has been the most productive course I have done. I mean 'productive' in terms of a *release* that has taken place within me, which began happening last term. I think that my response to poetry . . . has suddenly become *my* response, and not that which *I think I ought* to feel.

She is echoing the last words of *King Lear*, spoken by Edgar the wronged orphan:

> The weight of this sad time we must obey,
> Speak what we feel, not what we ought to say;
> The oldest hath borne most, we that are young
> Shall never see so much, nor live so long.

To encourage that kind of speaking in this sad time means encouraging subjectivity. The rejection of false objectivity is in line with the flow of science:

> The word 'objective' becomes, of course, quite quietly obsolete; and at the same time the word 'subjective', which normally confines 'you' within your skin, disappears as well.
> (Gregory Bateson, quoted in *About Bateson*, ed. J. Brockman, Wildwood House 1977; and in *Human Inquiry: a sourcebook of new paradigmresearch*, eds P. Reason and J. Rowan, Wiley 1981)

But in academic practice it is also necessary to provide safe structures, so that individuals may work confidently with their own resources, and acknowledge that they are a part of other people's resources too. That confidence, in the access to learning, goes against the ethos of competition, failure, 'stars' which equates so much of the economy, and of education, with TV gift games. To learn what it might be like to fly beyond all that, we have to take up the double meaning of *voler* in French – to fly, and to steal – as used by Cixous:

> Nor is the point to appropriate their instruments, their concepts, their places, or to begrudge them their position of mastery . . . Let's leave it to the worriers, to masculine anxiety and its obsession with how to dominate the way things work – knowing 'how it works' in order to 'make it work'. For us the point is not to take possession in order to internalise or manipulate, but rather to dash through and to 'fly' [*voler* – fly/steal].
> ('The Laugh of the Medusa')

The god of thieves was Hermes; it was he also who gave Orpheus his lyre.

REVIEW

This is not an excerpt. I notice the following concerns or symptoms in these papers, so far as they themselves constitute a cultural document.

1. The writing is most lively, and probably most accurate, when I engage in freely associative fantasy about myth, or read current

events as if they were a mythic text. At a lower level, there is much reliance on collage, *bricolage*, eclectic quoting from multifarious sources to bolster authority; but this does seem to represent a refusal to stay put, an effort at being inter-indisciplined. The weakest writing occurs when I try to explain DUET itself. This is in spite of my own experience of the workshops being vital and deeply felt. Perhaps we lack a language, uncontaminated by bureaucratic forms, in which actually to describe new institutions; hence the difficulty of inserting them into society.

2. There is a constant search for a new language, akin to the little language lovers use, or even to babytalk. This is allied to a whole paradigm of allusions to – indeed, dependence upon – birth, children, students, and women: figures which, for a man writer, represent the tender and the generative and the new (the different?). These classes are at some disadvantage in society now; this suggests that perhaps they are a real threat to some, and therefore a real hope to others?

3. The document itself, like the workshops it is attached to, is essentially collegiate rather than public. By this I mean that it came to be written not within the normal teaching and research activities of an academic department, but on the margins, in relation to as it were a mythical sub-department put into orbit. And it has come to be published not in the standard journals of English literary criticism but in a volume edited by a person who also had a hand in producing the original programmes. I don't want to see this as cottage industry. I said 'collegiate' to mark a particular kind of interdependent autonomy which is characteristic of the relations between Oxbridge colleges and their universities: it is exactly the opposite of the present British government stance towards local government (centralization of power) and towards industry (*laissez-faire*).

4. The 'cuts' are elided with nuclear threat. In a trivial way this parallels the way we elide, in the word 'holocaust', genocide conducted by a Nazi government in the past, with future nuclear war.

PS. I have been baffled, the last few weeks, by wondering what texts might now richly reflect our condition. They seem so weak beside the metaphors of even domestic news recently. Two bunches of metaphor stand out this month. One is of mines (here and in Nicaragua); miners being stopped in the Dartford Tunnel (another version of their workplace) from leaving Kent, by a new kind of policing; while a mole, underground in the Foreign Office, is unearthed, turns out to be a twenty-three-year-old woman of immense seriousness and modesty, and is imprisoned (in another pit, then) for six months. The other is of two great ganglions of knowledge and power – of intelligence – being seized: Government Communications Headquarters where the staff may no longer belong to a union; and the Greater London Council, which is to be abolished, replaced by appointed bodies, and before that its due elections voided. Both sets of metaphor relate to the city, which Blake, Angela Carter, Maureen Duffy, Bellow were writing about in the earlier part of this contribution; but suddenly the language is much closer to the body, intimate in its attention to viscera and to head or heart, sudden in its arrest.

Chapter 16

WOMEN BEYOND CULTURE

CORNFLOWER REFLECTION: BEYOND THE CIRCLE OF OUR VISION

LORNA SMITH

> two women, eye to eye
> measuring each other's spirit, each other's
> limitless desire,
> a whole new poetry beginning here.
> (Adrienne Rich)[1]

This article began as a piece of research into the ways in which women write about the experience of madness. I was led to question the available definitions of insanity; to rethink the language with which we explore texts; to enter into the possibility of my own madness. I wanted to communicate my experience of the text but the critical language available to me, while facilitating an intellectual understanding of the text, alienated me from, and denied access to, other forms of expression. The language I was seeking was carved out of pleasure, pain, confusion; it was not a language which sought to disguise, distort, re-form these experiences, but enable, enrich and realize them. It was important that I engaged with the texts in a way which did not demand an authorial structure; which in some ways evolved from the possibility of trust and vulnerability between 'reader' and 'writer' of different texts. The language of criticism, which is divisive and fraught with authority conflict, was of little use. I wanted a 'common language' and although I may not have found one, and there must be many, my search has uncovered a far richer, more lifegiving earth than I would otherwise have dreamed of.

I begin from a desire to move beyond the circle of patterns and structures which contains us; not simply to repeat the archetypal myth but to accept that it cannot be resolved, only reflected forever between two opposing mirrors; to let go and begin again. . . .

I could no longer call out with the certainty of a returning echo: only the misty silence drifting between the earth and the mirage: only the mountain in the clear southern sky. Madness like a soft-suffocating cradle threatened and beckoned me.

I have spun webs of understanding between myself and the world of others. Each of us with bodies kneaded to the shape of other eyes and hands; hopelessly searching for nourishment, without vision and song. Alone, we protect and punish, afraid of solitude and of ourselves. An intricate web, carefully spun, linking and communicating with that which is fragmented and in tension. But as the air no longer trembles and vibrates, in silence and stillness, afterwards, the web becomes weighed down; its surface no longer strong, fluid and mobile but laden with the dust of death. The channels of communication and interpretation which I have been taught have become meaningless, tortuous – the world has gone mad, not I. But where do I go to when I carry the soft weight of my own soul through the cobwebs into the attic beyond?

What labyrinths do women wander in as they articulate their experience of madness? How far can we stumble through these dim tunnels, before we retreat in fear back to the familiar channels of communication, which we create and perpetuate in order that we are not left totally alone, like dumb animals struggling to touch the loneliness of the other. But the fear is born of the touch of madness; our bodies and minds knowing beyond the language which stretches across the cracks and chasms. 'A great gap opened in the ice floe between myself and the other people whom I watched, with their world, drifting away through a violet-coloured sea where hammer-head sharks in tropical ease swam side by side with the seals and the polar bears. I was alone on the ice.'² I too begin to drift as I sift through the images offered to me in this passage. Drawn into the water in the illusion of its warmth, remembering the womb, a merging of consciousness and then the emerging of life, the blue veins on the neck and breasts of a pregnant woman, a violet field of gently swaying colour. Deluded by a sun-filled vision, ripped by the animal whose means of survival I chose to ignore, I am alone on the ice. Not because I had a choice but because I had lost the power to screen out and censor that which jarred with the pattern demanded. I was lured at first by the series of binary oppositions in which I was taught to read and recognize my culture, but encountering images which would not split or be reconciled, I had to engage with the world around me in a way which did not depend on either-or for its sanity.

A pattern, a form, a shape, whose material substance has a clearly defined function; whose five senses experience the surface reality in accordance with rigid codes and values; whose language pre-exists birth, is weighted and tied down by past history.	One who is open to the possibility of fluid and mobile axes of reference, spiritual and material; whose senses experience without judgement; one who dreams of a new language which will not be distorted by history; who is 'adept at detecting the reality beneath the erasure.'³

Floundering in the schizophrenic split of binary mythology, we struggle in a chasm of confusion for contact and meaning; threatened always by the ensuing darkness of a divided earth who trembles and heaves with the desire to be reunited with herself.

The literature of madness often begins from the difficulty of continually attempting to reintegrate and fit together the social codes which pre-exist our entry into subjectivity, while moving towards the creation of an alternative subjectivity. One of the clearest examples of this can be found in *Woman on the Edge of Time,* in which Marge Piercy imagines an alternative way of being whose change is centred in the roots, not the petals of the new growth. The madness springs not from the possibility of the future but from the way in which the past and the present track us down: cornered and bleeding the hounds move in for the kill, scarcely aware except in pleasurable frenzy that the taste of the flesh is their own. There is no peace in this novel to escape into fantasy and we grieve at the choice we make every day to live as we do. A similar kind of polarity is presented in Doris Lessing's *The Marriages Between Zones Three, Four and Five* (1980), extended simply by virtue of multiplicity. The resolution does not echo around madness but is bound to the blossoming of the spiritual in which a woman once again carries the burden of responsibility and the body of nurturing.

As readers, we are also aware of a choice: to enter into the experience of madness or to deny and refuse through definition and incarceration. In the prop rooms of our lives we assume the costumes which are recognizable. Layer upon layer of identity structures the flurrying mass of feelings, fragmented and diverse, which we believe must be contained behind the curtains. How can we be sure that being with our own confusion, if not easy, will at least be accepted? We have forgotten how to trust. And so by defining, naming, the person who doubts and does not conform to the social pattern, we are projecting on to the external world, on to the other, our fears of the 'other' within us. The desire to restore an order which is illusory is a defence against (the possibility of) impending chaos. Thus the definitions, originating from a self bound in a particular cultural experience, speak with the single voice to those of us for whom these truths resonate. A mad person is a political dissident (David Cooper), one who rejects 'one's sex-role stereotype' (Phyllis Chesler), one who is alienated in an 'environment that is permanently haunted by contradictions' (Foucault). By defining madness in relation to a socio-historical narrative, we judge and evaluate, constructing a 'norm' which the language of our society validates. To live within the authorial boundaries of sane-insane, right-wrong, acceptable-unacceptable, is not necessarily to believe in those boundaries: but creating alternatives depends on a shift of vision, a new horizon, not simply a response to that which is in existence. To go beyond the power of history and the oppressive weight of specific patterns of behaviour which are categorized, internalized, made more familiar than the contours of our own bodies, 'everything from history must be eliminated, the circles and the arrogant square pages.'[4] If we can work through the painful past, releasing the pleasure, freeing ourselves from the blurring of the past with the present, if we can begin from an inner strength to reach out to the community, then we begin to eliminate that which restricts, thwarts, destroys, cripples. The argument that madness is an expression of deep conflict between 'reality' and one's inability to conform to that reality without inflicting irreparable damage to the self is formed within a specific ideological relation to society. The social system demands a framework, the foundation and driving force of which is that all action and expression which does not reinforce the base model shall be deemed deviant, other. Madness, by definition, becomes external, in need of dissolution, distortion, disintegration. Thus personally, politically and socially, madness is alienated from our lives and is alienating in our experience of it. The creativity and perception which madness potentially offers is distorted and reorientated often because of a fear of intensity and strangeness. And our choice of ways of being is determined by the fact that, if we seek protection by merging our voices with the dominant authority, we pay with the silence of our souls. Our bodies paralysed with guilt and fear, we gaze at all the shuddering brutality we so wilfully perpetrate. Angry, yes, but no longer powerless, reeling against the despair which clouds the thought that the symbolic order has the limitless capacity to assimilate any position and represent it in terms of its own codes.

Writing about madness, women are articulating their experiences of alienation, guilt, fear, isolation, disorientation, creativity; not one confined experience of madness but a multitude of responses to a distorted and distorting system. That this energy is locked up in institutions or deadened with medication is testament to the absolute refusal to confront the 'other'. Literature offers us a looking glass but does our vanity allow us to see beyond the surface image? Stepping through involves resistance within the text to interpretation along traditional theoretical lines. The text does not resolve itself but challenges and undermines the false definitive base of knowledge which we adopt. Its potential support lies in its reflection of social insanity. Inverting what we assume to be the norm and foundation of 'reality', the literature of madness attempts to speak a new language. 'I knew the mad language which created with words, without using reason, has a new shape of reason; as the blind fashion from touch an effective shape of the sight denied them.'[5]

Madness embodies its own *raison d'être*. It is the weaving of this other thread of meaning which renders the communication of insanity so powerful. We are confronted by the totally isolated and enclosed world of the human mind; alien, non-us, unimaginable and therefore 'insane'. The world of the mad person threatens the sociocultural and linguistic scaffolding. The deeper the instability, the more fantastic the voyage, the more necessity there is to clearly define the physical and psychological barriers between the mentally 'ill' and the mentally 'healthy'. Perhaps it is the existence of these structures and delineations which, functioning in terms of exclusion and deletion, is at the root of madness. In order that a particular social system is maintained, confirmed and justified, a peculiar definition of madness is reinforced. The social and linguistic nature of madness is pre-determined. Madness must be seen as a deviation from the norm in order that the norm retain its power and authority.

The mentally 'ill' are contained within the circle of their own being; 'the cord retrieves them again and again to the central prison of their perplexity'.[6] An inability to give birth to the self; an umbilical relationship which will/can not be severed; the constant tension between being and reflecting, I and the other. The segregation and division of 'them' protects, reassures, confirms 'us', perpetuating the value system on which the division is based. We speak a language of protection and exclusion rooted in the belief that certain forms of social development cannot accommodate, except by alienation, transforming shapes and colours of creativity. The literature of madness reflects back images of the inner tomb of isolation, but it subverts the means by which this isolation is constructed by breaking down the barriers and drawing us into that prison of perplexity – through the chambers of our minds, thick with the sand of burial, the clear tapping of the self, alone and betrayed, echoes from the cold depths.

Who within and beyond me is silenced by the language with which I speak my sanity? From what source does the word derive its absolute authority? How can we bridge the gulfs which lie forever between us? We are drawn back into our central prison where we struggle to accept our own truths, ourselves; and from where the tentative sparks of contact rarely flare into life. The language which we enter into in the Lacanian sense offers an escape from isolation but it is an underground maze threatening to cave in, muffling our cries and our songs. 'Piona. . . could neither read nor write and found it hard to match her ideas with speech as if every time she wanted to say something, to emerge from herself, it was like trying to open a door and being prevented by great masses of dullness like the rubble of toppled buildings pressing down and entombing her.'[7] Each time we open ourselves to the 'other' in whatever form, anger, fear and violence rush in and, numbing myself to the experience, I no longer ask what access do I have to the many languages spoken in my culture, what value systems do they emerge from and blanket over, what power relationships do they permit us to function within? – but my body protectively gathering in around me becomes still, nurturing the seeds from which will spring forth new life shoots. Speaking in a tongue so heavily weighted with past meaning I become silent and confused. We have been denied access to the vibrant colourful energy of the other and of ourselves. The silence now like the gentle humming of women in protest, is the womb quietness of a new shape forming. And we must hold on to it, demand its acceptance and protection in the face of overpowering aggression.

> Silence can be a plan
> rigorously executed
>
> the blueprint to a life
>
> It is a presence
> it has a history a form
>
> Do not confuse it
> with any kind of absence.[8]

In the acts of learning and speaking our language, we absorb the myths and forms which regulate and control social evolution. We perpetuate and are responsible for certain forms of living. In some way we collude psychologically, agreeing to wear the designated linguistic disguise. The sources of this collusion are manifold and complex, from the self-awareness of fear and loneliness to the exercising of power (over). All linguistic expression is rooted in the need to relate to others. The act of communication reinforces 'I' but it is an 'I' whose form is predetermined in and by the language. Self and what it is to experience self drifts in a timeless mist around which language forms a fragile brittle shape. The analogy speaks of many images, of the womb, our source of life from which expelled we always seek to return; to penetrate the fragile egg of our first being; to be enclosed and protected; to seek escape from the prison. The continuing conflict between the need to be separate, whole and the longing for the other to complement our sense of incompleteness and fragmentation. A conflict born of a language of division and possession. The truth which is carried like a seed deep within ourselves cannot be cast in the form of language as it is; an abyss stretches between them.

> Death I said; but it is like truth and from continent to continent we fly within the two words, first class in the comfort of them, but when it is time for us to leave the words themselves and parachute to their meaning in the dark earth and seas below us, the parachute fails to open, we are stranded or drift wide of our target or, peering over into the darkness and stricken with fright, we refuse to leave the comfort of the words.[9]

Language contained, suspended in light and air above a deep living force. Language charged with the power and authority to protect us from ourselves, but draining away the vital essence. We judge our 'time from the sun's position in the sky when the sun itself has melted and trickles down the ridges of darkness into the hollows of evaporated seas'.[10] The power has dissolved but its liquid movement fills up a void, replenishes that which is barren, merges in the hope of creating.

If we gather in some of these thoughts and focus on texts, we can begin to explore whether or not this interweaving of voices can multiply their possibilities, enabling our awareness of them to widen and deepen. We need the voices from the outside world to complement in whatever way our own; we need to be secure enough in our own perceptions to allow ourselves to be open to the perceptions of others. The self in madness, hovering in freedom, bound by chains.

> The freedom of the wholly mad
> to smear and play with her madness
> write with her fingers dipped in it
> the length of a room.[11]

> the importance given to limits, to
> frontiers, to walls, to anything
> that encloses and protects, is a
> function of the absence of internal
> unity in the arrangement of things.[12]

One of the most powerful images in Janet Frame's book *Faces in the Water* is that torn and fragmented space between the face we can touch with our fingertips sensing that it is there, and the trembling image in the water which knows no crystal form, only an ever-changing current rippling beyond the surface. How do we reconcile those; how do we move through the space without falling into the void? 'I did not know my own identity. I was burgled of body and hung in the sky like a woman of straw.'[13] Images of possession, of property, of a capitalist mentality transferred on to the body of the woman, internalized by her, are interlaced with the pornographic images of women bound and raped. Physically and psychologically violated, the woman's body is suspended above and beyond reach; almost Christ-like, echoing the painting by Dali, but without the powerful symbolism of the Christ figure. Impaled as a warning to all who dare to break the rules, a limp, impotent figure of fear and mockery. In order to affirm herself – denied affirmation by others – Estina seeks a framework within and around which she can create her own identity, and the psychological instability results in a projection outward on to the physical environment. Surrounding objects become a focus for internal confusion. Reconstructing the material world, creating order, finding power over self. The material world becomes a symbol of stability, of permanence; a talisman to ward off the threat of non-existence which is posed by drugs, shock treatment, incarceration. The object symbolizes life, but is once removed from the process of living. It is another form of denial; 'this needling of their whole life into a piece of fancywork'[14] which takes on all the hope of suppressed colour, shape, movement, change.

Introduction to contemporary cultural studies

The arts and crafts of her story are real and creative forms of expression but within the institution they become a travesty; these objects embody suppressed cries of grief. Can we translate this into the social institutions of government and welfare which so often take the responsibility from the individual?

> She would get in such a panic if she could not find it, whimpering and moaning and turning everything on to the floor, and then kneeling and beginning to pray. She had transferred the meaning of her life to her handkerchief, as a child, after a long confusing day at the beach, takes home safe in her handkerchief her treasure of a few shells and bright stones, the meaning of her day.[15]

Clutching that part of oneself which is constantly drifting away; the symbol of individuality; rebellion against the system, against this form of life.

The power of the institution is absolute – if we give it that power. It consumes its victims, those without freedom and strength, denied those qualities from the moment of birth. They become absorbed by the shape of the institution, invisible. 'Did they live in the wall and emerge only at mealtime? Or were they perpetually immured and the smell that oozed from the wood was their personal smell of imprisonment that drained through their skin and their mind and their whole body?'[16] And the question which haunts our minds is not that which focusses upon the institution, the collective body which negates the self, but the insidious messages we receive constantly from all the forms of communication which invade our lives.

All the horror of being buried alive is transferred to this side of the grave. Immured, they 'emerged as some pitiful human spawn from the Brick Building itself'.[17] The sense of obliteration, of superimposition of a uniform, 'the brown colour that most of us had and that I had thought to be sunburn and windburn but that I realized was a stain of something else, a color of stagnancy spreading from inside and rising to the surface of the skin'.[18] Survival is assured by internalizing the unwritten codes of the institution but it is survival at the cost of the self. We recognize and identify with this process, those of us who inhabit a culture whose every form is potentially institutionalized. Ironically, the object which confirms Estina's sense of her belonging in the institution, 'her final entry into the land of the lost people'[18], is the same object which enables her to recover the lost experiences of sensuality. 'It was pink cretonne with a drawstring and roses around the top in a border and a circular base of cardboard; and my hand going into it was like a bee entering a flower.'[19] The overpowering sensation of touch, smell, enclosure and fecundity; a sensual awareness; a reciprocity of give and take; an easy coming together and moving apart. The moment of intensity, of self-awareness, is betrayed both by the institution and by the world beyond. Both demand an altered level of mediation between self and other which disturbs the foundation on which we build our perceptions of sanity and insanity.

> Have we progressed from illness when we do not care any more for the pink cretonne bag with its pattern of roses, but begin to look for people that we may thread a drawstring round their neck and carry them back and forth inside ourselves, and not be willing to let them go not even in the night in sleep and dreams?[20]

The power we are confronted with is the power of conformity, of distortion of what is unique into a shape that is uniform, comprehensible, integrable. And if the raw material cannot be moulded by coercion and persuasion then they will remove the 'self'.

> I will have a bandage over my head and a scar at each temple or a curved one, like a halo, across the top of my head where the thieves, wearing gloves and with permission and delicacy, have entered and politely ransacked the storehouse and departed calm and unembarrassed like meter readers, furniture removers, or decorators sent to repaper an upstairs room.[21]

They will attempt to possess utterly that which eludes them. The metaphors of capitalism and materialism have again been transposed on to the body and we perceive ourselves as objects in an economy, with relative viability. The body is no more or less than an object to be moulded and impressed by others more powerful than itself, and 'much of living is an attempt to preserve oneself by annexing and occupying others'.[22] When the tension between opposing factions begins to vibrate with its own frustrated energy; when the adult realizes that 'a child which they thought to be a toy becomes the dangerous reality of an individual being, as if the miniature piano had sounded forth symphonies'[23]; then the erupting violence has the power to obliterate utterly, even to self-destruction.

We protect that which is unique within a synthetic cocoon of acceptable form until it can no longer remain silent, tortured, entombed. Consciousness of this state divides us within and between ourselves. Our sense of reality is confirmed by the mirror images around us. When the mirror becomes a transparent entrance into another world we must destroy the threat of the other and force reaffirmation. What are we afraid of? – trading the free exploration of creativity for the keys to the prison of custom and habit.

The borders of orientation and definition, although there very clearly in terms of the asylum, continually move and fluctuate. Movement in *Faces in the Water* involves an interweaving of isolation and disintegration. The structure of the asylum is all-powerful (even the voice which speaks of the outside world fades into silence, the existence there becomes unreal, fragmentary, almost illusory). The shapes of the lives within that structure are enclosed, contained. Survival depends on the individual's ability to restructure/reform the environment. To create her own form from the world around her. This is an act of self-affirmation, the only possible act. In its existence the asylum is a manifestation of her own sterility in society's terms; thus reconstructing that environment is an act of defiance, of creativity.

The asylum threatens continually to obscure, absorb, annihilate the individual by being static, without natural development, seasonal change or growth. Imposed on each person is a rigid procedure of bodily functions; the sense of time movement throughout the day is negated by the endless repetition of identical days. 'There is no past present or future. Using tenses to divide time is like making chalk marks on water. I do not know if my experiences at Cliffhaven happened years ago, are happening now, or lie in wait for me in what is called the future.'[24] The promise of change is in the memory of a new dawn aroused, evoked and betrayed in the first moments of waking from sleep. Foucault speaks of the work of Minkowski on paranoia when temporality no longer conforms. 'The accumulation of the past can no longer, for him, be liquidated; and correlatively past and present cannot anticipate the future; no acquired security can serve as a guarantee against the threats that it contains; in the future everything is absurdly possible.'[25] The strangeness of this statement seems not to lie in the world of the paranoid but in the world which has forgotten that in the future everything *is* absurdly possible.

The only way in which time passing is acknowledged is in the body's awareness of its own change. The fear of this decay/decomposition, which is in part an inability to let go of destructive patterns of relating, is one of the reasons behind the refusal of time.

> Often for days on end, out of caution or inertia and the need to gather secret weapons, the season stayed poised in the same weather, bringing a deceptive feeling of timelessness, a separation from time which was, in reality, time's invasion which could not be borne and so was rejected from consciousness and remained monotonously in the background, unnoticed, like a clock ticking or traffic or the sea flowing.[26]

This expresses not only a refusal of death but an awareness of what is socially acceptable. A menopausal woman may fear the approach of 'old age' and the body changes she is experiencing but much of her anxiety is produced by the constant pressure on her to be young, attractive, slim and active. Too much is socially and economically invested in these images for us to be given the encouragement and space to explore new and fulfilling forms of sexuality. And this is a pale reflection of the archetypal mythology engraved in our lives. Perhaps one of the ways in which we can begin this process is to come together as individuals, refusing as Estina does to be coalesced into one institutionalized mass. The characters in the novel have an awareness of each other as people; Mrs Pilling 'is inclined to act out of character herself in order to preserve someone else's individuality'.[27] We 'moved closer to one another in spite of our separately sealed worlds, like glass globes of trick snowstorms'.[28] A solidarity evolving from many individuals seeking to touch the other without losing the self: to fight a battle with the forces which would mould us like jellies and find the strength to break through and begin again.

Woman on the edge of time.

The many faces in the water, past and future, self and other seem to dance in mockery at the question , 'who am I?'. We struggle to create a recognizable and acceptable identity; a shape of survival; avoiding confrontation with feelings and situations which demand an altered pattern of thought and behaviour, which require adaptation, flow, reshaping. We have a strong desire to locate other people, to order, to keep the sands from shifting beneath our feet. But behind this projected façade we are not only protected but isolated, untouched. Within each of us there are many different voices, faces, forms, colours, contact, love: in conflict, in harmony, in varying stages of transmutation. We have come to locate this process within a structure which is rigid. We think in terms of goals, time, production, reward. Before we draw our first breath, our unconscious is conditioned by the structures we are born into. The need to hear a voice in relation to some authority, age, gender, social or familial structures, denies the immediate response to the voice. A fixed authority negates our own sense of what is being said.

In articulating her feelings about herself, Estina Mavet reveals an image of her sense of isolation. The division is not only between self and other but between different selves within her. She describes herself in a language of metaphor which is a product of the society from which she is alienated. Self divided from self affords a brutal clarity of vision, rooted as it is in the internalization of an alien language – a mother tongue – which denies the child, the rebirth. Estina's rejection of the social mould, of her own prescribed sexuality, is expressed in terms of disgust and decay. The distortion emerges from the sense that she is perceiving herself in terms which are alien, preconstructed. 'Everywhere was the stench of dried blood, of stale food thrown from the shelves of an internal house that was without tenants or furniture or hope of future lease.'[29] She is denied the right or unable to realize her sense of who she is; in a clearly-defined sociocultural context, the refusal to accept and live within designated images and roles (e.g., motherhood) is perceived in terms of failure. What is left is an empty shell of sterility, non-creativity. Estina's slipping grasp on her own identity is finally fantasized in the draining of her own blood 'seeping through upon the slates and flowing swiftly through the door'.[30] The loss of menstrual blood, the loss of the potential child becomes the loss of one's sexuality. Other forms of expressing sexuality are excluded, denied and therefore the loss is also the loss of life. In the particular

Introduction to contemporary cultural studies

social context, motherhood is the ultimate form of creativity, an exclusive form in which all other creative expression is denied. In Estina the denial of her own form of conception and birth is resolved in her own death. She disrupts this pattern by writing the book, giving birth through her mind and imagination.

The alienated woman, the mad woman, the empty womb-an is a threat within society by being beyond it (and we can trace historically the attitudes towards women alone and separate from a male society by recovering and engaging with the work and lives of women who have chosen women to share their lives with). She is imprisoned, incarcerated, so that the threat will be contained, the threat of contamination. She is an echo of a possibility beyond a system based on exchange, barter, possession. She will not obey the rules; therefore she will not be given the love and care which is the reward for obedience. Perhaps she is not even perceived as needing nurturing. Thus the arid desert within her which longs for the soft rain of tenderness, for the torrent of affection and passion, which has been created because of ab-sense, will be perpetuated by ignorance, denial and power. 'Have you ever been a spinster living in a small house with your sister and her husband and their new first child? Watching them rub noses and pinch and tickle in the night, when you lie on the coffin-narrow camp cot that would not hold two people anyway, listening to them because you cannot help it?'[31] A clear image of heterosexist, exclusive society. A woman starving to death, starving for love; already given the respect of the dead; assigned to her coffin; coldly tolerated, never held close.

Janet Frame's images rock and reel within us, touching the source of our fear.

How do we begin to validate the imaginary in a way which does not rely upon the 'authentic' versions of reality and truth? If the creative imagination breaks the boundaries of being – boundaries ruthlessly and painstakingly constructed, perpetuated, revered – at what levels of perception do we encounter and engage with the beyond? Down the misty tunnels of madness and dream we tumble, like Alice, into the neglected garden of remembrance far below. And all our past and future fantasies against which we have shored up the walls of language, family and society ooze and treacle through our lifetime's work – and then flow inexorably like furious hot volcanic lava. And from this heaving mass the light and colour sparks and is born.

Walking with Janet Frame through *Scented Gardens for the Blind*, recalled to our senses and to our silence, the values which taint our being are constantly derided, shadowed. The truths and categories with which we interpret our sensual experience become like quicksand; shifting as we seek to understand, to discover the source of our madness; to clear the red sea divide across the murky depths of

340

confusion and multiplicity in which we swim. 'Blame rests always. It is a condition of human life that blame rests, like a butterfly on a leaf. We do not care to see blame hovering about us unable to decide where to rest. No one guesses the burden of the butterfly.'[32] A polar divide. Dichotomies, dualities, oppositions. A false security: a safe but sterile rigidity. The novel begins by offering us the complex simplicities (pattern) of a mother/daughter/absent father scenario and eagerly we absorb the information and run off computer-like a programme of psychoanalytic solutions. But gradually the statistics do not correlate, our information becomes more bizarre; to assimilate we begin to mutilate and in this act of interpretative criticism, Frame puts us in touch with the process of living non-creatively: 'how many times until death and nakedness will one be forced to cut off part of oneself, to whittle at, mutilate the whole in order to accommodate the intransigent shape of air?'[33] Our selves are rooted fundamentally in the earthy substance of our own awareness, beginning and ending always in the dark places of healing from which we emerge. Frame seeks to reweave a sensual cord; to release, retrieve the body and the imagination from the narrow coffins of an institutionalized intellect. Her writing, creatively controlled, is fraught with the tension and frustration of communicating an experience of the senses, the body, the feelings. 'It was useless to tell myself that I had been educated and was therefore not superstitious, when grief, panic, bewilderment, acting like a sponge, had seemed to absorb my knowledge and reason as if they were but temporary stains upon the fabric of feeling.'[34] The primary focus is sensual, but it is located in sight and speech, the two senses with which we engage most readily with the outside world. And beginning from here Frame seeks to reinterpret, to refocus our perception of the unconscious prohibitive boundaries which we construct around our senses. Sight and speech are the two senses the deprivation of which we can control immediately. Blind, we ask, what is vision, seeing? What kinds of free flow operate in a world over which we have no visual control? 'I had a primitive feeling that because I was now blind the sun might fall from the sky or the earth might stop spinning. I felt so powerless.'[35] But the phenomenological propositions are perhaps less important than the fear and the sense of threat from a world which demands sight and is barely tolerant of those without, 'cripples and misfits'. It is the fear of being without power in a world which not only possesses power but uses its knowledge mercilessly to maim. In response to deprivation, Vera's vision is not simply transformed from a material to a spiritual one; her awareness of other people becomes more diffuse, manifold. And with this awareness she senses the sometimes oppressive web of demands and presence created in relating. 'I realised gradually that I walked through accumulations of four lives – my own, Edward's, Erlene's, and my father's; and the wonder was not that these accumulations had suddenly made themselves palpable, but that I had been able to move through them at all. They might have held me prisoner by their very weight and mass.'[36] One of the difficulties experienced in this text is the realization that Vera's withdrawal has released her; but as an alternative version of reality she has created a pattern, the inherent form of which is almost identical to the one she has retreated from. Apparently this denies the breaking of boundaries to which I refer earlier. However, it draws our attention to an alternative way of recreating. The energy reserved for sight is channelled into the other senses and we 'see' differently. 'I would feel for the wall or the table . . . and touch it, and a warmth which I never knew belonged to such objects would flow into my fingers and along my arm, through my whole body; a sun-coloured light invading at all costs.'[37] Sight becomes a form of touch – 'no one knows how much the world is worn out, defaced, by the continual rubbing of human sight upon its edges, corners and open pages'.[38] The process of defamiliarization, of sight as touch, physical and with the power of destruction/eradication and reforming is a process of sensual confusion and blending. Are we encouraged to reshape our sensual boundaries, thereby enriching our experience, or do the blurry edges fill us with fear? 'My senses were overlapping, misplaced. I was afraid.'[39] When our senses fail us in recognized/accepted ways then we confront a serious communication problem. The rigidity of our patterns of behaviour determines the context of our moments of relating and when that rigidity begins to dissolve, when the very nature of what is inflexible brings about its own holocaust, then we seek to re-assess, to re-communicate, to be in another way. And we are made aware of our desire to remain distant from that which is other or strange, and from that awareness we question the definition of that 'otherness'. 'We must "deal with" these vast surfaces of strangeness which demand all our lives a protective varnish of sympathy. Protective for us; against them and ourselves.'[40] Vera has not been able to refuse the imaginary other in herself. She has created a world which she has populated with all the characters of herself. But why do the characters initially correlate so perfectly with our social expectations and how do we respond when that correlation becomes less and less easy; difficult to recognize and reconcile?

The voices in the story are clearly defined in terms of character and pronoun. Vera is written in the first person, the others in the third person. And immediately we are confronted with the 'I' which knows, which controls – our empathy as readers connects with Vera in a more intimate way than it does with the others. The identity behind the voice and the silence, however, will not be fixed, located. Our sense of the form of three characters betrays us when we are told the identity of the one woman whose mind we have been enchanted by. But if we deny ourselves the possibility of creation, if we forget the presence of the characters, then we are conforming to the system which locked up

Vera Glace because she became silent in a verbal world. We are once again shutting ourselves out of a vision by refusing to contemplate the 'other'. The 'closed, private circuit' is sacrosanct but it may also lead out on to a vast plain of shared imagination. Madness may be a protest, a withdrawal, a rejection; it is also a process of living. Without the freedom to explore and express, to be, there can be no sense of self. Thus the final location in an institution may encapsulate the questions and puzzles of the novel, interpret and answer them; but if we have the courage to begin again, to perceive the world of the senses, the body, the feelings as a place of nurturing and creativity, to listen 'to the sounds which came from beyond' ourselves, 'to the new language',[41] to breathe in through our skin the colour and warmth and sensation of life, then the novel offers us another perception.

A central focus of the book is the need for contact with human beings and the reality of isolation. We begin with fragmentation and alienation. 'Erlene is in the next room.' Divided from herself, 'I' and 'her', listening to her own silence, projecting it on to an imaginary other, not simply as a denial of the intolerable nature of her existence but also as a form of expressing this. The alienation is encapsulated in the image of the child and her friend. 'I had a little friend on stalks, and she was called Poppy; she was velvet.' This brief moment of tenuously holding together the disparate elements of the self – the sense of merging together the friend and the flower (the symbol of growth, sensuality) is a form of being which she wants to communicate. We are shown the way in which this is cut through; the child divided against and judging herself. The voice of the adult interjecting with the observation that 'cut flowers last longer . . . if they are bruised or singed or if you crumble in the water one or two of those pills which people swallow to deaden a continual feeling of pain'.[42]

The premature violation of a life which given the right environment would grow naturally coalesces with the images of a third of the female population functioning with drugs, of wards of people tranquillized, of death in life. What becomes clear is that there are definite boundaries required to protect the self, that these boundaries are frequently violated and that there is inherent in the text a vicious imagery which permeates the words themselves. The pain is not always inflicted from beyond – sometimes it seems to have its own form, a form absorbed from myth and from everyday living, a form over which we long to throw a 'gentle cloak'. And in the text itself we waver between the sense that Vera is inherently destructive, hence her presence in a mental institution, and that, born into a destructive world, she has attempted to articulate another, more accepting reality. But the irony of the utterings at the end of the novel, the hard cutting image of man emerging from the swamp, jar with the possibility of new utterance which Mary Daly offers us in *Gyn-Ecology*:

343

> The hope which springs when women's deep silence – the silence that breaks us – is broken is the hope of saving our Selves (of delivering our Selves from the Sins of the Fathers) . . . The point is not to save society or to focus on escape (which is backward-looking) but to release the Spring of be-ing. To the inhabitants of Babel, this Spring of living speech will be unintelligible. If it is heard at all, it will be dismissed as mere babble, as the muttering of mad Crones . . .[43]

Perhaps the essence of what Janet Frame offers in her writing is not a newly formed language which would somehow be synthetic, but a transformed language which like all life develops from, and is nurtured by, the surrounding life-forms.

The third text which I am focussing on is Charlotte Perkins Gilman's *The Yellow Wallpaper*. I began to think about this book in terms of inside, outside, mind, body, house, garden and became confused and disturbed about establishing a set of conventional dichotomies, balanced though they may be. Think again . . . and the shape which began to form was that of a funnel. It begins from an open circle around which are located differing perspectives, characters written into the narrative to balance. The writer who is woman and artist and mother and wife; he who is husband and physician and father; a child, a nurse, other members of the family. These characters bring with them a social structure and expectations of social behaviour. The pattern of their lives merges with the larger social pattern and they are at ease. But they are like staves driven into the body of the book; painful, deeply resisted, interrupting and violating a shape which needs to create its own logic. I as reader, swirling around inside the funnel, aware of the caring people who guide, dictate, dismiss, restructure in their own shape, am relentlessly drawn down through the dark tunnel into the body of the woman in whom this distress is located. (An image of the reader bound to the writer in the birth process.)

There, locked, thwarted and silenced are the senses and experiences which receive no validation. The only part of her which is recognized, the child, is cared for, embraced and finally smothered. 'He is very careful and loving, and hardly lets me stir without special direction. I have a schedule prescription for each hour in the day; he takes all care from me, and so I feel basely ungrateful not to value it more . . . He said we came here solely on my account.'[44] A woman, treated as a child, deprived of will, internalizing guilt, seeking to reclaim the lost parts of herself. A woman, trapped inside her own body by an authority which abuses its power. Within the confines of the room, in panic, fear and isolation, she recovers the will to restore and transmute her lost and fragmented selves. She is almost creating a circle of self, a magic circle, which will cup and hold inviolate her body, mind and soul.

The first few pages follow a pattern of narrative structure which is staccato. The short sentences, abrupt paragraphs informing the reader of the physical location of the writer's relationship to others, create a sense of control carefully imposed. The language must be circumscribed by a simple precise ordered structure like the 'schedule prescription', because it moulds into a coherent shape and sound that which threatens to rush outwards, overflow. Behind the dam, seeping into the walls and the sandbags is a vast source of creative energy. Powerful emotion thwarted, deflected, distorted for so long cannot come thundering and crashing through the barriers but trickles down, sometimes only drop by drop; silent, tortuous. Tears gathered throughout a lifetime until the body refuses to contain any more spill over, splash down, dry up, go on until there can be no 'going on'.

She is taking us to the side of the room, a room occupied by people who carry authority, power, who are representative of a well-ordered world, and casting darkness. She is whispering in my ear asking me to look and to see – and I ask, 'where do I belong?'

She is whispering the most ordinary words into my ear and yet they have the most bizarre quality. They echo and reverberate around the room piercing the protective shell. 'That mere ordinary people' are involved, some quite unwittingly, in a process of destruction; that her expectations of marriage incorporate denial, mockery, fear, subordination. And the self which has been silenced projects its shape on to the house, 'a haunted house' with 'something queer about it'. The house becomes a symbol of her own sense of emptiness and worthlessness: 'why should it be let so cheaply? And why have stood so long untenanted?'[45] And in that projection, within a safe place with a boundary, clearly defined and with a place beyond in the garden: the 'most beautiful place . . . quite alone . . . hedges and walls and gates that lock, and lots of separate little houses for the gardeners and people . . . delicious',[46] she realizes the extent of her own repression. She begins to feel and the feeling struggles with the thinking, the rational, embodied in her husband, John. 'John laughs at . . . is practical in the extreme . . . scoffs openly at any talk of things not to be felt and seen and put down in figures . . . is a physician.'[47] This is an almost simplistic description, male/female, a cardboard cutout authority figure which confuses the authority he carries with the authority which she invests in him. Her perceptions are not distorted until they come into conflict with a perception which articulates itself as 'truth'; or when she internalizes that 'other' pattern and attempts to integrate the two. 'I get unreasonably angry with John sometimes' is an example of two thought patterns in conflict. The word 'unreasonably' implies the intervention of a process which judges and thereby represses. And again, 'I would not be so silly as to make him uncomfortable just for a whim', when she begins to perceive what she is feeling in his terms. Her own logic/rationality is coherent: 'I believe that congenial work with excitement and change, would do me good';

but the space in which she can express the thinking and the feeling becomes smaller and smaller. Confronted by the possibility of almost total effacement she seeks to create and express her experience. The structure of the narrative is the logic of why, when, where, wherefore. It spreads over and leads through the mass of conflicting emotions beneath: 'when you follow the lame uncertain curves for a little distance they suddenly commit suicide – plunge off at outrageous angles, destroy themselves in unheard of contradictions'.[48] Not because these emotions are intrinsically bizarre or destructive but, contained within a rigid, non-yielding framework, they become incomprehensible and stifled and crippling. To release, to let flow, to give birth to the self are the cries which cannot rend the stagnant air.

The physical enclosure becomes a (final) statement of the psychological isolation; she has not succumbed but consciously and creatively moulded a form from her pain. Her environment is her clay and with her body she expresses very clearly that in order to survive she must make manifest her experience. Inner and outer spaces mirror each other, confirming her existence, her shape, her order. She experiences her life as a circle of isolation and denial, therefore her order is her sanity and it also becomes ours. We have moved beyond the logic of the social authority into her experience: and this is the movement of the story. Invited into and then trapped in a room 'at the top of the house', a room with a history of its own, not only as 'nursery first and then playroom and gymnasium' but with gates and bars and 'rings and things in the walls',[49] as a memory of violence and pain gratuitous. The image of the Inquisition, of the torture chamber haunts, echoing through the story as a voice almost heard, inarticulate. The paper is stripped off 'in great patches all around the head of my bed, about as far as I can reach, and in a great place on the other side of the room low down'. Desperation in the image of clawing at the paper; restraint in that it is in a space around the bed, the implication of sexual violation curiously displaced and re-formed by the reference to the 'boys' school'. The innocent boy child as victim provokes both sympathy and a sense of initiation into the rites of male adulthood – a chain of images which links us back to the woman in the room. The satisfaction implicit in stripping off the old wallpaper, in the context of recreating a room in the colours and textures of our own choice, is undermined by the close rigid brittle imagery of the paper 'torn off in spots' . . . 'it sticketh closer than a brother – they must have had perseverance as well as hatred'. The 'scratched and gouged and splintered'[50] floor and plaster may well have been accidents of play but our safety in this conviction has become a sham and a lie. The image of the bare wall at the other side of the room low down is of someone crouched, cowering, closed in, weeping, the animal finally cornered and broken and left to its own despair. As she draws her body into the smallest space and cleaves to the wall: 'I can creep smoothly on the floor, and my shoulder just fits in that long smooch around the wall, so I cannot lose my way'.[51] The sense of fluid movement, soft and sliding is her space. It is terrifying.

Internalizing her husband's codes of behaviour, eroding away herself like the waves mercilessly pounding and caressing the land until it gives way – the tiny piece of sanity which she has left focusses on the wallpaper and clings there tenaciously – suspended above the water the frayed rope begins to judder over the clifftop.

It is this focus which allows her to project her emotions, to try and resolve the patterns of behaviour she is victim to and experiences; to articulate in some form her madness.

Perhaps the way in which I perceive this happening is less relevant than the development of this articulation. To correlate the images and descriptions of the wallpaper with the social and psychological states of the writer would be to establish a kind of definitive relationship, explicative, dependent on an accepted rationale. These are the ways in which we interpret, render safe, that which at one level is uninterpretable, dangerous, disturbing. Correlating the structure with the mass of fluid contradictions reinforces and substantiates the structure, defusing the raw material of experience; implying a general objective where there is a complex subjective. Before the knots of this argument become inextricable, let us see what happens when we follow the pattern on the 'smouldering, unclean yellow' surface.

Do we become involved in a process of seeing that which has become unrecognizable? A process of discovery; an uncovering of a way in which she can become mad, allowing the unconscious to formulate its own logic and release.

'There is a recurrent spot where the pattern lolls like a broken neck and two bulbous eyes stare at you upside down.'

The grotesque humour of clowns parodying the observer; of a body hung.
We begin to understand that there is a way of perceiving the world which continues to make sense of it – that the knowledge which enables logical perception is created, given finite terms of reference – that it is precarious – that it protects us from the pain of 'seeing'.

'I get positively angry with the impertinence of it and the

It is no longer inanimate. It has become human and deformed. Its

everlastingness. Up and down and sideways they crawl, and those absurd, unblinking eyes are everywhere. There is one place where two breaths didn't match, and the eyes go all up and down the line, one a little higher than the other.'

expressiveness awakens childhood memories and a sense of security and protection which has been lost. A recognition of power in herself from which she has been alienated: of anger, distorted, deformed, displaced and her attempt to recover it; to give form to the anger, to make congruent her feelings and her experience.

'sub-pattern . . . you can only see it in certain lights and not clearly then'

Coming to form; inarticulate, indistinct, shadowy and a deep desire to pursue the form.

'a strange, provoking, formless sort of figure, that seems to skulk about behind that silly and conspicuous front design'

The front design has no logical form and the search for a structure to explain the cage evokes the most bizarre and frightening images.

'bloated curves and flourishes, a kind of 'debased Romanesque' with *delirium tremens* – go waddling up and down in isolated columns of fatuity'

Women in hospitals, mental wards, bloated with drugs, bored, afraid, without self, walking up and down the endless, dead-end corridors. Aged, pregnant, hopeful and hopeless women, all unacceptable in one way or another because of the patriarchaic structure which dictates desirability.

'the interminable grotesques seem to form around a common centre and rush off in headlong plunges of equal distraction'

Panic flight from a place where the self is compromised in order to fit; a centre which will tell her she cannot fit, that she is losing all the time; loss of control.
Images of radiation sickness and mutation, of total self-denial.

We are bound by the conflict between power and self-denial, forgetting that the only real power comes from the self and that when the self is denied, the power and the energy we feel is alien and destructive. Our perceptions are blurred when we project on to the other that which we long for in ourselves, and which in our anger we may attempt to destroy.

The process of acknowledging and extricating ourselves from the pain of the connectedness of self-mutilation and power echoes in the writing of Adrienne Rich:

> Today I was reading about Marie Curie:
> she must have known she suffered from radiation sickness
> her body bombarded for years by the element
> she had purified
> It seems she denied to the end
> the source of the cataracts on her eyes
> the cracked and suppurating skin of her finger-ends
> till she could no longer hold a test-tube or a pencil
>
> She died a famous woman denying
> her wounds
> denying
> her wounds came from the same source as her power[52]

The one clear image which surfaces from the experiences of reading and writing which I have focussed on in this essay is that madness, that confusion and contradiction within ourselves which the text offers to engage with, is real. And it is a base from which to begin. We could argue forever about the necessity for coherent structures in the 'text' and beyond it – our fears of anarchy, our need to relive primal experiences, the ever-diminishing circle. We cannot ever be 'free' but we can choose to let go, to step outside of the circle and begin again. The process of writing; the network of communication which is a deep humming connectedness throughout our culture; literature is a small but vital part of giving and receiving the energy within us. But we must begin from the self, from the 'I' which we are taught is mad: we must find the clear spring, not the manifold reflections in the murky pool and we must communicate that clear spring.

NOTES AND REFERENCES

1. Adrienne Rich. 'Transcendental Etude', in *The Dream of a Common Language,* Norton, New York 1978, p. 76.

2. Janet Frame, *Faces in the Water,* The Women's Press 1980, p. 10.
3. Michelle Cliff, *Claiming an Identity They Taught Me to Despise,* Persephone Press, Massachusetts 1980, p. 29.
4. Margaret Atwood, *Surfacing,* Virago 1979, p. 176.
5. Frame, p. 107.
6. Frame, p. 247.
7. Frame, p. 108.
8. Rich, 'Cartographies of Silence', in *Dream of a Common Language,* p. 16.
9. Frame, p. 202.
10. Frame, pp. 9–10.
11. Rich, 'The Phenomenology of Anger', in *Diving into the Wreck,* Norton, New York 1973, p. 25.
12. Foucault, *Mental Illness and Psychology,* trans. A. Sheridan, Harper and Row, New York 1976, p. 52.
13. Frame, p. 65.
14. Frame, p. 83.
15. Frame, p. 156.
16. Frame, p. 83.
17. Frame, p. 205.
18. Frame, p. 113.
19. Frame, p. 104.
20. Frame, p. 247.
21. Frame, p. 216.
22. Frame, p. 217.
23. Frame, p. 217.
24. Frame, p. 37.
25. Foucault, p. 51.
26. Frame, p. 193.
27. Frame, p. 35.
28. Frame, p. 195.
29. Frame, p. 12.
30. Frame, p. 166.
31. Frame, p. 65.
32. Frame, *Scented Gardens for the Blind,* The Women's Press 1982, p. 26.
33. Frame, *Gardens,* p. 17.
34. Frame, *Gardens,* p. 11.
35. Frame, *Gardens,* p. 18.
36. Frame, *Gardens,* p. 20.
37. Frame, *Gardens,* p. 20.
38. Frame, *Gardens,* p. 16.
39. Frame, *Gardens,* p. 18.
40. Frame, *Gardens,* p. 14.
41. Frame, *Gardens,* p. 251.
42. Frame, *Gardens,* p. 10.
43. Mary Daly, *Gyn-Ecology,* The Women's Press 1979, p. 22.
44. Charlotte Perkins Gilman, *The Yellow Wallpaper,* Virago 1981, p. 12.
45. Gilman, p. 9.
46. Gilman, p. 11.
47. Gilman, p. 9.
48. Gilman, p. 13.

49. Gilman, p. 12.
50. Gilman, p. 17.
51. Gilman, p. 35.
52. Rich, 'Power', in *Dream of a Common Language*, p. 3.

Chapter 17

TOWARDS THE CULTURAL STUDY OF TIME

BERNARD SHARRATT

This essay attempts little more than to outline the shadow of a concept, a possible object of inquiry, a notion that in a puzzling way already haunts a great deal of 'contemporary cultural studies' yet is rarely the explicit centre of attention or research. Its focus is that difficult and slippery term: time. My approach is to begin from the apparently obvious in order to suggest the increasingly complex problems concealed by that obviousness. The structure of the essay is, however, mosaic rather than linear, offering materials for consideration and discussion rather than any overall argument or thesis.

1: TIMING ACTIVITIES

Consider the following statistical statements, summaries and tables[1]:

Cinema attendances reached a peak in 1946 (when one third of the population were going once a week, 13 per cent twice a week).

The number of viewing-hours had risen fairly sharply at the end of the sixties, but held steady, with perhaps a very slight increase, in the seventies. In the 1977–79 period, average hours viewed per week were sixteen in the summer and twenty in the winter . . . The average number of hours listened to per week in 1978/9 was about nine hours.

In America, the normal working year consists of 1,976 hours against an average of 2,137 hours in Britain.

In 1968 manual employees in industry worked on average just over 46 hours per week . . . In her study of managers Stewart found that the average working week lasted for 42½ hours; . . . and in his investigation Copeman found heads of department averaging 41¼ hours per week whilst managing directors had a somewhat more arduous time with a typical working week of 49½ hours.

. . . a Gallup Poll survey in Britain in 1964 found that one out of six male workers had a spare-time job taking up an average of twelve hours per week.

. . . only 6 per cent of those earning under £650 p.a. have three weeks or more paid leave compared with 44 per cent of those earning £1,950 and over.

Proportion of Leisure Time Spent on Different Activities 1969 (percentages)

Activity	All males	All females
Television	23	23
Reading	5	9
Crafts and hobbies	4	17
Decorating and house maintenance	8	1
Gardening	12	7
Social activities	3	9
Drinking	3	1
Cinema and theatre	1	1

One could easily multiply examples of these familiar forms of comment upon or summarizations of various relations between time and activity. An influential sub-branch of statistical sociology has even emerged under the label 'time-budget studies'. In the introduction to the published report of the most ambitious multinational comparative time-budget survey, Alexander Szalai writes:

This conventional name has some metaphoric justification, since very many studies of this kind are concerned primarily with the proportions in which the twenty-four hours of the day are allocated the various activities by people belonging to certain groups or strata of the population – how many hours and minutes such people spend daily on chores and pastimes such as doing work, putting things straight in the household, shopping around, taking meals, visiting friends, reading books, listening to the radio, having a good night's rest, and so forth. This type of investigation is indeed somewhat similar to the procedure by which the allocation of funds for different purposes in financial budgets is analysed. As far as personal or family budgets are concerned, the similarity will even extend to many specific types of expenditure, because a great number of everyday activities involve not alone the expenditure of time but of money as well. At this point however, the resemblance comes to an end. Time can only be spent, not 'earned'. Therefore time-budgets have no income side. The fund of time which is being 'allocated' to various activities (24 hours in daily time-budgets, 7 x 24 hours in weekly time-budgets, etc.) serves simply as a frame of reference for setting out the temporal proportions of people's engagement in the whole gamut of their daily activities. Thus, it is not time itself, either as a physical or as a subjectively perceived entity, but rather as the use people make of their time, which is the real subject of time-budget studies.[2]

If, however, the 'use' of time is the subject of such studies, one could perhaps ask: what, then, is actually being 'measured' when the results are put in statistical or percentage form? As the conclusion to one of the studies in that same report comments:

> From the viewpoint of biology if breathing is normal, its duration is insignificant; but if it stops the difference between one and ten minutes is fatal for man. If one goes without sleep for one night no serious consequences will ensue, yet over a longer period of time a minimum of sleep expressed in hours and minutes per day is necessary for man's existence, health and well-being.
>
> Similarly, from the point of view of economics 20 hours of shopping can be taken as merely an indicator of the decision to purchase which again is nothing but a point in time, thus has no dimension in time even though it might as a process have taken one minute or one month.
>
> From the point of view of the sociological content and significance of an activity it can be seen that both a worker and a manager can work ten hours daily, but this fact can be utilised in only a limited number of very specific theories. By and large this fact is theoretically often irrelevant.[3]

Yet the potential significance of precisely this curious 'irrelevance' for any theoretically-informed 'cultural studies' seems considerable – if only because a preoccupation with the 'use' of time has deeply shaped one of the major influences upon cultural studies: Marxist theory.

2: MARXISM AND TIME

In the foreword to the English translation of Marx's *Herr Vogt* the editors write:

> *Herr Vogt* is Marx's 'forgotten' work. Mentioned in passing – if at all – in biographical studies, and scarcely at all in discussions of his writings, it has remained for over a century largely neglected.
>
> Yet this is the work which Marx took the best part of a year away from the writing of *Capital* to complete. It is an answer to the slanders against himself, Engels and their supporters which appeared in Karl Vogt's 1859 pamphlet, *Mein Prozess gegen die Allgemeine Zeitung*. He knew before its publication that many 'clever men' would be 'completely unable to grasp how I could squander my time on refuting such infantile nonsense'.[4]

Capital itself is concerned, at various points in its argument, with a variety of 'times' – circulation time, time of production, time of consumption, buying and selling time, capital turnover time, etc. – but at the core of its analysis of capitalism are a number of interlinked concepts, among which a certain conceptualisation of time is crucial.

Marx's analysis begins from a distinction between 'use-value' and 'exchange-value' and he advances the argument that the ultimate basis of exchange-value is 'socially necessary labour time', which fundamentally underpins the dynamics of capitalist production and capitalist exploitation. Two factors are central. First, and in its simplest formulation, exploitation is conceived in terms of the difference between the length of the working day during which the worker's labour-power produces the value of the wage paid to the worker and the 'additional' length of the working day during which the worker produces a further (surplus) value from which the capitalist's profit is derived but for which the worker receives no wage, no 'exchange-value' in return for the 'use-value' of his labour power. This simple analysis can, obviously, be modified and developed into a far more complex analysis (in terms, for example, of relative and absolute surplus value) but its core argument still appeals to a notion of capitalist control over the use of workers' labour-power for a certain time. Secondly, and as part of that more complex analysis, the differences between the rates of profit of competing capitalist concerns can ultimately be analysed in terms of the relation between the amounts of labour time actually utilized in production and the 'socially neccesary' labour time currently required for production; this line of analysis would take in such factors as the relation between 'fixed' and 'variable capital', the 'rate of exploitation', the adoption or otherwise of technological innovation, etc.

The most explicit political implication of this two-fold analysis, within Marx's own argument, is that the decisive struggle within capitalism is engaged over control of labour-power during the process of production. Again at its simplest, this can be a struggle over the length of the working day itself (as in Marx's own vivid account) or in more complicated forms over such issues as productivity, piece-rates, and the speeding-up of production processes – all of which focus ultimately on relations between work and time. It is these conflicts which are fundamental, if not of themselves decisive, in the relations between labour and capital and between competing capitalists.

Yet a less obvious struggle over time is also involved, which has been brilliantly explored by E. P. Thompson: the struggle over the relationship to and conception of 'time' which is dominant in our daily lives.[5] In a long process, a particular and historically specific notion of time was inculcated and imposed in the general development of capitalism. Towards the end of his lengthy analysis Thompson writes[6]: 'In all these ways – by the division of labour; the supervision of labour; fines; bells and clocks; money incentives; preachings and schoolings; the suppression of fairs and sports – new labour habits were formed and a new time-discipline was imposed.' One could summarize that shift in 'time-sense' and change in 'the inward apprehension of time' in the notion not only that 'time is money' but that time is *like* money: a matter of equal quantifiable units. As Thompson remarks: 'Time is now currency: it is not passed but spent.' From that it is a very short step to 'time-budget studies', in which, however 'Time can only be spent, not earned'.

There is, however, a further aspect of Marx's analysis which is more difficult to conceptualise. If one asks what is to replace capitalism and with it perhaps those now correlative notions of time and money, Marx's own answers are, at a certain level, problematic. His best-known formulation of communist daily life comes from *The German Ideology:*

> . . . in communist society, where nobody has one exclusive sphere of activity but each can become accomplished in any branch he wishes, society regulates the general production and thus makes it possible for me to do one thing today and another tomorrow, to hunt in the morning, fish in the afternoon, rear cattle in the evening, criticize after dinner, just as I have a mind to, without ever becoming hunter, fisherman, shepherd or critic.[7]

Lest one should be tempted to assimilate this account to a time-budget analysis of part-time activities and full-time work, or presume a distinction between 'professional' and 'amateur' activities, it is worth quoting a less well-known passage from the same work[8]: 'with a communist organisation, there disappears . . . the subordination of the artist to some definite art, thanks to which he is exclusively a painter, sculptor, etc. . . . In a communist society there are no painters but at most people who engage in painting among other activities.' The implications of this conception for modes of 'social organization' are very far-reaching indeed, as G. A. Cohen has pointed out.[9] Nevertheless, there remains a constant emphasis in Marx's thinking upon the overall reduction of 'socially necessary' labour-time, that deployment of time required to produce the 'necessities' of social life ('society regulates the general production'), and therefore to some extent a continuing practical distinction between what would now be characterized as 'work' and as 'leisure' or 'free time'. An alternative emphasis within the Marxist tradition can, of course, be traced, upon the reconstruction of 'work' as itself to be characterized by the qualities we now associate with such 'leisure' notions as creativity, self-realization, enjoyment – an emphasis most forcefully registered in William Morris, and sharply in contrast to some conventional assumptions in current categorizations of 'leisure' and 'work'.[10] But there remains a further, and even more intractable, conceptual distinction still operative in Marx's thought: that between use-value and exchange-value. If capitalism is premised upon production for exchange-value, then communism will be predicated upon production for 'use' even if some mode of distribution of 'use-values' is necessary, albeit not governed by 'exchange-values'. Yet the notion of concrete use (-value) is not assimilable to any conceptualisation of 'abstract' labour or therefore of 'abstract' time. At its simplest, there is no commensurability between 'use'-times as there may be, at a certain level of analysis, between 'production'-times. Implicit therefore in any

Marxist notion of a post-capitalist mode of life is – however proleptically – a non-capitalist conceptualisation of time, or at least the construction of a historically specific 'time-sense' and 'inward apprehension of time' different from that which has been constructed in the development of capitalism. Given the formidable difficulties of attempting to anticipate any such fundamental reconceptualisation, what follows can at best be a series of tentative suggestions, the first of which concerns the relevance of some of these considerations to 'contemporary cultural studies'. As will become clear, the suggestion also takes, in fact, the form of an oblique experiment.

3: CULTURAL STUDIES, MARXISM, SEMIOTICS, PSYCHOANALYSIS

The various attempts to engender a programme of 'contemporary cultural studies' under the aegis of a putatively Marxist approach have tended to retain, through many reformulations and theoretical redirections, a working distinction between 'levels' of analysis, whether in such traditional terms as base/superstructure or in various revamped terminologies (e.g., the economic, political and ideological instances of a social formation), but even when the reformulations have yielded a recognition of the 'relative autonomy' of the objects of study defined as 'cultural', the allegiance to Marxism has been most deeply registered in the emphasis on the concept or metaphor of 'production'. As with the classical Marxist critique of political economy, any consideration of 'consumption' has been conceptually subordinated to analysis of the processes of production, a subordination which is itself an inner premise of the more general theoretical formulae. Thus, even in relation to the relatively autonomous instances or domains, the angle of analysis has characteristically been upon the 'production of meanings' and upon modes of control over that production. In the allied and overlapping fields of literary, filmic and media studies, the primary concern has been the apparatuses of 'textual' production, for example in terms of the 'positioning' of the reader-spectator. Even in the reluctant encounter between Marxist literary theory and reader-response approaches, the difficulty of reconciling the site of production with the site of reception and response has been acute, visible in the predominant emphasis upon the construction of sites of reception internal to (implied in) the production process, the operation of the 'text'. There is an obvious continuity throughout these Marxist approaches with such familiar political concerns as the 'control' and 'ownership' of the 'means of production', a recognition or definition of that as the decisive terrain of power.

Yet some awkward problems have always hovered over this characteristic Marxist preoccupation – or, more strictly perhaps, have fallen outside the specific conceptual reach of Marxism. The concepts of 'use-value' and 'need' have remained, almost as it were of necessity, relegated to a merely contingent and 'concrete' specification, often assigned to the conceptually barren level of the 'individual'. The recognition of 'concrete' labour has been correspondingly cursory. In repudiating any methodological individualism Marx was pursuing a political as well as an intellectual trajectory: socialism was allied to forms of collectivity and solidarity as against 'private' modes of appropriation and competition, and the countervailing power to that of private capital had to be the construction of a proletarian class and class-interest. Obviously, certain alleged lacunae within this schema could then be focussed on: the role of the individual in history (not least Marx himself) or the problem of personal commitment and choice (class allegiance). But an undeniable perplexity remained endemic to the schema itself: if socialism-communism was to be characterized by production for use rather than exchange, 'from each according to his ability, to each according to his needs', then the conceptually unelaborated notions of use-value, need and concrete labour (all of which seemed to involve specification at the 'level' of the 'individual') were intrinsic to any positive, rather than simply reactive, conception of countervailing class-interest. Almost by its own definitions, therefore, the Marxist analytic of capitalism was unable, and not simply reluctant, to generate a coherent conceptualisation of socialism.

It is worth sketching some partial parallels to these problems within two other major influences upon recent cultural analysis: semiotics and psychoanalysis. Saussure's founding gesture of modern linguistics, which underpins later semiological approaches, was to distinguish *langue* from *parole* in order to constitute the former as methodological object. Yet the conceptual subordination (or even theoretical expulsion) of *parole* and the emphasis upon the systemic arbitrariness (unmotivatedness) of the relation between signifier and signified left open not only the problems of historical change (diachronic linguistics) and 'semantics' but also the problem of transgressive or 'creative' language and in particular the problem of 'trying to mean' – that reaching beyond the resources of an available combinatory that is endemic to actual language-use and exchange. Recent interest in the emphasis of Bakhtin-Volosinov upon the 'dialogic' and 'multi-accentual' character of language indicates a move to recovery of a perspective from which these issues might be rethought, and with them the conceptual status of the individual, concrete 'speech-act' which structural linguistics left inadequately explored. Saussure himself, in distinguishing the syntagmatic axis from the 'associative' axis,[11] arguably retained more awareness of the multi-accentual than later formulations in terms of the 'paradigmatic', and it may well be through a return to Saussure's wider notion of the associative, including individual 'associations', that a firmer bridge to psychoanalysis could be sought, for the assimilation of psychoanalysis in cultural studies has also been shadowed by a similar (and perhaps less justified) conceptual subordination of the 'concrete' to the systemic. The problem of methodological individualism is acute in Freud's own work, in the interaction between particular case-studies and theoretical elaboration, but in classic psychoanalytic practice the necessary focus has to be upon the particular analysand in a specific transference-situation with an analyst; divorced from that (dialogic) interaction any 'application' of psychoanalytic procedures or even concepts becomes vulnerable to a peculiar vacuity. Yet even within the patient collaborative construction and articulation of the particular analysis there are endemic perplexities, registered in Freud's recognition of the potential 'interminability' of any analysis and (correspondingly) the difficulty of any coherent conceptualisation of 'cure'. Lacan's notion of the necessary irreducibility of *désir* to full articulation is in part a reformulation of this problem.

These compressed comments do not entail any simple rejection of the methodological premises of Marxism, semiotics and psychoanalysis, in their various emphases upon the structural, synchronic and systemic, but are indicative of certain internal conceptual limits which are the necessary obverse of those premises. That a certain dissatisfaction with such approaches has emerged within cultural studies for other reasons (leading for example to a re-prioritization of the 'experiential', whether in feminist inquiries or ethnological methods) is not my concern here. Rather, I want to outline some major problems within cultural studies which perhaps echo the difficulties I have indicated.

An important impetus behind the development of cultural studies was the project or promise of locating, articulating and analysing a countervailing force against capitalism, whether in terms of opposing collective-communal values or residual-emergent cultural resistances; variations of this optimism found formulation in such notions as counter-culture and hegemonic struggle. Yet the characteristic tone of cultural analysis has been deeply ambivalent, a complex awareness of incorporation-resilience (to use an early vocabulary for this recognition). Arguably the problem registered here is precisely that of conceptualising 'post-capitalist' needs, demands and desires, of formulating what reaches beyond an available system of articulation, of what are to count as the constituents of the projected 'cure'. Another early impetus had been the questioning of a received dichotomization of 'cultural value', that between 'high' and 'low', élite and mass 'culture', posed most often in terms of judgements directed at artifacts but applying more generally to 'ways of living'. Yet here too a certain ambivalence is traceable, not only in implicit re-discrimina-tions across received boundaries but more paradoxically in the utiliza-tion of a formidable intellectual armoury drawn undeniably from the 'highest' resources of 'bourgeois culture', an affirmation in itself of a certain conception of countervailing resources available 'within' capi-talism. Yet such a recognition reinforces awareness precisely of the (linked) problems of individual allegiance-commitment and of the peculiar specificity and differentiation of cultural artifacts and pro-cesses, not only in their production and composition but in the con-crete and 'individual' *use* made of them. It is this latter aspect that I now want to highlight.

4: QUESTIONS AND QUOTATIONS

Sections 2 and 3 of this essay have been written not solely as exposition but also as a kind of experiment, an attempt, upon the reader. A series of grouped questions concerning time can now be put to that reader – i.e., to you, the specific, gendered, class-located individual of a certain age and ethnic identity currently reading this page.

What kind of sense, if any, does it make to ask how long you took to read sections 2 and 3 of this essay? If one tried to answer the question 'how long?' in terms of minutes, would what is measured by those minutes be the same whether you had understood what you were reading or not? Could one sensibly ask how long it took you to understand (or partially understand, or not understand) those sec-tions? Would an answer to that question involve assessing the 'dura-tion' of your previous reading of Marxism, semiotics, psychoanalysis? Would it also involve calculating 'how long' it took you to learn how to read? Or to 'learn' English? And would these various 'durations' be in any sense additional or cumulative with respect to each other?

If section 3 was recognized as in part a reworking of some of the contents of section 2, does this imply that section 3 could be read more quickly than section 2, or understood more quickly? Does it make sense to ask 'how much' of section 3 was a repetition or recurrence of section 2?

In what sense, if any, might reading these sections have 'saved' or 'wasted' time for you? When we read a footnoted reference to a work we haven't read, does this imply a potential 'multiplier effect' on our reading? Does it take as long to understand a précis of *Capital* as it does to understand *Capital*?

Does it make any sense to ask how long it took me to write those sections? If Marx had not written *Herr Vogt* what kind of implications might that have had for the time he took to write *Capital*?

In what contexts would it make sense to seek to compare the time taken by different individuals to read sections 2 and 3? For example, would it take you longer to type a manuscript that you understood than one you did not?

Can these questions be adapted to ask about watching a television programme, attending a play, listening to a piece of music, watching a film – and what difference does it make that it is plausible in all these cases to assign a 'stop-watch' timing to the 'performance' that is invariable by an individual in the audience? How far could such questions be extended to cultural activities which are not bounded by explicit performance limits?

Many more questions along these lines could certainly be formulated, though I would suggest that the two most basic that would eventually emerge would be an epistemological question and a political question: first, is the sense of a question determined by the possibility of its being answered?, and, second, in what senses could the division of labour between manual and mental labour be overcome? Involved in both questions, perhaps, is a further question, concerning the use you can or intend to make of (the time passed reading) this collection of essays.

Rather than pursue these questions directly, however, I now want to offer a series of quotations which I think have a bearing upon the problems I am trying in various ways to bring into focus:

1830–1840

> Read asked: 'How much should be allowed as the wage of the "owner of capital" superintending the industrious undertaking?' John Rae answered that the profit of stock must include a return for the mental exertion and anxiety of the owner of stock. J. S. Mill argued that such a wage was not determined in the same way as other wages, but was a commission on capital employed. And Ramsay went yet further, by distinguishing the function of supervisor and entrepreneur from that of the capitalist. The entrepreneur did not do manual labour, and his profits could not be said to be proportional to his 'mental qualities' as these could not be quantified . . . The level of payment for these qualities of entrepreneurship and abstinence was expected to be determined by social criteria. Returns, argued Scrope, were to be sufficient to pay the ordinary rate of profit on total capital, 'as well as remunerate him for his skill and trouble, according to the standard of remunerations generally expected by his class'.[12]

1983

> . . . we have taken the advice of an eminent barrister, and, while it is a nice point and has not yet been argued in the higher courts, he thinks that the election might stand provided that I became a fugitive from the kingdom. He was very attentive to us, and gave us a full seven minutes of his advice, and he charged for his counsel only £800.[13]

361

1830–1835

> Fees or Charges for Chemical Analysis or for Business Relative to the
> Application of Science to the Arts and Manufacturers.
> Consultation:
> Written opinion on a short case or letter of inquiry. Fee £2.2.0
> For a series of chemical experiments per day. Fee £5.5.0
> Attendance in London to view any manufacture; to examine apparatus or
> inspect any chemical process. Fee £4.4.0
> For similar attendance which shall occupy the whole or chief part of the day.
> Fee £6.6.0
> Attendance at a distance from London exclusive of travelling expenses per
> day. Fee £7.7.0[14]

1878: TRIAL OF WHISTLER

> – 'A stiffish price', suggested the Attorney-General, 'two hundred guineas.
> How soon did you "knock it off"?'
> – 'As well as I remember, about a day . . . I may still have put a few more
> touches to it the next day if the painting were not dry. I had better say, then,
> that I was two days at work on it.'
> – 'The labour of two days then is that for which you ask two hundred
> guineas?'
> – 'No. I ask it for the knowledge of a lifetime.'[15]

1874: LETTER FROM WILLIAM MORRIS

> Monday was a day here to set one longing to get away: as warm as
> June . . . though town looks rather shocking on such days, and then instead
> of the sweet scents one gets an extra smell of dirt. Surely if people lived five
> hundred years instead of threescore and ten they would find some better
> way of living than in such a sordid loathsome place, but now it seems to be
> nobody's business to try to better things – isn't mine you see in spite of all my
> grumbling . . .[16]

1886–1888: ACTIVITIES OF WILLIAM MORRIS

> It is absolutely impossible to understand how he found time for all his
> activities, at the same time keeping some supervision over the Firm, and
> (before the end of 1886) launching on a translation of Homer. In these two
> years he wrote *The Pilgrims of Hope, A Dream of John Ball,* and the first
> part of *Socialism from the Root Up:* articles, notes and editorials for
> *Commonweal*: he delivered something like 120 lectures, about fifteen of
> which (at the least) were written out in long-hand and are permanent
> contributions to Socialist theory: he attended the weekly Executive Council
> meetings of the League, the Ways and Means Committee, and goodness
> knows how many other meetings besides: he made tours of the provinces,
> breaking new ground, and consolidating old branches – Dublin, Scotland,

Yorkshire and Lancashire, the Potteries, East Anglia and a dozen other centres. He was present at sixty out of the ninety-nine meetings of the Committee of the Hammersmith Branch, at some of which only two or three others troubled to attend: and in addition was often in the Chair at the Sunday evening lectures – if he was not lecturing elsewhere himself. He spoke at scores of open-air meetings, chaired them, carried the banner, sold literature, took round the hat for collections. He acted as a sandwichman, between placards advertising *Commonweal*. He gave a hand with the smallest mechanical details of office or branch organisation, and wrote basketfuls of correspondence. He edited *Commonweal*. He attended the police-courts. He drew up balance-sheets, and subsidized the movement with his money. He helped with social evenings, gave readings of his own work or wrote special poems, entertained speakers, and made personal contacts with people sympathetic to the movement . . . Successive biographers have lamented this 'waste' of Morris's energies.[17]

1978

He was pondering the first three bits. Suddenly, without thinking about it, he was drawing another box below the first box . . . The segment number – the area code – would be the same as the ring number, which defined the level of security to which the compartment would be assigned. Three bits can be combined in eight different ways. So there would be eight rings (eight levels of security) and eight segments (eight area codes) in the memory system. The area codes themselves would indicate which ring was forbidden to whom . . . Although they are generally shy about claiming to have had one, engineers often speak of 'the golden moment' in order to describe the feeling – it comes rarely enough – when the scales fall from a designer's eyes and a problem's right solution is suddenly there . . . As for Wallach, after he had drawn the diagram, he stared at it, wondering for a moment, 'Where did that come from?'[18]

EARLY 1970s

The Eclipse was to be Data General's first microcoded machine. Alsing signed up for the job . . . and then he procrastinated. Month after month, his boss would ask him how the code was coming along and he would say: 'Fine. A few problems, but pretty well.' In fact, though, he had not written a single line of code. Finally, he could sense that his boss and some of his colleagues were growing angry; failure had become an almost palpable object – a pair of headlights coming towards him down the wrong side of a road. Scared, he packed up the necessary circuit diagrams, specs and manuals and went to the Boston Public Library . . . The Eclipse contained 195 assembly-language instructions, which in the end Alsing encoded in some 390 microinstructions, many of which performed multiple duties. He said he wrote most of those microinstructions in two weeks at the library. Perhaps it really took him less; West believed that Alsing did it all in two days and nights. 'Without question he did', West insisted.[19]

1979

> There's a clock inside Eagle. It ticks every 220 billionths of a second.
> Between each tick of the clock, Eagle performs one microinstruction.[20]

1970

> The rate-fixers cannot but set a production time which demands a super-
> human effort, since the whole point of the norms is to hold wages down to a
> level fixed in advance. If, for example, the sum of 61 forints has been fixed
> as the wage for a day's work at one hundred per cent performance, the
> rate-fixers are obliged to set the time per piece so that a minute of work does
> not yield more than the level fixed for the category; that is, the wage for a
> full minute's work. Even if the workers don't think like this, the rate-fixers
> are doing so all the time. Their point of departure is the pay itself – the
> 'incentive' of a danger to one's living standards – and not their experience of
> the true time taken to make a piece. Their stop-watches give a result which
> has been determined in advance, and this is the reason why the allocated
> times per piece, with very few exceptions, are unrealisable.[21]

Most of these quotations concern what we would probably classify as
'work-time', yet particularly insofar as they involve 'mental' labour (as
reading this essay does) they highlight the difficulty of assimilating
production time to a measure of homogenous units. One could add
further quotations to do with such activities as teaching, nursing,
counselling, child-rearing, etc., yet I would suggest that our habitual
way of considering and, more crucially, organizing even these activities in their character as socially-defined 'work' often tries to align
them with a dominant time-awareness that is at odds with their
specific, concrete, character.

5: TIME AND CULTURAL STUDIES

Pursuing the mosaic patterning of this essay, I now want to indicate
ways in which the problem of 'cultural time' already lurks within some
of the preoccupations, and possible intellectual resources, of cultural
studies – not least in that ambivalent qualifier 'contemporary'. That
'time' has been a concern within a variety of disciplines is apparent.
Both Anglo-American and continental philosophers have devoted
considerable recent work to the problem of time.[22] Modernist literature has produced a rich exploration, in Joyce's *Ulysses,* Proust's *A la
recherche du temps perdu,* Eliot's *Four Quartets,* Butor's *L'emploi du
temps.* SF writing has sometimes shown a more complex awareness of
'time' problems than those of mere time-travel.[23] Post-Einstein

physics, the *Annales* historians, the Lund school of time-geography, cognitive theory and developmental psychology, anthropology and ethnography, and of course economics,[24] have all broached the problems of 'time' as variously defined by those disciplines, and it would be an intriguing task in itself to trace the cultural significance, and percolated impact, of such intellectual concerns. Yet cultural studies have rarely focussed directly upon the contemporary cultural construction of time-sense and time-awareness or upon the current social organization of time. In a tentative way notions of 'generational' group identification and of individual biographical trajectory have been deployed in specific studies, and occasionally a particular inquiry yields intriguing material. Some instances can be very briefly commented upon, from work done at the Birmingham Centre for Contemporary Cultural Studies.

Dorothy Hobson, in her 'Housewives and the mass media',[25] points out that 'In some cases switching on the radio is part of the routine of beginning the day; it is, in fact, the first *boundary* in the working day. In terms of the 'structurelessness' of the experience of housework the time boundaries provided by radio are important in the women's own division of their time.' As Hobson also points out, the constant time-checks on radio and the time-referring programme titles (*The Breakfast Show, Mid-Morning Programme, The World at One*) help to structure the daily work-sequence. Some comments quoted in her study suggest a particular time-awareness linking across days:

Q: What do you like about the programmes that you watch?
A: Something to look forward to the next day 'cos most of them are serials.

and

Q: Why do you like *Crossroads?*
A: Just that you like to know what happens next, you know. I mean they're terrible actors, I know that, and I just see through that, you know.

The response introducing this comment on *Crossroads* is itself interesting:

. . . in between half-five and eight, that's me busiest time, feed him, change him, sometimes bath him. I don't bath him very often, erm, get Richard's dinner and I always clean up straight away, the washing up, and then I get everything settled and that takes me up to 8 o'clock, 'cos I stop at half-past-six to watch *Crossroads* [*laughs*]. And then from 8 onwards I just sit and watch the box [*laughs*].

One would need, of course, a great deal more to go on, but – and especially insofar as this pattern is also recognizable within one's own life – even these pointers suggest the potential usefulness of such notions as 'boundaries', time-embedding ('cos I stop at half-past-six'), time-deepening (simultaneity of activities), temporal matching (parallel sequences of activities), temporal horizons (something to

365

look forward to next day, next week, etc.), displaced and suspended overlapping temporalities (the various serial narratives each pursuing their own rhythms yet intersecting with one's own daily routines, the different levels of regularity inflecting each other), and perhaps most importantly the overarching notion of recurrence rather than repetition (one might think here of differences between childcare, housework, and industrial production-line work).[26] One might attempt to develop and apply such notions to a time-sense operating upon, or perhaps being reproduced at the level of, a different temporal span (for example, a 'marriage' as a latent temporal category) and one could probably compare the time-sense, time-organization and horizons operative in 'housework' and in 'political' awareness and activities: their respective necessities and the congruence or incompatibilities between them. It is also arguable that 'being a housewife' involves a degree of necessary dissociation from the time-discipline Thompson has analysed as constructed within capitalist development: socially as well as biologically constructed gender differences in 'inward apprehension of time' may sometimes be an important basis of conflict and incomprehension.

Paul Corrigan's 'Doing Nothing',[27] an excerpt from his study of Sunderland street-corner culture, suggests other directions of inquiry:

– What sort of things do you do with your mates?
– *Duncan:* Just stand around talking about footy. About things.
– Do you do anything else?
– *Duncan:* Joke, lark about, carry on. Just what we feel like really.
– What's that?
– *Duncan:* Just doing things. Last Saturday someone started throwing bottles and we all got in.
– What happened?
– *Duncan:* Nothing really.

and

– What do you do?
– *Albert:* Sometimes we get into mischief.
– Mischief?
– *Albert:* Well somebody gets a weird idea into their head, and they start to carry it out, and others join in.
– Weird ideas?
– *Albert:* Things . . . like going around smashing milk bottles.

Corrigan comments:

It is the 'weird idea' that represents the major something in 'doing nothing'. In fighting boredom the kids do not choose the street as a wonderfully lively place, rather they look upon it as the place where there is the most chance that something will happen. Doing nothing on the street must be compared with the alternatives: for example, knowing that nothing will happen with Mum and Dad in the front room; being almost certain that the youth club will be full of boredom. This makes the street the place where something might just happen, if not this Saturday, then surely next.

This is apposite, though one might want to explore further that tricky notion of 'boredom' and the differences between (sub-)cultural groupings in their labelling, and experiencing, of particular ways of 'doing nothing' as 'boring' (for example, sunbathing). One could also draw a certain comparison between waiting 'where something might just happen' and the 'waiting', or aimless prowling, that often characterizes a scientific researcher or 'creative' writer who also hopes that a 'weird idea', outside the given and expected matrix, will 'happen'. Such a comparison might include a consideration of 'deadlines' as a particular (often occupationally related) way of structuring time, a mode of time-horizon different from both the endlessly deferrable 'if not this Saturday, then surely the next' and the relatively reliable 'something to look forward to the next day'. In interviews with wives of soldiers embarked upon the Falklands expedition in 1982 a certain shift of horizon mode could be traced between the initial 'waiting' period as the battle fleet sailed towards the Falklands and the quite different 'expectancy' once actual combat had begun. From that example a more general exploration might reach out to include shifts in time-sense implicated in a latent or actualized awareness of the possibility of nuclear war – a matter in which deep generational differences might also be significant.

In his 'The Cultural Meaning of Drug Abuse',[28] Paul Willis quotes one 'acid'-taker:

> *Robin:* 'Dope' has a certain amount of freedom, as a result of, of . . . being much more aware of what is, you know, . . . what is rather than what was or will be. You know . . . er'm . . . I believe that one must live in the present, you know, this instant, now, experiencing now for what it is, because it is, because it is for no other reason. I suppose I could have gone into a monastery and meditated and, perhaps, found out the same thing in about fifty years, I've just found out how to do it, acid just speeded up the process of it, you know, well quite considerably.

Willis himself comments:

> This encapsulation by the 'now', and the feeling of freedom to 'walk around and feel the moment', led to a total breakdown of conventional notions of time. Industrial and job-oriented time is crucially concerned with order, i.e., what needs to be done before something else can be done – a massive critical path of consciousness . . . External coercion of time experience in this way is not always humanely relevant, as we can see from the very common feelings of boredom and frustration on the shopfloor . . . The heads felt the inappropriateness of conventional time particularly powerfully in the course of a 'trip'.

and then quotes another 'acid'-taker:

> *Norman:* You realise that time is man-made, there is no such thing as 'time', it's a load of cock, something that man has made to computerise himself by.

There are various aspects of these extracts that would repay comment, but Norman's remark suggests three important lines of inquiry. First, is there a degree of irreducibility in 'time' such that no possible human society could ignore certain 'givens'? At various levels one could argue that the domain of 'given' organizations of time has been steadily reduced, by the encroachment into night-time with artificial lighting, the extension of life-expectancy, the relaxing of natural agricultural temporalities with fertilizers, deliberate breeding processes and bio-technology, the deliberate modification of fertility rhythms, etc. But then, secondly, the claim that 'time is man-made' would have to be probed to disclose the specific 'men' involved in the control and encouragement of particular ways of reducing the domain of given time, and Norman's final phrase, 'something that man has made to computerise himself by', suggests one instance where that analysis is necessary. Thirdly, it is possible that a new form of capitalist reorganization of time is under way, in the development of a range of new technologies, all of which may reshape our time-sense, whether in the rapidation of information distribution or the restructuring of work-processes, the development of video (a private re-scheduling of the 'given' *TV Times*) or the perpetuation of large-scale and long-term unemployment. Already the tendencies being encouraged for employment to move from 'over-time' and 'shift-work' to 'flexi-time' and from 'full-time' to 'job-sharing' are indicative of changing forms of control over labour-time.[29] The emergence of 'inflation' as an important constituent of popular economic awareness opens up gaps between different, largely class-based, forms of response, in terms of financial planning and speculative opportunism. The extension of mortgaged house-ownership has probably already had an effect upon working-class conceptions of 'life-plans', perhaps in sharp conflict with the shrinking horizons registered in a consciousness of increasing job-obsolescence and the possibilities of periodic redundancy and retraining.

Clearly a great many facets of contemporary life under capitalism could be analysed in terms of the construction and reconstruction of time. But if one impetus in contemporary cultural studies has been a commitment to exploring residual and emergent areas of resistance or countervailing values it may become part of the agenda of cultural studies to attend to alternative conceptions of time already in process of formation. In that difficult project an awareness of the sometimes contradictory character of previous attempts to restructure social time-sense may be of value. Two examples from different periods can indicate this.

Christopher Hill and Keith Thomas[30] have both traced the campaign by seventeenth-century English Puritans to eradicate the many feast-days of the mediaeval church, which occasioned up to a hundred non-working days each year, and instead to regularize the week as consisting of six working days and one rest day, the Sabbath. This was an important step towards the modern homogenization of time, as uniform in quality. Yet by their very emphasis upon the observance of the Sabbath the Puritans themselves tended to foster the endowment of Sunday with 'mystical' attributes, with a peculiar quality of its own. As Thomas remarks: '[not] even the Puritans were able to emancipate themselves fully from the assumption that time was uneven in quality and that some occasions were inherently more propitious for perform-ing critical actions than others.'

The second example is from Catalonia in the 1890s.[31] The tenancies of the peasant farmers were based upon a contract measured not in years or in human lifetimes (as, e.g., in Ireland) but in terms of the life of the vines: the land reverted to the landowner when three-quarters of the planted vines had died (*rabassa morte* – the peasants were known as *rabassaires*). Brenan writes: 'The Catalan peasants had made an art of prolonging the life of the vines and in the old days they lasted as a rule for fifty years. This assured the labourer a contract that would cover his working life and remunerate him for the six or eight years of fruitless labour that young vines require before they mature'. But in the 1890s the phylloxera plague attacked European vineyards, eradi-cating the old stock of vine. The landowners imported phylloxera-resistant vines from America but these 'required much more care and labour and had a maximum life of only twenty-five years', which span was now, as far as the landowners were concerned, the legal limit of the tenancies. The eventual response of the *rabassaires* was to organize themselves for the first time into an agricultural syndicate under the leadership of Luis Companys, a lawyer who was to become in 1933 the leader of the Catalan coalition of 'left' political parties – hardly an outcome the landowners would have welcomed.

6: CONCLUSION

This tentative mosaic of an essay could conclude with suggestions as to lines of research into the cultural construction of time, and the asso-ciated methodological difficulties – for example, the problem of how to probe the relations between personal, gendered and class-shaped images of time, or the intriguing possibility of developing an 'architec-ture' of time akin to the construction, even creation, of habitable space in physical architecture, The relation between cultural sub-groupings, specific forms of time-awareness and particular modes of political consciousness might be explored, for example in different immigrant communities. Different modes of personal periodization, especially in relation to acknowledged crisis moments or significant years within a general history (e.g., 1945, 1956, 1968), might repay analysis. The continuing, even if decayed, role of 'special occasions', individual or collective, in both punctuating and revealing the character of mundane time may still illuminate the residual resistances in all our lives to dominant modes of time-organization. Even within a capitalist frame-work, the question of 'how much' we really consider our time to be 'worth' can often provoke deep-felt responses which would be suscep-tible to investigation. But the peculiarly 'individual' character of time – its literal non-alienability, the fact that in one sense we cannot choose *not* to 'use' our time, or that from one angle each new birth can indeed be seen as a unique 'income-addition' to social time – indicates the difficulty of elaborating any coherent method of research for a 'cul-tural study of time' or even a sociology of time, as section 3 has already suggested.

Perhaps, therefore, this essay can most appropriately conclude simply by offering two further quotations for consideration – quota-tions themselves being a form of temporal embedding. The first is from an American social historian, the second from a German Marxist critic:

> People who have not been 'famous' or who have not participated jointly in a common cause, such as a labour movement, a strike, or an organised political or social activity, experience great difficulty in making the connec-tion between their own lives and the historical process. Without such linkages, in most instances in the United States oral-history interviewing remains a private exercise . . . The former Amoskeag workers frequently replied with 'Why ask me? My story is not special' or 'What is so important about my life?' . . . Attitudes changed drastically, however, after the exhi-bition 'Amoskeag: A Sense of Place, A Way of Life' opened in Manchester in 1975 . . . Thousands of people, mostly former mill workers and their families, came to see the exhibit. Farmer workers, now elderly, searched the huge historic group portraits for their relatives; grandparents led their grandchildren through the exhibit, often describing how they did their jobs of thirty to forty years earlier . . . The sudden opportunity to view their own lives as part of a significant historical experience provided a setting for collective identification. Under these circumstances, interviewing ceased to be an isolated individual experience. It turned, instead, into a shared community event.[32]

> The awareness that they are about to make the continuum of history explode is characteristic of the revolutionary classes at the moment of their action. The great revolution introduced a new calendar. The initial day of a calendar serves as a historical time-lapse camera. And, basically, it is the same day that keeps recurring in the guise of holidays, which are days of remembrance. Thus the calendars do not measure time as clocks do; they

are monuments of a historical consciousness of which not the slightest trace
has been apparent in Europe in the past hundred years. In the July
revolution an incident occurred which showed this consciousness still alive.
On the first evening of the fighting it turned out that the clocks in towers
were being fired on simultaneously and independently from several places
in Paris . . . Historicism rightly culminates in universal history.
Materialistic historiography differs from it as to method more clearly than
from any other kind. Its method is additive; it musters a mass of data to fill
the homogeneous, empty time. Materialistic historiography on the other
hand is based on a constructive principle. Thinking involves not only the
flow of thoughts, but their arrest as well. Where thinking suddenly stops in a
configuration pregnant with tensions, it gives that configuration a shock, by
which it crystallises into a monad. A historical materialist approaches a
historical subject only where he encounters it as a monad. In this structure
he recognises the sign of a Messianic cessation of happening, or, put
differently, a revolutionary chance in the fight for the oppressed past.[33]

NOTES AND REFERENCES

1. The following quotations are from: Marwick, *British Society since 1945*, p. 75; Marwick, p. 250; Kenneth Roberts, *Leisure*, Longmans 1970, p. 10; Roberts, p. 21 (twice); *Trends in British Society since 1900*, ed. A. H. Halsey, Macmillan 1972, p. 541; ed. Halsey, p. 553. I am grateful to Hugh Cunningham, Steve Hipkin, Ray Pahl, Dave Reason and Kevin Robbins for bibliographical and other suggestions during the writing of this essay which was completed in 1983. Some of the themes are pursued further in my *The Literary Labyrinth*, Harvester 1984.
2. *The Use of Time*, ed A. Szalai, Mouton, The Hague 1972, p. 1.
3. Katja Boh and Stane Saksida, 'An attempt at a typology of time use', in ed. Szalai, p. 245.
4. Marx, *Herr Vogt*, trans. R. A. Archer, New Park Publications, New York 1982, p. ix.
5. Thompson, 'Time, work-discipline and industrial capitalism', *Past and Present*, No. 38 (1967), pp. 56–97. Cf. also Nigel Thrift, 'Owners' Time and Own Time: the making of a capitalist time consciousness, 1300–1880', in *Space and Time in Geography*, ed. A. Pred, Gleerup, Lund 1981, pp. 56–84. Foucault's discussion of discipline in schools is also relevant, cf. his *Discipline and Punish;* cf. also the recent historical survey by David S. Landes, *Revolution in Time: Clocks and the Making of the Modern World*, Belknap Press, Harvard University Press, Cambridge, Mass. 1984; and André Gorz, 'Towards a Politics of Time', in *Farewell to the Working Class*, Pluto 1982.
6. Thompson, p. 90.
7. Marx and Engels, *The German Ideology*, pp. 44–5.
8. Marx and Engels, p. 432.

9. G. A. Cohen, *Karl Marx's Theory of History: a defence,* Clarendon Press 1978, p. 133.

10. Cf. the discussion of the mutually exclusive categories of 'remunerated work' and 'activities oriented towards self-fulfilment' in Joffre Dumazedier, *Sociology of Leisure,* trans. M. A. McKenzie, Elsevier, Amsterdam 1974, p. 67ff.

11. Saussure, *Course in General Linguistics,* trans. W. Baskin, Fontana 1974, pp. 125–7.

12. Maxine Berg, *The Machinery Question and the Making of Political Economy 1815–1848,* Cambridge University Press 1980, pp. 123–4.

13. Thompson, *The Defence of Britain,* CND 1983, p. 35.

14. Quoted in Berg, p. 198.

15. Adapted from William Gaunt, *The Aesthetic Adventure,* Cape 1975, p. 90.

16. Quoted in Thompson, *William Morris: romantic to revolutionary,* Merlin 1977, p. 194.

17. Thompson, *William Morris,* pp. 423–4.

18. Tracy Kidder, *The Soul of a New Machine,* Penguin 1982, p. 77.

19. Kidder, p. 94.

20. Kidder, p. 116.

21. Miklós Haraszti, *A Worker in a Worker's State,* trans. M. Wright, Penguin 1977, p. 40.

22. Cf., e.g., *The Philosophy of Time,* ed. R. M. Gale, Harvester 1978; Hugh Mellor, *Real Time,* Cambridge University Press 1980; Edmund Husserl, *The Phenomenology of Internal Time-Consciousness,* trans. J. S. Churchill, Martinus Nijhoff, The Hague 1964; Martin Heidegger, *Being and Time,* trans. J. Macquarrie and E. Robinson, Harper and Row, New York 1962; Derrida, 'Ousia and Grammé', in *Phenomenology in Perspective,* ed. F. J. Smith, Martinus Nijhoff, The Hague 1970, pp. 54–93.

23. See, for example, the use made of a galactic perspective upon earth's history in Lessing's *Canopus in Argos: Archives.*

24. See, for example: Braudel, *The Mediterranean and the Mediterranean World in the Age of Philip II* (2 vols.), trans. S. Reynolds, Collins 1972–3; Ernest Labrousse, *Esquisse du mouvement des prix et des revenus en France au XVIIIe siècle,* Dalloz, Paris 1933; Pred, 'The choreography of existence: comments on Hägerstrand's time-geography and its usefulness', *Economic Geography,* No. 53 (1977), pp. 207–21; Pred, 'Production, family, and free-time projects: a time-geographic perspective on the individual and societal change in nineteenth-century US cities', *Journal of Hist rical Geography,* VII, 1 (1981), 3–36; *The Developmental Psychology of Time,* ed. W. J. Friedman, Academic Press 1982.

25. Hobson, 'Housewives and the mass media', in *Culture, Media, Language,* eds. Hall et al., pp. 104–14.

26. For the distinction between 'repetition' and 'recurrence', see David Reason, 'Classification, Time and the Organisation of Production', in *Classifications in their Social Context,* eds. R. Ellen and Reason, Academic Press 1979, p. 230.

27. Corrigan, 'Doing Nothing', *Working Papers in Cultural Studies,* Nos. 7/8 (1975), pp. 103–5.

28. Willis, 'The Cultural Meaning of Drug Abuse', *WPCS,* Nos 7/8, pp. 106–18.

29. See, for example, *Work and Society Newsletter,* No. 1 (1983), p. 2.
30. Christopher Hill, *Society and Puritanism in Pre-Revolutionary England*, Secker and Warburg, 1964, Ch. 5; Keith Thomas, *Religion and the Decline of Magic,* Penguin 1973, pp. 742–5.
31. Cf. Raymond Carr, *Spain 1805–1975,* Clarendon Press 1982, p. 420f.; Gerald Brenan, *The Spanish Labyrinth*, Cambridge University Press 1960, p. 277f.
32. Tamara K. Hareven, *Family Time and Industrial Time,* Cambridge University Press 1982, pp. 378–9.
33. Benjamin, *Illuminations,* pp. 263–5.

BIBLIOGRAPHY

This bibliography gives full details of the main texts mentioned in the chapters, and in the Notes and references. It also includes a few other works of particular importance. In general, the editions cited are those which should be most readily available to students.

It should be noted that the most systematic and extensive body of work on contemporary culture has emerged in the several series issued from the Birmingham Centre for Contemporary Cultural Studies; many references will be found in the Notes to Chapter 14 and elsewhere. A particularly noteworthy collection of primary sources is the Holloway Collection, formerly the Library of Contemporary Cultural Records, which is now housed in the library of the University of East Anglia.

Abel, Elizabeth, 'Editor's Introduction to *Writing and Sexual Difference* Issue', *Critical Inquiry*, VIII (1981), 173–8.

Abrams, Philip, *The Origins of British Sociology 1834–1914*, Chicago University Press, Chicago 1968.

Addison, Paul, *The Road to 1945*, Cape 1975.

Adelman, Clifford, *Generations: A Collage on Youthcult*, Penguin 1973.

Adorno, Theodor, *Prisms*, trans. S. and S. Weber, Neville Spearman 1967.

Alderson, Connie, *Magazines Teenagers Read*, Pergamon 1968.

Allen, John, 'In Search of a Method: Hegel, Marx and Realism', *Radical Philosophy*, No. 35 (1983), pp. 26–33.

Althusser, Louis, *Reading Capital*, trans. Ben Brewster, New Left Books 1970.

Alvarado, Manuel, and Edward Buscombe, *Hazell: The Making of a TV Series*, British Film Institute 1978.

Anderson, Benedict, *Imagined Communities*, Verso 1983.

Anderson, Perry, *Arguments within English Marxism*, Verso 1980.

Anderson, Perry, 'Components of the National Culture', *New Left Review*, No. 50 (1968), pp. 3–57.

Anderson, Perry, 'The Origins of the Present Crisis', *New Left Review*, No. 23 (1964), pp. 26–53.

Aptor, D.E., and James Joll, eds, *Anarchism Today*, Macmillan 1981.

Arato, Andrew, and Eike Gebhardt, eds, *The Essential Frankfurt School Reader*, Blackwell 1978.

Barbu, Zev, *Society, Culture and Personality*, Blackwell 1971.

Barker, Martin, and Anne Beezer, 'Scarman and the Language of Racism', *International Socialism*, No. 18 (1983), pp. 108–25.

Barrett, Michèle, Philip Corrigan, *et al.*, *Ideology and Cultural Production*, Croom Helm 1979.

Barthes, Roland, *Camera Lucida: Reflections on Photography*, trans. Richard Howard, Cape 1982.

Barthes, Roland, *Elements of Semiology*, trans. A. Lavers and Colin Smith, Cape 1967.

Barthes, Roland, *Image–Music–Text*, trans. Stephen Heath, Fontana 1977.

Barthes, Roland, *A Lover's Discourse*, trans. Richard Howard, Hill and Wang, New York 1978.

Barthes, Roland, *Mythologies*, trans. A. Lavers, Cape 1972.

Barthes, Roland, *S/Z*, trans. Richard Miller, Cape 1975.

Barthes, Roland, *Writing Degree Zero*, trans. A. Lavers and Colin Smith, Cape 1967.

Bassnett, Susan, and Keith Hoskin, 'Women and Creativity', *Gulliver*, No. 10 (1981), pp. 56–67.

Batalov, Eduard, *The Philosophy of Revolt: Criticism of Left Radical Ideology*, trans. K. Judelson, Progress Publishers, Moscow 1973.

Bateson, Gregory, *Mind and Nature*, Wildwood House 1979.

Bateson, Gregory, *Steps to an Ecology of Mind*, International Textbooks 1972.

Baudrillard, Jean, *In the Shadow of the Silent Majorities . . . Or the End of the Social*, trans. P. Foss, P. Patton and J. Johnston, Semiotext(e), New York 1983.

Baudrillard, Jean, *The Mirror of Production*, trans. M. Poster, Telos Press, St Louis, Mo. 1975.

Bauman, Zygmunt, *Socialism The Active Utopia*, Allen and Unwin 1976.

Beezer, Anne, 'Response to Alison Assiter', *Radical Philosophy*, No. 36 (1984), pp. 16–19.

Bell, Colin, *Middle-Class Families: Social and Geographical Mobility*, Routledge and Kegan Paul 1968.

Benjamin, Walter, *Illuminations*, ed. Hannah Arendt, Fontana 1973.

Bennett, Tony, *Formalism and Marxism*, Methuen 1979.

Bennett, Tony, 'James Bond as Popular Hero', *Open University Popular Culture Course*, Unit 21, Block 5.

Bennett, Tony, 'Text and Social Process: The Case of James Bond', *Screen Education*, No. 41 (1982), pp. 3–14.

Bennett, Tony, *et al.*, eds, *Culture, Ideology and Social Process*, Open University Press and Batsford 1981.

Berg, Maxine, *The Machinery Question and the Making of Political Economy 1815–1848*, Cambridge University Press 1980.

Berger, John, *Ways of Seeing*, Penguin 1972.

Berger, Peter, and Thomas Luckmann, *The Social Construction of Reality*, Penguin 1979.

Berke, Jo, *et al.*, *Counter Culture: The Creation of an Alternative Society*, Peter Owen 1969.

Black, Peter, *The Mirror in the Corner: People's Television*, Hutchinson 1972.

Bodeman, Michael Y., 'Mystical, Satanic and Chiliastic Forces in Counter-cultural Movements: Changing the World or Reconciling it', *Youth and Society*, V, 4 (1974), 433–47.

375

Bottomore, Tom, *Critics of Society: Radical Thought in North America*, Allen and Unwin 1969.

Bourdieu, Pierre, and Jean-Claude Passeron, *Reproduction in Education, Society, and Culture*, trans. R. Nice, Sage 1977.

Bourdieu, Pierre, *Two Bourdieu Texts*, trans. R. Nice, Centre for Contemporary Cultural Studies Stencilled Occasional Paper No. 46.

Boyle, Andrew, *Only the Wind Will Listen: Reith of the BBC*, Hutchinson 1972.

Brake, Mike, *The Sociology of Youth Cultures and Youth Subcultures*, Routledge and Kegan Paul 1980.

Braudel, Fernand, *On History*, trans. Sarah Matthews, University of Chicago Press, Chicago 1980.

Briggs, Asa, *The Birth of Broadcasting*, Oxford University Press 1961.

Briggs, Asa, *The Golden Age of Wireless*, Oxford University Press 1962.

Briggs, Asa, *Sound and Vision*, Oxford University Press 1979.

Briggs, Asa, *The War of Words*, Oxford University Press 1970.

Brown, Norman O., *Love's Body*, Vintage Books, New York 1968.

Brown, R. H., *A Poetic for Sociology: Towards a Logic of Discovery for the Human Sciences*, Cambridge University Press 1974.

Brown, Richard, ed., *Knowledge, Education and Social Change*, Tavistock 1973.

Bruner, J. S., *Towards a Theory of Instruction*, Oxford University Press 1960.

Buswell, Carol, 'Sexism in School Routines and Classroom Practice', *Durham and Newcastle Research Review*, IX (1981), 195–200.

Butterworth, Eric, and Robert Holman, *Social Welfare in Modern Britain*, Collins 1975.

Butterworth, Eric, and David Weir, eds, *The Sociology of Modern Britain*, rev. edn., Collins 1977.

Byrne, Eileen, *Women and Education*, Tavistock 1978.

Calder, Angus, *The People's War*, Cape 1969.

Campbell, Beatrix, 'A Feminist Sexual Politics: Now you see it, now you don't', *Feminist Review*, No. 5 (1980).

Capp, Bernard, *Astrology and the Popular Press*, Faber 1979.

Cardiff, David, and Paddy Scannel, 'Radio in World War II', *Open University Popular Culture Course*, Unit 2.

Cardiff, David, and Paddy Scannel, 'Serving the Public: Public Service Broadcasting before the War', in *Popular Culture: Past and Present*, ed. Bernard Waites et al., Croom Helm 1982.

Carrol, Jackson W., 'Transcendence and Mystery in the Counter Culture', *Religion in Life*, XLII (1973), 361–75.

Centre for Contemporary Cultural Studies, *Making Histories: Studies in History-writing and Politics*, Hutchinson 1982.

Centre for Contemporary Cultural Studies Education Group, *Unpopular Education: Schooling and Social Democracy in England since 1944*, Hutchinson 1981.

Centre for Contemporary Cultural Studies Media Group, 'Fighting over Peace: Representations of CND in the Media', Centre for Contemporary Cultural Studies Stencilled Occasional Paper No. 72.

Centre for Contemporary Cultural Studies Women's Studies Group, *Women Take Issue*, Hutchinson 1978.

Chambers, Peter, and Amy Landreth, eds, *Called Up*, Wingate 1955.

Chanan, Gabriel, and Linda Gilchrist, *What School is For*, Penguin 1974.

Chicago, Judy, *The Dinner Party*, Anchor Books, New York 1979.

Chodhorow, Nancy, *The Reproduction of Mothering: Psychoanalysis and the Sociology of Gender*, University of California Press, Berkeley 1978.

Cixous, Hélène, 'The Laugh of the Medusa', in *The 'Signs' Reader: Women, Gender and Scholarship*, eds E. and E. K. Abel, University of Chicago Press, Chicago 1983.

Clarke, John, Chas Critcher and Richard Johnson, eds, *Working Class Culture*, Hutchinson 1979.

Cliff, Michelle, *Claiming an Identity They Taught Me to Despise*, Persephone Press, Massachusetts 1980.

Cohen, G. A., *Karl Marx's Theory of History: a defence*, Clarendon Press 1978.

Cohen, Stanley, and Jock Young, eds, *The Manufacture of News*, Constable 1973.

Connell, Myra, *Reading Romance*, unpublished MA thesis, University of Birmingham 1981.

Conrad, Peter, *Television: The Medium and its Manners*, Routledge and Kegan Paul 1982.

Cook, Jim, *et al.*, *Television Situation Comedy*, British Film Institute Dossier 1982.

Corner, John, and Jeremy Hawthorn, eds, *Communication Studies: An Introductory Reader*, Edward Arnold 1980.

Corrigan, Paul, 'Doing Nothing', *Working Papers in Cultural Studies*, Nos 7/8 (1975), pp. 103–5.

Cottle, Thomas, *Black Testimony*, Wildwood House 1978.

Coward, Rosalind, *Patriarchal Precedents: Sexuality and Social Relations*, Routledge and Kegan Paul 1983.

Coward, Rosalind, and John Ellis, *Language and Materialism: Developments in Semiology and the Theory of the Subject*, Routledge and Kegan Paul 1977.

Critchley, T. A., *The Conquest of Violence*, Constable 1970.

Crossman, R. H. S., *The Diaries of a Cabinet Minister* (3 vols.), Hamilton 1975–7.

Cullen, M. J., *The Statistical Movement in Early Victorian Britain*, Harvester 1975.

Culler, Jonathan, *Saussure*, Fontana 1976.

Curran, James, and Vincent Porter, eds, *British Cinema History*, Weidenfeld 1983.

Curran, James, *et al.*, eds, *Mass Communication and Society*, Edward Arnold 1977.

Currie, Robert, *Industrial Politics*, Oxford University Press 1979.

Cutler, Anthony, *et al.*, *Marx's Capital and Capitalism Today* (2 vols.), Routledge and Kegan Paul 1978.

Daly, Mary, *Gyn-Ecology*, The Women's Press 1979.

Davies, Christie, *Permissive Britain*, Pitman 1975.

Dawson, J. A., and David Thomas, *Man and his World*, Nelson 1975.

Debord, Guy, *La Societé du Spectacle*, Buchet/Chastel, Paris 1967.

Debray, Régis, *Teachers, Writers, Celebrities*, trans. D. Macey, Verso 1981.

Delaney, Sheila, ed., *Counter-Tradition: A Reader in the Literature of Dissent and Alternatives*, Basic Books, New York 1971.

Denisoff, R. Serge, and M. D. Pugh, 'Consciousness III or Counter-culture: A Preliminary Study', *Youth and Society*, V, 4 (1974), 397–410.

Denisoff, R. Serge, and M. D. Pugh, 'Roszak and Reich Return to the Garden: A Note', in *Theories and Paradigms in Contemporary Sociology*, eds M. H. Levine and O. Callahan, Peacock, Itasca, Illinois 1974.

Derrida, Jacques, *Of Grammatology*, trans. G. C. Spivak, Johns Hopkins University Press, Baltimore, Md. 1976.

Derrida, Jacques, 'Ousia and Grammé', in *Phenomenology in Perspective*, ed. F. J. Smith, Martinus Nijhoff, The Hague 1970.

Derrida, Jacques, *Writing and Difference*, trans. A. Bass, Routledge and Kegan Paul 1978.

Donald, James, and AnnMarie Volpe, eds, *Is There Anyone Here from Education?*, Pluto 1983.

Dorfman, Ariel, *The Emperor's Old Clothes*, Pluto 1983.

Duffy, Maureen, *Capital*, Cape 1976.

Dumazedier, Joffre, *Sociology of Leisure*, trans. M. A. McKenzie, Elsevier, Amsterdam 1974.

Dyer, Richard, *Light Entertainment*, British Film Institute 1973.

Dyer, Richard, *Stars*, British Film Institute 1979.

Dyer, Richard, *et al.*, *Coronation Street*, British Film Institute 1981.

Easlea, Brian, *Science and Sexual Oppression*, Weidenfeld 1981.

Eaton, Mick, 'Comedy', *Screen*, XIX, 4 (1978/9), 61–89.

Eaton, Mick, 'Laughter in the Dark', *Screen*, XXII, 2 (1981), 21–8.

Eichenbaum, Luise, and Susie Orbach, *Outside In Inside Out*, Penguin 1982.

Eliot, T. S., *Notes Towards a Definition of Culture*, Faber 1948.

Eliot, T. S., *Selected Poems*, Faber 1954.

Ellen, Roy, and David Reason, eds, *Classifications in their Social Context*, Academic Press 1979.

Elliott, Philip, *The Making of a Television Series*, Constable and Sage 1972.

Ellis, John, 'Made in Ealing', *Screen*, XVI, 1 (1975), 78–127.

Ellis, John, ed., *Screen Reader: Cinema/Ideology/Politics*, SEFT 1977.

Empson, William, *Some Versions of Pastoral*, Penguin 1966.

Epstein, Leon, *British Politics in the Suez Crisis*, Pall Mall 1964.

Evans, Robert A., *Belief and the Counter Culture: A Guide to Constructive Confrontation*, The Westminster Press, Philadelphia, Pa. 1971.

Ferguson, Marjorie, *Forever Feminine*, Heinemann 1983.

Feyerabend, Paul, *Against Method*, New Left Books 1975.

Fiske, John, *Introduction to Communication Studies*, Methuen 1982.

Fiske, John, and John Hartley, *Reading Television*, Methuen 1978.

Foucault, Michel, *The Archaeology of Knowledge*, trans. A. Sheridan, Tavistock 1972.

Foucault, Michel, *Discipline and Punish*, trans. A. Sheridan, Allen Lane 1977.

Foucault, Michel, *A History of Sexuality*, trans. R. Hurley, Allen Lane 1980, Vol. I.

Foucault, Michel, *Mental Illness and Psychology*, trans. A. Sheridan, Harper and Row, New York 1976.

Foucault, Michel, 'What is an Author?', *Screen*, XX, 1 (1979), 13–33.

Fowler, Roger, Bob Hodge, Gunther Kress and Tony Trew, *Language and Control*, Routledge and Kegan Paul 1979.

Freud, Sigmund, *Standard Edition of the Complete Psychological Works of Sigmund Freud* (23 vols.), ed. J. Strachey, Hogarth Press 1953–73.

Friedman, W. J., ed., *The Developmental Psychology of Time*, Academic Press 1982.

Frye, Northrop, *Anatomy of Criticism*, Princeton University Press, Princeton, N.J. 1957.

Fussell, Paul, *The Great War and Modern Memory*, Oxford University Press 1975.

Gale, R. M., ed., *The Philosophy of Time*, Harvester 1978.

Gallop, Jane, *Feminism and Psychoanalysis: The Daughter's Seduction*, Macmillan 1982.

Garnham, Nicholas, *Structures of Television*, British Film Institute 1973.

Gathorne-Hardy, Jonathan, *The Public School Phenomenon*, Hodder and Stoughton 1977.

Gauthier, Guy, *The Semiology of the Image*, trans. D. Matias, British Film Institute 1976.

Gauthier, Xavière, 'Existe-t-il une écriture de femme?', *Tel Quel*, No. 58 (1974), pp. 95–7.

Gellner, Ernest, 'The Crisis in the Humanities and the Mainstream of Philosophy', in *Crisis in the Humanities*, ed. J. H. Plumb, Penguin 1964.

Gellner, Ernest, *Thought and Change*, Weidenfeld 1964.

Giedion, Sigfried, *Mechanisation Takes Command*, rev. edn., Norton, New York 1969.

Gilbert, Sandra, and Susan Gubar, *The Madwoman in the Attic*, Yale University Press, New Haven, Conn. 1979.

Gillett, Charlie, *The Sound of the City*, Souvenir Press and Sphere 1971.

Godley, J. R., *Living Like a Lord*, Gollancz 1955.

Goldie, Grace Wyndham, *Facing the Nation: Television and Politics 1936–1976*, Bodley Head 1977.

Goldthorpe, John H., *Social Mobility and Class Structure in Modern Britain*, Clarendon Press 1980.

Goldthorpe, John H., *et al.*, *The Affluent Worker* (3 vols.), Cambridge University Press 1968–69.

Goodhart, G. J., *et al.*, *The Television Audience*, Saxon House 1975.

Goodman, Mitchell, ed., *The Movement Toward a New America: The Beginnings of a Long Revolution*, Pilgrim Press, Philadelphia, Pa.; Knopf, New York 1970.

Goodman, Paul, *Growing Up Absurd*, Vintage Books, New York 1960.

Gorer, Geoffrey, *Exploring English Character*, Cresset Press 1955.

Gorer, Geoffrey, *Sex and Marriage in England Today*, Nelson 1971.

Gorz, André, *Farewell to the Working Class*, Pluto 1982.

Gouldner, Alvin, *The Dialectic of Ideology and Technology: The Origins, Grammar and Future of Ideology*, Macmillan 1976.

Gouldner, Alvin, *For Sociology: Renewal and Critique in Sociology Today*, Penguin 1975.

Gramsci, Antonio, *The Modern Prince and Other Writings*, trans. L. Marks, International Publishers, New York 1957.

Gramsci, Antonio, *The Prison Notebooks*, eds Q. Hoare and G. Nowell Smith,

Lawrence and Wishart 1971.

Greer, Germaine, *The Female Eunuch,* MacGibbon and Kee 1970.

Griffin, Christine, 'Cultures of Femininity: Romance Revisited', Centre for Contemporary Cultural Studies Stencilled Occasional Paper No. 69.

Griffin, Susan, *Pornography and Silence,* The Women's Press 1981.

Gurevitch, Michael, et al., eds, *Culture, Society and the Media,* Methuen and Open University Press 1982.

Habermas, Jürgen, *Strukturwandel der Öffentlichkeit,* Neuweid, Berlin 1962.

Habermas, Jürgen, *Habermas: Critical Debates,* eds J. B. Thompson and D. Held, Macmillan 1982.

Hall, Stuart, 'Cultural Studies: Two Paradigms', *Media, Culture and Society,* II (1980), 57–72.

Hall, Stuart, 'Some Paradigms in Cultural Studies', *Annali Anglistica,* XXI (1978).

Hall, Stuart, Dorothy Hobson, Andrew Lowe and Paul Willis, eds, *Culture, Media, Language,* Hutchinson 1980.

Hall, Stuart, and Tony Jefferson, eds, *Resistance through Rituals: Youth Subcultures in Post-War Britain*, Hutchinson 1976.

Hall, Stuart, *et al.*, *Policing the Crisis: 'Mugging', the State and Law and Order*, Macmillan 1978.

Halloran, J. D., ed., *The Effects of Television,* Panther 1975.

Halsey, A. H., A. F. Heath and J. M. Ridge, *Origins and Destinations: Family, Class, and Education in Modern Britain,* Clarendon Press 1980.

Halsey, A. H., ed., *Trends in British Society since 1900,* Macmillan 1972.

Haraszti, Miklós, *A Worker in a Worker's State,* trans. M. Wright, Penguin 1977.

Hareven, Tamara K., *Family Time and Industrial Time,* Cambridge University Press 1982.

Harris, José, *Beveridge,* Oxford University Press 1977.

Hartley, John, *Understanding News,* Methuen 1982.

Hartman, Geoffrey H., *Saving the Text: Literature/Derrida/Philosophy,* Johns Hopkins University Press, Baltimore, Md. 1981.

Harvey, Sylvia, *May 1968 and Film Culture,* British Film Institute 1980.

Hawkes, Terence, *Structuralism and Semiotics,* Methuen 1977.

Hebdige, Dick, *Subculture,* Methuen 1979.

Held, David, *Introduction to Critical Theory,* Hutchinson 1981.

Hennessy, Peter, and Keith Jeffery, *States of Emergency: British Governments and Strike Breaking since 1919,* Routledge and Kegan Paul 1983.

Hicks, David, 'Bias in Books', *World Studies Journal,* I, 3 (1980), 14–22.

Hill, Christopher, *Society and Puritanism in Pre-Revolutionary England,* Secker and Warburg 1964.

Hirsh, Arthur, *The French Left: A History and an Overview,* Black Rose Books, Montreal 1982.

Hobson, Dorothy, *Crossroads,* Methuen 1982.

Hoggart, Richard, *The Uses of Literacy,* Chatto 1957.

Horton, Donald, and Richard Wohl, 'Mass Communication and Parasocial Interaction', *Journal of Psychiatry,* XIX (1956), 215–29.

Huxley, Aldous, *Music at Night and Other Essays,* Penguin 1950.

Hyman, Richard, *Strikes,* rev. edn., Collins 1977.

Hyman, Stanley E., *The Tangled Bank: Darwin, Marx, Frazer, Freud as*

Imaginative Writers, Atheneum, New York 1959.

Jacobus, Mary, ed., *Women Writing and Writing about Women*, Croom Helm 1979.

Jacoby, Russell, *Social Amnesia: A Critique of Conformist Psychology*, Harvester 1977.

Jameson, Fredric, 'Marxism and Historicism', *New Literary History*, XI (1979/80), 41–73.

Jameson, Fredric, *The Political Unconscious: Narrative as a Socially Symbolic Act*, Cornell University Press, Ithaca, N.Y. 1981.

Johnson, Richard, 'What is Cultural Studies Anyway?', Centre for Contemporary Cultural Studies Stencilled Occasional Paper No. 74.

Kantor, R. N., *et al.*, 'How Inconsiderate are Children's Textbooks?', *Journal of Curriculum Studies*, XV, 1 (1983), 61–72.

Kelf-Cohen, Reuben, *British Nationalisation 1945–1973*, Macmillan 1973.

Kelsall, R. K., *The Higher Civil Service in Great Britain*, Routledge and Kegan Paul 1955.

Kidder, Tracy, *The Soul of a New Machine*, Penguin 1982.

King George's Jubilee Trust, *Citizens of Tomorrow*, King George's Jubilee Trust 1955.

Kress, Gunther, and Robert Hodge, *Language as Ideology*, Routledge and Kegan Paul 1979.

Kristeva, Julia, *Desire in Language*, ed. L. S. Roudiez, Blackwell 1980.

Kuhn, T. S., *The Structure of Scientific Revolutions*, 2nd edn., University of Chicago Press, Chicago 1970.

Lacan, Jacques, 'The Mirror Phase', trans. J. Roussel, *New Left Review*, No. 51 (1968), pp. 71–7.

Lahr, John, *Prick up your Ears*, Penguin 1980.

Landes, David S., *Revolution in Time: Clocks and the Making of the Modern World*, Bellknap Press, Harvard University Press, Cambridge, Mass. 1984.

Larrain, Jorge, *The Concept of Ideology*, Hutchinson 1979.

Larrain, Jorge, *Marxism and Ideology*, Macmillan 1983.

Leavis, F. R., *Education and the University*, Chatto 1948.

Leboyer, Frédérick, *Birth without Violence*, Fontana 1977.

Leech, Kenneth, *Youthquake: Spirituality and the Growth of a Counter-Culture*, Sphere/Abacus 1976.

Lefebvre, Henri, 'What is the Historical Past?', *New Left Review*, No. 90 (1975), pp. 27–34.

Lessico politico delle donne 6: letteratura, cinema, arti visive, edizioni Gulliver, Milan 1979.

Lessing, Doris, *The Marriages Between Zones Three, Four and Five*, Cape 1980.

Lessing, Doris, *Memoirs of a Survivor*, Octagon Press 1974.

Lessing, Doris, *Shikasta*, Cape 1979.

Levinson, Daniel J., *The Seasons of a Man's Life*, Knopf, New York 1979.

'Literary Theory in the University: A Survey', *New Literary History*, XIV (1983), 411–51.

Lockwood, David, 'The "New Working Class" ', *Archives Européennes de Sociologie*, I, 2 (1960), 248–59.

Lovell, Terry, *Pictures of Reality*, British Film Institute 1981.

Lowery, Shearon, and Melvin L. De Fleur, *Milestones in Mass Communi-*

cations Research, Longmans 1983.

MacDonald, Barrie, *Broadcasting: A Selected Bibliography,* IBA 1981.

Mannheim, Karl, *Essays in the Sociology of Knowledge,* ed. P. Kecskemeti, Routledge and Kegan Paul 1952.

Mannheim, Karl, *Ideology and Utopia: An Introduction to the Sociology of Knowledge,* Routledge and Kegan Paul 1960.

Manvell, Roger, *The Film and the Public,* Penguin 1955.

Marcuse, Herbert, *Eros and Civilisation,* Beacon Press, Boston, Mass. 1964.

Marcuse, Herbert, *An Essay on Liberation,* Allen Lane 1969.

Marcuse, Herbert, *Negations: Essays in Critical Theory,* Penguin 1968.

Marcuse, Herbert, *One-Dimensional Man: Studies in the Ideology of Advanced Industrial Society,* Routledge and Kegan Paul 1964.

Marks, Elaine, and Isabelle de Courtivron, eds, *New French Feminisms,* Harvester 1981.

Marris, Peter, *Loss and Change,* Routledge and Kegan Paul 1974.

Martin, Bernice, *A Sociology of Contemporary Cultural Change,* Blackwell 1981.

Martin, David, *The Dilemmas of Contemporary Religion,* Blackwell 1978.

Marwick, Arthur, *Britain in the Century of Total War,* Bodley Head 1968.

Marwick, Arthur, *British Society since 1945,* Allen Lane 1982.

Marwick, Arthur, *Class: Image and Reality in Britain, France and the USA since 1930,* Collins 1980.

Marwick, Arthur, *The Home Front,* Thames and Hudson 1976.

Marwick, Arthur, '*Room at the Top* and *Saturday Night and Sunday Morning* and the "Cultural Revolution" in Britain', *Journal of Contemporary History,* XIX, 1 (1984), 125–51.

Marwick, Arthur, *Social Change in Britain, 1920–1970,* Birkbeck College

Marx, Karl, *Capital* (3 vols.), trans. B. Fowkes, Penguin 1976–.

Marx, Karl, *A Contribution to the Critique of Political Economy,* Lawrence and Wishart 1971.

Marx, Karl, *Early Writings,* introd. L. Colletti, Penguin 1975.

Marx, Karl, *Grundrisse,* trans. M. Nicolaus, Penguin 1973.

Marx, Karl, *Herr Vogt,* trans. R. A. Archer, New Park Publications, New York 1982.

Marx, Karl, *Selected Writings of Karl Marx on Sociology and Social Philosophy,* 2nd edn., eds T. B. Bottomore and M. Rubel, Penguin 1963.

Marx, Karl, and Friedrich Engels, *Collected Works,* Lawrence and Wishart 1975–.

Marx, Karl, and Friedrich Engels, *The German Ideology,* ed. C. J. Arthur, Lawrence and Wishart 1970.

Mast, Gerald, *The Comic Mind,* University of Chicago Press, Chicago 1973.

Masterman, Len, *Teaching About Television,* Macmillan 1980.

Matterlart, A., and S. Seigelaub, eds, *Communication and Class Struggle,* International General, New York 1983.

Mays, John, Anthony Forder and Olive Keidan, eds, *Penelope Hall's Social Services of England and Wales,* 9th edn., Routledge and Kegan Paul 1975.

McLellan, David, *Marx,* Fontana 1975.

McLuhan, Marshall, *Culture is Our Business,* McGraw–Hill, New York 1972.

McLuhan, Marshall, *The Mechanical Bride,* Routledge and Kegan Paul 1967.

McLuhan, Marshall, and Harley Parker, *Through the Vanishing Point: Space in Poetry and Painting,* Harper and Row, New York 1968.

McRobbie, Angela, '*Jackie:* an Ideology of Adolescent Femininity', Centre for Contemporary Cultural Studies Stencilled Occasional Paper No. 53, 1978.

McRobbie, Angela, and Trish MacCabe, eds, *Feminism for Girls,* Routledge and Kegan Paul 1981.

Mellor, Hugh, *Real Time,* Cambridge University Press 1980.

Menand, Louis, 'Glad Hearts at the Supermarket', *The Nation* (15 May 1982).

Mercer, Colin, 'Pleasure', *Open University Popular Culture Course,* Unit 17, Block 4.

Michele, Laura di, 'The Royal Wedding', Centre for Contemporary Cultural Studies Stencilled Occasional Paper, forthcoming.

Middlemass, Keith, *Politics in Industrial Society,* André Deutsch 1979.

Middleton, Richard, and John Muncie, 'Pop Culture, Pop Music and Post-War Youth: Countercultures', *Open University Popular Culture Course,* Unit 20, Block 5.

Miles, Jonathan, 'The Naked, the Uniformed and the Dead', *Z/G,* No. 7 (n.d., probably 1982).

Mills, C. Wright, *The Power Élite,* Oxford University Press 1955.

Millum, Trevor, *Images of Woman: Advertising in Women's Magazines,* Chatto 1975.

Milner, Roger, *Reith: The BBC Years,* Mainstream Publishing 1983.

Mitchell, Juliet, *Psychoanalysis and Feminism,* Allen Lane 1974.

Molina, Victor, *Marx's Arguments on Ideology,* unpublished PhD thesis, University of Birmingham 1983.

Moran, Michael, *The Politics of Industrial Relations,* Macmillan 1977.

Morley, David, *The Nationwide Audience,* British Film Institute 1980.

Morrison, Blake, *The Movement,* Oxford University Press 1976.

Mulvey, Laura, 'Visual Pleasure and Narrative Cinema', *Screen,* XVI, 3 (1975), 6–18.

Mumford, Lewis, *The City in History,* Penguin 1961.

Mumford, Lewis, *The Culture of Cities,* Harcourt Brace, New York 1938.

Mungham, Geoff, and Geoff Pearson, eds, *Working Class Youth Culture,* Routledge and Kegan Paul 1976.

Musgrove, Frank, *Ecstasy and Holiness: Counter Culture and the Open Society,* Methuen 1974.

Musgrove, Frank, with Roger Middleton and Pat Hawes, *Margins of the Mind,* Methuen 1977.

Nairn, Tom, 'The English Literary Intelligentsia', *Bananas,* No. 3 (1976), pp. 17–22.

Neale, Steve, *Genre,* British Film Institute 1980.

Neale, Steve, 'The Same Old Story: Stereotypes and Difference', *Screen Education,* Nos. 32/33 (1979–80), pp. 33–7.

Negt, Oskar, and Alexander Kluge, *Öffentlichkeit und Erfahrung: Zur Organisationsanalyse von burgerlicher und proletarischer Offentlichkeit,* Suhrkamp, Frankfurt am Main 1972.

Nichols, Bill, ed., *Movies and Methods,* University of California Press, Berkeley 1976.

Nobile, Philip, ed., *The Con III Controversy: The Critics Look at the Greening of America*, Pocket Books, New York 1971.

Noble, Grant, *Children in Front of the Small Screen*, Constable 1975.

Noble, Trevor, *Modern Britain: Structure and Change*, Batsford 1975.

O'Connell, Judith, *Sexist Images in Children's Comics and Television Programmes*, BA dissertation, University of Sheffield 1982.

O'Malley, John, *Sociology of Meaning*, Human Context Books 1972.

Ong, Walter, *Fighting for Life: Contest, Sexuality and Consciousness*, Cornell University Press, Ithaca, N.Y. 1981.

Ong, Walter, *Interfaces of the Word*, Cornell University Press, Ithaca, N.Y. 1977.

O'Sullivan, Tim, et al., *Key Concepts in Communications*, Methuen 1983.

Packard, Vance, *The Hidden Persuaders*, new edn., Penguin 1981.

Parker, Tony, *The People of Providence: a housing estate and some of its inhabitants*, Hutchinson 1983.

Parrinder, Patrick, *Science Fiction: its Criticism and Teaching*, Methuen 1980.

Pateman, Trevor, 'How is understanding an advertisement possible?', in *Language, Image, Media*, eds H. Davis and P. Walton, Blackwell 1983.

Paulu, Burton, *British Broadcasting in Transition*, Macmillan 1961.

Pirani, Alix, 'The creative process', *Self and Society*, X (1982), 284–6.

Pollard, Sydney, *The Development of the British Economy*, Edward Arnold 1962.

Pollard, Sydney, *The Wasting of the British Economy*, Croom Helm 1982.

Pred, Allan, 'The choreography of existence: comments on Hägerstrand's time-geography and its usefulness', *Economic Geography*, No. 53 (1977), pp. 207–21.

Pred, Allan, 'Production, family, and free-time projects: a time-geographic perspective on the individual and societal change in nineteenth-century US cities', *Journal of Historical Goegraphy*, VII, 1 (1981), 3–36.

Pred, Allan, *Space and Time in Geography*, Gleerup, Lund 1981.

Punter, David, *The Hidden Script: Writing and the Unconscious*, Routledge and Kegan Paul 1985.

Punter, David, 'Theory, Writing, Experience', *New Literary History*, XV (1984), 413–24.

Reason, Peter, and John Rowan, eds, *Human Inquiry: a source-book of new paradigm research*, Wiley 1981.

Reich, Charles, *The Greening of America*, Allen Lane 1971.

Reith, Lord, *Broadcast Over Britain*, Hodder and Stoughton 1924.

Reith, Lord, *Into the Wind*, Hodder and Stoughton 1949.

Remmling, Gunter, *The Sociology of Karl Mannheim*, Routledge and Kegan Paul 1975.

Rich, Adrienne, *Diving into the Wreck*, Norton, New York 1973.

Rich, Adrienne, *The Dream of a Common Language*, Norton, New York 1978.

Rich, Adrienne, *Of Woman Born: Motherhood as Experience and Institution*, Norton, New York 1976.

Rich, Adrienne, *On Lies, Secrets, Silence*, Virago 1980.

Richards, Jeffrey, and Anthony Aldgate, *The Best of British: Cinema and Society 1930–1970*, Blackwell 1983.

Riesman, David, *The Lonely Crowd*, Yale University Press, New Haven,

Conn. 1950.

Roberts, Kenneth, *Leisure,* Longmans 1970.

Roszak, Theodore, *The Making of a Counter Culture: Reflections on the Technocratic Society and its Youthful Opposition,* Faber 1970.

Roszak, Theodore, *Where the Wasteland Ends: Politics and Transcendence in Postindustrial Society,* Faber 1973.

Roszak, Theodore, ed., *The Dissenting Academy: Essays Criticising the Teaching of the Humanities in American Universities,* Penguin 1969.

Roszak, Theodore, ed., *Sources: An anthology of contemporary materials for preserving personal sanity while braving the great technological wilderness,* Harper and Row, New York 1972.

Roszak, Theodore, with Betty Roszak, eds, *Masculine/Feminine: Readings in Sexual Mythology and the Liberation of Man,* Harper and Row, New York 1969.

Rowntree, B. S., and G. R. Lavers, *Poverty and the Welfare State,* Longmans 1951.

Rubinstein, W. D., *Men of Property,* Croom Helm 1981.

Rubinstein, W. D., *Wealth and the Wealthy in the Modern World,* Croom Helm 1980.

Russell, Peter, *The Brain Book,* Routledge and Kegan Paul 1979.

Ruthrof, Horst, *The Reader's Construction of the Narrative,* Routledge and Kegan Paul 1981.

Samuel, Raphael, ed., *People's History and Socialist Theory,* Routledge and Kegan Paul 1981.

Sarsby, Jacqueline, *Romantic Love and Society,* Penguin 1983.

Sartre, Jean-Paul, *Critique of Dialectical Reason,* trans. A. Sheridan Smith, Verso 1982.

Saussure, Ferdinand de, *Course in General Linguistics,* trans. W. Baskin, Fontana 1974.

Schiff, Martin, 'Neo-transcendentalism in the New Left Counter-Culture: A Vision of the Future Looking Back', *Comparative Studies in Society and History,* XV, 2 (1973), 130–42.

Schlesinger, Philip, *Putting Reality Together: BBC News,* Constable and Sage 1978.

Schofield, Michael, *Sexual Behaviour of Young People,* Longmans 1965.

Schwab, J. J., 'The concept of the structure of a discipline', in *Guiding Learning,* ed. M. D. Glock, Wiley, New York 1971.

Scott, J. M., *The Upper Class in Britain,* Macmillan 1982.

Sendall, Bernard, *Independent Television in Britain: Origin and Foundation 1946–1962,* Macmillan 1982.

Sennett, Richard, *The Fall of Public Man,* Cambridge University Press 1974.

Sharpe, Sue, *Just Like a Girl,* Penguin 1976.

Sharratt, Bernard, *The Literary Labyrinth,* Harvester 1984.

Sharratt, Bernard, *Reading Relations: Structures of Literary Production: A Dialectical Text/Book,* Harvester 1982.

Shea, F. X., 'Reason and Religion of the Counter-Culture', *Harvard Theological Review,* No. 66 (1973), pp. 95–111.

Short, K. R. M., ed., *Film and Radio Propaganda in World War II,* Croom Helm 1983.

Showalter, Elaine, *A Literature of Their Own,* Virago 1978.

385

Silber, Irwin, *The Cultural Revolution: A Marxist Analysis,* Times Change Press, New York 1970.

Simon of Wythenshawe, Lord, *The BBC From Within,* Gollancz 1953.

Spender, Dale, *Man Made Language,* Routledge and Kegan Paul 1980.

Spender, Dale, ed., *Feminist Theorists: Three Centuries of Women's Intellectual Traditions,* The Women's Press 1983.

Spender, Dale, and Elizabeth Sarah, eds, *Learning to Lose,* The Women's Press 1980.

Spilka, Mark, ed., *Towards a Poetics of Fiction,* Indiana University Press, Bloomington, Indiana 1977.

Stacey, Margaret, *Tradition and Change: A Study of Banbury,* Oxford University Press 1960.

Stanworth, Michelle, *Gender and Schooling,* Hutchinson in association with the Explorations in Feminism Collective 1983.

Statera, Gianni, *Death of Utopia: The Developments and Decline of Student Movements in Europe,* Oxford University Press 1975.

Stedman Jones, Gareth, *Outcast London,* Clarendon Press 1971.

Steiner, George, *On Difficulty and Other Essays,* Oxford University Press 1978.

Stewart, Michael, *The Jekyll and Hyde Years,* Dent 1977.

Stuart, Charles, ed., *The Reith Diaries,* Collins 1975.

Sumner, Colin, *Reading Ideologies,* Acadmic Press 1979.

Suvin, Darko, 'Narrative Logic, Ideology and the Range of SF', *Science Fiction Studies,* IX (1982), 1–25.

Swingewood, Alan, *The Myth of Mass Culture,* Macmillan 1977.

Sypher, Wylie, 'The Aesthetic of Revolution: the Marxist Melodrama', *Kenyon Review,* X (1948), 431–44.

Szalai, Alexander, ed., *The Use of Time,* Mouton, The Hague 1972.

Taylor, Robert, *The Fifth Estate: Britain's Unions in the Modern World,* Routledge and Kegan Paul 1975.

Thomason, Burke C., *Making Sense of Reification: Alfred Schutz and Constructionist Theory,* Foreword by Tom Bottomore, Macmillan 1982.

Thompson, Denys, ed., *Discrimination and Popular Culture,* Penguin 1973.

Thompson, E. P., *The Defence of Britain,* CND 1983.

Thompson, E. P., *The Poverty of Theory and Other Essays,* Merlin 1978.

Thompson, E. P., 'Time, work-discipline and industrial capitalism', *Past and Present,* No. 38 (1967), pp. 56–97.

Thompson, Jane, *Sociology Made Simple,* Heinemann 1982.

Todorov, Tzvetan, *The Fantastic: A Structural Approach to a Literary Genre,* trans. Richard Howard, Case Western Reserve University Press, Cleveland, Ohio 1973.

Tracey, Michael, *The Production of Political Television,* Routledge and Kegan Paul 1978.

Vilar, Pierre, 'Marxist History, a History in the Making: Towards a Dialogue with Althusser', *New Left Review,* No. 80 (1973), pp. 65–106.

Volosinov, V. N., *Marxism and the Philosophy of Language,* trans. L. Matejka and I. R. Titunik, Seminar Press, New York 1973.

Walker, John, *Art in the Age of Mass Media,* Pluto 1983.

Walvin, James, *Beside the Seaside,* Allen Lane 1978.

Walvin, James, *Leisure and Society 1830–1950,* Longmans 1978.

Ward, J. P., *Poetry and the Sociological Idea*, Harvester 1981.

Watson, James, and Anne Hill, eds, *A Dictionary of Communication and Media Studies*, Edward Arnold 1984.

Waugh, Evelyn, *Put Out More Flags*, Chapman and Hall 1959.

Weber, Max, *From Max Weber: Essays in Sociology*, ed. H. H. Gerth and C. Wright Mills, Routledge and Kegan Paul 1948.

Webster, Frank, *The New Photography*, Calder 1980.

Westergaard, John, and Henrietta Resler, *Class in a Capitalist Society: A Study of Contemporary Britain*, Heinemann 1975.

White, Hayden, *Metahistory*, Johns Hopkins University Press, Baltimore, Md. 1973.

Whitty, Geoff, and Michael Young, *Explorations in the Politics of School Knowledge*, Nafferton 1976.

Whorf, Benjamin Lee, *Language, Thought and Reality*, MIT Press, Cambridge, Mass. 1964.

Whyte, William, *The Organisation Man*, Doubleday, Garden City, N.Y. 1956.

Wiener, Martin, *English Culture and the Decline of the Industrial Spirit, 1850–1980*, Cambridge University Press 1981.

Williams, Raymond, *The Country and the City*, Chatto 1973.

Williams, Raymond, *Culture*, Fontana 1981.

Williams, Raymond, *Culture and Society*, Penguin 1971.

Williams, Raymond, *Keywords: A Vocabulary of Culture and Society*, Fontana 1976.

Williams, Raymond, 'Literature in Society', in *Contemporary Approaches to English Studies*, ed H. Schiff, Heinemann 1977.

Williams, Raymond, *The Long Revolution*, Penguin 1965.

Williams, Raymond, *Marxism and Literature*, Oxford University Press 1977.

Williams, Raymond, 'Marxism, Structuralism and Literary Analysis,' *New Left Review*, No. 129 (1981), pp. 51–67.

Williams, Raymond, *Politics and Letters*, New Left Books 1979.

Williams, Raymond, *Problems in Materialism and Culture*, Verso 1980.

Williams, Raymond, *Television: Technology and Cultural Form*, Fontana 1974.

Williamson, Judith, *Decoding Advertisements*, Marion Boyars 1978.

Willis, Paul, 'The Cultural Meaning of Drug Abuse', *Working Papers in Cultural Studies*, Nos 7/8 (1975), pp. 106–18.

Willis, Paul, *Learning to Labour: How Working-Class Kids get Working-Class Jobs*, Saxon House 1977.

Williams, Paul, 'Male School Counterculture', *Open University Popular Culture Course*, Unit 30, Block 7.

Willis, Paul, *Profane Culture*, Routledge and Kegan Paul 1978.

Wilson, Elizabeth, *Only Halfway to Paradise: Women in Post-War Britain 1945–1968*, Tavistock 1980.

Wilson, H. H., *Pressure Group: The Campaign for Commercial Television*, Secker and Warburg 1961.

Winter, Jay, ed., *The Working Class in Modern History*, Cambridge University Press 1983.

Woolf, Virginia, 'Women and Fiction', in *Women and Writing*, The Women's Press 1979.

Wright, David, 'Evaluating Resources: Why not ask the Pupils?', *Multicultural*

Teaching (1983).
Ziegler, Philip, *Crown and People*, Collins 1978.
Zweig, Ferdynand, *The Worker in an Affluent Society*, Heinemann 1961.

NOTES ON THE CONTRIBUTORS

EILEEN AIRD is an organizing tutor in women's education for the northern district of the WEA. Has a subject background in literature and is particularly interested in the work of nineteenth- and twentieth-century women writers. In addition she recently qualified as a psychotherapist and sees many similarities between the processes of education and those of therapy. Author of *Sylvia Plath* (1972), and various articles on literature and education. Co-editor of *Writing Women*. Mother of two sons aged nine and eleven.

SUSAN BASSNETT is senior lecturer in comparative literature at the University of Warwick, and has published widely in several areas, notably in translation studies and women's studies. She has two daughters.

ANNE BEEZER, JEAN GRIMSHAW and MARTIN BARKER are all senior lecturers in communication and cultural studies in the humanities department at Bristol Polytechnic; they have jointly developed a cultural studies option within the degree that tries to integrate audiovisual methods of exposition into the critical analysis of the media.

JOHN BROADBENT was a student at Edinburgh and lecturer at Cambridge; he is now a professorial fellow in English literature at East Anglia. His earlier work focussed on poetry, especially of the seventeenth century; latterly it has been more concerned with the actual environments in which reading and learning occur.

JON COOK is a lecturer in the School of English and American Studies, University of East Anglia. He has published on romantic writing, critical and cultural theory, and contemporary poetry.

TONY DUNN has been engaged on the construction and teaching of cultural studies courses since 1972. His main areas of interest are seventeenth-century history and literature, twentieth-century American culture, and contemporary British theatre. He is at present working on Defoe as historian, and the plays of Howard Barker and Caryl Churchill.

ALEC GORDON used to lecture part-time in theoretical studies in the

Department of Fine Art at Leeds Polytechnic. His translation of a selection of Philipp Soupault's poetry (1917–1926) is to be published in a bilingual volume. He is currently writing a study of Soupault's poetry and a critique of contemporary cultural studies. He is also a poet.

KEITH HOSKIN is lecturer in educational history at the University of Warwick, and has published articles on the history of examinations and of childhood and, in conjunction with Susan Bassnett, on the construct 'woman'. He is currently writing a book on the relation between the history of writing and the history of education.

LOUIS JAMES was brought up in Africa and England, and has taught in universities in Europe, the United States, the Caribbean and Africa. His books include *Fiction for the Working Man: 1830–1850* (1963); *Print and the People* (1976); and *Jean Rhys* (1978). He has written and broadcast on popular literature and drama, the Victorian novel and Third World writing, and is working on a social history of nineteenth–century fiction. He is presently professor of Victorian and modern literature at the University of Kent in Canterbury.

RICHARD JOHNSON is director of the Centre for Contemporary Cultural Studies and has written about the history and politics of education, working–class culture, the problems of history writing, and cultural theory. He is currently working on a book on subjectivity, memory and history being prepared by the Popular Memory Group at CCCS.

DEREK LONGHURST is principal lecturer and course leader in communication studies at Sunderland Polytechnic (visiting professor, University of Minnesota 1984–5).

TERRY LOVELL is lecturer in sociology at the University of Warwick. She is the author of *Pictures of Reality: Aesthetics, Politics and Pleasure* (1980), and has written a number of articles on the sociology of literature and film.

ARTHUR MARWICK is professor of history at the Open University, and, during 1984–5, visiting scholar at the Hoover Institution, Stanford University, California. He holds a D Litt from Edinburgh University for published work in the field of twentieth–century historical studies, and his books include *War and Social Change in the Twentieth Century* (1974), *British Society since 1945* (1982), and *Britain in our Century: Images and Controversies* (1984).

DAVID PUNTER is senior lecturer in English studies at the University of East Anglia; he has also worked in China, Poland and the US. He has published a number of critical books, including *The Literature of Terror* (1980) and *The Hidden Script* (1985), and also some poetry; and has some experience in educational and organizational consultancy.

ROGER SALES is lecturer in English studies at the University of East Anglia. His publications include *English Literature in History 1780–1830: Pastoral and Politics* (1983).

BERNARD SHARRATT read English at Cambridge 1965–8. PhD on working–class autobiographies. Since 1971 lecturer in English at University of Kent, with brief periods as visiting lecturer at Universities of the West Indies, Bogazici and Krakow. Published work includes *The Literary Labyrinth* (1984), *Reading Relations* (1982), *Performance and Politics in Popular Drama* (ed. with David Bradby and Louis James, 1980).

LORNA SMITH researches into women's writing; teaches in further and higher education; works with different groups of people towards more integrated, exciting and transforming ways of being; and is mother of two young children.

DAVID WRIGHT has taught in schools in the UK and the US, and is now lecturer in the school of education in the University of East Anglia.

INDEX

Index

Index

Index

Index